The French Revolution and Empire

D1714895

For Holly and the infs

The French Revolution and Empire

The Quest for a Civic Order

D. M. G. Sutherland

Blackwell
Publishing

© 2003 by D. M. G. Sutherland

350 Main Street, Malden, MA 02148-5018, USA
108 Cowley Road, Oxford OX4 1JF, UK
550 Swanston Street, Carlton South, Melbourne, Victoria 3053, Australia
Kurfürstendamm 57, 10707 Berlin, Germany

The right of D. M. G. Sutherland to be identified as the Author of this Work has been
asserted in accordance with the UK Copyright, Designs, and Patents Act 1988.

First published 2003 by Blackwell Publishers Ltd, a Blackwell Publishing company

Library of Congress Cataloging-in-Publication Data

Sutherland, Donald (Donald M. G.)
The French Revolution and Empire : the quest for a civic order /
D.M.G. Sutherland.
      p. cm.
   Includes bibliographical references and index.
      ISBN 0–631–23362–8 (hard : alk. paper) – ISBN 0–631–23363–6 (pbk. : alk. paper)
      1. France–History–Revolution, 1789–1799.
      2. France–History–Consulate and First Empire, 1799–1815.
      3. France–History–1789–1815. I. Title.
DC148 .S856 2002
944.04–dc21

                                                                    2002005372

A catalague record for this title is available from the British Library.

Set in 10 on 12 pt Sabon
by Kolam Information Services Pvt. Ltd. Pondicherry, India.
Printed and bound in the United Kingdom
by TJ International, Padstow, Cornwall

For further information on
Blackwell Publishing, visit our website:
http://www.blackwellpublishing.com

Contents

Map 1   France: Departments of 1790

'The mire of debauchery infects public morals. Dissolution passes from the court into society: luxury and licentiousness pass from bishops and high benefactors down to the Levites. In a word, corruption overflows from the ranks that surround the throne to the nearest neighbour, from the capital to the entire empire. The people are little by little possessed by languor; they have become the slave of the government, of the privileged, as well as of their own pleasures and great sufferings.'

Elysée Loustallot, 'Notice. Revolutions de Paris,'
12 July 1789

'Incomparable year! You have seen the end of a government of frightening memory, a government that was so closely bound to the Bastille, its first favourite and the most gross and monstrous female anyone has ever seen, dead of a sudden and violent attack. It is by that we saw the same day my brave and happy compatriots save the National Assembly...break the chains of slavery and terrify the blade of despotism....Grand year! You will be the year that regenerates, you will always carry that name.'

Louis-Sébastien Mercier, 'Adieux,' *Annales patriotiques*,
31 December 1789

'Frenchmen, rise up! Let the anger of the nation burst and return to dust the handful of intriguers who desolate us with the force we let them have....People, be of good cheer! The saviours, the avengers of the world are coming! Oh! With what transports of delirium are they welcomed. I see this stream grow from a holy source, form a torrent which drags along its course the tyrants, the slaves, the priests, the nobles, the hypocrites and all the trash, which for centuries, have soiled and poisoned the sojourn of man [on earth].'

Jacques-Antoine Dulaure, *Thermomètre du jour*, 26 June 1792

'...a nation must show itself great, strong, invincible and terrible; it is then, that instructed by the experience of her misfortune, by seventeen centuries of oppression, slavery and cruelty, she must launch the thunderbolt of her anger against the monsters who fertilize the soil with blood in order to resuscitate privileges [that] are odious to nature [and] injurious to religion....

There can be no hesitation between death and the destruction of tyrants: we have to devour the Prussian who advances, and fall like a torrent on the traitors and the conspirators. Our pikes must do justice to the counterrevolutionaries of the interior and our cannon annihilate the crusade of the conspiring despots....'

Jacques Roux, *Sur les moyens de sauver la France et la Liberté.*
Prononcé dans l'église Métropolitaine de Paris, dans celles de
St.-Eustache, de Ste.-Marguerite, de Saint-Antoine,
et de Saint-Nicolas-des- Champs, membre de la Société des
Droits de l'Homme et du Citoyen (1793)

'Such is the nature of human affairs that great benefits are always mixed with great misfortune. What then ought to be the principles of truly patriotic legislators? It is to pardon the great wrongs, the append-age of the great benefits which operate for the regeneration and enfran-chisement of the human race. And certainly, if this principle is not admitted, no Revolution would ever be possible, never would an en-slaved people rise to liberty; for an abuse, which is inseparable from any Revolution, would stop its progress and prevent its effects.'

Jean-Bon-Saint-André, regicide, Protestant pastor, future
member of the Committee of Public Safety, speaking in favour
of a motion to quash all proceedings against those arrested
for murder during the September Massacres, 8 February 1793,
Archives parlementaires, lvii, pp. 377–8

'The Terror of '93 was not a necessary consequence of the Revolution, it was an unfortunate deviation. It was more fatal than useful to the formation of the Republic because it went beyond all the limits, be-cause it was atrocious, because it immolated both friends and enemies ...and because it led to a nasty reaction not only against the terrorists but also against liberty and her defenders.'

Antoine-Claire Thibaudeau, regicide,
Mémoires sur la Convention, et le Directoire (1824), p. 57

'Our hopes have been deceived: the Revolution was scarcely only a change of name for things and [a change] of fortune for individuals.'

Henri-François Grégoire, regicide,
constitutional bishop of the Loir-et-Cher,
Mémoires, (1814), i, p. 457

Introduction:
The Problem and the Thesis

There are three questions worth asking about the French Revolution. What caused the Revolution? What caused the Terror? Why did it end in the dictatorship of Bonaparte?

Of course, there is an endless number of other questions that can be asked after these, but they are all subsumed under these three. The reader of this, or any other history of the period, can tell what question the author is addressing simply by paying attention to the time-line. If the subject under discussion is the Old Regime and 1789, for example, the author is trying to answer the first question. And so on.

Unfortunately, the answers to the questions are not at all as simple as the questions themselves. The debates over the answers can be traced back to contemporaries who often provided vital clues about how they understood the event itself. The early historians of the Revolution, the historians of the 1820s and 1830s in France, often posed the questions that historians still debate. Indeed, a case could be made that there was a real French Revolution, one that actually happened, and the French Revolution of these early writers. They did not falsify the record, far from it, but they were concerned to write a history that would contribute to the realization of what they thought were the ideals of the Revolution. Theirs was always a noble version of the Revolution, a Revolution that sought to find in the events of 1789 and after, a legitimation of a humane, compassionate, egalitarian liberal society or even a democracy. We frequently, and perhaps unavoidably, see the real Revolution through the filter that they provided.

Writing a history of the Revolution is a political act. In the nineteenth century, being an active politician and an historian of the Revolution was frequently a seamless activity. The day of the scholar-statesmen has probably passed forever, but the political preferences of most historians of the Revolution since the founding of the chair of the French Revolution in 1884 have been well known. None has tried to hide their preferences under a veil of an elusive objectivity. Writing the history of the French Revolution and Empire therefore is to join an enterprise that itself has a long and honourable history, and one whose practitioners in France are public figures.

One example of how contemporaries cued subsequent historians to the kind of history that could be written was what is called 'the thesis of circumstances', a term we will be discussing often. This means the revolutionaries did what they did because outside forces forced them to institute extraordinary and violent solutions to the problems that faced them, namely foreign war and domestic counterrevolution. That is, the Terror was a provocation external to the Revolution itself. This was the language of the revolutionaries themselves when they instituted the Terror, that what they did was an indisputable act of self defence. This is fair enough, but there is so much more that could be said about the concept and how it was used, or rejected, at the time.

François Furet reversed this claim about the thesis of circumstance. He and those whom he inspired flipped the thesis of circumstances upside down. The claim was that far from being external to the Revolution, the internal needs of revolutionary ideology generated the violence of the Revolution. A lot of what follows in this book is a discussion of this flip. This assertion is not at all wrong – it does, however, force a serious re-thinking of the subject.

When Al Bertrand of Blackwell asked me to write a second edition of *France, 1789–1815: Revolution and Counterrevolution*, we both assumed the process would be short. Since the publication of that book, I had thought I had kept up fairly well with the publications in the field. This turns out to have been far too optimistic. As I began to delve into the production since the publication of the first book, and especially as I tried to master the enormous production since the Bicentennial of the Revolution of 1989, I realized how much I had missed. Not only that, I realized as my reading went on how much the field had taken another qualitative leap forward in terms of analytical capacity. A great deal of this production has been published in a newly refurbished *Annales historiques de la Révolution française*, a journal that improves with almost every issue, and with the publications of Michel Vovelle and his students. Another invaluable source has been the publication of the hundreds of papers of conferences about the Revolution. And unlike most conference proceedings, these are often of high quality. This has been one of the major venues of valuable work in the last decade.

Still another source has been the Library of Congress. The collection blossomed. Not only has the LC been able to acquire the unspeakably expensive French Revolution Research Collection, the European librarians, especially Carol Armbruster, have scarcely missed a book. She also is a quiet resource for this book.

Steven Kaplan pointed this out some time ago. The Bicentennial was a major intellectual event. For those of us who jet-setted around the planet, it was enough to bask in the unusual attention that the media conferred upon us all. But Professor Kaplan saw very early that beneath the glitter, some major changes were occurring in the conceptualization and the expression of the French Revolution. Some of these changes are reflected in this book.

It tries to incorporate as much as anyone can the renewal of the field since 1989. These changes have been so great that they have forced a major re-writing and thus a new title. Almost all of the chapters down to the Directory have been completely re-written. Those that follow have changed less, because the field itself has changed less. But there is a major re-writing of the relation between the Revolution and the economy that reflects some of my own research since 1989.

This book does retain the major thesis of the earlier one, namely that the Revolution has to be understood as a struggle between revolution and counterrevolution. I think a lot of this argument has now been absorbed into general writing of the subject. It is no longer possible, as it was at the conference at Rennes in 1985, for someone to deny that an authentic and popular counterrevolution existed, to deny that 'the people' could possibly be counterrevolutionary.

But from that base, I hope that this version is richer and more complex than the earlier version.

At the same time, I have tried to make the book more accessible to students coming at the field for the first time. I have done this by trying to simplify the prose and by introducing the editorial comments that pop up in the text from time to time. These diminish, indeed disappear, because as time goes on in this period, the amount of serious controversy also declines. Alas, there is nothing I can do about reducing the geographical challenge this book poses. Trying to expand the standard narrative to the provinces requires a geographical familiarity that few Anglo-Saxons coming at the subject for the first time have. The map should help. There are also several geographical sites that are discussed: Paris and the Midi in the largest sense. The third geographical entity is the west, but contrary to what some good friends have alleged, this is not a book about the French Revolution viewed from the west. The argument then and now is that the opposition to the Revolution was real, serious, authentic, legitimate in its own way, and popular. It was not marginal, not confined to the west alone. Indeed, the anti-revolution and the counterrevolution were in their way *the* popular movements of the period.

There are many people I would like to thank for offering comments, criticisms and suggestions. First among them has to be Timothy Tackett, who let me see an early version of his wonderful study of Louis XVI and the Flight to Varennes. He did it knowing that I am his most severe critic and I hope, his greatest admirer. Then, *my* most severe and best critic, Tim Le Goff, followed by Jack Censer, David Bell, Howard Brown, Philip Hoffman, Colin Lucas, Patrice Gueniffey, Françoise Brunel, Gerard Béaur, the Baltimore–Washington Old Regime Group, and many others, in no particular order. And, it goes without saying, Michel Vovelle from whose books and articles I have learned so much. Within my own department, I cannot express how much I have learned over the years from Madeline Zilfi and Brigitte Bedos-Rézak, both of whom work on a history totally remote from the Revolution, but both of whom have taught me more than I can express about religion, politics, society, and how women fit in. Or, as they would now correct me, having just read the last sentence, how I still have to think more about this subject.

College Park
February 2002

1

The Origins of the Revolution in France

The Classic Theory of the Bourgeois Revolution

There was a time when historians were confident in describing the origins of the French Revolution. The operative concept was 'aristocratic reaction'. It meant several things at once. Politically, it referred to the undermining of the absolutism of Louis XIV. The Sun King was thought to have subverted the independence and privileges of the aristocracy. But after his death in 1715, the *parlements*, the regional sovereign and appeal courts of which that of Paris was by far the most important, undertook an offensive, a reaction, on behalf of the entire nobility. They were able to transform their right of registering laws and edicts into a veto on progressive royal legislation. The Crown was consequently much weaker.

This had implications in the social sphere as well. In the course of the eighteenth century, the aristocracy ended up monopolizing the highest offices in government, the military, the Church and the judiciary. This in turn affected the bourgeoisie. No longer able to advance to the top of the predominant social and political institutions of the day, the bourgeoisie became increasingly alienated from the state and from respectable society. Frustrated in achieving its highest ambitions, its loyalties painfully strained, ever open to imaginative criticisms of the system, it was well placed to take advantage of the political crisis of 1788–9 to overthrow the old order altogether. One of the many crises of the Old Regime was a crisis of social mobility.

The argument was irresistibly attractive, partly because of its internal elegance and partly because it explained so much. It made sense of the reign of Louis XIV, the eighteenth century and the Revolution too. The struggle between revolution and counterrevolution could be reduced to two actors, the bourgeoisie and the aristocracy, who had first come to blows in the closing years of the reign of Louis XIV. The aristocracy lost, of course, and specialists of the nineteenth century could move on to the next round, the struggle between the bourgeoisie and the working class.

This argument is also utterly untenable. In the first place, it assumes rather than demonstrates the aristocracy's progressive monopoly of high posts. It assumes, too, that the society of the seventeenth century was more open than its successor but relies on incomplete evidence and a limited range of contemporary complaints. The duc de Saint Simon's famous observation that Louis XIV raised up the 'vile bourgeoisie' turns out to be untrue in the case of the episcopate, partially true but grossly misleading in that of the ministry and unknown in the case of the officer corps of the army. More refined methodologies have turned up some odd anomalies. All the intendants (the immensely powerful representatives of the king in the provinces) of Louis XV and Louis XVI were nobles, but the trend in appointments, such as it was, was increasingly to prefer nobles of more recent creation. Closer examination of some of the major signs of noble exclusivism shows that restrictions were often aimed at excluding the rich parvenu nobles, not a rising bourgeoisie. The famous Ségur ordinance of 1781, for instance, limited the recruitment of army officers to men with four quarterings of nobility, that is, four ascendant blood relatives had to have been noble. Oddly enough, the intention was to help professionalize the army by excluding nobles who had recently amassed a fortune in commerce or finance. These types were thought to value cupidity and self-interest, not the genuinely military values of self-sacrifice and discipline that were supposed to be the preserve of staid, landed families. Even the few *parlements* which took similar four quarterings decrees had much the same object in mind. The Parlement of Rennes, for instance, most of whose magistrates could trace their noble lineages back two centuries, adopted a four quarterings decree in 1732 and managed to maintain its caste-like character against all comers, noble and roturier, until the very end. The Parlement of Paris, whose jurisdiction covered one third of the country, never bothered to restrict its entry and remained conspicuously open to the rich men of banking, high finance and government service, most of whom were nobles already. To be sure, exclusivist tendencies were worrying to many bourgeois, even though they were not affected directly, because they feared an even greater tightening in the future.

It was always possible for many to acquire noble status. The Crown did grant nobility directly, and after 1760 or so broadened the basis of selection significantly. The annual number of direct grants more than tripled to nearly a dozen per year and, while outstanding service in the military and judiciary continued to be rewarded as before, so now also were contributions in government service, commerce, industry, culture and science. The Old Regime monarchy, in fact, rewarded a broader range of talents than did Napoleon.

By far the most important device for creating new nobles was venal office. There were roughly 70,000 offices in the royal bureaucracy and outside it that could be bought, sold and inherited just like any other piece of property. These included most offices in the judiciary, all army officers, financial services, many municipal posts and even humble occupations like market-porter and barber-wigmaker. Office was attractive because it guaranteed exemptions from some taxes or provided a monopoly of a certain service. Restricting entry thus sustained the owner's income. The more expensive the office, the more exemptions and privileges. And they were getting more expensive. From the closing years of the reign of Louis XV to the Revolution, the value of offices doubled and even trebled, a far greater increase than rents on farms and domaines. Right up to the end, they remained a safe and lucrative investment.

Roughly 3750 venal offices in the civil, criminal and financial courts and some municipalities conferred hereditary nobility on the owner or his family, mostly after one or two generations. The very expensive office of *secrétaire du roi* brought heredtary nobility after twenty years' service. There were 800 of these and their owners did nothing more onerous than seal legal documents. No one is certain how many families were ennobled by the process of venal office during the reigns of Louis XV and Louis XVI, but one estimate suggests 10,000. By 1789, most noble families were descended not from the military nobility, but from office-holders. The Old Regime aristocracy was thus comparatively young and was in a constant process of renewal.

The doors of the Second Estate were always ready to swing open to men of talent, but above all to men of money. Society was therefore capable of absorbing the most thrusting, entrepreneurial and ambitious men of the plutocracy.

An ennobling office was far from cheap. In 1791, they were commonly priced well above 50,000 *livres*, enough to support two hundred families of rural weavers for a year. The owner of an ennobling office was therefore a very wealthy man indeed. The classic origin of these nobles is usually thought to have been an aspiring merchant family that gradually withdrew from trade over a generation or two, and bought land, offices and a title instead. Such families were certainly very numerous and the temptation to follow this route may well have increased for many merchant families along the Atlantic coast because the successes of British privateering made investment in overseas trade much more risky. But this was not the only pattern. Many other families rose to the top through tax-farming or the fiscal system generally. Another route was to make a fortune in the sugar islands of the Caribbean and begin the ascent that way. The most famous example was the writer Chateaubriand's father who returned to France enormously rich, 'reclaimed' his status as a Breton noble and settled into a brooding life at his newly acquired château at Combourg. The fast route could lead to some dizzying ascents with rises from the artisanate or even the peasantry in one or two generations. Still other families had been primarily landowners and rentiers for some time, content to build up the family's status monotonously through the patient acquisition of ever more prestigious offices until it slid almost imperceptibly into the Second Estate.

There were few qualitative economic differences between the aristocracy and the bourgeoisie. Approximately 80 per cent of the private wealth of the country was in land, urban real estate, bonds and so on, and both groups invested heavily in them. Although the proportions varied greatly from place to place, the nobility and the bourgeoisie together were everywhere important landowners. In some of the rich agricultural areas of the country, like maritime Flanders, around Versailles, parts of Burgundy, the river valleys of Provence and so on, they owned land out of all proportion to their numbers. Nobles were also heavily involved in industrial activities closely related to land and its resources like forest products, mining and metallurgy, not to mention the marketing of grain and wine. Although there remained a strong prejudice against direct participation in trade, nobles were major investors in colonial trading companies, land-clearing and speculation companies, and in banking, industrial and tax-collection enterprises of all sorts. The prominent contributions of nobles to capitalist ventures and the strong presence of bourgeois on the land show that from the point of view of economic function, the two groups were a single class. At the very least, the bourgeois–noble split of 1789 did not have economic origins.

The effect of the revisionist critique of the classical interpretation has been to reassert the importance of the cultural and political origins of the Revolution. If the nobility had always been a dominant class, if whatever trends there were towards exclusivism are problematic to interpret, if opportunities for advancement were far greater than has ever been suspected, and if nobles and bourgeois shared similar economic functions and interests, then the notion that the Revolution originated in a struggle between two distinct classes has to be abandoned. Politics and culture remain. Both groups could agree to unite to overthrow absolutism in favour of a liberal constitution but, according to which revisionist historian one follows, they fell out either over means, or because of a failure of political leadership or the form the political crisis took, or even over something as amorphous as 'style'.

Some of the cultural interpretations are, to be sure, a stretch. Explanations based upon psychology are always hard to prove. The claim that the decline in the role of fathers in eighteenth century novels was related to the decline in the myth of kings as fathers of their peoples and therefore is related to the execution of Louis XVI is hardly convincing. Similarly, claims that the politicization of pornography in the Old Regime had a bearing on the origins of the Revolution can also be carried too far. After all, randy nuns, lascivious prelates and debauched lords are very old stock characters in European literature. No one thinks of dirty books as coded manifestos of the future or imagines how they could be linked to the Declaration of the Rights of Man.

Other investigations of the cultural dimension of the Revolution illustrate that a small part of the literate class was increasingly critical of the status quo. Lawyers' briefs, for example, were not censored and could be printed in large numbers. Advocates who borrowed from tropes in popular theatre cast heros and enemies in stark contrast, and were able to portray prominent cases in terms of dastardly aristocrats cheating their roturier partners, taking advantage of their connections to exploit ordinary people, and otherwise failing to live up to even their code of honour. But this mode of pleading was fairly rare even among jurists in Paris. It was even more rare among barristers and other legal professionals who would be elected to the Estates-General. Other writings broke new ground. Some of these were histories of France in which the monarchy's role in the national history was marginalized or even delegitimized.

The century also witnessed an unprecedented explosion of print literature, in the form of national and provincial newspapers, pamphlets, books, and so on. Academies and reading societies along with salons and masonic lodges were established in most of the large provincial centres. Thus was created what the German Marxist Habermas called 'the bourgeois public sphere', a nexus in the realm outside the control of government where men and women aroused by the passions and fads of the day, could debate and discuss. There was, of course, nothing bourgeois about these institutions, nor were they somehow outside normal society, nor were they harbingers of Revolution. Most of the academies were dominated by aristocrats and, in the cities that had parlements, by the leading magistrates. Many devoted themselves to public policy and intellectual questions and so downplayed status distinctions among their members. The significance of this social mixing can be exaggerated. In 1789 at the early meetings of the Estates-General, noble deputies spoke of the bourgeois deputies as if they had never seen a barrister close up in their lives. And the astonishment was mutual.

Moreover, a great deal of print culture was completely apolitical. Printers in the provinces, for example, contracted only for government announcements, posters and almanacs. The *Affiches de Rennes*, a weekly in one of the most politically robust provinces in the country, was an utterly tedious compendium of real estate ads and grain prices. The admirers of the work of Augustin Cochin on the literary societies of Brittany, thought to be among the most important institutions for spreading the radical Enlightenment, stifle the genuine quirkiness in Cochin's work. He was convinced that the literary societies were front organizations of an ultra-secret 'Machine', and the very absence of a shred of evidence of the Machine's existence was proof of how successful a conspiracy it really was. Cochin's own evidence shows that the crisis of 1788–9 politicized the literary societies; they did not politicize the crisis, so much as respond to it.

But if there was no straight line between Old Regime cultural institutions and beliefs on the one hand, and the Revolution on the other, some cultural phenomena certainly did contribute to a profound disaffection for the status quo. One of these was Jansenism. This was a doctrine of salvation and the means of grace that several popes condemned, most notably in 1713 in the bull *Unigenitus*. After decades of persecution from ecclesiastical and royal authority, Jansenism became a movement hostile to bishops, to papal sovereignty and to the wrongful exercise of royal authority. It found a home in a small but energetic faction among the Parisian *parlementaires* and to an extent in the streets of the capital. The Parlement took up the cause of the liberties of the French or Gallican Church against the Crown and the papacy, and in the 1750s, it defended Jansenist clerics against attempts to deny them extreme unction on their deathbeds.

Jansenism, therefore, popularized the idea of obedience to legal rather than arbitrary authority. Jansenist factions also claimed the *parlements* somehow were the guardians of the kingdom's fundamental laws and that the magistrates represented the Nation and spoke for it. In other words, France had a Constitution that kings were bound to respect. Many *parlementaires* and attorneys of the Paris bar were convinced they had a special role in evaluating the extent to which royal activities intruded upon ancient rights and privileges. While many of these men were sympathetic to Jansenist ideas, they were also upholding a centuries old tradition of French public law they had learned at university or studied in their legal textbooks. Moreover, in defending these concepts, they were also defending their interests as a corporation. Unlike the *philosophes*, for instance, they were largely indifferent to reform of the criminal law and they were more or less loyal to the Parlement of Paris in its battles with the Crown.

After they engineered the dissolution of their archenemies, the Jesuits, in 1763, the Jansenist movement scattered in different directions, denouncing the Enlightenment as impious, but advocating religious toleration for Protestants and Jews, and endorsing anti-slavery. These ideas had a great future but in the immediate term, individual Jansenists got more directly involved in politics. One of the most interesting examples was the journalist and publicist Pidansat de Mairobert. In the 1760s he had been deeply involved in a Jansenist salon hosted by Mme Doublet, and later made his living collecting and publishing news, scuttlebutt, rumours and gossip. The Maupeou coup of 1770–1 (see below) crushed his spirit, however, and in 1779, he slit his wrists, overwhelmed with debt and with despair for his country. He was convinced that the absence of any real resistance to the coup not only proved the monarchy to have been a despotism but that the French themselves had been too corrupted with centuries of oppression to regenerate themselves. His moralizing, his manecheeism, and his emphasis on a regenerative, morally based politics was an eerie foreshadowing of a major revolutionary discourse on how to effect regeneration after centuries of corruption of the human personality. Mairobert was a pessimistic Robespierre.

Mairobert was also a venomous critic of the court and he was tossed into the Bastille for writing a scurrilous biography of Madame du Barry, Louis XV's mistress, that highlighted her base origins as a cook and one-time prostitute. Indeed criticism of the court and its nefarious role in setting public policy grew throughout the century. From army officers in dusty provincial garrisons complaining about the conferring of the best commissions on well connected courtiers, to the intense humiliations at court of provincial squires like the comte d'Antraigues who consequently loathed Marie-Antoinette greatly, and who became one of the best publicists for Rousseau, the court loomed over polite society. It was resented almost everywhere.

One of those resentments was how much the court cost. No matter that most of its expenditures were entirely routine: meagre sums conferred on widows of military officers and on the relatives of other modest former state servants. No matter that the court budget was so small relative to overall expenditures: no one knew this at the time. There were too many spectacular examples of the Crown underwriting the debts of favourites; too many examples of far too much extravagant spending for the acquisition or construction of new châteaux, like St Cloud and the Bagatelle for the public to forgive the lush expenditures. After all, the Parlement of Paris itself told the public, in documents that could not be censored, that the source of public debt was extravagant government spending.

The unpopularity of the court related directly to the unpopularity of the King's mistresses, or in the case of Louis XVI, of his wife. Mme de Pompadour, the stunningly beautiful and charming mistress of Louis XV, eventually came to be loathed both by courtiers and by pamphleteers because of her sexual power. Commentators and gossips interpreted her improvized plays before the King at Versailles as humiliations of various courtiers. From the beginning, she had been described as 'the whore'. As time went on, she seemed to have an unnatural power over the King; indeed to have taken such advantage of him as to emasculate him. Her low birth only made the scandal worse, and the Jesuits at court were quite beside themselves when she acted in her own plays before the queen and uttered taunting lines. Her successor, Mme du Barry was seen as so grasping and so domineering that she was blamed for a grain shortage in Paris in 1770, a shortage that was allegedly designed to allow Louis XV to rake in mega profits to buy her fantastic jewellery and magnificent coaches.

But the most hated consort was Marie-Antoinette. Louis XVI was not respected. Courtiers commented on his awkwardness, his lumping gait, his absence of majesty, his irresolution, his lack of self confidence, even his impotence until that was fixed. But most of that mean spiritedness was kept within bounds. Not so with Marie-Antoinette. Rhetorical devices of sexual excess and irresistible seduction that had been applied to Mme de Pompadour were next applied to her. As a Hapsburg princess, she was a victim of the unpopularity of the alliance of 1756 with Austria but her gaucherie and her spite exacerbated her disastrous reputation. From the moment she stepped onto French soil until the day of her execution, many suspected her loyalties were anti-French, and that she was a Hapsburg spy in the highest quarters. Rumours about her libidinous sex life began early: she had had lesbian affairs with courtiers, it was said; she committed incest with her brother-in-law, the comte d'Artois who taught her new positions, it was said; she was 'soiled with crime and debauchery', said another pamphlet. The police commissioner of Paris actually bribed some people to cheer her when she visited but to little avail. Passers-by correctly suspected police involvement.

The Diamond Necklace Affair of 1785 gave such rumours an enormous fillip. This was a confidence scheme in which a gang of tricksters persuaded the ageing Cardinal de Rohan to purchase a hugely expensive diamond necklace as a gift for Marie-Antoinette to gain her favour. The thieves stole both the necklace and the money and made off to London. When the scam was discovered, Louis XVI concluded that Rohan could not possibly have been so stupid and that he must have been an accomplice. The King invested a great deal of energy into getting Rohan convicted but when the Paris *parlement* narrowly exonerated him, it showed that few feared Louis's wrath. Worst of all, anonymous pamphlets assaulted the Queen, accusing her of catching venereal disease from the Cardinal and spreading it to the court. Needless to say, courtiers outside her charmed circle with the Polignac family often funded these attacks.

The consequence of these attacks on mistresses and queens was not to discredit the idea of monarchy as an institution, far from it. In both the case of Louis XV and Louis XVI, the discourse represented the king as a passive victim of sexually powerful, not to say, domineering women. One solution was to reduce the malign role of the court, to reduce its political influence over public affairs to nothing and to choke off its finances. For some others, the prominence of corrupt women in politics and the fame of certain salons that were dominated by celebrated women, showed the utter impurity of public life. Thus another avenue opened up that led to the same conclusion Mairobert had reached: France itself had been debauched. An entire generation grew up dreaming of doing great things. Some school boys at Louis-le-Grand in Paris that several future revolutionaries attended (Robespierre, Desmoulins, Fréron) smuggled books about Roman heroism to their beds to read them under the covers. This led others to dream of restoring a masculine identity, to revive a male altruistic virtue. Art historians have argued convincingly that David's *The Oath of the Horatii*, first exhibited at the salon of 1785, exemplifies this. The sons take the oath from their father to sacrifice themselves for their country while the women sit limp off in a corner.

Where Are We Now in the Argument?

The great historian of the Revolution in the nineteenth century, Alexis de Tocqueville, said that the Revolution was made in men's minds before it became a reality. As with anything Tocqueville said, the statement forces us to think, but it is certainly wrong. Those who embrace the interpretation of the Revolution based upon language and culture believe Tocqueville, though. Indeed, the late François Furet went even further than Tocqueville and asserted that the utopian language of the Enlightenment dominated the scene once the Old Regime collapsed and that since it was impossible to decree virtue, the Terror, the obsession to compel people to be good, was a logical and inevitable result. Furet also insisted on the importance of the influence of a particular reading of Rousseau, that his thought set up the conceptual framework of Jacobinism. This erected popular sovereignty into an absolute so that there was no limit on public power. If after a long and sincere debate, Rousseau says, someone persists in resisting the General Will, that is, they resist an unambiguous moral truth, they can be killed. Thus there is but a short step, or perhaps no step at all, to the conformity of sentiments in the Terror.

Others have asserted that certain discourses of the Old Regime, particularly those that emphasized a political theory in which the ideal polity was based upon justice, as opposed to liberty or the rule of law, 'opened the way for the Terror'. Still others have argued for a decline in the respect kingship evoked, or even that the monarchy was desacralized. Thus when the pathetic law clerk/servant Damiens plunged a pocketknife into Louis XV's fur coat in January 1756, the would-be assassin set off a chain of events, so it is said, that led to the de-legitimization of the monarchy.

If only things had been so simple. Police reports at the time certainly showed the public understood the hypocrisy of maintaining Louis XV's public image as the *Bien aimé* (the 'well beloved') and his scandalous private life, as well as his persecution of those much admired spiritual Olympians, the Jansenists. But the most some hotheads could imagine was a replacement of the Bourbons with another dynasty. Indeed, few revolutionaries at the beginning could imagine France without monarchy. Even after Louis XVI's many betrayals once the Revolution began, even after the overthrow of the monarchy in August 1792, most Jacobin clubs assumed monarchy in one form or another would continue. Monarchy as an institution in people's minds could be eradicated only after the immense provocations that occurred after 1789, not before.

The importance of the linguistic–cultural interpretation is that it is an outgrowth of the anti-Marxist critique of the origins of the Revolution. Their adepts assume that since the class struggle interpretation is untenable, a social interpretation in any form is untenable too. The defining event of the period thus becomes the assault on the monarchy. The research agenda in turn becomes a search for anti-monarchial statements in the Old Regime. But the dislike of individual kings, or the utterly disgusting attacks on their reputations, ought not to be confounded with hostility to the institution of kingship. Unfortunately for those who believe in the desacralization of the monarchy thesis, the French Revolution occurred under Louis XVI, not under the reign of his grandfather.

Perhaps it is time to revisit the social context in which the Old Regime collapsed. But before doing so, we need to realize that even on the eve of the Revolution, the Revolution had not yet occurred in people's minds. The political experience of the thinking classes before 1789 was that the monarchy was too despotic, and that the court was quite beyond redemption. The solution was more liberty, a liberty that was quite compatible with monarchy, but almost until the eve of the final crisis in 1788, no one, literally no one, imagined that aristocratic, clerical, and other privileges would have to disappear too. In other words, a great deal of what made the Revolution revolutionary did not occur until circumstances compelled the revolutionaries to do what they did.

Circumstances mattered largely because the good will of moderate leaders of both sides was not able to overcome fundamental differences over the nature of the liberal constitution to be imposed on the monarchy. This in turn arose because of critical differences in the social position of the two groups, that is over the related questions of wealth and privilege. Nobles were the wealthiest single group and were among the most privileged. Although many nobles were willing to surrender all or most of their privileges and maintain their leading social position simply through their massive ownership of property, the majority of the elected representatives of the Second Estate was not. Pure selfishness apart, they retained an older view that privilege was a useful defence against unbridled absolutism. All that was needed was a constitution to supplement these privileges. In the event, many bourgeois agreed on the necessity to reinforce privilege. It was the role of the liberal leadership, both noble and bourgeois, to convince their constituencies that group privileges were no longer adequate. They failed, and since privilege was removed by violence and chicanery in August 1789, they created one of the strands of the counterrevolution.

Aristocrats and Bourgeois

It is hard to imagine how wealthy the eighteenth-century aristocracy was. Of course, there were many poor nobles. To cite only one example, Sublieutenant Bonaparte earned only 1000 *livres* per year in the artillery, which was less, far less, than the court aristocrats, the La Tremoilles, spent on their boxes at the *Comédie Française* and the *Théâtre Italien*, let alone the 44,000 *livres* a year they spent on dinner parties. Other court families like the Orléans, with their revenues of two million a year, or the Contis with their 3.7 million, were among the wealthiest people in the country. There were similarly breathtaking bourgeois fortunes. The Luynes family, merchants at Nantes, had a fortune of over four million *livres* in 1788. On the whole, however, the nobility's fortunes were greater than those of most others. Even in Lyon, the largest industrial city in the country, the average noble fortune, much of it in the hands of office-holders, was three times that of the silk wholesalers, the wealthiest single group in the bourgeoisie. In Troyes, another manufacturing city, noble fortunes were more than double those of the wholesale merchants. Of the sixteen wealthiest people in the little port of Vannes, twelve were nobles. Of the marriage contracts signed at the administrative centre of Dijon in 1748, all those of the nobility but not one of those of the bourgeoisie were worth more than 50,000 *livres*. Finally, in the administrative centre of Toulouse, nobles held over 60 per cent of the private wealth in the city and two thirds of that noble wealth belonged to the magistrates in the *parlement*. Despite the overlappings these figures reveal, the overwhelming tendency was for the aristocracy to be wealthier than anyone else.

Wealth, status and professional ties also made nobles a fairly closed group. Although much work remains to be done on the question of marriage alliances, what evidence there is suggests a high degree of endogamy. Among the magistrates of the Parlement of Provence, 90 per cent of the marriages were with other nobles, mostly other robe families, but there was a significant set of alliances with sword, or military, nobles too. A little over one in ten marriages was with non-noble families but alliances with the merchant and wholesaling bourgeoisie were very rare despite the proximity of Aix-en-Provence and Marseille and despite the fabulous fortunes of the Marseille shipping clans. Elsewhere, eight out of ten marriages of the magistrates of the Parlement of Brittany took place within the circle of fully-fledged aristocrats. Marriages with merchants and financiers were very rare for the magistrates of the Parlement of Paris, who had close family relationships among themselves and with some of the most illustrious names at court. Among the nobles of the Paris region in general, there was almost no intermarriage with the Third Estate, indeed almost no marriage across the various sub-classes of noble. Among courtier families, the intermarriage among cousins in the same family was increasing because they were increasingly concerned to keep the blood lines pure. It also helps explain why opinion considered courtiers almost a race apart – they almost were.

The revolutionaries defined nobles with some justification as a wealthy group. They also claimed they were excessively privileged. Although this allegation is harder to assess, there was considerable truth to it. One of the difficulties is that there were few privileges common to the aristocracy throughout the realm and many varied in their impact. Their honorific rights defined in heraldic and sumptuary legislation marked them out without harming anyone else materially. Others could have real but intangible consequences: exemption from the jurisdiction of the bankruptcy courts, exemption from hanging or flogging except in cases unworthy of their station like treason or perjury, the privilege of *committimus* by which some nobles (and some clerics, among others) could demand a trial in civil cases before a higher jurisdiction, and so on. Still others could have a direct material benefit for individuals or their families. Nobles alone could own seigneuries or fiefs outright. Roturier owners had to pay a tax known as *franc-fief*. In regions of customary law, nobles enjoyed a different testamentary code that could permit primogeniture, thus preserving their estates from the disintegration that threatened those of roturiers every generation.

Above all nobles benefited from tax exemptions. Contrary to a common belief, nobles did pay taxes in the Old Regime. In 1695, Louis XIV subjected them to the *capitation*, a tax on overall revenues, and in 1749 his successor imposed the *vingtième*, a 5 per cent tax on net landed revenues. But nobles were exempt from compulsory billeting, militia service, the *corvée* or compulsory roadwork, and the *gabelle*, or salt tax. They were exempt too from the *taille personnelle* which covered three quarters of the country. In practice, this meant they could cultivate a home farm directly and pay no tax. Turgot, who as finance minister and a former intendant was in a position to know, estimated that this exemption was worth up to 2000 *livres*, and the reduced taxes on the farms of tenants allowed the noble landlords to demand higher rents.

They also paid less than they ought to have done on the taxes they owed. The richest noble families around Toulouse paid an average rate of less than 15 per cent while a typical peasant family paid considerably more. The princes of the blood ought to have paid 2.4 million *livres* in *vingtième* but actually paid only 188,000 *livres*, while one of them, the duc d'Orléans, bragged that he paid whatever he pleased. In Brittany the noble-dominated provincial estates collected taxes on behalf of the Crown on separate rolls for the nobility. They assessed themselves at half the per capita *capitation* of roturiers. The result was that the Marquis de Piré who had a gross fortune of 2.5 million *livres* paid only 27 *livres* in taxes, less than a prosperous baker paid. Privilege then was worth having. So too was ennobling office despite the low formal return on investment.

Many non-nobles thought privilege was worth having too. In fact, the most privileged corporation in the kingdom was the Church, which paid no taxes at all and instead negotiated a *don gratuit* or 'free gift' with the Crown every five years. In return, it received a monopoly of public worship, education and public charity. Many *roturiers* were privileged as well. No Bretons paid the *taille* or *gabelle* with the result that their tax load was less than one fifth that of their counterparts in the Ile-de-France. Indeed, as Necker, the Director-General of Finances, revealed in 1781, the regional disparities in the incidence of taxation were immense. Within the provinces too, various towns had bought or acquired exemption from the *taille*, as had various individuals, office-holders and occupations. Given the primitive fiscal machinery of the time, it is likely too that towns in general paid less than the countryside, although the system tried to compensate for this by elaborate indirect taxes on articles of consumption such as alcohol, soap, legal documents and playing cards.

In other words, nobles and bourgeois may have been functionally a class of property holders but there were still significant differences among them. Nobles were richer, and relatively more privileged. These differences affected the politics of the two groups in 1789.

The Crisis of the Old Regime

Aside from obvious self-interest, one of the reasons Frenchmen of whatever rank clung to privilege so much was that it protected them from a fiscal system that was both a mystery and accountable to no one. Indeed, the government itself had no idea what its resources or expenditures were. Although there were substantial efforts to adopt a more responsible system of internal accounting under the reign of Louis XVI, the Old Regime monarchy never thought of opening the books to outside scrutiny, or even to a centralized internal audit, let alone of justifying its fiscal policies to the public. Yet the monarchy did expect its subjects to pay and its officials were flabbergasted when other bodies questioned them.

The first great crisis of this sort occurred in the wake of the Seven Years War (1756–63). To raise money for this disastrous war, the government doubled the *vingtième* in 1756, and tripled it in 1760. Some exemptions from the *taille* were suspended, those remaining exempt had their *capitation* doubled, indirect taxes were raised and surtaxes were created. No one questioned that everyone had to make sacrifices in wartime but these measures were so drastic that they raised the question of the government's right to tax as it saw fit. Since the government proposed to continue these measures into the peace for reasons that were clear to no one, the question quickly arose of the limits of the monarchy's fiscal powers and of the proper relation between the Crown and its subjects.

The men best placed to pose these questions were the magistrates in the *parlements*, not only because the fiscal expedients of the war directly affected their pocket books but because venality of office offered them a measure of protection against reprisals. But they also spoke for everyone else who was affected, privileged or not, or for all those haunted by the nightmare of unchecked fiscality devouring the wealth of the nation.

Although the *parlements* lost in the struggle against the monarchy, they did habituate the politically conscious public to the idea that the solution to royal voracity was the rule of law. During the Jansenist crisis, the Parlement of Paris had already claimed to represent the nation. In 1763–4, it applied this principle to taxation. The magistrates argued that the King held his throne and legitimacy from the fundamental laws of the realm, which were immutable. The *parlement* had the right to determine whether ordinary legislation conformed to the principles of the ancient constitution. In fiscal matters, the magistrates claimed, 'the infraction of the sacred right of verification simultaneously violates the rights of the Nation and the rights of legislation; it follows that the collection of a tax which has not been verified is a crime against the Constitution...'. The purpose of government was to maintain the citizens in the enjoyment of rights which the laws assured them, those rights being liberty and honour. Provincial *parlements* went even further with strikes, collective resignations and orders to arrest local governors for enforcing the edicts. The most agonizing and dramatic conflict came with the Parlement of Brittany. This struggle lasted until 1770 with arrests, counter arrests, suspension of the *parlement*, resignations and arrest of magistrates. When the Parlement of Paris refused orders to cease its intervention, the Chancellor Maupeou in effect abolished it in February 1771. Subsequent protests from provincial parlements led to their 're-modelling'.

Yet once the government had its way, the Controller-General, Terray, did nothing to reform the government's finances. Force had shown that the monarchy could push its critics aside and stumble from one expedient to another, as it always had. Thus when Louis XVI, who ascended the throne in 1774, immediately restored the *parlements* in an attempt to win popularity and govern by consensus, men drew a number of conclusions from Maupeou's 'revolution', as it was called at the time. The *parlements* issued a number of declarations that showed they were unrepentant. They strongly protested Turgot's attempt in 1776 to transform the *corvée* into a money tax. In practice, however, the judges showed an extreme reluctance to risk provoking the monarchy again. Other commentators were simply dismayed. The timid Paris bookseller Hardy accused Maupeou of destroying the ancient constitution of the French government but could think of nothing better than to look to the princes of the blood 'on whose protests depends perhaps the salvation of the French and the conservation of the true rights of the nation'. Others were more imaginative. The Maupeou affair confirmed what some had been thinking for a long time: that France had become a despotism, no different from that of the dreaded Turks or any other oriental despotism. French kings no longer ruled according to the laws of God. They had succumbed to their base appetites.

But there were other possible lessons that could be taken from the Maupeou affair. Malesherbes, the magistrate of the *cour des aides* who later defended Louis XVI at his trial, remonstrated on behalf of his colleagues that the courts 'supplemented' the role of Estates in consenting to taxes and, in 1775, demanded the King hear 'the nation assembled .... The unanimous wish of the nation is to obtain the Estates-General or at least, provincial estates'.

Some of the provincial *parlements* like Grenoble, Bordeaux and Besan-çon demanded provincial estates as well, bodies which would give their provinces a bargaining power over taxes and a lever against the intend-ants such as the Bretons had and which they alone could not provide. In fact, the *parlements* had a strong sense of their own fragility, which was only reinforced by the docility of the Paris *parlement*. It registered a double *vingtième* in 1780, a triple *vingtième* in 1782 and loans of 125 million *livres* in 1784 and 80 million *livres* in 1785, with only perfunc-tory demands for further economies in the royal household and finances. The long-term effect of Maupeou's revelation of the *parlements'* weak-ness and their subsequent docility was thus to discredit the *parlements* as a defence against despotism. Rabaut-Saint-Etienne, the Protestant minis-ter and deputy to the Constituent Assembly, wrote that part of the nation regarded the *parlements* as a 'barrier to despotism of which everyone was weary'. The general public may well have thought so, but others explained the absence of heroics from this generation of magistrates as obsequiousness, ambition or corruption. The abbé Morellet, a minor writer, accused the *parlement* of 'letting us be overwhelmed [with taxes] for over a century, [of permitting the government] all its waste and its loans which it knew all about . . . '

Many Frenchmen of the 1780s had concluded that the risks of the monarchy degenerating into a despotism were very real and that the solution was not to reinforce the powers of the *parlements* but to revive the provincial estates or the Estates-General. So far as one can tell, few yet thought about the question of privileges. Indeed, the *parlementaires* who demanded the revival of representative institutions clearly thought of them as augmenting their constitutional powers and consequently protecting their privileges, not supplanting or suppressing them.

The government's freedom of maneuver in this general crisis of confi-dence in existing institutions was consequently limited. Nor had the two important finance ministers of the period, Necker and Calonne, raised the level of confidence. When a powerful coalition of tax-farmers, resent-ful courtiers and spiteful ministers pushed him out of office in 1781, Necker claimed in his famous *Comte rendu au roi* that there was a surplus on hand of 10 million *livres*. Whether this was misleading, as his detractors later suggested, is less important than the fact that, as the first public declaration of royal finances, it created a sensation and established Necker's reputation as a miracle worker. The triple *vingtième* and the huge loans after his fall only reinforced this impression. Calonne underlined it by heaping huge pensions on avid courtiers and by author-izing the Crown's acquisition of the lovely châteaux of Saint-Cloud and Rambouillet. By contrast, Necker had tried to impose greater internal accountability, closer surveillance of the tax-farmers and economies on the royal household: the very programme the *parlements* over a generation had educated the public to believe was the solution to the Crown's financial woes.

Calonne's strategy was to increase government credit and to stimulate the economy which in turn would increase government revenues. But the huge spending touched off a stock market boom, particularly in shares that were known to have government backing or ministerial protection. In addition, the boom fed, and was fed by, a mammoth speculation in urban real estate in which the court was directly involved. The duc d'Orléans, for example, developed his properties around the Palais Royal, the comte de Provence financed a great deal of building in the Vaugirard quarter of Paris, and the comte d'Artois ran up debts of 28 million, a victim of his own speculative appetites and peculation in his own household. A mountain of paper and credit surrounded the houses of the great and the ministry. By 1787, the government found itself subsidizing inflated shares in the New India Company, the Paris Water Company (which delivered no water), and in fire and life insurance companies (which ensured no lives). Yet the financiers and tax-farmers the government supported were in serious trouble by late 1786. Wine prices had been low since 1783 and the country was entering a manufacturing depression. The financiers' revenues from taxation were consequently declining and so, indirectly, were those of the government. With share prices in the India Company, the Water Company and Discount Bank falling in the wake of the speculative boom, many financiers were hard pressed. Calonne had also reached the limit of his ability to support them. In the first half of 1787, five went bankrupt, further shaking the government's credit, amid charges of fraud and embezzlement. At the very least, all this demonstrated the financial incompetence of the old monarchy.

Calonne proposed to deal with this gathering crisis once and for all, not by revamping the system of collection, but by tapping into the nation's resources in a new way. In August 1786, he announced to Louis XVI that the Crown no longer had any money. The third *vingtième* was due to expire the next year, the government had borrowed 1.25 billion since 1776, debt service alone would cost 50 million a year by 1790 and short-term loans were already too high at 280 million. Further taxes were politically impossible, would not yield enough anyway, and further economies would be insufficient. The only solution was a revamping of the entire fiscal and administrative structure of the state and a reform of its relationship to the economy. Whether any of this was true, of course, still has to be shown. The document was also entirely political, designed to back a dithering monarch into a corner and convince him that no other course of action was possible.

At the heart of Calonne's proposals was the replacement of the *vingt-ièmes* with a territorial subvention, a tax collected in kind on the basis of the landed income of all proprietors irrespective of their privileged status. Local assemblies representing all proprietors, again irrespective of their privileged status, would apportion the new tax. Other fiscal measures included reforms in the royal domain, extension of the stamp tax, rescheduling the national debt, commuting the royal *corvée* into a money tax, and reducing the salt tax. There were a number of proposals designed to stimulate the economy as well. Uniform tariffs, abolition of internal customs and freedom of the grain trade would all liberate the economy from administrative tutelage.

Whatever the merits of Calonne's plan, he had a long history of antagonism with the *parlements* – he had written the famous *séance de flagellation* speech of 1766 in which Louis XV expressly denied the *parlements* had any independent judicial authority. Further the Parlement had recently shown signs of life during the Diamond Necklace Affair and in questioning some of Calonne's fiscal machinations. He needed a ringing statement of confidence from outside the government that would shore up the monarchy's credit. This device was the Assembly of Notables, which had last met in 1626. By tradition, this body was composed of the princes of the blood, prelates, great nobles, magistrates and representatives of the *pays d'états* and some cities. Calonne hoped to pack the assembly with enough sympathizers to get the reform package through. Then flush with the support of the great names of the country, he could overawe the Parlement, but if this scheme did not work, he was prepared to force the reforms on them by a *lit de justice*, a perfectly legal constitutional device that required a *parlement* to accept a government law or decree. He also needed the full support of Louis XVI. In the end, none of these assumptions worked out. Of the princes who owed him so much, only the comte d'Artois was loyal. Provence and Orléans were in open opposition while the others remained quiet; the clergy was outraged by the attack on its privileges; the *parlements* were encouraged to believe once again that they represented public opinion; and Louis XVI, stung by the extent of the opposition and timid as always, allowed the situation to drift. Most importantly, the defiance of the Notables aroused public opinion.

The Collapse of Absolutism

The Assembly of Notables is a kind of interlude in the story. It defied the Crown, and passed the crisis off to the Paris *parlement*, but it was significant for two reasons: in demanding more economies in government expenditure, it convinced the public that the government was right: ever since the 1740s at least, the government had been maintaining that the source of the financial problem on the revenue side was tax privilege. The public endorsed this partial analysis, and the financial policy of the patriots ever after was to endorse this line. The public in turn was led to believe that eliminating tax privilege would lower the tax liability of the non-privileged. When this turned out not to be so, the disillusion was great. The second reason the Assembly of Notables was important was that it showed the Old Regime constitution worked they way the philosopher Montesquieu said it worked. In defending their own privileges, the Notables defended the nation against a rampant fiscality.

The Assembly of Notables met at Versailles from 22 February to May 1787. Opposition to the reform package itself was vociferous from the start. Much of it came from the clergy and the representatives of the *pays d'états* who were afraid of losing their privileges. But not all of the criticism was completely self-interested. The territorial subvention was an immensely stupid idea. The proposal to collect it in kind would not only attack the privileged but also it would be immensely expensive to collect and remove what little external control on revenue and expenditure remained. The provincial assemblies that would decide its distribution would work in such a way as to co-opt local élites to the royal despotism since these assemblies would have no independent rights. As it turned out, they were much like the departments the revolutionaries established and that still exist, with very little independent power either then or now. Nor could the representatives of the privileged provinces agree to the abolition of their rights to import freely certain colonial products, the extension of the state's tobacco monopoly and the generalizing of the salt tax even at a reduced rate.

Calonne's high-handed refusal to lay the royal accounts before the notables and his self-serving attacks on the ever popular Necker undermined his position. Once opposition began to grow, he published a pamphlet assaulting the notables' unwillingness to make sacrifices and presented himself as the defender of the non-privileged. This was a demagogic and fraudulent appeal to the Third Estate, since the government was yet again insisting that the problem was privilege, nothing else. Louis XVI had had enough and promptly sacked Calonne. He had to flee to England, the first émigré.

Meanwhile, the King called in one of his bitterest critics, the Archbishop of Toulouse, Loménie de Brienne. Brienne made a number of important, if futile, concessions. The territorial subvention would no longer be collected in kind, would have a fixed term and would be limited to government needs. The stamp tax was revised, economies promised, government accounts opened and the distinctions of the privileged in the provincial assemblies were to be recognized. But Brienne fared no better with the notables than Calonne. They had no desire to compromise themselves with an aroused public opinion and refused to vote any taxes, which they claimed they had no mandate to do. Brienne had no choice but to dismiss the notables and take his proposals to the Parlement of Paris which was now thoroughly aroused.

The government had calculated that the prestige of the notables would overawe the *parlements*. Yet articulate opinion that had first seen the notables as mere tools of the ministry was delighted at their show of independence. This reaction only encouraged the magistrates to believe that they represented the entire nation's distrust of royal fiscality. No doubt much of the *parlement's* action in the ensuing crisis was motivated by self-interest. Fiscal reform would certainly hurt them as landowners. But the *parlement* operated under other pressures as well. The magistrates' defiance was popular. As in the previous reign, the public saw the *parlements* as a defence against ravenous fiscality. As Rabaut Saint-Etienne recognized, in demanding the convocation of the Estates-General, the Parlement of Paris gave in to public opinion: 'No one knew it better because it studied it incessantly in order to rest upon it'. Pasquier, then a young magistrate, said the same thing and recalled that from 'the moment our interest was clearly at stake, we saw nothing more beautiful than to sacrifice it to what we considered the public good. Generous sentiments overwhelmed us and there was no way of holding us back'. Such idealism centred around the young councillors in the *parlement*, Adrien Duport and Hérault de Sechelles, who were working towards a constitution that would make ministers truly accountable. Although it was hardly apparent at the time, other magistrates were more conservative. Duval d'Eprémesnil and Saint-Vincent, for example, saw the great enemy as ministerial despotism and tried to exploit the crisis to enhance the prerogatives of the *parlements* and protect the corporate structure of French society of which the aristocracy was, of course, a vital part.

The *parlement* accepted some of the government's proposals but they rejected the stamp tax and the territorial subvention because only an Estates-General could consent to new taxes. Most of the peers and magistrates in the Parlement were aware that this was a revolutionary claim. Some recalled that the American Revolution had begun with resistance to taxes. Others feared that an Estates-General would amount to a revolution, although many were probably consoled with the idea that it was the traditional Estates that were being demanded, not a National Assembly. The recourse to a very old French parliamentary tradition was also a result of rumours that began to circulate from the summer of 1787 onwards that the *parlements* would be emasculated or abolished as punishment for their resistance, as in 1771. The Estates-General would protect the *parlements* who knew from experience that the government had the means, and, if sufficiently provoked, the will, to repeat the Maupeou experience.

Initially, therefore, the demand for the Estates-General was not revolutionary: those who demanded it did so because they expected it would reinforce existing institutions. How much esteem the government had lost, and how much support the *parlements* had, was shown in the reaction to the attempt to enforce registration of the fiscal edicts. On 6 August 1787, a *lit de justice* registered them and when a defiant *parlement* declared this null and opened an enquiry into Calonne's conduct for abuse of authority, the government struck. On 15 August, the magistrates were exiled to Troyes, but this only raised an unprecedented clamour throughout the country. Dozens of lower courts protested, some echoing the *parlement's* call for an Estates-General. Opinion at large followed, especially in Paris where crowds of young law clerks and porters roamed the streets stoning officials' houses and shouting anti-government threats in the markets. Neither Brienne nor the magistrates desired such an outright confrontation, however, and by mid-September a compromise had been worked out whereby the government withdrew the controversial land and stamp taxes in return for a continuation of the *vingtièmes*.

At first sight, the compromise appears to have favoured the *parlement*, but by withdrawing the new taxes Brienne undercut the magistrates' rationale for demanding the Estates-General. The crowds who welcomed the return of the judges to Paris did not understand this, but some acute observers did. Clearly, some hoped that the crisis would go much further and produce a reconfiguration of the constitution. The abbé Morellet, for example, wrote, 'On whom would you have the nation rely today? The parlements, which defended it so badly, have again deserted it.... We need some bar to the repetition of abuses: we need the Estates-General or the equivalent. That is what people everywhere are saying.' The bookseller Hardy who heard much of the gossip emanating from the law courts, reported that 'all the young jurists...exploded in anger at the parlement's moderation, which they regarded as sheer cowardice'. For those who wanted to keep the crisis going, who hoped that it could be transformed into a struggle for representative institutions, the compromise was a sharp disappointment.

Their instincts were correct because Brienne had decided to abandon fiscal reform in favour of an ambitious programme of retrenchment, rescheduling debts and pruning the military. Recovery was planned for 1792. An Estates-General that met in 1792 would only be in a position to applaud the government's success. But the bridging loans this strategy required did not convince the peers who sat in the Parlement. When the King's cousin, the duc d'Orléans protested that enforcing the loans was illegal, Louis XVI countered: 'That is of no importance to me. . . . You're indeed the minister. . . . Yes, of course . . . it is legal because I will it.'

Eventually, the government decided to have done with the *parlements*. Clearly, the government thought it was in a very strong position. On 8 May 1788, Lamoignon, the Keeper of the Seals, forced the registration of Six Edicts that emasculated the *parlements*. Registration of new edicts was transferred to a new Plenary Court, composed of princes of the blood and royal officials.

Lamoignon's coup was a classic case of over-reach. It initiated the final crisis that brought about the collapse of the old monarchy and it did so by exhausting the government's capacity to borrow. This was difficult to foresee. Investors quickly took up the advantageous loans in the November edicts, and government stocks, buoyed along by a promising *compte rendu* published in April 1788, climbed in the immediate aftermath of the coup. But the aristocratic revolt which followed helped to sap investor confidence. While Paris remained calm, there were violent riots in Rennes, Grenoble and Pau. The intendant of Brittany, Bertrand de Molleville, had to flee the province in July, while in Grenoble troops were showered with roof tiles by the outraged citizenry; four people were killed and scores injured in the subsequent repression. The Assembly of the Clergy, dominated by aristocratic prelates, gave the government a miserable 1.8 million *livres* in *don gratuit* instead of the requested 8 million and published a strident denunciation of Lamoignon's 'revolutions', as they called it. Elsewhere provincial *parlements* and *présidiaux* protested, lawyers promised to boycott the superior bailiwicks and in Brittany aristocrats formed 'correspondence committees' among the towns to stir up public opinion – presumably a deliberate borrowing of a term from the English and American revolutions. The government might have mastered this unprecedented wave of discontent because, in the end, the army, for all the discontent among some junior officers, remained loyal. In any case, the opposition was far from united. The new provincial assemblies were on the whole cooperative, not all the *parlements* protested, and some presidial magistrates and some towns were delighted to have their status raised or to become the site of a new court.

But a divide and rule tactic was no longer possible in the summer of 1788 because the political crisis finally ruined government credit. By early August, Brienne found the treasury empty. A sure sign of trouble had come earlier in July when, in an attempt to bolster confidence, he moved forward the meeting of the Estates-General to May 1789. Thus the confident assumption that the 1792 assembly would simply congratulate the government for restoring public finances had already evaporated, and the Crown for the first time admitted it could not govern without a representative assembly of some sort. The final blow came on 8 August when the government suspended treasury payments, which many panicked investors interpreted as a partial bankruptcy. Defeated by a credit crisis and the aristocratic revolt, Brienne could only resign. With great reluctance but with no alternative, Louis XVI turned to Necker as the only man who could salvage the situation. Finally the *parlements* were restored and the May edicts withdrawn. Absolutism had collapsed.

The Men of Liberty

What would replace it became the central point of the struggle for the next nine months. The Parlement of Paris saw itself as the great victor in this triumph over despotism and declared on 25 September that the Estates-General would meet according to the form of the last one in 1614. This is usually taken as the moment when the aristocracy threw off its mask, determined to preserve its privileges at any price since adherence to the forms of 1614 required each estate to vote separately and each would have a veto over the actions of the other two. Thus the aristocracy would be able to control the pace of reform. This was undoubtedly a revelation for many, as the scores of municipal deliberations and outraged pamphlets testify. But the situation was less clear. The magistrates could not have thought through the implications of their action, since adherence to the 'forms of 1614' would have put them in the Third Estate. Clumsy as it was, the *parlement's* attempt to anticipate the structure of the Estates-General sparked a new campaign among those whose support for the aristocratic revolution had always been tactical or tepid. But even future revolutionary leaders were far from adopting a common outlook during the crisis. All of them were feeling their way and improvising. Whatever their attitude in the crisis following Lamoignon's coup, the ultimate aim was a National Assembly, presumably modelled on something like the English parliament or some American state legislatures, an aim that was quite at variance with the forms of 1614. For them, the *parlements* were a weak reed against despotism, as the compromise of September 1787 had shown. The magistrates had also opposed enlightened reformers like Turgot in 1776 or had long before ruined their reputation with the Protestant community. For men like these, support for the *parlements* or enlightened ministers had always been contingent upon reform. With the meeting of the Estates-General now certain, their agenda switched towards securing a National Assembly which offered a better hope than any other institution.

They called themselves 'patriots' which at the time meant a lover of liberty. Who were they? In fact, the composition of the group is not well known at least in part because the patriots constantly represented themselves as the entire nation. Since they won the propaganda battle of 1788–9 so decisively, it is tempting to read the history of the period as that of the nation against despotism. From what little is known about them, however, they were certainly not the nation, nor were their followers entirely bourgeois. In fact, the Paris leadership was hardly bourgeois at all. The most influential body that took upon itself the task of educating the nation in its rights was the Society of Thirty, a hastily formed club drawn from the various salons of the capital. Of the fifty-five identifiable members, fifty were nobles, split roughly evenly between courtiers and the younger magistrates. Almost all of them came from families that had been ennobled for generations, and among the courtiers, all but one had been ennobled before 1500, making them among the most ancient and illustrious families in the entire aristocracy. Paradoxically, many had been alienated because of Louis XVI's policy of professionalizing his councillors, intendants and army officers by recruiting them from the provincial squirearchy – in other words, they resented being deprived of their entitlements. All of them despised Marie-Antoinette for spitefully freezing their families out of lucrative court honours and sinecures. A few, like Lafayette, were veterans of the war in America where they had picked up notions of individual rights, contract theories of government and the rhetoric of popular sovereignty. None expected these notions would shake their own position in society. As Lafayette put it, the purpose of a reform in France would be 'to establish the executive power of the monarchy, the predominance of the nobles, and the rights of property [on the basis] of a free constitution that would permit all citizens to participate in the advantages which nature had accorded to all men . . .'. Finally, some were connected with Turgot and fell from court favour when he fell from the ministry. That great disappointment must have prepared many to look outside the existing order for a genuine reform.

The connection with Turgot was a direct connection with the Enlightenment for it was men like the members of the Society of Thirty whom the *philosophes* influenced most. The *philosophes* did not have a particularly wide impact. Professional, religious and historical themes dominated provincial reading culture and the bestseller of the century was not one of the enlightened classics but a justly forgotten, but endlessly reprinted, book of devotions called *The Guiding Angel*. Although literacy rates were climbing dramatically, particularly for women and for southerners, popular reading tastes scarcely changed at all. These remained mired in a culture of the marvellous, the supernatural and the fantastic.

As for the deputies to the Estates-General, an obvious group to test for the relationship between ideas and action, the overall assessment is untidy but fairly clear. There were genuine men of ideas, men who had intellectual lustre in their own right like the Marquis de Condorcet, or there were men professionally associated with famous men of letters. But many of them had a hard time getting elected. One example would be the abbé Sieyès who failed to get elected in the First Estate and came twentieth out of twenty in the Paris delegation for the Third. Few of the deputies were members of local academies and although more were members of the masonic societies and some even held high position in the lodges, such men were still a serious minority. Many of the future deputies were authors in their own right, but few showed much response to traditional Enlightenment themes. Many of the books were technical or professional legal treatises. Fewer still appealed to Enlightened principles once the revolution of 1789 was under way. On religious issues, deputies to the Third Estate were rarely fervent, but this mattered little in the run-up to the Revolution; it would matter when it came to the implementation of the reforms they would impose on the Church.

The relation of nobles to the Enlightenment was very different. In so far as it is possible to attach ideas to a class, enlightened culture was practically the culture of the cultivated nobility. It was they who patronized writers, corresponded with them, and publicized them through the salons of the capital. In the provinces, the parlementary magistrates encouraged the spread of reason and light through the provincial academies they dominated. Nobles were also prominent among the buyers of the greatest enlightened work of the century, Diderot's huge, expensive and enormously popular *Encyclopédie*, to which many nobles including d'Alembert and Jaucourt contributed.

The advanced ideas of the century were not even necessarily political. Much enlightened thought dealt with themes like man's place in the universe, original sin and the nature of sense impressions that had little to do with the issues of the 1780s. There was also an extensive and well-argued Catholic counter polemic that meant that the *philosophes* did not carry all before them. Indeed, some of the future deputies contributed to it.

Nonetheless, in a general sense, the Enlightenment was indeed very influential even if it is nearly impossible to pin down the impact of specific writers or individual books. As a cast of mind, it taught its followers to judge institutions by reason and utility, not by their antiquity or sacredness. This provided the justification of the reforms of 1789–90. In particular, its desacralization of life required religious toleration and the suppression of many privileges of the Church. So it may well be that Enlightened writings did little to subvert the monarchy or the society of privilege but made it easier in a general way to justify what happened to the Church. For those associated with Turgot, it also meant a society dominated by landowners, not privileged persons, a more rational fiscal system, freedom of the grain trade, the end of immunities in taxation, the suppression of monopolies like guilds, and the creation of representative assemblies. Again 'economical' ideas had little to do with the origins of the Revolution itself, but they did provide a huge archive of ideas about what to do once the Old Regime collapsed. In short, the Enlightenment was enormously influential on a small group of men who were themselves enormously influential in the winter of 1788–9 and in the Estates-General. Ordinary deputies may have had only a passing knowledge of these ideas before the Revolution; once it came to liquidating the Old Regime in late 1789–91, there were plenty of experts available to educate them.

It is difficult to be more precise about the impact of the propaganda of the Society of Thirty on the provinces. As wealthy men, its members were able to flood the country with pamphlets and broadsides attacking privilege and suggesting the form the Estates-General ought to take. Their immediate demand was for vote by head, that is, a single chamber; and double representation for the Third Estate. Both devices would counterbalance the defences of the orders of the clergy and the nobility. As an appeal to the relatively non-privileged, this was enormously successful but the provinces had their own reasons, aside from this propaganda or the Enlightenment, for responding as massively as they did. People feared there was no limit to the government's ability to tax the nation and the Estates-General would stop that. People also accepted the government's analysis that the deficits existed because of the exemptions of the privileged classes. There was little or no discussion of the similar privileges of the Third Estate, partly because of self-interest but partly because neither Calonne nor Brienne had laid much emphasis on them as causes of the state's financial problems.

On the whole, the patriots in the provinces were the relatively non-privileged but this was not an invariable rule, nor were the patriots exclusively bourgeois. In Dauphiné in the summer of 1788, nobles and clerics associated themselves with a movement led by the lawyers Barnave and Mounier to have the provincial estates organized on the basis of the doubling of the Third, vote by head and elected representatives, not *ex-officio* ones. This culminated in a meeting of all three orders on 21 July 1788 at Vizille that promulgated these demands and that agreed to have all taxes assessed on the basis of fiscal equality.

In Brittany, similar events took a more violent course because the *parlement* and the noble-dominated provincial estates had a long history of resistance to reform. As early as 1768, the issue of noble tax privileges had arisen in the Estates and continued for every session thereafter. It provoked the young law professor Lanjuinais to advocate a wider and more effective voice for the Third Estate. When the final crisis broke, the *parlement* encouraged violent demonstrations against Lamoignon's Edicts, and the comte de Botherel, the procurator of the Estates, toured the province's law courts in the summer of 1788 claiming new taxes violated the terms of union between Brittany and the Crown. The Paris *parlement's* demand for the forms of 1614 would have nullified the Third's hope for tax relief, however, since ancient usage would have permitted the local estates to choose the deputies to the Estates-General. The reform of the Estates itself thus became an urgent priority. The patriots created the impression of an overwhelming wave in favour of reform. Perhaps because Brittany had a more active political life in the Old Regime, they were much more successful, even though they too appealed to specific groups. In Rennes, the legal professions, merchants and wholesalers and master-craftsmen (particularly in the building and clothing trades) adhered to the patriot movement far out of proportion to their numbers in the population, while the journeymen, labourers and domestic servants were considerably under represented. As early as December 1788, the revolutionary coalition that was to dominate the political life of the city for the next six years, and indeed the nation, had emerged. Contrary to their rhetoric that represented them as deprived, the patriots were well off. The poor were singularly under represented. The average patriot paid four times the city average while the really wealthy who formed one third of the patriots paid 80 per cent of the group's taxes.

Not all the wealthy, not every lawyer and not all the trades were as enthusiastic as others and why this should be so is not clear. In faraway Toulouse, it was impossible to distinguish patriot from non-patriot barristers on the basis of age or wealth. One clue comes from the little Breton port of Vannes where the patriot municipal councillors tended to be those who were more zealous participants in local affairs than non-patriots. Their political education had been primed by trying to cope with the obstruction of the privileged in town affairs for a half-century. For them, eliminating privilege at the local level could only come with undermining it in the provincial constitution. But for others the choices were less clear. Clientage, family relations, professional interests and fear of disorder kept them with the privileged. In Rennes, the barristers as an order, as opposed to enthusiastic individuals, tried to mediate the pretensions of both groups. Their leader, Le Chapelier, who had just inherited noble status from his father, stayed aloof from the demagogues of the dominant aristocratic faction and the inflammatory law students. The barristers were provoked into siding with the Third Estate. On 26 January 1789, aristocratic thugs, domestics and sedan-chair carriers in the pay of the great houses, assailed the law students. The *parlement* refused to investigate and the barristers took this as support for the assault. Thus for reasons that had everything to do with law and order, the barristers as a group joined the patriot side. The old order's deception and hypocrisy explains much of the Breton delegation's moral indignation and intransigence in the Estates-General.

Elections and Issues

Throughout the gathering agitation in the provinces, the government remained cautious to a fault. Financial considerations and the looming crisis in the economy distracted Necker. Ever since September, the pamphleteers had been demanding the doubling of the number of deputies of the Third Estate. Neither a second Assembly of Notables nor a Parlement of Paris totally stung by the pamphleteers took a stand on the issue of doubling. Necker thus took the plunge and in December 1788, ordered that the number of deputies to the Third Estate be doubled. But without vote by head, this was nearly meaningless. It did encourage the patriots, however, to pursue their pamphlet war in favour of vote by head.

The mode of elections to the Third Estate contributed to a latent unity among the deputies. In the countryside, the inhabitants met in March and early April to choose delegates. These men in turn met at the seat of the bailiwick to choose deputies to the Estates-General. In the towns, the guilds, corporations and town councils chose deputies to the bailiwick assembly in a two-, three- or even four-stage process. At each stage the assemblies drafted *cahiers de doléances*, or statements of grievances, which the general bailiwick assembly consolidated into a general *cahier*. At the same time, it chose deputies to the Estates-General.

The elections were among the freest of the entire revolutionary period and deputies were chosen on a wide franchise. Turnout in many places was higher in the countryside than the towns but even so, the turnout was poor. In Paris, for example, the turnout of 25–30 percent would be the highest for the decade. In any case, the system of indirect elections favoured men of substance, particularly the legal professions, at every step of the way. This was because lawyers were used to public speaking anyway and because the deputies to the bailiwick assemblies and to the Estates-General were generally expected to pay their own expenses.

The conditions of election produced a remarkably homogeneous group. Counts vary but on the whole the legal professions were overwhelmingly represented among the deputies to the Third Estate. Nearly two thirds had legal training. Over 200 were qualified advocates who were at the peak of their careers and who were to be very active speakers and committee men, while 127 were bailiwick magistrates who tended to be spectators. Over 40 per cent of the deputies were venal officeholders while businessmen and landowners totalled only about one fifth of the delegations. Most significantly, Third Estate deputies were far less wealthy than the noble deputies. Marriage contracts for nobles noted assets that were fifteen times those of the Third Estate. Far more Third Estate deputies had a formal education, and many of them had advanced training, mostly in the law. Many of them too had political experience before the Revolution. While the soldiers trained in barracks or went to America, the lawyers and magistrates were on town councils or other bodies and they had become caught up in the political mobilization of 1788. Nearly three quarters of the deputies came from towns with a population greater than 2000 at a time when 80 per cent of Frenchmen lived in smaller centres. No less than one quarter of the deputies came from the larger towns and cities which were inhabited by only 10 per cent of the population. The strong urban representation was particularly significant because the general *cahiers* of urban regions were more critical of noble privileges and seigneurial rights, and more demanding of representative institutions, than the *cahiers* of parish and guild assemblies. Northern deputies also outnumbered southern by over two to one and since northern France tended to be more heavily urban, there was a strong contingent of deputies who were highly critical of existing institutions. The system of indirect elections then produced an embryonic political élite with remarkably similar ideas.

The elections to the privileged orders also produced some unpredictable results. The government allowed the parish clergy a direct role in choosing delegates to the First Estate, and in the diocesan assemblies they took advantage of it. The upper clergy – about a hundred deputies – was certainly well represented, which shows that respect for them had not gone into eclipse as much as contemporaries thought. On the other hand, nearly two hundred parish priests were elected. These were highly professional men, often highly qualified with university degrees and disproportionately recruited from urban bourgeois families and highly dedicated to pastoral work. The liberal *curés* also had a more extensive education than their conservative counterparts. Most had grievances. They were critical of the opulence of the upper clergy, worried that the Church was losing its sense of vocation, and anxious about the increasing secularization of the country represented by the spread of impious, philosophic writings. Some had experience demanding rights for the pastoral clergy against bishops whom they depicted as indifferent oppressors, more interested in billiards than in pastoral work. Most were unhappy at the granting of partial civil status to Protestants and resentful at being excluded from high office and the deliberative bodies of the Church. The solution for many was greater control of the Church from below and greater clerical influence over national life. Although there was a significant party of patriots led by the abbé Gregoire, most never envisaged the Church losing its corporate identity. On secular matters the clerical *cahiers* were in broad agreement with those of the general bailiwicks. They too saw regular constitutional government and the abolition of fiscal privileges, including those of the Church, as the route to national regeneration.

The elections to the Second Estate, the nobility, also produced some surprises. For all their visions of themselves as defenders of the nation against despotism, the *parlementaires* fared badly. Only twenty-two were ever elected, revenge no doubt for the disdain in which *parlementaires* had long held country gentlemen, and a reflection too of the nobility's determination to defend their interests themselves. The court and Parisian aristocracy did better than might have been expected considering the provincials' dislike of high living in the capital. Indeed, the great names of the kingdom did very well in the elections. Thus, the noble deputies did not much resemble the nobility as a whole. Eight out of ten of their families had been ennobled before 1600, while the aristocracy as a whole was much younger. They were also enormously wealthy, far wealthier than the deputies to the Third Estate and even wealthier than their fellow nobles. Most lived in towns, few were country squires, none fitted the legendary stereotype of a penniless bumpkin. Above all, they were soldiers. Eight out of ten were officers in the army or navy, again in contrast to the bulk of the order who were office-holding civilians. This made a difference in the politics of 1789. Many of them had obtained a dismal education and they were not articulate men. Many resented their inability to hold their own in debate against the lawyers of the Third Estate, but many lawyer-deputies became enormously bitter at the noble deputies' disdain and snobbery.

Contrary to what was once thought, political divisions did not align court liberals against provincial reactionaries. Such a split scarcely existed. Instead, the 90 (out of 282 noble deputies) liberals were younger. One half were under forty in 1789 whereas three quarters of the conservatives were over forty. Liberals were also more likely to have an urban background. Nearly 90 per cent of them lived in a town of more than 2000 inhabitants while less than three quarters of the conservatives did. Liberals too were more likely to have travelled to England or even America, and more likely to belong to a local academy or learned society and therefore to have participated in the vibrant cultural life of the century. In other words, the liberal nobles, whose influence in the design of the constitution was to be disproportionate, had much in common with the activists in the Third Estate: youth, an urban background and hostility to privilege.

In short, beneath the traditional division of the élite into orders, there lay a fundamental social and cultural split, not between classes in the now discarded Marxist sense, but between certain kinds of social experiences. Above all, there were huge differences of background, wealth and life experience between noble and the Third Estate deputies. This translated itself into programmatic issues and it meant that only some extraordinary leadership and persuasion could have produced an accommodation between the two groups. On the other hand, much of the patriot grouping did transcend these differences and they had much in common. Patriots were younger, well educated, well travelled, and above all immersed in an urban setting. They had few doubts of their intellectual and cultural gifts and they were determined to bring their insights to the nation as a whole. For those provincials who were less gifted, or as the patriots were so quick to stigmatize, more ignorant and boorish, these attitudes were insufferably arrogant and contemptuous. But it would be a while before this gulf of misunderstanding revealed itself.

There was a broad consensus on constitutional questions. The aristocracy believed that absolutism had to be checked and that concessions had to be made on the fiscal issue. In its 5 December, 1788 declaration, the Parlement of Paris envisaged an Estates-General that would meet regularly, that would consent to taxation and to which ministers would be responsible. Individual liberty, the rule of law and freedom of the press were also essential features of a regenerated nation. The *parlement*, the second Assembly of Notables and the famous Memoir of the Princes submitted to the King on 12 December 1788 all claimed that nobles were willing to sacrifice their pecuniary privileges. An impressive 89 per cent of the noble *cahiers* also favoured the surrender of fiscal immunities. Thus the dispute between the nobles and the Third Estate was not over fiscal privilege. Most nobles were willing to surrender this.

Nobles were less certain than the larger cities on some other constitutional issues. Just half of the nobles' grievances demanded a constitution while three quarters of the cities did, and 60 per cent of the noble *cahiers* demanded individual liberties while over 80 per cent of the cities did. While neither foresaw the complete overthrow of traditional institutions as yet, the nobility was much more likely to want to limit the role of the Estates-General to the defence of those institutions, whereas the cities were more likely to want to fix the relationship between individuals and state institutions.

These differences on constitutional questions derived from the differences between the nobility as a wealthy privileged ruling class and the relatively non-privileged bourgeoisie. The nobles trusted the institutions they controlled to curb the arbitrariness of the monarch; whereas scepticism was greater among the Third.

The social differences produced even more marked differences of opinion on issues of civil equality. Where a mere 5 per cent of noble *cahiers* demanded equality of opportunity regardless of birth, 73 per cent of the cities did. Where less than one fifth of the noble *cahiers* demanded the abolition of the *franc-fief*, the tax roturiers paid to own seigneuries or fiefs, nearly two thirds of the cities did. Where less than one third of the noble *cahiers* demanded abolition of venality in office, 82 per cent of the cities did – an indication incidentally of how little influence office-holders had in drafting general urban *cahiers*. The nobility and the bourgeoisie did share similar economic functions and interests but differences of power, wealth and privilege produced conflicting outlooks on the nature of the constitution, on how open the élite was to be and on the role of birth, property and talent in the composition of that élite.

This is why the issue of vote by head was so important in the Estates-General. The nobility was almost evenly divided on the issue. About 40 per cent of their *cahiers* demanded vote by order. Roughly another 40 per cent vote by head, and the rest would have permitted vote by head depending upon the issue. Some nobles clung to vote by order so tenaciously because it was a way of defending what d'Epremesnil called the just prerogatives of the nobility and the clergy, by which he meant the monopolies in the army, education, the Church, state and judiciary. The Memoir of the Princes (signed by all but the liberals, Provence and Orléans) threatened a noble boycott of the Estates-General if vote by head were conceded. On the other hand, a substantial minority of nobles, and a majority on fiscal issues, was willing to take the risk that vote by head would not undermine their eminent social position or their property.

The bulk of Third Estate opinion did not aim at a total subversion of the existing order either. It was mainly in the larger cities that there were clearly articulated demands for change, numerous grievances and a strong sense of the importance of individual rights as a device for regulating the relationships between the state and the citizen. This was important since the larger cities were over represented in the Estates-General but their radicalism did not go so far as to undermine urban privileges and provincial rights. Indeed the universal demand for provincial estates, the absence of any thorough anticlericalism or hostility to the nobility as an institution, the respect for the authority of the king, and the very infrequent references to national or popular sovereignty all suggest that opinion even within the upper Third Estate was still poised between the defence or revival of traditional institutions and the newer doctrines. Needless to say, opinion in the smaller towns, guilds and village assemblies was even more conservative. Nothing could be more misleading, therefore, than to take the abbé Sieyès's famous pamphlet *What is the Third Estate?* as typical of opinion in the nation. He argued that the two privileged orders were parasites on the nation, their privileges usurpations to be severed, not generously surrendered. It would be some time before this view acquired much popularity.

Thus there was a considerable scope for political leadership. One can imagine a situation whereby the very real differences among the estates could have been fudged and compromised. Indeed, many deputies of the Third Estate had no idea what their *cahier* even contained and therefore what they were theoretically obliged to demand. Instead, they were suffused with a vague well-meaning goodwill towards the problems of the country. Men like this could certainly have been led. That a grand compromise within the aristocratic and bourgeois élites proved impossible has to do with circumstances that unfolded in the summer of 1789 and also because the patriot political leadership, composed of both progressive nobles and bourgeois lawyers, never wanted any such compromise. As it turned out, this was a perfectly defensible calculation in 1789. But when the provinces began to understand the consequences of this calculation later and how it affected them, the patriot élites lost control of the situation they had created.

The Revolution of the Lawyers

When the Estates-General opened at Versailles on 5 May 1789, all observers agreed that the government wasted an opportunity to give a lead on the major questions of the day. Government spokesmen proposed letting the Estates-General itself resolve the problem of vote by head. The Third countered by raising the issue of the verification of election returns. This was to dominate the political scene for the next seven weeks. In itself the issue was trivial but if a committee composed of delegates of all three orders verified the returns, a precedent would be set for vote by head. From this a single-chamber legislature would follow. The Third Estate, whose doubled representation aided by the liberal nobles and clerics, in turn would dominate this single chamber. It could shape a regenerated France according to its own wishes. Separate verification of powers, on the other hand, would ultimately allow the nobility to retain its privileges. The Third Estate, therefore, refused to verify its powers or declare itself constituted which, since it was not a formal body, led to the anomalous result that curious sightseers from Versailles and Paris were allowed to wander among the deputies on the floor of the *Salle des Menus Plaisirs* where they met, shouting encouragement to their favourites.

The leaders of the Third began an appeal to the lower clergy to begin verification in common and the bishops barely held them back. Meanwhile, votes in the Second Estate, the nobility, showed how insignificant the liberal nobles were. There were only 46 (out of 231) votes against the decision to declare the order constituted on 11 May, and only 16 votes (out of 218) against the declaration on 28 May that vote by order and mutual veto were fundamental to the monarchial constitution. As the Marquis de Ferrières explained, 'It's not right to let ourselves be led by the nose by all these advocates.'

The increasing polarization between the Second and Third Estates dismayed moderates on both sides but drew both to the militants in each order. The comte d'Artois and the appalling Polignacs kept an open table for the provincial nobles while d'Epremesnil and Cazales took the most combative defense of noble interests in the Assembly. Among the Third Estate the Breton delegation, under the informal leadership of Le Chapelier, gained greater ascendancy. Finally, the abbé Sieyès persuaded the Third that the way out of the impasse was to 'cut the cable'. On 10 June, on Sieyès's motion, the Third by a vote of 246 to 51 announced it would begin the verification of powers of all deputies to the Estates-General with or without the cooperation of the other two orders. A very similar motion by Le Chapelier had failed a month earlier, which shows that exasperation among the uncommitted deputies of the Third now drew them towards more adventurous solutions. On the 17th, again on a motion by Sieyès, the Third took the title National Assembly by a vote of 491 to 90. On a motion by Le Chapelier and Target, they guaranteed existing taxes for the existing session only and invited a tax strike should the Assembly be dissolved by force. The deputies were under no illusion: ever since the deadlock among the orders had manifested itself in mid-May, there had been rumours that the Estates would be dismissed and the financial crisis resolved by new loans. The assumption of national sovereignty and constituent power implied in the decrees of 10 and 17 June gave a new fillip to these rumours and Le Chapelier's motion represented an invitation to open rebellion as a defence. The lawyers in the Third Estate had become revolutionaries.

Meanwhile, the clergy was still torn by the problem of common verification of powers. They had voted against it on 6 May but after the failure of Necker's attempts at compromise, an increasing number became anxious to take an initiative on their own. Already twenty had responded to the Third's roll call after 10 June and on the 19th, by a narrow majority of about a dozen, they voted to verify powers in common. In the minds of many, this was not meant to prejudice the question of vote by order or the clergy's separate status, but, whether they knew it or not, the clergy had in effect voted to join the National Assembly.

With the situation disintegrating all around him, Necker finally persuaded Louis XVI to try to take the matter in hand by holding a royal session of all three orders. Yet the King, with only his good will to guide him, was irresolute. Numbed for a time by the death of his son on 4 June, he was pressured by the Queen, Artois and the leaders of the noble deputies to take a strong stand. The ministry too was divided with Necker, Montmorin and Saint-Priest urging conciliation, while Barentin, the Keeper of the Seals, demanded firmness. The resulting royal programme reflected these conflicts, offering at once a broad programme of reforms that did not satisfy the liberal deputies on the main issues. The royal programme was nonetheless important because it represented the transformation of absolute to constitutional monarchy, which Louis later said was his last free act. It was, however, shortly forgotten. The King departed from it significantly in the letter he left behind when he tried to flee the country in 1791. His brother, the Pretender who later became Louis XVIII, committed himself to an out and out restoration of the Old Regime for most of the period. He agreed to accept a constitution only in his Declaration of Saint-Ouen in 1814 and the Restoration Charter was a very different document than the programme of the *séance royale*.

The bungling of the preparations for the royal session only reinforced the National Assembly's resolution to stand firm. The *Salle des Menus Plaisirs* where the Third Estate met was closed to prepare for the session, but no one officially informed Bailly, the president of the Third. When the deputies arrived on the morning of the 20th to find placards closing the assembly hall and two hundred soldiers standing guard, many immediately concluded that a formal dissolution was imminent. Angered at the contempt for their rights and fearful of conspiracy, they went to a nearby enclosed tennis court and there took an oath not to separate from the National Assembly, and to reassemble wherever necessary if it was dissolved, until they had established a constitution for the kingdom. The Tennis Court Oath was one of the great days of the Revolution. The painter David immortalized it in his celebrated painting. The oath was a symbol of national unity (only one deputy formally refused and two others timidly absented themselves) and it reaffirmed the assumption of sovereignty the National Assembly took on the 10th and the 17th.

Equally important, the oath undermined the King's solution even before it was offered. The *séance royale* of 23 June was hardly designed to satisfy men who had shown such hard resolution. Louis promised a regular Estates-General that would have a wide measure of financial control over government operations including the sanctioning of taxes. He also promised to establish provincial estates in every province that would have considerable local autonomy. He also invited proposals on the abolition of *lettres de cachet* consistent with state security and on press freedom consistent with morals and religion. He also proposed a reform of the civil and criminal administration, of indirect taxes, of militia service and the abolition of internal customs, of the *corvée* and of the *taille*. The *parlements* and the provincial estates had been demanding much the same for a year, however. In other words, the King offered nothing which would flaunt the desires of the privileged. On the major issues, he aligned himself completely with the privileged orders. He said he would sanction fiscal equality only if the privileged orders first agreed, that all property, including the seigneurial system and the tithe, would be respected and that privileged exemptions from such things as compulsory billeting and militia service would remain unless the Estates-General commuted them into a money tax. Vote by head in the Estates-General would be permitted on issues of common utility but specifically excluded from this rubric were affairs concerning 'the ancient and constitutional rights of the three orders... feudal and seigneurial property and the useful rights and honorific prerogatives of the first two orders.' The Third Estate had already rejected similar proposals. If the Third persisted, Louis continued, 'if you abandon me in such a worthy enterprise, I alone will achieve the welfare of my people.'

The nobles were exultant and many even welcomed the threat to dissolve the Estates. The nobility and many clerics filed out of the hall but the Third refused, reaffirmed the Tennis Court Oath and carried on as before. Within hours, the royal initiative had collapsed.

There was nothing left now except a military solution. On or about 25 June, the decision was taken to resign the state to bankruptcy and dissolve the Estates-General by force. Orders went out to the commanders of the garrisons on the northern and eastern frontiers to march to Paris and Versailles. The troop movements were disguised on the pretext of keeping order. Partly as a ruse and partly to protect them from daily mob attack for remaining separate, Louis ordered the remaining nobles and clerics to join the National Assembly on the 27th.

The revolution of the lawyers appeared doomed. The people saved it.

So Why did a Revolution in France Occur?

One can think of a lot of reasons why it did not occur, not because of a class struggle between a rising bourgeoisie and a declining nobility; not because the monarchy as an institution lost respect; and not because the effect of the cultural transformations of the eighteenth century was to create the Revolution in men's minds before it occurred. The best example of this would be the abbé Sieyès. He wrote an utterly banal pamphlet about the financial and political crisis in the late autumn of 1788 and then he wrote the inflammatory *What is the Third Estate?* the following spring. What happened between the two pamphlets? One must postulate either that Sieyès held back his true opinions in the first pamphlet – but there is no evidence for this – or that the rapidly evolving situation radicalized him. Even so, events quickly bypassed him as well. He had a huge influence in June 1789; by July, no one paid any attention to his impenetrable drafts of a declaration of rights.

If we assume that what was revolutionary about the Revolution was the Declaration of the Rights of Man and the Citizen, then it is obvious that very few Frenchmen were revolutionaries before 1789. No doubt there were some who carried Anglo-American ideas like the Virginia Declaration of Rights back with them when the American War ended. Lafayette was the best example, and he continued to look for ideas and inspiration from Thomas Jefferson. But there is a counter-example, a man who is equally interesting: the Marquis de la Rouerie, a Breton nobleman, and a lifelong admirer of Washington, who also fought in America. But he believed American ideas were fine for Americans. France was another matter and he went to the Bastille in 1788 defending Breton liberties (meaning the marriage contract of Anne of Brittany and Louis XI of 1531). He eventually organized an anti-revolutionary conspiracy that, had it been successful, would have returned the old duchy to the pristine state it had been in the sixteenth century, before the Bourbons violated the marriage contract.

So even the American example, much as the patriots admired it, does not always work in explaining the Revolution. Thus we have to return to the idea that there was a social basis to politics and that the very real differences in status, wealth, and mental preoccupations between the aristocracy and the bourgeoisie mattered in explaining political commitments. But not entirely. Circumstances mattered too. One can imagine any number of points along the time line when a compromise or a bold measure might have made a difference. If only the Crown had given a lead in May 1789 on the issue of vote by head. If only the Crown had paid more attention to the grievances of the Third for equality of opportunity or fiscal equality. Many deputies to the Third Estate were quite naïve about many of these things and there was a wide scope for action to lead men who were this fuzzy. But naive as they were, they may well have surprised themselves at their courage in refusing to surrender on the issues of liberty, and, although it was more difficult to define, on equality.

If that meant they had to defy their king, they were, in the end, prepared to do it and to follow the lead of other men who pointed the way. And as events would prove for the next three years, and although they were very reluctant to articulate it, they were always prepared to do so.

2

The First Year of Liberty

The Revolution of the People

Up to the early summer of 1789, the conflict between 'aristocrats' and 'patriots' in the National Assembly had resembled the kind of struggles over a constitution which had racked most western European countries from mid-century on. What popular violence that had taken place was more or less peripheral to the struggle, flashes of summer lightning on the horizon. When the common people did intervene in July and August 1789, they transformed conflict among the élites into something quite different. Ordinary people were never able to impose a programme on otherwise reluctant politicians. Rather, popular violence at least in Paris or in the case of the anti-seigneurial risings in 1789–92, could be the pretext for political factions to act in directions they intended to act beforehand. The legal classes in the Third Estate, a very large number of deputies, had long been hostile to seigneurial justice, and the so-called abolition of feudalism on the Night of 4 August, 1789 also abolished many things that were not at all feudal but to which the lawyers were hostile. Popular pressure was successful when factions in the political class had reasons of their own for acceding to popular wishes. Other popular protests, like protests over the religious issue after 1790, or over conscription after 1793, were not only disregarded; they were repressed with uninhibited uses of force.

Moreover, the relationship between the politicians and rioters both in Paris and the provinces was not particularly a dialogue. Instead, people rioted for reasons that had little to do with making an impact on national politics, and much more to solve local problems or deal with local enemies. The best example of this would be the riots in Paris in July 1789 which culminated in the taking of the Bastille. Those involved

intended to protect their city against a military attack that the Crown
was preparing. But the rioters did not particularly intend to thwart the
Crown's plot against the National Assembly. Their motives were defensive and particular. The fact that they also thwarted the plot was a happy
side effect of the military vacuum that the fall of the Bastille caused.

The Crisis of Daily Life

For all the patriots' talk about 'the nation', there was little in the social
and economic life of that nation that bound it together. Life experience
was quite limited. It was more than likely that a person would marry and
die within ten kilometres of where he or she was born. A river, a small
range of hills or more subtle changes of landscape could mark off one
pays from another and people could tell a 'stranger' from even a short
distance away by their distinctive dress or from different voice inflexions
or accents. Indeed a substantial number of the subjects of the King of
France did not even speak French. Catalan, Breton, Flemish, German and
Provencal were foreign languages but the innumerable local dialects
rendered people difficult to understand to each other as well. All but
the very rich or the very poor stayed close to home. Even the large cities
drew on their hinterlands. In Lyon, for example, over half of the silk-
workers were born in the city or the Lyonnais. Paris fitted into this
pattern as well. Although the legendary stonemasons from Limousin
were long-distance migrants and although roughly two thirds of the
working people of the city were born in the provinces, more than 80
per cent of the migrants came from nearby provinces, rarely from south
of the Loire. It was likely too that a man married a woman whose
family's social status, wealth and even trade were roughly the same as
his own. In a society where so much wealth was in precious land or tools,
parents could not permit the young a random choice of a partner.

For all that the rural world appeared to be mired in ancient custom,
important changes had taken place in the two centuries before the
Revolution. One of the original characteristics, to use Marc Bloch's
phrase, of rural society in France was the sizable amount of property
peasants owned. This had come about between the thirteenth and fif-
teenth centuries as seigneurs or manorial lords, battered by demographic
collapse and war, saw their jurisdictional rights weaken and their
domains fragment. Many peasants became for all intents and purposes
landowners in their own right, subject only to a weak jurisdiction from
the seigneurie or manor. The religious wars of the sixteenth and seventeenth centuries, the ruthless taxation that underwrote the rise of royal
absolutism, and demographic crisis after 1640, weakened the peasantry

and permitted nobles and urban bourgeois to amass more land and reconstitute the large estates. Yet the reconquest was never complete, and by the
eighteenth century it had lost its impetus. Thus, on the eve of the Revolution all classes owned land. There were, of course, extreme variations.
Non peasant property was more extensive in the north than the south.
Around the capital and the *parlementaire* towns, it could drop to very
small proportions. Relative to their numbers, nobles and bourgeois always
owned a disproportionate share of the land. Even among the peasantry,
land was very unequally shared. In just about every region a majority and
sometimes a substantial majority, of households barely grew enough to
make a living. At the other end of the scale, a small minority of rich
farmers either owned or more likely rented, the largest holdings. In general, it has been estimated that the upper 10 per cent of the population
owned half the land, the rest having to make do with the other half. But
this is a rough estimate. Nineteenth century figures show that about one-
third of the population owned or rented out over two-thirds of the land.

The typical rural community then, if there was such a thing, was a
hierarchy, not an unrelieved lump of destitute cultivators. Invariably well
represented among the village élite were the larger peasants, 'gros laboureurs', as they were known in some places, the 'rural bourgeoisie'.
according to some historians. In the west, they were men of fairly modest
means and there were many of them, but on the northern plains they
were rare and well off indeed. Sometimes they owned land in their own
right but more often they made their living as tenants of the larger farms,
sometimes of more than one which was a cause of resentment. Sometimes, as in the Brie region south of Paris, they lived apart from the
village proper in large farmsteads, the entire building complex surrounded by high walls. As many as fifty people worked there. Like the
Chartier family, wealthy peasants from around Pontoise north west of
Paris, they resembled a caste, marrying the best local families, and
assuring good places for their sons in the legal professions and the
Church. Their living standards were almost always on the rise – no
Labroussian crisis for them – and they used their growing riches partly
for investment but considerably for their own comfort and for their
family's advancement. Such people controlled parish and municipal government both before and after 1790 and they probably had a disproportionate influence on the parish *cahiers* in 1789. Through their influence
and position in the rural community, they could nearly determine how
the entire region would react to the Revolution.

Few of their neighbours were so fortunate and with so many people not
having enough land on which to survive, they turned to what Olwen
Hufton has called the economy of makeshifts. One of these expedients
was rural industry. Housewives were spinners almost everywhere but each

region specialized, with sailcloth-making in Upper Brittany, cotton in Upper Normandy, silk-spinning in the Vivarais, woollens in Languedoc and, in parts of the Massif Central, knife-making. A substantial proportion of French industrial production was generated in the countryside. Helping with the harvest was another expedient everywhere and there were truly massive migrations in the viticultural districts when grapes had to be picked quickly. Thousands came from the Charollais and the Bresse to help out in the Mâconnais and almost whole villages in the southern Massif migrated to the Mediterranean coast and worked their way north again. Other regions exported people. The Limousin was famous for its wandering masons but many trinket merchants came from there as well. The Alps even exported teachers who wandered the country offering to show people how to read and, for a slightly larger fee, how to read and write.

But many others could not make do. The penniless comprised an unbelievable 40 per cent of the national population. They made their living, such as it was, by public and private charity for the most part. They squatted on wastelands and forests, huddled by church doors, slept under bridges or in dosshouses, their only possessions a few miserable rags. A large proportion were women, ruined by the death of their husbands and incapable of remarrying because they were encumbered with children. People like this were a problem only to overstretched charitable institutions, but the more daring could be more of a nuisance to the better off. The line between poverty and petty crime could be crossed easily. The criminal dossiers of the Old Regime are bursting with prosecutions for theft of bread or drying laundry or of pennies from charity boxes in parish churches. Bands of beggars wandering a countryside that was nearly unpoliced were an even greater threat. Able-bodied paupers who menaced isolated farmers for food and lodging could easily grow into a vast criminal gang. The *bande Hulan* was the scourge of the Beauce and the Ile-de-France at mid-century. The *bande d'Orgères* was a floating group of several hundred men, women and children in the same region later. They spoke their own specialized slang. They were also responsible for countless thefts, murders and maimings, until the army finally rounded them up in 1798. No other gang's activities were so sensational but every part of the country suffered from brigandage in one form or another, whether it was the legendary smuggler Mandrin who amassed forty murders over his bloody career in the Dauphiné, to the part-time toughs with their trained dogs and subterranean hideouts who smuggled salt over the Brittany–Maine border. Smugglers were often popular heroes but the wandering poor were potential thieves. The pauper, who was still regarded as an object of Christian charity, was becoming more and more ominous as the century wore on.

The poor as such played almost no role in national politics in 1789 or after. Fear of them was one of the complex elements in the Great Fear and the peasant revolts of the summer of 1789, and many paupers turned to brigandage of the most appalling sort following the collapse of the economy after 1794. But poor people generally fended for themselves throughout the period, as they always had. On the other hand, declining living standards are supposed to have played a role in the coming of the Revolution. This was because, it is said, the economy could not keep pace with a growing population and this in turn reverberated through the structure of society, both town and country.

According to the most recent estimates, the population of France grew from 22.4 million to 27.9 million between 1705 and 1790. After 1730 or so the population began a gentle swing upwards which only slowed but did not stop after 1770. Probably several factors at once contributed to this 'demographic revolution'. The absence of plague after the outbreak in Marseille in 1720, the disappearance of prolonged wars and invasion, the more frequent garrisoning, rather than billeting, of troops were all preconditions of population growth. A genuine change in the climate is still being debated although it is certain that there were no meteorological calamities between 1709–10 and 1788, so that the food supply was reasonably certain most of the time. Another factor whose impact is difficult to measure was the elaborate controls imposed on the grain trade by government, the *parlements* and the seigneuries. Their overall purpose was to assure supply to local people at a reasonable price. Certainly contemporaries tried enormously hard, and public officials spent the government's and their own money prodigiously, to make sure that poor folks were fed: surely such generosity made a difference. Another reason in some regions was the adoption of 'economical milling', a way of deriving more flour from each seed grain. In other words, there was not a single reason the population grew. No matter what the combination of reasons, whether in a decline in the incidence of disease or in a healthier or more abundant diet, more infants and children survived into adulthood in the second quarter of the century. The next step in the argument, a crucial one among specialists, has been that France could support this rising population only at the price of a decline in the standard of living. That is, the argument has been that productivity remained what it had been since the Middle Ages and what it would be until the 1840s. There was no agricultural revolution to match the demographic, or so it is said. The country remained tied to yields and to production plateaux that undulated within limits that had been common since the fourteenth century. In other words, people revolted in 1789 because they were poor or else because they were getting poorer. This is a very gratifying conclusion for those who believe that the source of popular revolution in general is poverty or that revolution is a result of too much inequality, however 'too much' is defined. Unfortunately, such pieties do not describe reality on the ground.

More recent research, however, has suggested that this view is far too pessimistic. At least in the Ile-de-France, the pull of Paris was so great as to stimulate the beginnings of an agricultural revolution. Prices rose and so farmers had an incentive to invest in their lands. Productivity rose to match, or at least keep close to, the rising population. There were signs of an agricultural revolution everywhere around Paris: in the increasing amount of land devoted to wheat, as opposed to the less noble grains like rye and barley; in the increasing number of implements, and in the increasing number of animals that pulled the heavier ploughs, harrows, and rollers; and especially in the concentration on nitrogen-fixing crops like lucern, sainfoin and clover. In other parts of the country, peasants were moving away from classic patterns of land use to complicated and imaginative rotations. In Upper Normandy, near the coast in a region known as the *pays de Caux*, farmers devoted almost no land to fallow, while further inland around Rouen, cattle raising overwhelmed cereal production. In Upper Maine, fallow occupied just a quarter of the surface rather than the traditional one third or one half; wheat, rye, barley and, most interestingly, clover, had replaced much of the old fallow. In short, the countryside was not an inert mass, imprisoned in unchanging routines. It was responding to changes in the structure of markets, improved transportation, and rising prices for wheat and cattle with changes of its own.

Indeed, the immiseration thesis depends entirely upon inferences from indirect evidence. It goes back to the indefatigable historian of prices, C. E. Labrousse. He showed that between 1726–41 and 1785–9, wheat prices increased by 66 per cent; rye, a common staple, by 71 per cent; meat by 58 per cent; firewood by 91 per cent. Over the same period, wages lagged behind. Agricultural wages increased by only 16 per cent; construction wages by only 24 per cent. The result, said Labrousse, was inevitably a declining standard of living. Every historian who has followed him has accepted the inevitable conclusion: this immiseration had something to do with the origins of the Revolution.

But there are both methodological and empirical problems with this approach. Constructing a wage series over a long period is an extremely difficult task. Not only are the sources rare, most laborers were paid by the task, no matter how long the task took – this renders the vast majority of wage data that remain in the archives quite useless; and following a single individual through a lifetime of work shows immense variations that were due to changes in life cycle, ill health, and advancing age. An illness for an otherwise totally loyal employee produced unbelievably harsh consequences.

Attempts to get behind Labrousse's abstract figures produce ambiguous results. A contemporary estimated that a family of day-labourers around Arles just held its own between 1750 and 1788, despite the Labroussian inevitability. An analysis of a budget of a family of weavers in Abbeville shows they spent about the same proportion of their income on bread in the 1780s as they had in the 1760s. According to the Labrousse model, they ought to have been worse off, but they were not.

In short, the immiseration thesis and its relation to the origins of the Revolution is problematic. Ordinary people did not revolt because they were poor or because their long term living standards were declining.

The decline in living standards, where it took place, was a slow process, probably not even perceptible to most people. What counted for them was a short-term harvest shortage. These hit the last generation of the Old Regime with increased frequency – in 1769–71, 1778–9, 1781–2, 1785–6, 1788–9 – and such a crisis reverberated throughout the entire economic system. Labrousse showed that in normal years, working people could spend anywhere between 45 per cent and 60 per cent of their incomes on bread, but a harvest shortage that could double or triple prices in a few months could push this figure beyond 90 per cent. As if this was not bad enough, the contraction in purchase of non-food items could cause a crisis in the manufacturing sectors with falling orders and increased unemployment. In the country, there was less work in harvesting and rural industry and poor peasants were forced to market grain they would need the next spring to pay taxes, rents, dues and tithes. A harvest shortage too was often accompanied by disease, and convalescence of either breadwinner could wipe out modest savings and capital. A reasonable security could be transformed overnight into destitution. During any crisis, the folklore of dearth told of people dying of hunger, of desperate suicides and of people being forced to eat rotten food or grass.

But people rarely believed they were the passive victims of inclement weather. Hard times provided wonderful opportunities to speculators of all sorts, from grain dealers and bakers to wealthy peasants who, in popular opinion anyway, withheld grain from the markets to drive prices still higher, bought low in one market to sell high in another and engaged in all sorts of sharp practices like adulterating bread and cheating on weights and measures. And since in time of shortage there was likely to be more grain than usual on the road because speculators were unusually active, popular opinion that a shortage was man-made appeared to be confirmed. The result was that any shortage was usually accompanied by grain or bread 'riots', a misnomer since the violence involved was rarely wanton and rarely went beyond roughing up or threatening the local grain dealers, farmers or bakers. After the grain was prevented from leaving a threatened area, or pillaged on the market square, or sold at a price the crowd considered fair and the proceeds given to the dealer, people usually went home.

Nonetheless, the hundreds of disturbances and demonstrations over grain in the last two decades of the Old Regime reveal the mentality of ordinary working people fearful of being pushed over the edge. They reveal too a pre-capitalist mentality which assumed that people had a right to a decent subsistence and that the well being of the community overrode the private interests of those in the food trades. The community also expected the authorities to enforce these assumptions and on the whole up to the 1760s, government and courts did so with elaborate controls on the grain trade. When the government relaxed or abolished these controls as in 1769–70, 1774–5 and 1787–8, in an attempt to stimulate production, crowds attempted to enforce the controls on their own. In other words, people were protesting the commercialization of food and the decline of paternalistic monarchy which the adoption of free trade implied.

In the capital anyway, this protest was direct. The belief in hoarding and the belief in plots to starve the people were given a great fillip in the 1760s. The scribbler, Leprevost de Beaumont, published a pamphlet purporting to uncover a vast plot on the part of ministers and perhaps even Louis XV to solve the government's deficit by forcing up grain prices under the guise of liberalism. As a characterization of government policy towards provisioning Paris, this was a grotesque distortion but it reflected a deep unease people were beginning to feel about government generally. In September 1770, the bookseller Hardy reported the appearance of a seditious wall poster threatening 'if you don't lower the price of bread and put order into the affairs of state, we'll know what to do'. It was also said that Louis XV was criminally indifferent to the sufferings of his people. Later, Hardy reported that a drunk was arrested on the Place Maubert for accusing the King of 'letting his people die of hunger while he's just given the Comtesse du Barry, his mistress, a carriage which they say cost 60,000 *livres*...' Publicists and scandal mongers acclaimed the Parlement of Paris in these circumstances because not only did it protest against rising taxes, it was also a consistent critic of liberalization. Thus, after the *parlement* was 'remodelled' in 1771, a wall poster appeared demanding 'Bread at two *sols*, chancellor hanged or revolt in Paris'. One wonders how much popular support the parlement lost when it reversed its traditional policy and meekly registered Brienne's edict freeing the grain trade in July 1787. In any case, when the old debauched king died in 1774, he was universally despised because in some people's minds grain and fiscal policies were linked. Louis XV may have aroused revulsion because of his disordered personal life and his indifference to public affairs, but the fiscal crisis and the policy of grain liberalization also made him loathsome to the public.

The existence of the monarchy was never at issue, however. In time honoured fashion, the public invested great hopes in his successor and Louis XVI satisfied those hopes. He acquired instant popularity by restoring the *parlements* and with them paternalistic monarchy. Indeed, the rioters in the so-called Flour War which broke out in Paris and its region in May 1775, following another round of grain liberalization, believed they had the well-meaning King's authorization to lower bread prices to 'just' levels, no matter what his ministers may have ordered. The belief in Louis's benevolence lasted to 1789 and beyond, but throughout the period there remained dark suspicions that ministers might also be speculators.

It is doubtful whether fears of a government-sponsored famine plot penetrated far beyond Paris but provincials had problems of their own. In the Midi particularly, the reign of Louis XVI coincided with a disastrous crisis in viticulture. The over extension of vineyards and a series of abundant crops in the 1770s and 80s resulted in falling prices. Between 1726–41 and 1785–9, the price of wine increased by only 14 per cent. Squeezed by higher food prices, many small viticulturalists were ruined, along with industries which depended on them such as barrel-making and transport.

Nonetheless, the constitutional crisis coincided with economic calamity. Two dry summers in a row in 1785 and 1786 ruined forage crops and forced peasants to sell cattle, horses and sheep at low prices. In 1787, the silk harvest failed throwing thousands of Lyon workers on to charity. Continual rains in the autumn delayed the sowing of wheat. The mild winter was followed by heavy rains the following June and a hot summer drought which shrivelled the ripening grains. The harvest of 1788 would be poor anyway and was ruined by a hailstorm on 13 July which devastated crops on a mile-wide path through Burgundy, the Ile-de-France and Picardy. Some hailstones were so large that grazing horses were killed.

The price of bread began to rise almost immediately and by the spring of 1789 it has been estimated that 88 per cent of a Parisian working man's income was being spent on bread. Bankruptcies increased dramatically. The 199 bankruptcies in Rouen in 1789 were among the highest of the century and the size of debts left by bankrupts in 1788 and 1789 was more than double what they had been in 1787. Unemployment increased as well. In one parish in Lyon, half the working population was living off charity. In Rennes, one of the sailcloth factories was only kept going through the generosity of its owner, a priest. The textile trade in Normandy was particularly hard hit. In Bayeux one fifth of the population was receiving charity, in Elbeuf half the workforce was unemployed, while in Rouen, the figure reached 10,000. Unemployment in the countryside was less severe but, even so, it averaged 12 per cent of the workforce in Upper Normandy. Those who did find work in town and country had their wages drastically reduced. Charitable institutions, already overburdened by financial problems of their own, were swamped. The army and the *maréchaussée*, or mounted police, were scattered throughout the country in innumerable patrols to police markets and grain convoys. Significantly, the underpaid soldiers and policemen sometimes showed sympathy for the rioters.

Even before the revolutionary crisis broke in the summer of 1789 citizen committees began to form here and there to handle the breakdown of order for themselves. In March 1789 a committee representing all three orders took over the municipality of Marseille and established a citizens' militia. Similar militias, forerunners of the National Guard, were later established at Montpellier, Caen, Etampes and Orléans. The Old Regime, already paralysed by the constitutional crisis, was beginning to crumble from below.

The Politics of the People

It was in this atmosphere of protracted economic crisis and disintegrating authority that ordinary people met to choose delegates for the bailiwick assemblies and to draw up preliminary *cahiers de doléances* or statements of grievances. As Georges Lefebvre argued, the very act of participating in the political process transformed people's expectations and gave them a hope that they would not otherwise have had that their plight could be solved by political means. After all, their reasoning went, if the King was asking them to state their grievances, he intended to do something about them. Thus was born the almost millenarian hope that was so characteristic of 1789: that the Estates-General, the King, or 'the great ones' would alleviate the sufferings of the common people. Yet the process of drafting *cahiers* did not excite everyone. Although the *cahiers* were often vague on the subject and although there was great variation even within one region, it appears that turnout in the parish meetings was often fairly low. In Upper Brittany, it was less than one third, in the Vexin region west of Paris, it averaged only 22 per cent, and around Rouen only 23 per cent. Other regions witnessed similarly dismal averages. The exception was Burgundy where the tradition of the annual assize required everyone to attend so that there was a practice here of large village assemblies. Everywhere, however, the assemblies elected the wealthiest men of the parish, generally the 'gros laboureurs', notaries and merchants, to carry the local *cahier* to the bailiwick assembly.

Nonetheless, expectations were very high for radical change in the spring of 1789. Both in the countryside, and among the urban legal classes, there were uncompromising demands for drastic changes in taxation and especially for the abolition of the seigneurial regime and for the alleviation of some of the burdens that the Church imposed.

It is not true, therefore, to say that the urban bourgeoisie was forced to abolish 'feudalism' in the countryside against its will. In Brittany, for example, patriots in Nantes drafted a model *cahier* following the break with the aristocracy in January 1789. This model denounced the seigneurial regime as a total usurpation and demanded its outright abolition. Patriots in Rennes then distributed the model to the countryside where almost every parish adopted entire clauses with no changes, or adapted them to suit their particular situation. The abbé Sieyès collaborated on another similar model *cahier* for distribution around the domains of the duc d'Orléans. Sieyès's hostility to the seigneurial regime was based on an old tradition common to both the Crown and the Parlement of Paris that a seigneur's powers were a devolution of public authority that properly belonged to the sovereign. Ever since the early seventeenth century, legal commentators had gleefully repeated legends of a seigneurial regime that was administered by drunken local rubes. Somehow seigneurial justice and with it the entire seigneurial regime, was illegitimate. The endless reiteration, without verification of this canard, was the common coin of legal treatises, and this no doubt explains why many patriot lawyers endorsed this argument. The deputies from the parishes probably had fewer legalistic reasons. As reasonably wealthy men, they suffered from unlimited hunting rights, from the costs of the requirement to use the lord's mill or press or from the chicanery of justice exercised in private hands, not to mention the various dues themselves. Men like these were often behind the rural rebellions of the summer of 1789. For the moment, however, the well-off in the countryside and the urban elites found themselves allies.

The elections were entirely peaceful in most places but there were indications that many ordinary people were not going to limit their activities to the formal legal process. Throughout the period, a great deal of popular political activity would occur in a much wider forum. Thus in Toulon, Marseille, Mâcon and Reims, journeymen and apprentices, who had been excluded because they paid too little in taxes to qualify as electors, disrupted electoral meetings. The same thing occurred in the countryside. In the small town of Aubagne outside Marseille, hundreds of peasants invaded the town meeting to make sure their voices were heard. There were many other occurrences like this throughout the country.

The most dramatic example of the growing political awareness of some of the common people occurred in Paris during the so-called

Reveillon riot which broke out at the end of April. It was said that Reveillon, a wealthy wallpaper manufacturer and Henriot, a saltpetre maker, had advocated a reduction in wages during the electoral meetings in their districts. Coming at a time when bread prices were high and many resented being excluded from the electoral meetings, such remarks were highly inflammatory. The disturbances which followed were not particularly serious – in the end, the crowds looted a few food shops and devastated Henriot's and Reveillon's houses. In fact, the forces of order unleashed far more violence as angry and frightened infantry and artillery opened up on an unarmed population which had pelted them with roof tiles and chimney pots when the soldiers tried to maneuver through the narrow streets of the faubourg Saint-Antoine. There was a traditional ritual element too in the riots as Henriot and Reveillon were burned in effigy and people paraded through the streets to the sound of drums. But the slogans they shouted showed that popular consciousness had begun to change. Besides the usual cries for cheap bread, and loyalty to the King, they feted the duc d'Orléans and Necker, both of them heroes of patriots. They stopped the carriages of sightseers to ask the startled occupants if they were for the Third Estate. Obviously the 'Third Estate' did not include Reveillon. Indeed, some rioters cried out ' . . . if we don't rise up against the rich, we should all be done for'. A war on the rich in the name of the Third Estate was far from the minds of the deputies who at that very moment were gathering in Versailles.

Rumours

Fantastic rumours were inherent in Old Regime political culture. Partly because communications networks were so primitive and partly because no one in the government thought they had any consistent responsibility to explain themselves to the public, the most amazing urban legends could take on a vivacious life. Thus in the 1740s, the rumour went round that the government intended to deport all street urchins to New France. The consistent characteristic of such stories was the attribution of utter malice to those in power. At a time of high excitement in the spring of 1789, the attribution of fiendishness to evil ministers and to the great families acquired political consequences.

Thus people feared the aristocracy and clergy would stop at nothing to retain their privileges. In one form, the idea of a noble plot was a revival of the idea of a 'famine plot' that was so popular during the reign of Louis XV. But it acquired quite a different political content in the circumstances. In February 1789, the bookseller Hardy noted that 'some say that the princes [Louis XVI's brothers and cousins] have been hoarding grain the better to overthrow M. Necker.... Others said that the Director-General of Finances [Necker] was himself the chief and the first of all the hoarders, with the consent of the King, and that he only favoured and supported such an enterprise to get money more promptly for his majesty...' This was certainly way off the mark in reality but it is an identikit replication of similar rumours twenty years before about Louis XVI's grandfather. Once again, the accusation that the government or the court was involved in price fixing at pubic expense was highly significant.

Then, once the deputies met and became stalemated over the issue of verification of powers, people began to fear the Estates-General would be dissolved. In early July, Hardy noted that people were certain that the government was hoarding grain because, if the Estates-General came to nothing, the Crown's financial problems could be solved by profiteering. An observer reported to the government in mid-June that he had discovered a plot in which the clergy, the nobility and the *parlement* had combined to bring about the fall of the ubiquitously popular Necker, by accusing him of being a grain speculator in the government's interest. Such a rumour terrified holders of government bonds who linked his fall with their own and the nation's bankruptcy. The observer also reported the existence of a false letter going the rounds which 'announced that the deputies of the Third Estate who, threatened with assassination by the nobles, were asking for help'. People were talking of arming themselves and marching to Versailles.

Nor was the idea of a noble plot to starve the people confined to Paris. A *curé* in the province of Maine later noted that 'many great seigneurs and others holding high office ... undertook secretly to ship all the grain from the kingdom to foreign countries, thus starving the kingdom, force it to revolt against the Estates-General, disunite the assembly and prevent its success'. The age-old fantasy of a famine plot had clearly been combined with the hope of regeneration and the fear of the aristocracy.

There were further additions as well. One was the ubiquitous fear of brigands. No doubt there were more vagabonds on the roads in the spring and summer of 1789, and fewer means to control them as the *maréchaussée* and the army were preoccupied with protecting markets and grain convoys. Wandering beggars had often posed threats in the past but they now became assimilated to the aristocratic plot. As the situation became increasingly critical throughout June and July, there were more and more rumours of secret armies moving through forests at night, of roving bands maliciously destroying growing crops, of plots nipped in the bud to blow up towns, and of landings on the coasts. And the fear of brigands easily slid into fears of foreign intervention. There were dozens of stories of the Queen having written to her brother, Joseph

II of Austria, for help, of the comte d'Artois, Louis XVI's youngest
brother, fleeing to Spain or Piedmont to seek support from his relatives,
or of pirates landing on the Mediterranean coast, and so on. The notion
of such vast conspiracies linking food problems, aristocratic machinations, hired criminals and foreign invasions was to appear not only in
1789 but in every subsequent crisis in one form or another down to 1815.

The Fall of the Bastille

In this frenzied atmosphere, the government decided to try once again to
control the National Assembly. There probably was no firm plan of how
to accomplish it but there was talk of issuing paper money, or of arran-
ging new loans. Some undoubtedly wanted to dismiss the National
Assembly but more likely, Louis XVI intended to have another royal
session in mid-July to impose his earlier programme. If there was resistance this time, he might do what the Crown had always done with the
parlements: move the Estates-General to another city, suspend it, or
arrest, exile or imprison some of the more outrageous deputies. In
other words, the government operated on an *ad hoc* basis. Moreover, it
felt strong enough to do so. After the recall of the King's Bodyguard from
its march to its home garrison, orders went out to the garrison towns of
the north and east to mass troops around Paris and Versailles. It was
expected there would be 20,000 infantry, cavalry and artillery in the
region by 18 July. This was an immense increase in the number of
available security forces.

Paris had the reputation of being heavily policed but in fact the hand of
royal absolutism was quite light. In ordinary times, Paris was protected
by only 1500 men to which were added about 3600 men from the French
Guards regiment. After the Reveillon riots and the growing restiveness in
the capital in May and June, the baron de Besenval, in effect the military
governor of the city, brought up thousands more troops to keep order.
With the additional troops from the frontier garrisons in place by mid-
July, a veritable army under the command of the aged Marshal de Broglie
would ring Paris and Versailles. Yet the government did not expect an
insurrection or expect to have to attack the capital. Broglie's orders to
Besenval were to secure the arsenals at the Invalides and the Bastille,
guard the approach roads to Versailles from an attack by a Parisian mob,
protect the royal treasury and government bonds and, above all, not to
provoke the population.

But these basically defensive measures served only to inflame opinion,
not intimidate it. From late June onwards, the most fantastic rumours
began to circulate in Paris: that the deputies would be imprisoned in the

Bastille, that others would be executed, that four thousand troops would be arriving from Spain, another nine thousand from Switzerland, that the *Salle des Menus Plaisirs* in Versailles had been mined, that Paris would be shelled from the heights of Montmartre, that the city would be laid waste and pillaged. And so on.

The deputies themselves were equally alarmed. When Mirabeau made a violent speech denouncing the troop movements as a dangerous provocation, he was rebuked. An address by the National Assembly on 8 July requesting withdrawal of the troops was met with the blithe reply that order had to be kept. Several deputies feared for their lives and began to sleep in the assembly hall or at the homes of friends.

Whatever the government ultimately intended to do, all might have gone well if serious problems of morale and discipline had not developed among the troops. This showed itself first among the French Guards, a police unit permanently established in Paris who, contrary to their reputation, was an increasingly professional and militarized force, composed increasingly of non-Parisians, cut off from their fellow citizens in disciplined garrisons. Their defection was, therefore, all the more significant and disastrous for the government. The French Guards had been fully loyal in the repression of the Reveillon riots, but some of them, like other soldiers and sailors throughout the country, had caught the revolutionary enthusiasm. So in the aftermath of disturbances at Versailles on the evening of 23 June, and during the mobbing of the Archbishop of Paris on the 24th, they refused their police duties. Four days later, a group of them told an apprehensive crowd at the Palais Royal they would never march on them. When their colonel had the ringleaders arrested, a crowd of four thousand besieged the Abbaye prison, forced their release, and carried them in triumph to the Palais Royal. By 14 July, five out of six battalions of the French Guards had deserted to the side of the crowds and many were prominent in the attack on the Bastille. Desertion and fraternization with civilians plagued other regiments as well. Soldiers quick-marched to Paris, and bivouacked in makeshift conditions along the way, arrived to inadequately prepared quarters that were low on food supplies. All were tired and many were ill. Yet the populations in the little towns around Paris – Saint-Denis, Vanves, Issy, and so on – received the soldiers well, fed them, lodged them and, above all, shared their fears with them. There were also direct attempts to incite soldiers to disobedience. At least two itinerant booksellers were arrested at the Champ de Mars parade ground for selling seditious pamphlets, and orators at the Palais Royal urged the troops not to use their weapons against the people. Other regiments too began to suffer from desertions, sometimes in company strength and sometimes from even the German-speaking regiments. In the end, only a small proportion of all the troops encamped

around Paris deserted before 14 July but this, and the fraternization, and
the incitement from civilians, unnerved their officers who became convinced they could no longer be sure of their men. The defection of the
French Guards also caused a sensation. Because of it, the noble deputy,
the Marquis de Ferrières was convinced that the government was on the
verge of a catastrophe.

Yet neither the King nor those who now had his ear – the Queen, his
brothers, the Polignacs – saw it this way. Preparations went ahead. An
essential first step was to dump Necker as part of an overall plan to create
a stronger ministry under the baron de Breteuil. Necker had never been
popular at court and had incensed the King (but delighted Parisians) by
absenting himself from the royal session on 23 June. He was dismissed on
11 July and told to leave the country quietly. Yet the news leaked out and
arrived in Paris on the morning of Sunday the 12th. Morning strollers
immediately concluded that the departure of Necker, the patriot, the
financial genius, the enemy of speculators, meant the dissolution of the
National Assembly, bankruptcy and high bread prices. The aristocratic
plot was unfolding.

Thousands now rushed to the Palais Royal, the town house of the duc
d'Orléans whose courtyards had for months been an oasis of free speech
and a centre for distributing pamphlets because the duke's property was
outside the jurisdiction of the Paris police. Dozens of orators standing on
tables urged resistance. Alas, the story of one of them, Camille Desmoulins, who said that he urged people to arm themselves against an
impending massacre, cannot be believed. But others, whose names are
unknown, urged action. Crowds then fanned out to close the theatres as a
sign of mourning while another group took the busts of Necker and the
Duc d'Orléans from a waxworks museum and paraded them through the
streets before black banners. They clashed with the Royal Allemand
cavalry on the Place Louis XV, and when they were driven into the
nearby Tuileries gardens they pelted the soldiers with stones and debris.
According to the English traveller, Dr Rigby, this incident was decisive.
Up until then, the orators at the Palais Royal had urged the crowds not to
give the military a pretext to intervene but as soon as the clash was
known, the cry went up for the crowds to arm themselves for their own
defence. The French Guards, thus alerted that a massacre had taken
place, then entered the square and charged the Royal Allemand. Swiss
regiments stationed on the left bank crossed the Seine but too late after
darkness to have any effect. Shortly after midnight, the Place Louis XV
was evacuated.

Meanwhile, crowds had begun pillaging gun shops, and the guards at
the Hôtel de Ville were disarmed. With the exception of a tiny detachment
at the Bastille, the right bank was now in the hands of the insurgents.

Around midnight, crowds began setting fire to the customs posts around the gates of the city because these were held responsible for the high price of wine and many consumer goods. French Guards, supposedly protecting the posts, instead took part in the pillage. Throughout the night and well into the next day, huge bonfires ringed the city. Thirty-one of the forty posts were destroyed. Early on the morning of the 13th, other crowds sacked the monastery of Saint Lazare and carried off not only huge quantities of grain, flour and wine but almost anything they could find. And while crowds were loading foodstuffs from Saint Lazare on to carts, other crowds released the inmates of the debtors' prisons which in turn sparked a prison riot at Le Châtelet where dangerous criminals were held.

The city appeared to be collapsing into anarchy. The electors of Paris took it upon themselves to try to control the situation. This was an overwhelmingly bourgeois body – 180 out of 407 were lawyers – and so they were probably less concerned about famine plots than ordinary working people. Nonetheless, since it presaged state bankruptcy, the fall of Necker was as alarming as the mounting disorder in the city. Consequently, they decided on the 13th to form a 'Permanent Committee', which effectively displaced the old municipality, and a citizens' militia to keep order, and perhaps defend Paris against attack. By early evening, rudimentary patrols wearing cockades of red and blue, the city's colours, had restored some kind of order. Yet they were desperately short of arms – pillaging the gun shops, getting others from old stores or stopping barges laden with powder yielded little. Only the royal armouries at the Invalides and the Bastille had arms in sufficient quantity.

Immense crowds easily overran the Invalides on the morning of the 14th and some 32,000 muskets were distributed pell-mell to whoever wanted them. But 10,000 pounds of powder and cartridges were stored in the Bastille. This was an ancient fortress normally used as a state prison and its ninety-foot walls towered over the faubourg Saint-Antoine, in eastern Paris. A crowd had been there too from early morning, and crackling gunfire between the besiegers and the small garrison had broken out from noon onwards. During poorly observed truces, the Permanent Committee, meeting at the Hôtel de Ville, sent four separate delegations in the course of the day to ask the governor, the Marquis de Launay, to surrender, but he refused. During one assault in which the crowd lowered a drawbridge leading to an inner courtyard, the defenders fired on the assailants killing ninety-eight and wounding seventy-three.

The decisive moment came in the mid-afternoon when the French Guards, hidden in the smokescreen of burning straw brought up in carts, breached the outer defences and trained cannon, taken from the Invalides, on one of the drawbridges leading to the inner courtyards. De

Launay threatened to blow up the powder magazines and with them half the neighbourhood but wiser counsels prevailed, and he ordered the main drawbridge lowered. The fortress had surrendered.

Six of the garrison were later murdered in retaliation for the earlier shootings. De Launay, whom the crowd suspected of treachery in the earlier negotiations, was dragged through the streets, beaten, stabbed and shot; his head was hacked off with a pocketknife and paraded through the streets on the end of a pitchfork because, as the man who did it later claimed 'in his job as a cook, he knew how to work on meat'. The same happened to Jacques de Flesselles, the acting head of the Permanent Committee, whom the crowd suspected of withholding arms on the 13th and 14th. On 22 July, the intendant of Paris, Bertier de Sauvigny, and his father-in-law, Foulon de Doué, who were both suspected of food hoarding, were also murdered and decapitated, and their heads and hearts paraded through the streets. The Old Regime had sometimes displayed the remains of executed criminals; the crowds were now exacting a grisly justice for themselves. Within days, children were imitating the grand event by parading the heads of feral cats they had killed on the ends of sticks. The journalist Mairobert in the previous generation argued that centuries of despotism had corrupted the French. Had he lived long enough, he might have cited such examples by adults and children in support of his case.

A Comment

The deputy Alexandre Barnave, an otherwise sympathetic and intelligent figure, excused this vigilante justice with the comment 'Is this blood then so pure that one should so regret to spill it?' In 1789, such comments were quite rare and many historians have hurried to say how untypical Barnave's disgraceful remark was. And rightly so: it was not very typical in 1789, but by 1792, in many cities in the south, the same attitudes had become much more common; a major scandal, in fact; and a source of resistance from those who felt victimized by such attitudes. By 1794 and beyond, these attitudes had not only corrupted the administration of justice, their perversion justified the murder of revolutionaries themselves. Barnave himself became a victim of his own principle of the politicization of justice that his famous remark endorsed.

A Return to the Story

The Fall of the Bastille is rightly celebrated as a symbol of the triumph of liberty over despotism. Despite the popular mythology at the time, however, there were only seven prisoners inside, only one of them political, a reflection of the reluctance of governments under Louis XVI to exploit *lettres de cachet*. Yet the mythology of the taking of the Bastille began immediately. Although the primary reason for the attack was to seize the powder inside, very early after, publicists created the myth that persists to this day that the Bastille was liberated to release the prisoners inside. Indeed, when the 'release the prisoners' story was found to be too far fetched, pamphleteers invented a prisoner, the comte de Lorette, imprisoned long before thanks to the vindictiveness of the ministry. The ghostly count was invariably depicted with an immensely long white beard, his skinny arms raised in supplication and gratitude. Within months the old fortress was demolished, its stones distributed to other liberators like Washington and Jefferson, and incongruously to the greatest despot in Europe, Catherine II of Russia.

Comic relief aside, the fall of the Bastille destroyed the King's plans and saved the National Assembly. It took some time to realize this at Versailles. After the withdrawal of troops from the Place Louis XV on the 12th, Besenval had done nothing to support the small garrisons at the Invalides and the Bastille. On the evening of the 14th, he withdrew troops from the Champ de Mars to secure the approaches to Versailles. In other words, he abandoned Paris to the insurgents but he did not disperse his troops. The King informed the deputies when he appeared at the Assembly the next day that no dispersal was contemplated. Later, Barnave and Mirabeau demanded the dismissal of Breteuil's government and the recall of Necker but there was no guarantee as yet that Louis would accede. It was only at a council meeting on the morning of the 16th that the King learned that the situation was hopeless. Marshal de Broglie informed him that the loyalty of the troops was in doubt and flight was out of the question. Louis had to capitulate. The troops were sent back to their garrisons and Necker recalled. The next day, caving in to a popular clamour, Louis made his way to Paris where, on the steps of the Hôtel de Ville before a cheering crowd armed to the teeth, he donned the tricolour cockade (white was the Bourbon family colour, blue and red those of Paris) and confirmed the appointment of Bailly as mayor of Paris and of Lafayette as commander of its National Guard, the new name of the citizens' militia. In short, the fall of the Bastille was less important than the slow realization that the troops were potentially unreliable.

Revolution in the Provinces

Whether the government simply lost its nerve during the crisis following the dismissal of Necker and misread the soldiers' morale is one of the most interesting speculations of the period. Part of the answer can be obtained by examining the reaction to the crisis in the provinces. As in the immediate Paris region, soldiers often surrendered their arms or joined the crowds. Municipalities, local electoral committees, literary societies and people avid for news followed events in Versailles and Paris closely. From late June onwards, addresses inundated authorities protesting the closure of the assembly hall on 20 June, protesting the King's having been misled on 23 June, expressing their joy and their suspicions at the reunion of the orders on 27 June and complaining of the build-up of troops around the capital in early July. But the provinces did not await the dismissal of Necker to take action on their own.

As for the municipal revolutions themselves, these were more common in the north than the south where price rises were less steep and where local institutions had not succumbed to royal absolutism, and more common in the interior than in the ports which could rely on shipments by sea. The form the collapse of government took varied considerably from place to place. Thus, at Rennes, crowds seized weapons from the armoury and the troops threw down their weapons. There were similar incidents at Auxonne and Strasbourg. At Nantes, Dijon, Marseille, Bordeaux and Le Havre, crowds seized the citadels or troops freely surrendered them; at Nantes, Château-Gontier and Bourg, tax offices were invaded and people in Lyon threatened a tax strike. The King's visit to Paris, a symbol of the victory of the Third Estate, did little to calm provincial opinion for people still believed the aristocrats capable of anything. So permanent committees spread. In some cities they took over the municipality, while in others power was shared. Some of them even took over the government of the countryside. Thus the Nantes committee instructed the priests to have strangers disarmed and arrested. National Guards were also established and despite attempts of the committees to control it, the militia was enrolled and armed in the same haphazard fashion as their Parisian counterparts.

The subsistence crisis, which had reached terrible proportions in the provinces, also played a role in the establishment of committees and militias. There were innumerable riots to stop the transport of grain, or to fix prices, or simply pillage, and in the Paris region and Touraine some grain dealers were murdered. Some municipalities like Dijon and Cherbourg collapsed before riots. As in Paris, the committees and militias were not only conceived as a defence against royal attack but as protection against popular disorder. Indeed, Barnave recommended that Grenoble follow the Paris model because it was 'bonne bourgeoise'. Almost everywhere, royal authority collapsed. The intendants, who for 150 years had done so much to create that authority, were powerless. Some simply closed their offices and went home.

Authority collapsed in the countryside too. The peasant revolution was one of the most distinct features of 1789. The lurid spectacle of peasants murdering seigneurs and firing châteaux horrified contemporaries and has fascinated historians ever since. The risings are far from easy to understand, but for nearly a century the explanation has revolved around the concept of 'seigneurial reaction'. It is generally believed that in the latter half of the century seigneurs, avid for profit, or fearful of economic decline, restarted the process of tightening the bonds of dependence over their peasants. This took the form of revising the 'terriers' or register books in which the various seigneurial obligations were inscribed. The result was either raising dues, reviving others that had fallen into disuse, or being less tolerant of arrears. It is generally believed also that seigneuries were most vigorous in the 'backward' regions of the country or where seigneurs depended on dues for a considerable proportion of their income. The result was that peasants resented the increased vigour of the seigneurie, complained about it in their *cahiers*, and revolted against it in 1789. The arrangements for liquidation were not at all satisfactory and so they continued to struggle against it until its final abolition in July 1793.

This explanation, of course, has a tight internal elegance. Peasants revolted in 1789 because they were oppressed and the bonds of oppression were tightening. Unfortunately, this view does not hold up. It is possible to create the impression of ubiquitous oppression by simply listing the various seigneurial claims which in their lush variety, from the truly burdensome to the downright silly, could fill several pages in an impressive list. Yet the reality was that peasants had an uneven relationship with the seigneuries. Almost everyone paid a modest quit-rent, but other exactions affected people unevenly. If one was not in the land market – and few were very often – and if one's relationship to market production was fairly feeble – the experience of the majority – then the seigneuries scarcely affected most people. Seigneurial courts were another matter, and in northern Burgundy, at least, peasant families appeared before the courts fairly often, about once a decade. But they were much more likely to face their neighbours than the lord himself. By far the majority of disputes in these courts were over trespass, debts, inheritances, wardships, and so on. Probably in most areas of the country, seigneuries did not extract much income from peasant communities and the income that was extracted has to be balanced against the services they sometimes provided. The *banalités* were one example where the lord built very expensive mills, and presses, and in return imposed the requirement that the 'vassals' in his jurisdiction use only his mills and presses. The burden here was the monopoly cost, not the overall cost, but the overall cost could be quite modest. In northern Burgundy, the fee for using the lord's bread oven was just five percent of the value of the bread. Another service was the court itself, an institution villagers valued because justice was cheap, local, swift and fair. The revolutionaries, once they abolished it, had to reinvent much of it in the form of the justice of the peace.

Even where the seigneurie was demanding, there were trade-offs. The *champart*, for example, was usually quite heavy, and since it was collected as a tax in kind on rural produce, it resembled the Church's tithe. It was inflation proof. Yet where the *champart* was high, rents and taxes would be low. Otherwise, peasants would migrate to areas where burdens were lower.

Were the Peasants Oppressed and Was it Getting Worse?

Much depends on the definition of the term 'oppression.' If we assume the word meant that the seigneuries extracted a high percentage of the peasant's income, then we will be disappointed. Even assuming the tithe was feudal, which medievalists would reject, feudal exactions did not take a great proportion of a typical peasant family's income – perhaps somewhere between 1 and 3 per cent. Even where their burdens were higher than the norm, this limited the ability of state and landlords to impose taxes and rents.

Yet peasants complained enormously about the seigneurial regime in their *cahiers de doléances*. The great historian of the nineteenth century, Tocqueville, explained this paradox of hostility and benign burdens by observing that rural communities resented feudal burdens because these burdens had become obsolete. This is a great insight. No doubt some burdens, like the obligation to provide guard duty to the local château had indeed become obsolete. Yet, this was not true in other respects. The *cahiers* themselves provide one clue about why country folk resented the system. Many complained that lords were not living up to their obligations and that in return for collecting tolls on markets, roads and bridges, they should be obliged to maintain these services. If the lords failed to fulfil their obligations, their rights should be forfeit. Second, another tack would explain the hostility to seigneurial justice, in many ways the lynch pin of the system, as a function of its own success. As the system became more open, more accessible, more responsive to local interests over the course of the century, the right of the lord to be judge and party in his own cause must have appeared more and more anomalous. In other words, rural communities were demanding a more public justice, something that the system was already close to offering. Not that the lord appeared very often in his own cause, but improving the system required eliminating this obvious conflict of interest.

The critique of the seigneurial system was very thorough and many communities demanded its outright abolition sometimes with compensation, but more often without any compensation at all. But the relation of this critique to the accountant's green eye shades in assessing the pluses and minuses of these burdens ought to be abandoned. One can, of course, find plenty of examples of lords or their agents imposing sharp practices. But, in general, there were better ways to fleece the peasants. Within the jurisdiction of the Parlement of Paris, at least, which represented one third of the country, it was legal to revise terriers only once every thirty years. Even then, revision was a process that could take up to twenty years, and even if vassals could be made to pay for their own declarations, there were plenty of other ways to nail vassals than this painfully slow process. But doing so took one out of the feudal complex. For some, the lords may have weighed on them more than before, but few lords had an interest in doing so. It was much easier to raise the rent.

So Why Did Peasants Revolt?

If the seigneurie was not that oppressive and if examples of lords' attempts to exploit their vassals are few and far between, why indeed did peasants revolt in 1789? Part of the answer to this question will always remain a mystery because not all areas where complaints were shrill later revolted. Whether a region revolted or not in 1789 depended a lot on circumstance but another element was also important: many of the leaders of the revolt in 1789 were individuals who felt the weight of the seigneurie as an institution that taxed their commercial transactions. In effect, manors were not backward institutions, vigorous only in the backward parts of the country, as Le Roy Ladurie contended. On the contrary, seigneuries long before the Revolution had positioned themselves to tax peasant economic activity. Thus, there were many excises on fairs, markets, bridges, land transfers, and so on, all of them taxes on peasant commercial activity. In most places, the most lucrative seigneurial right was the *lods et ventes*, a private tax on land sales. In other words, the seigneurie did not oppress the poor – why bother? – so much as tax the entrepreneurial peasantry. In short, peasant rebellion in 1789 depended upon the presence of wealthy peasants who were willing to lead their neighbours.

One of the factors that was most important in explaining the peasant rebellion in 1789 was the visit of Louis XVI to Paris after the fall of the Bastille. This was designed to assuage opinion in Paris and in the National Assembly after the fall of the Bastille, but almost everywhere in the provinces, the King's journey was taken to be an endorsement of popular rebellion. Country people knew the Third Estate had achieved a great victory and assumed they had the King's sanction to take matters into their own hands.

There were five regions of peasant rebellion which lasted from 19 July to 3 August: the wooded region northwest of Alençon in Normandy and in the Lower Maine; the Hainault region of Flanders; and Upper Alsace-Franche-Comté, the Mâconnais and Dauphiné. The risings themselves took different forms depending upon the local system of property holding under feudal law. Thus in Flanders and, to a lesser extent, in Normandy and Maine, bands of peasants forced lay and ecclesiastical lords to sign renunciations of dues and titles because the law presumed land to be subject to seigneurial jurisdiction, unless the vassal could produce legal proof to the contrary. In eastern and south-eastern France, by contrast, the law presumed land to be allodial (i.e., free of seigneurial claims) unless the seigneur could produce a title, and so peasants in these regions rarely bothered with renunciations but burned charters and terriers instead.

The peasant risings were thus far from the explosions of blind furies contemporaries tended to think they were. They were also occasions for celebration and opportunities to settle old scores. Almost everywhere people believed they had the King's sanction. In Franche-Comté, a contemporary chronicler wrote 'For several weeks, news went from village to village. They announced that the Estates-General was going to abolish tithes, quitrents and dues, that the King agreed but that the peasants had to support the public authorities by going themselves to demand the destruction of titles'. Some produced imaginary declarations of the King's Council authorizing violence.

The violence involved was rarely wanton. The attack on the château of Lignou in Normandy, for instance, was led by a wealthy 'gros laboureur' named Louis Gibault, who, it was said, owed the seigneur the impressive sum of 40 *écus* in dues. Gibault sent his farmhands around the region to spread stories of a false royal declaration. After three hundred villagers burnt the feudal papers in the courtyard, destroyed the hedges around the seigneur's meadow, pastured their animals on it, and fished in the seigneurial millpond, Gibault forced the seigneur to serve him wine. Nearby, other leaders included an iron merchant and his barrister son, and a postmaster-landowner. All of them incited poorer villagers to demand restitution of fines, some them going twenty and thirty years. In Flanders, there were similar acts of popular justice. In one case, the villagers demanded that the monks of Château return every penny collected in tithe since 1709, while in another case the abbot had to produce the original titles and agree to reduce the rate of collection. In this region, arson occurred only when the seigneurs tried to resist. Almost everywhere the risings were clearly another way of carrying out lawsuits which the villagers had lost or which were pending.

If the Norman risings show most sharply the coalition in the villages which carried out the peasant revolution of 1789, those of the Mâconnais show most clearly the atmosphere of fear, hope and celebration. The townspeople of Mâcon, Châlon-sur-Saône and Pont-de-Vaux gave the signal by attacking the municipal customs barriers and grain merchants on 20 July. A few days later a rumour began to circulate that the postmaster at Saint-Albain had received a letter to the effect that Louis XVI had decreed that no one would be punished if the people destroyed the châteaux within three days. A judicial holiday that authority regularly granted was common enough in the charivaris of the Old Regime, but this was not the only folkloric element in the risings. Peasants armed with farm tools trooped to the courtyards of the châteaux, mounted the towers and tore down weather vanes (a seigneurial monopoly), destroyed pigeon coops (another monopoly), and compelled the seigneurial agents to lay a table and give everyone food and drink. Masons were forced to climb roofs and towers and literally began to demolish the châteaux by removing tiles and bricks. Only later did someone think to head to the archive rooms and toss the charters out of the windows where others made a gleeful bonfire. Grain bins were pillaged, wine cellars were sacked and the contents consumed on the spot, and furniture and curtains were taken. Nor were the châteaux the only enemies. Seigneurial agents apart, country notaries, *rentiers* and *curés* were forced to give the rebels food and drink and sometimes money.

In the middle of the spreading insurrection, a rumour, probably an echo of the risings in Franche-Comté, that brigands were about to cross the Saône, put dozens of villages on the alert. Bands of partially armed men went down to the banks to fight them off, but others took them for brigands. Opinion blamed the monks of Cluny for sowing the rumours. On 29 July thousands of peasants attacked the town. The citizens' militia repulsed them. This finished the insurrection but dozens of châteaux had been sacked and a few burned, possibly in some cases by accident. Summary courts eventually sentenced twenty-six leaders to death by hanging.

The complicated relations of fear and reprisal were also evident in Dauphiné. The troubles started here when rumours that brigands were invading from Franche-Comté put everyone on the alert. When the rumours proved false, people began to mutter 'Was it the seigneurs who were the cause and who wished to do harm to us?' Others were less rhetorical. 'It was the seigneurs who caused this alarm because they wished to destroy the Third Estate and they sent brigands to do it.' The attacks on the châteaux began on 29 July, but seigneurial archives were not always the principal object. Instead, as in the Mâconnais, bands marching in military order behind beating drums looted wine cellars or they stole bedclothes, tapestries and money. Here too, many of the country people believed the King had ordered the sacking of the châteaux. Later, notaries were dragged in, forced to stand on tables with a little wine to fortify them, and compelled to read out titles of papers which were then burned amid gunshots fired in celebration.

Most alarming because it was so irrational was the Great Fear, a vast panic which spread over almost the entire country from six original centres between 20 July and 6 August. It was invariably linked with a fear of brigands who were seen as capable of anything. One such fear was the destruction of the crops whose harvest was vital because of the previous year's shortage and because of the unnaturally wet July. At times the rumour mill linked fear of brigands to an invasion of foreign troops from almost any country in Europe. Needless to say, such sombre and visceral fears joined with other terrors of an aristocratic plot. These fears of unspecified malevolence further envenomed relations with the aristocracy and encouraged the formation of more citizens' militias and permanent committees. Yet it reinforced the solidarity of society as well because in some regions priests, nobles and magistrates joined the emergency committees, and towns which had eyed each other with dark suspicion over food supply now sent each other offers of help. In other words, the Great Fear was not synonymous with the peasant rebellion, although a careless reading of Lefebvre's classic has entrapped many of his successors into asserting they were.

The 4 August and the Patriots' Revolution

The paramount effect of the Great Fear and agrarian revolts, however, was on the deputies in Versailles, because both the fear and the revolt convinced them that malevolent forces were at work. Yet neither the fear nor the revolt was enough to convince the deputies that feudalism had to go. There is a substantial historiography to the contrary. This claims that the revolts in 1789 forced the deputies in the Constituent Assembly to abolish 'feudalism'. Georges Lefebvre and anyone who has endorsed him since has thought this, but the issue is worth challenging. If the Constituent Assembly did cave in to a popular movement, it would have been the only time in the revolutionary decade to come that a national assembly did so. This very same Assembly paid little heed to the anti-seigneurial revolts of 1790 which were far more serious than those of 1789. And its successors repressed other popular revolts about religion and conscription later with a savagery that, in fact defines the Terror. If they capitulated to this one, circumstances may well have made it convenient to do so.

Moreover, when the Constituent Assembly abolished 'feudalism', ostensibly in response to pressure from below, according to Lefebvre and his followers, it went on to abolish things that had nothing to do with popular opinion, but that had a lot to do with patriot opinion in the summer of 1789. In other words, popular pressure was a pretext to justify what patriot deputies had already decided to do. As it turned out, just as popular opinion in the villages was hostile to seigneurialism, so too were the *cahiers* of the Upper Third Estate. The many lawyers in the Constituent Assembly had pored over the near universal opinion in the legal texts that seigneurial justice was a usurpation but that it had to be respected because it was property, no matter what. In the summer of 1789, they were prepared both to abolish it and at the same time respect it as private property by providing indemnities.

The lead came from the Breton Club. This was originally a café society of Breton deputies, attractive to other like-minded deputies for its intransigent hostility to the nobility. By early August, it had about 150–200 members. The Bretons persuaded their colleagues that the disturbances in the provinces were the result of a popular 'desire for liberty', a 'delirium of liberty', as one deputy put it, and that the moment had come to throw off 'slavery and tyranny', as another deputy, Coroller du Moustier, explained. A caucus of deputies agreed that they would support a proclamation exhorting calm only if it also contained a renunciation of fiscal privilege. In other words, the Bretons were prepared to use popular violence as a lever against the First and Second Estates. They persuaded the duc d'Aiguillon, one of the richest men in the country, a patriot and former member of the Society of Thirty, to propose a motion suppressing tax exemptions. Yet the caucus clearly anticipated resistance even from their fellow deputies in the Third Estate. Otherwise, it would not have been necessary to use 'a kind of magic', as the deputy Parisot put it; that is, maneuver the nobility into renouncing its fiscal and seigneurial privileges voluntarily at a night session when fewer of those not privy to the secret would be present. For all that it was planned, the 'Night of 4 August' was an astonishing patriot victory. It began with the comte de Noailles and d'Aiguillon demanding fiscal equality among the orders, the suppression of provincial and urban privileges, and compensation for the abolition of seigneurial rights. These were generous offers, as were all the other renunciations of rights and privileges which deputies from all three orders rushed to make in the next eight hours. But the session was not quite a delirium of unrelieved generosity punctuated by thunderous applause after each renunciation. Aiguillon's estates in the southwest amassed considerable sums in dues, and he proposed a compensation package that was probably greater than his estates were worth. Noailles and Aiguillon were also court nobles, less dependent on dues than many provincials. Right after, an obscure noble deputy from Perigord proposed the abolition of useless and excessive court pensions.

There were also hesitations. No cleric proposed abolishing the tithe but it was abolished anyway. When the Third Estate deputies got up to surrender the rights and privileges of their provinces and towns, many did so on the understanding that they would have to seek the concurrence of their constituents. A certain bloody-mindedness and an exaggerated respect for imperative mandates (which the King had annulled) underlay the attitudes of many. Yet there were genuine sacrifices too. The vicomte de Beauharnais's proposal to open high posts in Church and state to commoners and to establish equality of judicial punishments was one example. Many deputies, privileged and *roturier*, also had something to lose by the abolition of seigneurial justice and venality of offices. Moreover, the renunciations came so quickly that no one could have thought out the full implications of what they had done, no matter how much subsequent legislation tried to clarify the principles sketched on the night of the 4th. As we shall see, the abolition of everyone's fiscal privileges meant that many members of the Third Estate also had to pay more taxes.

Afterwards, many breathless deputies justified what they had done by claiming it was necessary to appease popular clamour and to restore order. This was true only to a point. Such claims were useful to persuade constituents, who had shown a great attachment to the privileges of their own towns, provinces and corporations in the spring, that a renunciation of their liberties was necessary. As far as many deputies were concerned, the Night of 4 August was a way of escaping from a parliamentary impasse, as well as a device to appease the peasantry. Ever since 9 July when they declared themselves the 'Constituent Assembly', the deputies had been debating the form and necessity of a declaration of rights as a preamble to the constitution. The privileged orders had been resisting this and had even gone so far as to propose that a two thirds majority be required on constitutional questions. This would have reintroduced all the disadvantages of vote by order. By early August, the patriots had concluded that the legal underpinnings of privilege had to disappear before any progress could be made on the constitution. As the Breton deputy Boullé put it: after the decisions of 4 August 'all interests finding themselves blending together, and from now on being the same, the rest of the work on the constitution will be much easier and quicker'. Parisot was even more explicit. As he scribbled his note to his constituents in the early dawn of 5 August, he made no reference to the risings or to seigneurial rights as a motive for suppressing feudalism. This was an amazing omission. Instead, he explained that the delaying tactics employed by the nobility and clergy to a declaration of rights convinced the patriots that 'so long as the two privileged classes had any privileges whatever, the particular interest would override the general good . . .' and that 'to fulfill our views... while making a truce on the Constitution, it was a question of destroying all the privileges of classes, provinces, towns and corporations'. In other words, subverting the social and legal basis of privilege was a continuation of the Third Estate strategy that had emerged earlier of making everyone equal within the nation. This required some effort at persuasion, especially to sceptical provincials who were still attached to their own privileges. Boullé exhorted his particularist constituents 'When the intimate union of all the provinces under the dominion of law and liberty presents such a great and majestic idea, what interest could one have in isolating oneself...?' The Night of 4 August thus went far beyond the mere abolition of seigneurialism. It introduced changes into people's lives that few had anticipated five months before. It remained to be seen whether they would cede to sentimental appeals like Boullé's.

The deputies' accommodation of the peasant revolution also raised hopes in the countryside. But the legislation of 11 August which 'abolished feudalism' is less of a fraud on country people than is often supposed. Abolishing mortmain and other marks of personal servitude like seigneurial *corvées* was a genuine gain. Retaining other dues until the seigneurs were compensated at a rate to be determined was also to be expected from an assembly concerned to protect the rights of property. On the other hand, the fact that the Assembly was willing to go so far encouraged peasants in some regions to expect still more. These heightened expectations overwhelmed the text of the law. Peasants soon found they could defy the law altogether. They could get away with it because local authorities were reluctant to enforce the law. Where authority tried to do so, it provoked even bigger rebellions than those of 1789. Thus seigneurialism abolished itself 'from below' in any case.

The enabling legislation had great implications for the Church as well. The abolition of the tithe was not a common demand in the spring and when the Duc du Châtelet proposed it (in retaliation for the Bishop of Chartres's motion to abolish hunting monopolies), he seems to have had in mind a substitute money tax with compensation to the Church. No compensation was allowed for in the law of 11 August, so this aspect of the law was not a sobering reaction after the delirium of 4 August, but a sort of radicalization. The idea was also abroad that the Church's wealth could be used to pay the state's debts. Clerics would be supported 'by other means', according to the law. Implicit in this was the disastrous Civil Constitution of the Clergy which would turn the priesthood into salaried officials.

The deputies also forgot their qualms about consulting their constituents about the abolition of provincial rights. The law of 11 August also abolished provincial, urban and corporate rights because, as the law explained, 'a constitution and public liberty are more advantageous to the provinces than the privileges which some of them enjoy...' This was the sum total of the political experience of the entire generation. Privilege had not been able to resist a rapacious state whenever the monarchs exercised their will and in the autumn of 1788, the patriot party had successfully complained that the balance of privilege was inequitable. By the summer of 1789 a majority of deputies had come to the same conclusion. But it was all the more necessary to define the relationship between the state and society, in other words to promulgate a declaration of rights.

The Declaration of the Rights of Man and Citizen, which was adopted on 26 August, was intended to be an educational device to enhance the nation's love of liberty and a statement of principles against which the institutions and performance of government could be measured. Despite the rioting which no one could be sure was over, the Assembly resisted the recommendations of three of its own committees headed by Mounier, Mirabeau and the archbishop Champion de Cicé that laid great stress on duties and obedience. Instead, the final Declaration closely followed Lafayette's drafts which had been in the making since the previous January and which in turn owed much to the Virginia Declaration of Rights and the Declaration of Independence (Thomas Jefferson, then American Resident in Paris, annotated Lafayette's second draft). These in turn can be traced back to the political theories of Locke, Montesquieu and, to a lesser extent, Rousseau, and, through them, to the whole European tradition of natural law. Although the deputies acknowledged their debt to America, the Declaration of the Rights of Man addressed itself to specifically French problems. The statements that men are inherently free and equal in rights, that social distinctions are based only on utility (Art. I), that virtue and talent are the only requirements for public office and the endorsement of equality of taxation (Art. XIII) confirmed the destruction of aristocratic privileges. The power of the monarchy was severely restricted. Sovereignty rested with the nation (Art. III), not the king (but, unlike America, not with the people either); all citizens had the right to take part in the legislative process (Art. VI); arbitrary arrests and punishments were illegal (Arts. VII and VIII); consent to taxation and accountability of public officials were essential rights (Arts. XV and XVI); as was freedom of speech and the press (Art. XI). All these clauses were directed against routine practices of government under absolute monarchy. Nor was the Church spared. Freedom of opinion 'even in religion' (Art. X) and the invocation of the 'Supreme Being' (preamble) rather than God, eliminated the Church's monopoly of public worship as well as its claim to special status.

The Declaration was more than an attempt to exorcize the Old Regime, however. The purpose of all political association was to preserve 'the natural and imprescriptible rights of man. These rights are liberty, property, security and resistance to oppression' (Art. II). (This last was drafted during the military build-up in early July, while Lafayette's addition, to preserve 'the common good', was later deleted.) The right of property was left undefined possibly because to have tried to do so would have reopened the question of whether seigneurial property and the tithe were legitimate property. Liberty was defined to mean any activity that did not harm another, a common-sense formulation that had nothing to do with the more positive Rousseau–Robespierrist exercise of civic virtue. The specific protection given to property (Art. XVII) was understandable enough in a country where there were so many people who owned land, but it did raise the question of the role in the polity of those with little or none. Journeymen, town and country labourers, tenants and sharecroppers all had claims which were not compatible with a strict defence of the rights of property. As had the guilds. The resolutions of 4–5 August, consistent with the *cahiers*, only promised to reform them. The Declaration of Rights implicitly subverted them.

The Significance of August 1789

The Night of 4 August, the law of 11 August, and above all, the Declaration of the Rights of Man and the Citizen are what made the French Revolution revolutionary. The National Assembly's claim to sovereignty on 17 June began this process and the military situation following the fall of the Bastille meant that for the moment, there was nothing the King or his advisors, could do about it except feign acceptance. August specified what that assumption of sovereignty would mean. Many deputies, perhaps a majority of the Third Estate, did not see this outcome clearly, if at all, when they first arrived in Versailles. But others did have a vision of what a post-absolutist France would look like. Witness the drafts of the Declaration in Lafayette's papers that date from January. The Bretons too, or most of them, arrived in Versailles with a vividly articulated anti-noble and anti-privileged agenda. Indeed, one of the most important things leaders like Lafayette and other liberal nobles, and members of the Breton Club did, was persuade the timid, often baffled backbenchers to support their bold leadership. The utter incompetence of the King, his fecklessness and also his ill-timed surges of activity certainly made the task of persuasion easier. So too did the undeserved contempt many nobles flaunted to the provincial deputies, always sensitive to their status. To repeat, in a crisis, the ordinary deputies had to focus, realize that the time for goodwill had passed, and once they did this, they usually always supported anti-absolutist, anti-privileged, and sometimes, even anti-clerical measures.

Here then are the principles of 1789: liberty under law, equality under the law and equality of opportunity, due process, limited government, religious toleration, protection of property, and so on. Yet the 'principles of 1789', unfortunately never defined, but it must be these, have a terrible reputation. Even at the time, some deputies grumbled that the Declaration was so much 'metaphysics'. Such a criticism never entirely disappeared, especially among conservative historians. It was revived over twenty years ago when the late François Furet, and those whom he inspired, claimed that the 'principles of 1789' caused the Terror, or the Terror was embedded in these principles, or that the principles 'scripted the Terror'. The argument is that the circumstances of an abrupt collapse left no other choice except to reconstruct society around ideology, that the rupture had destroyed social cohesion so that only ideas held people together. The Terror was 'an integral part of revolutionary ideology'. The 'principles of 1789' were too abstract, too utopian, the attempt to remake human nature was too ambitious; and that to ignore the past was bound to produce an authoritarian result, since most people resist having their natures remade. In any case, it is impossible to begin history all over again because the past is an incubus that weighs upon us all, whether we realize it or not.

Attractive as all this sounds, it ignores the fact that the Declaration for all its high-minded, and assuredly abstract, statements of principle, was quite specific about how these principles applied. Indeed, they encapsulate the programmatic aims of all European liberal parties ever since, without, it would seem, having caused a Terror anywhere, let alone a Gulag which was one of Furet's obsessions. Furet's argument also ignores the period between 1789 and 1793–4. But by telescoping the two periods, he eliminates the necessity to assess the importance of the war and the resistance to revolutionary reforms and what the war and the resistance had to do with the Terror. Finally, Furet's general histories of the period, as opposed to his manifestos, are quite conventional; indeed in returning to the discussion of high politics and philosophy, he was returning quite consciously to an older tradition that eschewed both social history and the provinces. This book will argue that this is a fatal omission, that every crisis of the Revolution after 1789 had its origin in the provinces, and that knowledge of how provincial and national histories interact is crucial to understanding the revolutionary decade.

October Days

Once a kind of afterthought in the narrative of a very busy year, the 'October Days' have become a critical source of excitement for American feminist scholars and their enthusiastic followers. In effect, many thousands of Parisian women launched themselves on a wet and cold journey from the market stalls, shops, and narrow streets of central Paris to Versailles in those early days of October. Their intention was to force the royal family to accompany them back to Paris.

The event was more complicated than just the women compelling the return of the royal family. The women were not alone. After nightfall on October 5, the all-male battalions of the Paris National Guard followed the women to Versailles, many hours later it is true, but the arrival of armed force was crucial. There were royal regiments at Versailles, and at least one of them was totally hostile to the Revolution, so the National Guard battalions were essential if there was going to be any resistance to the women's project. Furthermore, the idea to march to Versailles forcibly to retrieve the royal family was not spontaneous, nor did it originate with the women. Instead, the idea had been bandied about since late August in radical political circles and at least one previous attempt fizzled. Moreover using women to head crowds was a common tactic in Old Regime grain riots because it effectively disarmed troops sent to repress them and seldom led to prosecution.

As in July, the major beneficiary of revolutionary events was the Constituent Assembly. By late July, the former privileged orders had begun to regroup especially after the return of two of their most talented orators, the abbé Maury and Duval d'Espremesnil, who had fled the Assembly in fear in the July Days. The various factions of the right quickly formed a tight and well co-ordinated caucus. They won a number of key votes on staffing committees and they were able to stall consideration of the new constitution. These tactics were what persuaded the deputy Parisot and others to subvert their privileges in the Night of 4 August.

Relations were already bitter among the factions, partly because of the continuing antipathy of the former Second and Third Estates for each other, and partly because many in the clergy felt the patriots had seduced them in June 1789, only to betray them in August when the Constituent Assembly abolished the tithe. Since the issue for many parish priests had always been a desire to restore their ability to carry out their pastoral duties independent of interference from both the state and the hierarchy, the abolition of the tithe wrecked the financial autonomy of the village clergy. So in their bitterness, they were only being consistent.

Following the August decrees, the record of the patriots in getting their way was mixed. They won a vote making the new legislature a single chamber, as opposed to a bicameral legislature like that of Great Britain. In this, they got the support of many provincial nobles who had long distrusted the pretensions of the Versailles blue-bloods and reckoned these snobs would dominate a second chamber. The voting on a veto for the king on legislation was much more ambiguous. Eventually, the Assembly settled on a suspensive veto which was supposed to be a compromise between those who wanted no veto at all and those who wanted the royal veto to be absolute. This turned out to be a total catastrophe. Not only was the king given a suspensive veto, the veto could not be overridden for up to six years. No one foresaw that in a national emergency, like that of 1792, no one was prepared to wait that long. Unlike an American president's veto that can be overridden quite rapidly if there is sufficient opposition to it in Congress, the suspensive veto was much more powerful, too powerful as it turned out because it fatally weakened the legislature. The veto left only force to resolve the emergency.

Yet Louis XVI refused to sanction any of these innovations. He also refused to recognize the August laws. Rather than recognize the King's fervid opposition to these reforms, public opinion preferred to rely on the old device of blaming the King's evil councillors. But the way to evade these occult influences was to bring the King into the midst of his people. This was new, of course, and it says something about how the events of 1789 lead people in Paris to solve old problems in new ways. Instead of complaining, and letting it go at that, they were willing to act. Another factor working in the same direction was the political uncertainty that the economic situation produced. There was agitation among various types of journeymen, and the continuing drought delayed getting the harvest of 1789 milled. At the same time, financial confidence was at a low ebb. Necker's new loans floated in August found few takers. Hoarding of specie thus disrupted the market mechanisms. His reputation as a miracle worker began to sag. Somehow, bread shortages, in Paris, a continuation of the 'famine plot persuasion' of the Old Regime, were the fault of machinations in Versailles.

Finally, rabble rousers at the Palais Royal, like Camille Desmoulins and Georges Danton, accused Marie-Antoinette of having urged her brother, the Austrian Emperor, Joseph II, to intervene to rescue the royal family. Thus the Queen's black reputation that her loyalties lay with her Hapsburg relatives translated itself into radical politics in Paris – quite a leap given the origin of this reputation in extreme Catholic elements at court in the Old Regime. The street orators even anticipated early on that Louis would try to flee the country. They did not know it, but they had read his mind, although the King rejected such a plan at this point as cowardly. He would change his mind eventually.

The precipitating event was a banquet of the notoriously monarchist Flanders regiment. There were many toasts to the King, but conspicuously, none to the health of the nation. Some sang 'Richard, coeur de lion', a lament for a fallen king. As the evening was breaking up, stragglers, worse for wear, got even more provocative and cried out 'Down with the Assembly!' Needless to say, rumours of what had been said were even more inflammatory when they reached Paris. The women of the market halls could scarcely contain themselves. Led by Mailland, an official Conqueror of the Bastille, they began to march to Versailles on the morning of 5 October, hauling several heavy cannon with them. The men of the National Guard, injured by the womens' taunts and at least as outraged by the stories about the Flanders regiment, could scarcely contain themselves either. Eventually Lafayette, the commander of the National Guard, got the authorization from the Paris municipality to go to Versailles, and like another revolutionary leader of the nineteenth century, led his men by following them.

When the women arrived in Versailles in the late afternoon, drenched and on edge, some joined the disconcerted deputies on the benches of the Constituent Assembly while others roamed the corridors of the palace of Versailles. (One wonders what happened to the brave declarations of the intrepid royalist regiments of the night before – they seem to have melted away). When they ran into the Queen, Marie-Antoinette was so frightened by their vulgarity, their ferocity and their threats, she feared for her life. The Paris National Guard arrived around midnight, and restored some calm. Inside the Assembly, one deputy, realizing how opportune the situation was, demanded Louis sign all the decrees he had been refusing to sign. The King agreed, no doubt reasoning that anything signed under duress was invalid. But he still refused to move to Paris. What decided the issue was a scuffle when someone in the Kings' Bodyguard killed a National Guardsman, just after dawn on the 6th when the Guard burst into a courtyard on the palace grounds. The Guard retaliated by killing two Bodyguards, and parading their heads around on pikes. In order to avoid the situation from collapsing into total catastrophe, the King, the royal family and Lafayette appeared on a balcony of the palace to announce the royal family's departure for Paris. The Parisians had triumphed. But from the royal family's point of view, the Parisians had threatened them with death and indeed, had been prepared to kill to get their way. Later that afternoon, a huge procession, accompanied by heavy wagons of flour from the palace reserves, and the heads of the two Kings' Bodyguards on pikes, made its way to the capital amid shouts from spectators and chunky market-porters that they were bringing back 'the baker, the baker's wife and the baker's boy'. That night as the royal family settled into the Tuileries palace adjacent to the present-day Louvre, the city was illuminated in celebration, but nothing could disguise the fact that political authority had shifted decisively. Unlike July when Parisians' actions had been essentially defensive, the October Days represented the first and hardly the last occasion when direct Parisian intervention decisively affected national politics.

The October Days did not stand alone as popular disturbances went. Except for big military affairs, women always had an important role in riot and disturbance during the Revolution. As in the disturbances of the spring of 1795, women's taunting of the men was the start of the affair and they also were participants, literally drumming up help, invading workshops to round up others to follow and so on. During religious disturbances women were always in the forefront, men played a supporting role.

So Why Did a Revolution Occur in France in 1789?

A revolution based upon rights would have been difficult to foresee until almost the very end of the Old Regime. Certainly respect for property had been a part of French jurisprudence for a long time. The French Enlightenment also had a strong sense of certain rights like religious freedom and a criminal justice based upon due process and the presumption of innocence. But there was another sense in which the leading intellectuals of the day, for all their Anglophilia, did not embrace the full sweep of civil rights until quite late. Voltaire's *Philosophical Dictionary*, for example, recommends flight as a defence against political oppression. Surely, only the sage of Fernay and other rich people could avail themselves of this solution. The *Encyclopédie* has an equally crabbed view of equality.

It looks like the intellectual antecedents of the Declaration emerged quite late, that they had not been bubbling up for a long time. Similarly, it may well be that the literate public abandoned the defence Montesquieu had made of privilege quite late. This was that privilege for the restricted few in all its forms protected the population as a whole from the Crown's excesses. There were two occasions within the memory of the revolutionary generation where this had proved false, during the Maupeou crisis of 1770–1 when the *parlements* were first abolished, and in 1788 when they were abolished again. Only an aroused public in 1788 whose protests sapped confidence in the royal finances forced the government to reverse itself and call the Estates-General. In short, the political and financial desperation of the old monarchy forced ministers to break some of the traditional assumptions about the relation between government and the country, and this in turn forced many members of the public to re-evaluate traditional notions of governance.

Other elements of the political culture that brought the Revolution about had been around much longer: suspicion of the court, hostility to ministers, dislike of taxes, and so on. Indeed, some of these notions had been a part of general political culture in one form or another for centuries and both the high born and ordinary people believed the stories and rumours based upon them. It took unusual circumstances to divert them to a genuinely subversive role. A changed context made these traditional apprehensions seditious.

This change of perception did not happen to everyone simultaneously. For some, like Lafayette and his friends on the Committee of Thirty, the crisis of 1788 was an opportunity to get a National Assembly, presumably with constituent powers. But even future radicals came to their positions later than this and quite suddenly. Many deputies of the Third Estate arrived in Versailles, dazzled by the wonder of it all, full of goodwill but with little developed sense of what programme they favoured. Some did not even know what was in their region's general *cahier*, which ostensibly bound them to demand certain reforms. People like this became revolutionaries after the Revolution itself began.

Social considerations also conditioned but hardly determined reactions to the agony of the Old Regime. There was a sweeping range of agreement between the nobles and the Upper Third Estate on the kinds of reforms everyone hoped the Estates-General would initiate. Equality of taxation, a parliamentary regime with regular legislatures that would vote taxation, most civil liberties, and so on were a common demand in the spring of 1789. But there were significant differences of wealth, education, life experience, access to power and privilege, even marriage patterns that made nobles and bourgeois different, a difference that was reflected neatly in the composition of the noble and commoner deputies. So, there were divergent perspectives on the kind and extent of reforms, with the aristocracy being understandably less radical in general. Even after the merging of the orders into a single assembly on 27 June, the sizeable contingent of nobles and upper clerics might have forced a greater compromise, and therefore a less radical outcome. But the Crown, focused as it was on its own survival, failed to provide a lead, and at this stage anyway, no leaders emerged to lead an opposition within the Constituent Assembly to the patriots.

The patriots' skill at mobilizing their tepid supporters emerged very early, perhaps because the Breton delegation represented a province where semi-parliamentary institutions were vigorous until the end, and partly because an exuberant public opinion both in Paris and the provinces buoyed along the hesitant. But above all, events broke the patriots' way. The *journées* in Paris did not aim at preventing the dissolution of the Estates-General in July, nor at intimidating Louis XVI into accepting the constitutional decrees of August–September. But that was their effect. Nor did the anti-seigneurial risings of the summer intend to propel the patriot programme so far. But the politicians were able to profit from the disorder, from the 'delirium of liberty', to persuade other politicians and the public to go way beyond what the insurrections were demanding. One might imagine that the formerly privileged might have resented having their 'property' torn from them, without debate or compromise, and that recriminations would have arisen at their representatives who had so foolishly surrendered. No doubt some felt this way, but it did not matter. By the end of 1789, the defeat of the old order had been so total, the victory of the patriots so great, that the social basis of any opposition had been thoroughly undermined. Even the aristocratically dominated army had to fear mutinies, as, for that matter, did the navy, so quick were sailors returning from long voyages to learn the language of revolt from willing Jacobin teachers.

By the end of the year, the Revolution had tremendous support in the country as the daily reading in the National Assembly of countless, almost deliriously enthusiastic, addresses from all over the country showed. But for all the nation's adherence, what would really matter was what the 'principles of 1789' would mean once they were made operational. The deputies themselves would have to work out these details. Loyalties that appeared unshakable and passionate would soon be tested: some would solidify, others would drift towards hostility. For all that the Revolution appeared to be over in 1789, another one was about to begin, this time one that would severely challenge the 'principles of 1789'.

3

Subjects Become Citizens

Once the Constituent Assembly had established the 'principles of 1789', it had to implement them. While the principle of liberty and equality was straightforward enough, the complications were in the details. No one expected equality of taxation would mean higher taxes. While almost everyone in the Third Estate denounced abuses in the Church in their *cahiers* in 1789, only a few expected the abolition of the tithe, the nationalization of Church lands, and consequently the loss of autonomy of the former First Estate. For many clerics and indeed for many in the laity, this was a calamity. By the end of the eighteenth century, almost all élite laypersons believed in the principle of religious toleration. In many parts of the country, particularly in the Midi, ordinary people found this totally unacceptable. The earliest anti-revolutionary disturbances began in the Midi over this issue. Finally, while the constituency for the abolition of feudalism, however it was defined, was very large, few could have expected there would be little relief, that the Constituent Assembly would explicitly authorize landlords to add part of the former feudal burdens to the lease. Worse still, the law demanded the continued payment of the former dues until the former vassals compensated the former lords. As a result of the unintended consequences of these reforms, resistance to the Revolution began to appear. A Revolution that began with the sense that humanity could be reborn would very quickly slide into a brutal civil war.

Reform and the Bourgeois Revolution

One of the least controversial reforms of the Constituent Assembly was that of local government. Since the Assembly had eliminated venality of office as well as local and provincial privileges, it took advantage of the opportunity to create entirely new organs of government. The basis was the 'department', a territorial unit that has survived to this day. There were 83 departments of roughly equal size; these in turn were divided into districts, of which there were up to nine or ten per department. Below that were the villages, or the parishes of the Old Regime, now renamed communes. The individual cities were communes. Cities were also subdivided into 'sections' for electoral purposes. But once the electors in the sections decided not to disband, they started to meet more regularly and the sections acquired an informal but significant role in pressuring city governments.

Unpaid, elected volunteers staffed all of these levels in the hierarchy of government. Generally, a directory chosen from a much bigger council administered a department or a district. There were easily 10,000 local administrators above the level of commune throughout France that the new system called into existence. Including the communes, there may well have been a million. Experience showed there were plenty of men willing to serve, often at some inconvenience to themselves, or to their careers.

The new administrative system ignited a passionate campaign on the part of hundreds, perhaps thousands, of small towns to get for themselves the loaves and fishes that the new administrative system offered. From the largest to the smallest, towns, bourgs and villages launched every argument imaginable to inflate their claims and demean their rivals. No institution, no court was too insignificant to attract some town's eager eye. They pressured home town deputies, hired lobbyists, sent delegations, and bombarded the Constituent Assembly with petitions. This huge effort devoured much of provincial energy from the end of 1789 until early 1791 and beyond. But the effort was worthwhile. In the short term, this mobilization gave local bodies some experience in bending national institutions their way, and in the long term, successful efforts had major consequences for a town's prosperity. Generations later, being the seat of an administrative body or a law court contributed greatly to a town's well being. Losing out could bring stagnation. There must have been many diocesan towns like Dol-de-Bretagne, that lost even its status as a district seat in 1795, and that became ever after an unlovely town with a big former cathedral to remind folks of better days. Or towns like Aix-en-Provence that eventually lost the department seat of the Bouches-du-Rhône to Marseille and so remained utterly immobile until the late twentieth century.

The Political System

The electorate was divided into three classes. Everyone was considered a citizen, deserving of elemental protections of persons and property, but the law then split the citizenry into active and 'non-active', or as historians prefer, in to active and 'passive' citizens. An active citizen was a man who paid at least the equivalent of three days labour in taxes, was aged 25 or more and was resident for a year. This distinction between active and passive was bitterly criticized at the time and since, as a violation of the Rights of Man. As a principle such a criticism was telling, but in fact, the number of active citizens was very large: one estimate puts it at 4.3 million which would encompass two thirds of the adult males and make it proportionately larger than that of England, and many American states. The result was that in Dijon, for example, every trade was well represented among the corps of active citizens, and people in the manual occupations, who made up just over half the corps, were certainly numerous enough to make their presence felt in any election. But by basing the electoral system so heavily on taxes, the Constituent Assembly favoured the countryside over the towns because the electoral rolls were still based on the fiscal rolls of the Old Regime whose per capita direct taxes weighed more heavily on the countryside. Thus in the rural communes of the department of the Sarthe, over 90 per cent of the adult males were active citizens while in the towns roughly 70 per cent could vote. In the eastern Ille-et-Vilaine, three quarters of the rural male population was enfranchised while roughly two thirds of the overall population was. In one village in the Toulousain, 96 per cent of the men were active citizens but only 40 per cent were in Toulouse itself. In Paris, half, and sometimes considerably more depending on the section, of the adult males were disenfranchised. In the country as a whole, perhaps 60 to 70 per cent of the adult males who met the age and residency qualifications were active citizens. The system was much more inclusive than the rhetoric at the time alleged.

Active citizens chose 'electors' who in turn chose the local administrators. An elector was a person who paid the equivalent of ten days labour in taxes. Nearly two-thirds of active citizens, perhaps 40 per cent of all adult men, were eligible to become an elector. In short, the electoral system conferred the vote on a very substantial proportion of the population, but attempted to mitigate the 'democratic' element through a system of indirect elections.

A comment   This was not in any sense a federalist system. The hierarchy of administrations was a division of labour, not a system of divided sovereignty. In theory, the departments, districts and communes were meant to administer the will of the sovereign nation as enacted by the National Assembly and promulgated by the king. Reality was considerably different. Whatever the theoretical basis of local government, administrators were often required to act without the sanction of the ministry, if only because France was so large. Once local authorities lost confidence in the legitimacy of the central government, as they did in 1791–2, they began to act on their own often in defiance of the ministry and the law.

Nonetheless, a local administration whose purpose was to enact legislative decisions had its limits. However admirable it was to turn administration over to elected volunteers, the system crumpled under the strain. It never collected taxes efficiently or promptly, and its police powers in this area were to no avail. Although many local officials had the power of arrest, they had little authority to coerce beyond the goodwill of the citizens. There was no police as such, National Guards often had their own ideas about interpreting the general will, and the army was suspect. Even the Terror relied upon sometimes elected, more often appointed, amateurs. The ability of central government before, during and after the Terror to bend local administrations to its will was always limited. One of the reasons the Terror was not embedded in the Revolution of 1789 was that the institutional basis was entirely absent.

Was the Revolution bourgeois? If the measure of that was whether the bourgeoisie, however defined, took power in the elections to departments and districts late in 1790, the answer is certainly, yes. Nobles were clearly eligible to stand for local office but, either because the electorate mistrusted them, or because they chose not to stand, there were very few of them elected. In the Calvados, Morbihan, Ille-et-Vilaine, Tarn and Rhône-et-Loire, there were none at all elected, while in many other departments they were a mere handful. The shift of power these elections represented, therefore, was enormous. Given the structure of the bourgeoisie of the Old Regime, the legal professions were overwhelmingly represented, although the Cher and the Indre appear to have been exceptional in electing so many former officeholders and subdelegates. Elsewhere, the victors were more often small-town lawyers of various types. They were often men of experience, men who had received an apprenticeship in local government in the provincial assemblies after 1787, and who had been prominent patriots in the electoral campaign of 1789. Almost everywhere, however, it is possible to detect a reaction against the imperious rule of the permanent committees that had taken power, frequently by force, in 1789. In some municipal elections – Dijon, Nîmes and Montauban, among others – the advanced revolutionary party was actually defeated. The electorate and the administrators clearly wanted order and an end to adventures. It was all the more significant, therefore, that such conservatively minded men were to contribute so much to the radicalization of the Revolution when it was challenged in 1791–2.

A decentralized government run by local citizens was an ideal common to almost everyone in the early Revolution. Whether it would be accepted in the longer term depended on how the lawyers used the power the electorate conferred on them, and this in turn depended a great deal on the other reforms of the Constituent Assembly.

Finance and the Land Settlement

Questions of finance dominated the Constituent Assembly. The state's deficit had called it into being and it had kept itself in being in the critical months of 1789 by guaranteeing the national debt. The crisis shaped its reforms of taxation and ecclesiastical affairs. Moreover, the crisis grew worse every day. The royal bureaucracy crumbled, the nation took a tax-holiday and investors showed little confidence in the loans authorized in 1789. One solution, adopted on 2 November 1789 on an earlier proposal by Talleyrand, Bishop of Autun, was to sequester the property of the Church. This was a very rare demand in the spring and only the gravity of the crisis drew the deputies to it. Even so, the financial situation worsened. In March 1790, Necker, whose popularity was sinking with every failed loan and alarming financial statement, forecast a staggering deficit of 294 million, far more than Calonne's which had begun the final crisis of the Old Regime in the first place. Consequently, the deputies decided on 17 March 1790 that Church property would be sold to the public. In the meantime, the state would issue 400 million *livres* of treasury bills or 'assignats' at 3 per cent interest, which would be guaranteed by the newly nationalized property or 'biens nationaux'. The early *assignats* were, therefore, bonds that were based on solid collateral and the slight fall in their value can probably be explained as an effect of discounting. However, because of the great interest in *biens nationaux*, and because of the debt, the Assembly authorized a new emission of 800 million of *assignats* in September in denominations as low as 50 *livres* and this time they would bear no interest. In other words, the deputies had authorized the creation of paper money. This in itself was no bad thing because the 1200 million *assignats* in circulation at the end of 1790 was well below the value of the *biens nationaux*. The *assignats* would raise their price at auction and accelerate their sale. But the appearance of the *assignats* coincided with a shortage of specie which was itself due to hoarding, and with a balance of payments deficit brought on by the emigration of many aristocrats and the necessity to pay for grain imports. Without money, therefore, the economy was grinding to a halt as peasants held on to their grain and working people were not being paid. The solution to this was the creation, mainly by the Jacobin clubs, of 'billets de confiance' or notes of small denominations which in combination could be exchanged against the larger-denomination *assignats*. In other words, the state was losing control of the money supply. It also contributed to its expansion by authorizing the issue of 21 million in small coins which soon disappeared, and by issuing 100 million in *assignats* in denominations of 5 *livres*. This simply led to further hoarding of specie and a dreadful spiral of printing more *assignats* in ever smaller denominations, price inflation, a fall in the value of the *assignat*, quicker circulation of money and still further inflation. By the end of December 1791, *assignats* had depreciated by 25 per cent; on the eve of the war in the spring of 1792, by 40 per cent. Living standards of the poor and artisans invariably fell with immense consequences for labour relations, for the marketing mechanism of grain and for the continuation of disturbances in both town and country. A difficult and complex financial operation therefore eventually led to a challenge to the rule of the bourgeois citizens.

The obverse of this improvised monetary policy was the sale of ecclesiastical property. These lands were known as *biens nationaux* and they were important because they created, as was intended, a constituency of thousands who had a material stake in the success of the Revolution. They did not, however, contribute much to solving the problem of insufficient land for the poor peasantry because there was too little ecclesiastical property to accomplish that and because the lands were sold at auction which invariably favoured the highest bidder. All social classes were represented among the buyers including some of the future leaders of the counterrevolutionary rebellion in the Vendée. In many regions of the country, a surprising number of newcomers, who somehow managed to float enough credit, acquired property for the first time. Nonetheless, given the conditions of sale, the rich, particularly the urban bourgeoisie, were disproportionately successful. A considerable amount of money was mobilized for what amounted to a profitable way of showing one's patriotism. Bids were usually well beyond the original estimates and payment so assiduous that many buyers did not even profit much from the depreciation of the *assignat* (thus rendering the operation a financial success for the state). Contrary to what was a common opinion, officeholders were not major beneficiaries. Instead, they had to use their compensation money, not to buy land, but to repay those who had lent them money to buy the office. Still the Revolution reinforced the investment patterns of many of the old landed bourgeoisie and made their presence in the countryside more prominent than ever. The land settlement, therefore, favoured those who already had some wealth, or at least access to credit, and probably enhanced the importance of the urban grip on the countryside.

The Anti-Seigneurial Rebellion Spreads

Much of the effect of the new fiscal system, the use of *assignats*, and the sale of *biens nationaux* had to be worked out over a long period. The liquidation of the seigneurial regime was more immediate, and as a result of the August decrees, everyone knew the former seigneurs would be indemnified despite the demands for outright abolition in many *cahiers*. This knowledge that their earlier aspirations were going to be compromised might explain why anti-seigneurial rebellions broke out here and there in the early winter of 1789–90 in Upper Brittany, the Limousin, and elsewhere.

When it appeared, the law on liquidation was immensely provocative and invited challenge and defiance. The law of 15 March 1790, the work primarily of Merlin de Douai, a specialist in the mysterious components of feudal law, distinguished between rights bearing on persons, or those whose origins were thought to be usurpations and rights that could be interpreted as property. Thus, the law eliminated burdens on persons, but validated claims on land. Vassals had to redeem claims on land. The law was unworkable. In practice Merlin's distinction was impossible to make. The high redemption payments – twenty-five times the value for dues and twenty for transfer fees – encouraged few and securing an assessment of the value of the dues was a long and cumbersome process. In the end, redemption payments were very rare, perhaps because the political situation was so unstable as to assure former vassals that the situation was indeed going to change. The few who did exercise their rights under the law were the occasional urban bourgeois or wealthy peasant who took advantage of the falling *assignat* early in 1792 to redeem their land at much less than the rate envisaged in 1790. Or else, owners redeemed their land in order to make the property more attractive to a buyer.

If redemption was rare, so also was payment. Former vassals soon discovered in some places that the courts were not going to protect the former seigneurs' rights, probably because few seigneurs complained to an authority they considered tainted in the first place. Former vassals even refused to pay the dues that were still legal and they threatened neighbours who were too timid to join in the refusal. What made evasion possible was the abolition of seigneurial courts in August 1790. A seigneur wishing to enforce his claims no longer went to his own court but to the district tribunals whose judges were elected by the active citizens and the electors. In some districts, no cases where seigneurs claimed arrears ever came before the courts. There were such cases in the Corrèze but it is likely that peasants ignored court orders too when they lost their cases. In this context, the laws of July and August 1792, that required seigneurs to produce the original titles, let alone that of 15 July 1793 that abolished feudalism without compensation, sealed the facts on the ground.

But the seigneurial regime did not crumble from below everywhere. Between the end of 1789 and mid-1792 there were over 150 incidents in well over one third of the departments involving demonstrations, protests and mass violence. The country people refused to accept the Constituent Assembly's settlement as final. In other words, these risings were far more extensive and of far longer duration than the risings of 1789 which are much better known. The reason for this neglect, of course, is that this new round of insurrections had almost no impact on the national political scene, beyond a handful of politicians demanding leniency for the insurgents. Besides the resentment at the law on liquidation itself, the seigneurs' attempts to claim their rights that still existed kept the countryside even more effervescent. In Upper Brittany and in Quercy-Périgord-Limousin, there were dramatic insurrections. In February 1790 in Upper Brittany between Rennes and Ploermel, peasants rose up against the seigneurs' still legal attempts to collect arrears of dues and forced many to sign renunciations of their titles. At the end of January 1790 in Lower Limousin, peasants were convinced that 'the rich' were suppressing the decrees of the National Assembly. A band of eight or nine hundred in marching order headed by a billiard master, devastated a handful of châteaux between Brive and Tulle. They opened the sluice-gates of a number of seigneurial ponds. More significantly, they took the benches reserved for the seigneurial judges (presumably lawyers from nearby towns) from the churches and gleefully burned them on the public square. Since the bourgeoisie in this region also owned fiefs or were seigneurial officials, peasants attacked them too. They took receipts and oaths of fealty from their files and pillaged their houses. People were also convinced that their priests were allied with the seigneurs, and so refused to pays tithes and ground rents. There was an anti-clerical element to these risings as well. Disturbances continued throughout the year. In March and April in the Bourbonnais, Berry, Limousin and Nivernais where peasant micro property was very extensive, there were rumours that the National Assembly had reduced the price of bread. In June, these regions were racked by a wave of popular price-fixing and demands that seigneurs surrender usurped wastelands.

The most intractable rebellions were those which broke out in the departments of the Dordogne and Lot at the end of 1789. These continued with few interruptions until the spring of 1792. They began around Sarlat in the Dordogne in late November 1789, with attacks on seigneurial agents. The insurgents demanded that seigneurs remit dues that had already been collected, sometimes as much as twenty years before; and return guns, some of which had been confiscated from the insurgents' fathers. Like their counterparts elsewhere in the summer of 1789, peasants clearly had long memories for old grievances and took advantage of the unsettled conditions to right old wrongs.

This was not the only parallel with the risings in 1789 in the Mâconnais and elsewhere. The folkloric element was conspicuous, although here it took the distinctive feature of planting what were called 'May trees'. These were trees planted in the village square decorated with flowers, laurel leaves, and blue, white and red ribbons and topped with a crown. They did not differ from the thousands of 'liberty trees' which were springing up all over the country. But, like any powerful symbol, May trees had more ancient levels of meaning in the southwest. They certainly came to symbolize regeneration and deliverance and may have related to a customary belief that if they were kept standing for a year and a day, vassals would be free of seigneurial dues. They also symbolized the joy of spring and rebirth. Villagers traditionally paraded them throughout the countryside and planted them in the lord's courtyard. By suspending measures, small sacks of grain, chicken feathers or weather vanes from them, the villagers informed the lord symbolically that they considered his collection of dues abusive.

Planting May trees, therefore, was a symbol of freedom and a provocation to the lords. The practice of planting them to celebrate the union of the three orders in June 1789, or the anniversary of the fall of the Bastille in 1790, also shows how villagers blended traditional symbolism to commemorate unprecedented events and so to express their aspirations to be rid of the seigneurial regime entirely. When they planted them with a stolen weather vane on top, they were announcing their liberation from the lord's justice.

People planted May trees along the valleys of the Dordogne, the Corrèze and the Vezere in the spring of 1790. Bands of peasants, sometimes in National Guard uniform, marched to the sound of flute and drum to the lord's château where the lord had to give everyone food and drink, promise restitution of dues and guns, surrender his weather vane (a symbol of high justice) and watch his pigeons put to death. These demonstrations were quite peaceful, even joyful, indeed in one case, handshakes with the seigneur were spurned in favour of hugs because 'they were all equal'. As in the Limousin, pews were removed from the churches and burned in the village square and, as elsewhere, feelings against the bourgeois ran as high as against the nobles. When the lawyers of Saint Pierre-de-Chignac came to vote in the municipal elections, people cried out, 'We don't want any of these P... messieurs in the assembly... they were thrown out, tutoyés, vilified and threatened with death'. When authorities tried to tear down the May trees, women and children prevented it. The attempt of the Department of the Lot in September to use the army and the *maréchaussée* to do this systematically provoked a rising of nearly five hundred peasants, many of whom were National Guards armed with old hunting weapons and farm tools. Convinced that the laws of feudalism were the work of aristocrats, not the National Assembly, they overran the town of Gourdon, destroyed the houses of the administrators of the district, the former subdelegate and the rich, as well as a number of outlying country houses.

Nobles took up arms to defend their property. They roamed the countryside on horseback and fired on crowds of demonstrators. This provoked a wave of violent attacks on châteaux which lasted until January 1791. As in the Mâconnais, people set about literally demolishing the châteaux by destroying towers, and tearing off roofs or setting fire to them. Eventually, a band of rural National Guardsmen killed the leader of the noble horsemen, the Marquis d'Escayrac-Montratier, by shooting into a subterranean dugout in which he had been forced to take refuge. The troubles died down after this but only in degree, for throughout 1791 and into 1792 there were sporadic attacks on châteaux, firings of granges, demonstrations demanding the restitution of dues, destruction of pigeon coops and so on.

These risings were highly significant, because, as in 1789 peasants made little distinction between so-called revolutionary bourgeois and reactionary aristocrats. They had their own aspirations, and in these regions they meant to impose them.

Equally significant was the geographical distribution of resistance. In the country as a whole, anti-seigneurial risings occurred in areas of market production, where there was an important city nearby and where there were close market relationships between town and country as the well developed road network showed. In the Limousin anyway, the revolts were not the revolts of the downtrodden and the oppressed. The rebellions broke out in areas where peasants owned a great deal of the land already and where they were increasing their share. They were also engaged in commercial production through cattle raising and viticulture, and since commercial agriculture requires an ability to record transactions, these regions were highly literate, unlike other areas of the Limousin. As always with peasant rebellions, the rural élites had to be involved. But cultural elements mattered too as a great deal of the symbolic activity showed. Here it was not so much the oppressiveness of the seigneurie that mattered – such a case would be hard to make – as that the countryside appropriated the message of equality it received from the National Assembly. The highly active local Jacobins' clubs then inadvertently transmitted it to the countryside in a form they could not possibly have intended, and the country people applied it in their special and literal way. As the late Ralph Gibson argued for the nineteenth century, the uncompromising peasant egalitarianism of this region was an adaptation of middle-class radicalism. As such, it appropriated a vision of society that demonized the aristocracy and their hangers on, but eliminated from its restricted spectrum other sources of oppression, like the towns, or even the bourgeoisie itself.

The Civil Constitution of the Clergy and the Emergence of Popular Anti-revolution

The Civil Constitution of the Clergy was intended to define the relations between Church and state in the new order. It was a function of the new financial situation of the Church, and also a function of the deputies' desire to guarantee that the Church was loyal and compliant to the new regime. This aim to employ the Church to assure the loyalty of ordinary folk could not be proclaimed openly, but everyone knew how important the Church was in influencing public opinion.

Moreover, it was on issues that related to the Church that the deputies of the Constituent Assembly departed most from that the opinion that the villages expressed in 1789, or even from the opinions that the élite of the Third Estate proclaimed at the same time. Both the villagers and the élite wanted equality of taxation, both were hostile to the seigneurial regime, and the élite wanted equality of opportunity, the suppression of venality, an open national market, and basic civil liberties. Except in Brittany, or in the West generally, bald-faced anti-clericalism was rare. The innovations that befell the Church were almost alone in being a product of innovations that the National Assembly made up as it went along. The village *cahiers* demanded, not the abolition of the tithe, but its return to its original purpose of upkeep for priest, presbytery and poor. There was a broad, canonical shaped band of élite *cahiers* stretching from Paris to the coasts of Normandy and southern Brittany that did anticipate the Civil Constitution in major respects, but elsewhere few even of the élite *cahiers* demanded reform like this. There were mandates for every other major reform that the Constituent Assembly undertook; but not for this.

The decision to abolish the tithe and seigneurial dues and the nationalization of Church property stripped the Church of its financial resources. The idea that the government would thus have to pay the clergy was implicit in the decree of 11 August 1789. So if clerics were to be paid from public money, Constituents claimed a right to have a voice in the organization of the Church and how much of it they would support. The government would not support 'useless' religious orders and 'superfluous' dioceses. On 28 October 1789, they suppressed religious vows and dissolved contemplative orders, retaining only those involved in education, hospitals and charity. Later they decided that there would be just one diocese in each of the 83 departments, thus eliminating 52 others.

Financial considerations were not the only factors affecting the reorganization of the Church. By guaranteeing religious toleration and freedom of thought and expression, Articles X and XI of the Declaration of the Rights of Man undermined the Church's rationale for its existence as a separate, organized order. Protestants received full civil rights on 24 December 1789, although Jews had to wait until 27 September 1791.

Equal treatment of religious sects and their followers did not imply separation of Church and state. However many freemasons, deists or tepid Catholics there were among the deputies, all of them shared the Voltairean assumption that without religion, the popular classes would have no morals. If only in the interests of public order, the protection of property and the defence of the Revolution, they intended to tie the Church even more closely to the state than it had been under the Old Regime.

The most controversial element of the Civil Constitution was the election of new *curés* and bishops by the active citizens and electors. As its opponents pointed out, this allowed non-Catholics to help choose priests. Elections would also violate the traditions of millennia by undermining episcopal discipline, not to mention doctrine of apostolic succession. Men like these had absorbed the post-Reformation ideal of a disciplined, organized and hierarchical Church. This standard was an essential part of the ability of the Church to pursue its spiritual mission.

But it is difficult to see how the Constituents could have acted otherwise. From the point of view of the Constituents, several arguments dovetailed: unwavering claims of national sovereignty, the necessity to pay the clergy once the tithe and the land endowment were gone, and the precedent of royal interference in Church affairs, like the suppression of the Jesuits, all justified the reforms. In no way, said the Constituents, did the reforms imperil the Church's spiritual vocation. Those opposed to the Civil Constitution insisted that ecclesiastical discipline was broken, that indeed the Civil Constitution did invade the spiritual realm, and that in any case, no reforms could be accepted until a national council had accepted them. For the deputies, this was simply an act of bad faith since councils had defied the Crown most recently in 1788 and another one called to discuss the Civil Constitution would surely defy the representatives of the sovereign nation. Otherwise, why demand it? There were some opportunistic re-positionings on the Galician issue. The bishops, usually so cool to Rome, now insisted on the importance of papal acquiescence. No matter, the deputies thought this might be easy to get since an antipapal revolution at Avignon had voted for union with France. This allowed the Constituent Assembly a good deal of leverage against Rome.

With the papacy of little concern, the deputies could push ahead and ignore the protests of clerical spokesmen. Indeed, there were other reasons that were best left unsaid that also impelled the deputies. Aside from a desire to make all officials responsible to the electorate – and the clergy had become civil servants – the bishops of 1790 were all aristocrats. Some bishops had already emigrated and others, beginning with Le Mintier of Treguier in Brittany in November 1789, had denounced the Declaration of Rights. Could anyone trust the bishops to choose patriotic *curés*? Moreover, by the time the Civil Constitution was finally voted, on 12 July 1790, riots had broken out in some of the cities of the Midi whose slogans were not only anti-Protestant but anti-revolutionary. Religion could not be permitted to become the stalking horse of counter-revolution.

Once the question was posed with such clarity, compromise of any sort was very difficult. Finally tired of apparently sterile debates which had continued since May, and uneasy at a swell of religious troubles, the exasperated Constituents imposed an oath of loyalty to the entire constitution. This received royal sanction on 26 December. Those who refused it, bishops, *curés* and *vicaires*, would be expected to leave their posts with a pension as soon as a replacement was elected.

The oath to the Civil Constitution is rightly considered to be one of the great crises of the Revolution because it gave the counterrevolution a popular base. In order to understand why this was so, it is necessary to make a distinction between the reasons some clerics rejected it and why certain regions of the country supported that decision. There were many elements in the Civil Constitution that made the decision to take or reject the oath very difficult. The residence requirements for bishops, the reduction of scandalous incomes to respectable salaries, the prerequisite of pastoral experience that opened the episcopate to the lower clergy, and the assurance of a decent income for themselves, not to mention the welcome secular reforms, were close to many of the demands expressed in the clerical *cahiers* of 1789. Yet the clergy had dreamed that the national regeneration inaugurated by the calling of the Estates-General would have a religious gloss, which in some cases came close to advocating theocracy. Could this be done without the security of an established, self-governing order, the sacrifice of which was far greater than that asked of the nobility? Many of the *curés* who took the oath, soon to be called 'constitutionals', were convinced not only that it could, but that the Civil Constitution was the voice of God. Many of them, including many of the *curés* both in the Assembly and in the country, also dreamed of restoring the Church to the less opulent, purer existence of the first and second centuries when clergy and laity were a simple association of the faithful. There were many *curés* on the side of the National Assembly who saw God's handiwork in the Revolution, a Revolution that was, for them, a way of cleansing the Church of centuries of corruption. It was a providential intervention to purge an episcopate that cared more about the pleasures of billiards in the game rooms of Versailles than in residing in their dioceses. God Himself spoke through the Declaration of Rights. The vision of a primitive Church was powerful even among those who eventually rejected the religious settlement, and this explains why there were so few protests over the sequestration of Church property.

Those who refused, the 'refractories', were not so sure and could point to the Declaration of Rights, the dissolution of religious vows, the defeat of a motion by the reformer Dom Gerle in April declaring Catholicism the state religion, and the talk of permitting divorce as indications that the laity would not permit the clergy to lead them and that the vision of the leaders of the Third Estate for a post-revolutionary France implied a much crabbed role for the Church. Some went even further, and anticipated a major current in reactionary historiography in the next century. These men saw the impious influence of 'philosophy' in the Revolution and the Civil Constitution. Such denunciations had been significant themes in the clerical *cahiers*, but now some went even further and detected the corrosive influence of Voltaire and Rousseau in the oath.

By midsummer 1791, about 60 per cent of the *curés* and a little less than half the *vicaires* had taken the oath. Only seven bishops, including Talleyrand and Loménie de Brienne, did. The *curés* were subject to a great deal of pressure, not least from the Pope whose long-awaited condemnations on 10 March and 13 April 1791 sparked a flurry of retractions; not many retracted under papal pressure in the end, but each retraction was sensational. Family, friends, fellow priests, seminary professors, bishops, officials and Jacobin clubs inundated the *curés* with blandishments, advice, threats and fulminations. Thus no single or even multiple explanation can be found which would explain why some *curés* took or refused the oath. But the most convincing explanation rests upon cultural factors. In effect, on the eve of the Revolution two different theories of pastoral care divided the parish clergy. One group retained the theory of the Counter-Reformation developed in the Council of Trent at the end of the sixteenth century, that a parish priest ought to live at a distance from his flock, be a compassionate but stern advisor, dwell apart from his parishioners, socialize only with other priests, and undertake only secluded amusements like reading breviaries, or fishing, or solitary promenades. Another theory was what Timothy Tackett calls the theory of the 'citizen priest', a man who got involved with the laity, tried to understand their problems, and who lead his flock through sympathy and engagement. Where the Tridentine theory of pastoral care prevailed, there also did the priests refuse the oath. Areas of high oath taking correlated with regions where theories of citizen priests dominated. But local factors also mattered. In Brittany, for example, there is a strong correlation between a priest on his own and oath-taking, and a priest with assistants and refusal. Whatever this means – a little clerical society offering each member support or a deeper lay piety or both – the correlation is weak elsewhere.

Broadly speaking, one of the most important factors affecting the decision was pressure from the laity. The geography of oath-taking was not random. Instead, a broad belt beginning in Picardy and running through northern Burgundy in the east and the frontier of Maine in the west, and finishing in Berry and Lower Poitou, represented an area of massive oath-taking. So did another belt beginning in the Ain which ran east of the Rhone through the Alps to the Mediterranean. By contrast, a zone beginning in Upper Languedoc and continuing in a northern crescent through the southern Massif Central and ending in the Lyonnais, another in Alsace and still another in the Nord and Pas-de-Calais represented regions of massive refusals. Most impressive of all was the refractory region roughly west of a line drawn through Caen, Le Mans and Poitiers. In very general terms, the map of oath-taking and refusals is also the map of popular attitudes to the Revolution and of left-right voting in the Second and Third Republics.

The revolutionaries at the time explained the popular support for the refractories as the result of their preaching on an ignorant, servile population, and all of the punitive legislation against the refractories down to the deportations of 1792 and 1797 was ultimately directed at controlling a hostile laity. Persecute the priests, so the reasoning went, and the scales would fall from the eyes of the laity. Historians are not so naïve and a great deal of effort has gone into exploring the hypothesis that the map of oath-taking also correlates with the map of literacy, higher circulation of books, better communications and pre-revolutionary dechristianization. While this research continues another explanation is possible.

Let us assume that the revolutionaries were right in asserting that the Civil Constitution of the Clergy altered no fundamental dogma. It certainly did not touch the liturgy which was a more vital element in popular culture than belief, of which most ordinary people were astonishingly ignorant. The constitutional priests were as capable and as qualified to perform the rites of passage and invoke the deity against the evils of a malevolent and capricious spiritual world as the refractories were. This is what most people expected of the clergy and the Revolution did nothing to alter that. In some regions of the country, people allowed them to perform this role; in others, they did not. Whatever else it was, the Civil Constitution of the Clergy was also a kind of plebiscite for and against a Church that was associated with the Revolution, a church, that was expected to proselytize for it and to keep order for it. In other words, to reject the Revolution was to reject the rule of the citizen-lawyers who had come to power in the elections of 1790.

Discontent and the Distribution of Benefits

In some regions then, country people expected more than the Constituent Assembly and its local allies were able to deliver. Villagers contested the settlement on the feudal system from the beginning. The subsistence question remained in abeyance for the moment but ordinary people never accepted the Constituent Assembly's declaration on freedom of the grain trade. The same lack of finality was true of taxes. How this related to the question of popular hostility to the Civil Constitution will be easier to understand once we understand what happened to the great cry of 1789 for tax relief through fiscal equality.

One of the major issues that has to be decided in assessing the impact of the Revolution was whether people paid more. Certainly, people expected relief in 1789. The *cahiers* overwhelmingly complained about the fiscal system and overwhelmingly blamed the miseries of the Third Estate on tax privilege. Complaints about taxes were as common as complaints about the seigneurial regime. Indeed, while everyone at the time was awestruck at the anti-seigneurial risings and the attacks on châteaux, assaults on tax officers and tax collectors were about as frequent.

The Constituent Assembly tried to honour these demands for relief from the very beginning. The deputies decreed the principle of equality of taxation on the Night of 4 August, and established special tax rolls covering the end of the year that made the privileged pay their fair share. But the termination of fiscal privilege did not bring the solace that people expected. In fact, the principle of equality of taxation meant that the formerly un-privileged had to pay more. The reason for this paradox is that the Constituent Assembly considered it a point of honour to pay down the huge national debt it inherited from the Old Regime. And, of course, once the revolutionary wars began, tax relief was out of the question.

The new regime also undertook a major shift in the mix between indirect and direct taxation. Under the revolutionary system, direct taxes, mostly taxes on land, were supposed to represent about 70 per cent of government revenue. The best economic theory of the day dictated that this should be so because 'physiocracy' proclaimed that land was the sole source of value. Moreover, the men of the Constituent believed that the tax system should be transparent and with this danger-ously naïve belief for politicians, they engineered a tax system where the payer was as aware as he could be of how much he was paying. Another generation later, legislators were retreating as fast as they could from a transparent tax regime, the better to disguise the cost of dictatorship. Sometimes these were the same people.

There ought to have been compensation for higher taxes, namely in the abolition of the tithe and in the abolition of feudal dues. Indeed, this is the reason why some historians believe the reforms of 1790–1 actually transferred income to the peasantry. It's just not so. The law of 2 December 1790 explicitly allowed landlords to add the equivalent of the former tithe to the rent beginning with the harvest of 1791. Harsh as this sounds, given the land hunger in late eighteenth-century France, landlords would have done this anyway once the lease came up for renewal. The law was almost superfluous, which probably explains why there was no debate about it. The effect of the law was to advance the date when landlords would have rolled the former tithe into a rent increase. As for the abolition of feudal dues, strictly speaking, many dues would have been added to the rent once the lease fell in, and other dues like mutation fees, would have been added to the selling price of land. Since everybody sold land, the effect among social classes must have been a wash.

As for market taxes, and other fees, consider the experience of the little Norman town of Clères near Rouen. Before 1789, the seigneurs owned the town's market hall, and so imposed the feudal *droit de marché*. This was a fee exacted on every merchant who sold on this market, a device for the seigneur to recoup the costs of providing the hall, and perhaps to allow him to make a modest profit. The Revolution, of course, abolished such fees as feudal, eventually confiscated the hall, and sold it to private bidders. The town then went into eclipse, until, in 1825, a forward looking municipal council decided to purchase the market hall from its private owners. To make the hall viable, the town council imposed fees on any merchant who opened a stall. It turns out that the municipal-ization of the *droit de marché* was progress, but merchants and con-sumers could be forgiven for failing to notice the difference.

The issue then is to decide whether the abolition of feudalism, in the largest sense of the abolition of seigneurial dues and the tithe, compen-sated for the increase in direct taxes. There may well have been places where this happened, but where the subject has been investigated thor-oughly, the answer is that people paid more. And they paid it either in higher taxes or in higher rents. The revolutionaries claimed otherwise and put the net gain of the abolition of fiscal privilege and cheaper forms of collection at about the equivalent of eight days' labour. This was not a lot, in fact, but even so, there was some sleight of hand even in this assertion, since official figures rarely included the additional surtaxes necessary to finance local government, and they assumed that the tithe had been abolished, which was only a half truth. In fact, since the law assigned the defunct tithe to landlords, former seigneurs acquired some compensation for the loss of tax privilege.

On the other hand, the Constituent Assembly reduced indirect taxes substantially or abolished them outright. For many urban consumers, this was a substantial reduction in the cost of living. It thus reduced wine prices, the price of all sorts of goods that were taxed at the octroi gate (a kind of municipal customs) or by abolishing internal customs barriers, increased the circulation of goods, and so on. For country folk, it abolished the hated *gabelle*, or salt tax. This could well have compensated the many country people for the adverse shifts in rents and direct taxes but the evidence here is very slim. The District of Laval in the Mayenne, part of a region where the *gabelle* was most demanding, produced figures showing overall relief, but the officials neglected to distinguish between the market and monopoly prices of salt, so their argument looks promising but only half finished.

Evidence of real hardship, however, certainly exists. It is easy to find examples of farms where taxes doubled and tripled, and in the end, the loss was both the tenant's whose cost of operating land rose and the landlord's because the state had usurped a rent increase that otherwise would have been his. Still, these blinding increases may well be exceptional cases. More systematic enquiries suggest that taxes increased by between 20 and 40 per cent. In a handful of communes in the Hérault, the rise was at the bottom end of this scale – 20 per cent – but this was still a blow. Once the war started, taxes could go even higher. In the Nord, for example, they quickly rose to 50 per cent higher than they had been in the Old Regime. In the canton of St Caradec near Lorient in the Morbihan, the rise in direct taxes ranged between 150 per cent and 200 per cent depending upon the commune. Moreover such sky rocketing taxes could only be achieved by imposing amazing marginal rates. In the nearby commune of Crédin in the District of Josselin, marginal rates averaged 38 per cent. In short, by embracing fiscal equality, the Constituent Assembly took a major step towards fiscal justice, but those who hoped that the suppression of privilege would lighten their burdens must have been disillusioned.

The Contours of Counterrevolution

The counterrevolution that mattered was a mass uprising where all of these factors coalesced: loyalty to the old religious order, grumbling at higher taxes and rents, and other resentments that still had to be defined. This powerful sense of wrong also had to be joined to the cause of a root and branch restoration of the 'Old Regime', however it was defined. At first, there was what Colin Lucas calls an 'anti-revolution', a diffuse series of resentments, discontents, and rumblings that expressed ordinary folks' unhappiness that the promises of the Revolution had been so discouraging. At some point, the anti-revolution in some places became the counterrevolution, but not always. In the West, this transformation occurred early and clearly. In the Midi, the transition was messy, with some places propelled to counterrevolution very early through hatred of Protestants, in other places they stalled at the anti-revolution phase, or better, they focussed on anti-Jacobinism throughout. The adepts of anti-Jacobinism never did embrace the counterrevolutionary programmes. The anti-revolution was not moderate; it could be as murderous as the counterrevolution. Needless to say, the Revolution, and the revolutionaries soon lost all sense of moderation too.

A counterrevolution did exist from the beginning, but it was a minor phenomenon. At first, it was a series of conspiracies rather than a mass uprising. The counterrevolution began with the emigration of the courtiers most compromised in bringing about the dismissal of Necker in July 1789, that is of the comte d'Artois, the Condés, the Polignacs, and so on. By September, Artois had established a committee in Turin whose purpose was to plan 'une contre-révolution'. Other courtiers joined the émigrés after the October Days and groups of officers followed in the aftermath of the many mutinies among the troops in 1790.

At first, there was no plan of organizing the émigrés militarily, at least partly because the Turin committee had no money and the new arrivals, convinced the national delirium would soon pass, brought little with them. In any case, all that apparently had to be done was to rescue Louis XVI and appeal to the foreign powers in the name of monarchial solidarity.

This turned out to be impracticable. The King, true to his policy of not wanting to provoke a civil war, refused to be rescued, and the Queen did not want to be rescued by the émigrés because, in the curious way that she combined spite and political acumen, she disliked Artois and realized that a successful émigré-sponsored counterrevolution would enslave the restored monarchy to the courtiers. Rescue was also dangerous, as the Marquis de Favras, in an apparently lone attempt, possibly encouraged, possibly betrayed by the comte de Provence, found, as he was hanged for trying to kidnap the royal family in February 1790.

The Crown had its own strategy anyway. One element was to buy influence. The most notable catch was the deputy Mirabeau who went on the secret payroll in early 1790 and, among the club leaders in Paris, possibly Danton. The most important element in the Crown's plan was Marie-Antoinette's brothers. But Joseph II, embroiled with a rebellion in the Low Countries and at war with Turkey, and a believer in popular sovereignty outside his own lands, refused any help. When Joseph died in February, Leopold II contented himself with sonorous epistles to the Queen and the émigrés which amounted to nothing. Of the other powers placed to intervene, none was willing to help. George III considered the Revolution a divine visitation on the French for meddling with the American colonies. Of the foreign powers, only Artois's diminutive and bellicose father-in-law, Victor-Amedeus III of Sardinia, was willing to translate his hospitality into active intervention, at the price, of course, of some territory. The probability that all the powers might exact compensation for intervention did not worry the Turin committee overmuch, although it did bother others. Nor were its members anxious that its activities or rescue plans imperilled the royal family. Artois soon veered towards the idea, later developed by the vicious counterrevolutionary spymaster, the comte d'Antraigues, that the monarchy was more important than the king, which in Antraigues's case meant that if Louis XVI had to martyr himself for aristocratic honour and privilege, so be it.

But by itself the counterrevolution of the émigrés could not amount to much. With no money and minimal foreign assistance, its helplessness was only underlined by the Prince de Condé's quixotic plan to invade the country at the head of a column of gentlemen. Domestic support was obviously crucial but it was not obvious where this might come from.

The Constituent Assembly helped along the process of noble alienation by abolishing hereditary nobility and titles on 19 June 1790. This did not bother the deputy Marquis de Ferrières, who considered the essence of nobility to have disappeared already. He was more disgusted that the desultory debate had been preceded by a ludicrous salute to the deputies by people in national costumes representing the 'entire universe' led by the fatuous Prussian baron, Anacharsis Cloots. Ferrières worried that his constituents in Poitou might not take the symbolic destruction so lightly, however, and rightly so, for almost immediately, the baron de Lezardière began to form a 'coalition' that would act as a fifth column in the event of a foreign invasion. No doubt other provincial nobles began to think along the same lines, although similar conspiracies in Normandy and Brittany did not get organized until the next year.

The most promising base of domestic counterrevolution had to come from *roturiers*, however, and the first offer came from a former accountant of the cathedral chapter of Nîmes and of the royal domain, François Froment, whose unemployment and fanatical Catholicism were matched only by his bitter desire to avenge his father's removal as municipal tax assessor for fraud by Protestant textile interests. In January 1790, Froment visited Turin and argued that 'one cannot snuff out a strong passion except by a stronger one . . . that religious zeal alone could stifle the revolutionary delirium'. The plan was to organize a simultaneous insurrection throughout the cities of the Midi; the means, to capture the municipalities and infiltrate the National Guard, or use Catholic companies which had already been organized against 'patriot' authorities or 'Protestant' guards at the right moment. Artois was enchanted, and with the light-hearted promise that the princes could take care of foreign support and procure arms, Froment's agents fanned out to recruit adherents throughout the cities.

The plan of provoking religious strife was enormously successful. Communities that had lived together reasonably well for over a century were suddenly incited to be at each other's throats. Whether it can all be attributed to Froment's conspiracy is unknown, but by the spring there were reactionary companies or volunteer organizations in Toulouse, Uzès, Montauban, Nîmes and other cities. After a barrage of propaganda claiming among other things that Protestants were plotting a massacre of Catholics, the Catholic party swept most of the municipal elections in early 1790 throughout the region. During the spring, handbills circulated in Toulouse, Montauban, Castres, Uzès and Nîmes declared that the decrees of the Assembly had annihilated religion. Soon there were mass protests at the Constituent Assembly's rejection of Dom Gerle's motion proposing Catholicism as the national religion.

But the anti-Protestant crusade once begun could not be easily controlled. At Toulouse on 29 April, there were serious disturbances including gunfire when patriots attacked anti-Protestant petitioners. That had the support of the reactionary National Guard units under the command of comte de Toulouse-Lautrec. At Montauban on 10 May, some four to five thousand women, some of them with pistols stuffed in their belts, prevented the municipal officers from making inventories of the religious houses. While a black man named Balthazar harangued crowds in the Cordelier monastery, the men threatened to burn the houses of leading Protestants. The rioters soon murdered five National Guardsmen and thousands of Protestants fled the city, including the pastor and future member of the Committee of Public Safety, Jeanbon Saint-André.

The National Guard of Bordeaux and Toulouse eventually brought Montauban back to the patriot fold. But events soon led to appalling massacre at Nîmes. On 3 May, some members of Froment's unofficial companies, known variously as 'cébets' (onion eaters) or 'poufs rouges' for their red pompoms, quarrelled with soldiers and a soldier was killed. This only alienated the garrison and encouraged the Protestants, who had been shut out of the municipal elections, to make a strong showing in those of the department. While the electors were gathering on 13 June, a

Protestant National Guardsman arrested one of Froment's followers for creating a disturbance. A crowd gathered to demand his release, the guards panicked and fired into the crowd.

Throughout the night, each side called on its coreligionists from the countryside – much the same had happened earlier at Montauban to no effect – and the next day, rural and urban Protestant guardsmen assailed the Catholics. Once Froment's forces were defeated, an orgy of murder of Catholic monks and laity continued for the next two days. In the end, about two to three hundred were slaughtered. Not surprisingly, Catholic electors fled and the department was in the hands of the Protestants. As vengeance for age-old persecutions and hatreds, the *bagarre de Nîmes* may have given some satisfaction but it also unleashed an ever-widening circle of support for counterrevolution throughout the Midi.

The first response was a gathering of 20,000 Catholic National Guards with crosses sewn into their hats who met at Jalès in the Ardèche in August. Some of them broke off to protest the massacre at Nîmes. This was tame stuff, but later in October someone, perhaps the organizing committee, issued a virulent manifesto accusing the National Assembly of treason against God and the King. They also demanded an end to the oppression of Catholics. With the first *camp de Jalès*, religious sectarianism leapt beyond the town walls to the countryside.

The second *camp de Jalès* – there were five altogether – illustrated once again how broad the anti-Protestant appeal was. This began as a brawl in a bar in Uzès in February 1791 and soon Catholics were ringing church bells to bring in their rural supporters, just as the Protestants had done at Nîmes. No one knew quite what to do next, however, although the support was certainly impressive as 10,000 Catholics awaited orders from a confused leadership. Soon folks drifted home. Thus when troops and patriot National Guards from as far away as Lyon and Marseille converged on the plains of Jalès, they found no army to oppose them. One of the leaders of the Jalès committee, Bastide de Malbosc, was arrested and imprisoned at Pont Saint-Esprit. A few weeks later, his body was found on the banks of the Rhône.

Similarly in the Comtat, a vicious struggle broke out. This was independent papal territory until an assembly at Avignon voted for union with France. Other cities like Carpentras and Cavaillon were violently opposed and soon a bitter civil war broke out. The early culmination of these struggles occurred in October 1791 when the pro-French forces hurled 65 opponents off the awesome towers of the Palais des Papes in Avignon into the latrines below. The pro-French leader was named Pierre Jourdan, nicknamed Coupe-Tête. The nickname speaks volumes. By now the ability of the anti-revolution and the patriots to mobilize very large numbers in support was obvious, as was the totally uninhibited violent response of the patriots. The future was a series of hideous massacres and counter-massacres that would tear the region apart for the next ten years.

Turbulence in the south encouraged plots in other cities. In Lyon, the former *échevin*, Imbert-Colomès, had already had an attempt to form separate National Guard legions foiled by a popular uprising. The new plan was to rely on the troops of the comte de la Chapelle who would seize the city pending the arrival of the king, an army of the princes and a corps of nobles from the Forez and Auvergne. But one of the initiates denounced the plot to the municipality which arrested three of the leading conspirators on 12 December. Imbert-Colomès and his friends fled to the country or abroad.

Meanwhile another conspiracy based in Provence, led by the barrister Pascalis in Aix and the former commander of the National Guard of Marseille, Lieutaud, was preparing to facilitate the invasion of the Prince de Condé. But some members of Pascalis's newly formed club, the Amis du Roi de la Paix et de la Religion, got into a shoot out with some local patriots who were soon joined by a hastily formed expedition of National Guards from Marseille. Pascalis and two others were imprisoned. Then, on 14 December, the guardsmen and their hangers-on broke into the prison, held a mock trial in the courtyard, and hanged the prisoners. The Marseillais marched home with the grisly trophy of Pascalis's head on the end of a pike. It was the first prison massacre of the Revolution. No one was ever prosecuted for this.

The discovery of the Lyon conspiracy, the iynchings at Aix and the King's continuing refusal to be rescued, temporarily destroyed the prospects of the counterrevolution. The princes soon decamped to Coblenz on the Rhine and began to solicit help even more earnestly from the great powers.

The first phase of the counterrevolution was over but its permanent strategy was already in place – a mix of foreign intervention combined with internal conspiracy and insurrection, a strategy that was eventually to work in 1815. It is easy, of course, to mock the émigrés' and the conspirators' conceited assumption that they represented the true France which had temporarily succumbed to the yoke of a self-seeking cabal, a cabal which Antraigues believed was a secret committee of Orleanists controlling the entire network of Jacobin clubs. Such fantasies aside, they were not wrong in believing they had considerable support. From the vicar-general and former procurator of the *parlement* who incited the petition campaign at Toulouse, to the canon-counts of Lyon, to the country squires who organized the *camps de Jalès*, through to disgruntled army officers and rural gentry whose 'coalitions' were already being formed, everyone expected that the counterrevolution would get support from the former privileged orders. The combination of hurt pride, ancient loyalties, fear of disorder, loss of income, and the prospect of unemployment propelled many of these men into careers of conspiracy and exile. More interesting is the problem of *roturier* counterrevolution. One element was the counterrevolutionary bourgeoisie. Many of them clearly had close professional or emotional ties with the institutions of the Old Regime. The Froment clan and the Trinquelaques of Uzès, lawyers, tax assessors and church officials; Imbert-Colomés, one of the richest wholesalers of Lyon, only recently ennobled; Pascalis, a defender of Provencal liberties in 1788 who made a notorious speech defending the *parlements* in September 1790, are all examples. Craftsmen and peasants were clearly drawn into anti-revolutionary politics by religion which split the unanimity of the old Third Estate as clearly as shattered quartz. Whatever conflict the continuing economic slump engendered in the silk weaving towns of the Midi between weavers and spinners on the one side, and Protestant and petty Catholic merchants on the other, was subsumed in confessional strife.

Ancestral memories blended with the active role of the church in daily life. The suppression of the many religious houses and cathedral chapters which offered employment to laymen, from musicians to gardeners, and whose charity was vital in a region where population pressed on resources more than it did elsewhere, raised unprecedented anxieties. It was easy to blame and to fear Protestants whose newly acquired civil rights suddenly gave them the political power and military force to avenge past wrongs, as in the *bagarre de Nîmes*. Popular religiosity and folklore also played a role in mobilizing opposition. Possibly in Languedoc, certainly in Provence, the demonstrative baroque Christianity of the common folk suffered no decline, unlike that of the élite. It was surely no coincidence that the disturbances at Montauban began after a procession marking the first day of Rogations, that Froment worked through the lay penitent funeral confraternities, that the Catholic guardsmen set out for the first *camp de Jalès* just after Assumption, or that the demonstrations at Uzès took the form of the farandole or long snake-like dance through the streets. The old 'society of orders', bonded by religion, no longer by deference, survived.

The social composition of the factions in Montauban shows how a class interpretation of the conflict does not begin to capture the complexities of the struggle. The counterrevolutionary National Guard battalion of Montauban was quite different from the battalions of the patriots. Whereas wholesalers and the liberal professions dominated the patriot officer corps, retired army officers dominated the anti-patriot battalions. As for the rank and file, artisans, of which there were only twelve masters, outnumbered all the other groups combined in the counter-revolutionary battalion. Textile artisans alone made up nearly half the artisan contingent. Religious conflicts clearly overlay trade disputes between 'patriot' merchants and 'counterrevolutionary' wage-earners, but not entirely since artisans and the liberal professions were represented on both sides while petty merchants and retailers opted for the patriots on the whole.

In the Avignon massacre, most of the victims were artisans but the bulk of the pro-French followers were artisans too, although the leadership positions in the pro-French faction came from the liberal professions. Pierre Jourdan alias Coupe-Tête, their leader, had a chequered background as a wine merchant, and it was said he was a smuggler. Many of his followers were silk workers, and many of them were young and fairly new to the city.

The broad point is that anyone looking for the Parisian pattern of radicalism of the humble working poor against the bourgeoisie, which is so often assumed to represent the nation as a whole will be disappointed. In Montauban, Avignon and for certain elsewhere, the patterns require a much more subtle analysis that would take in age, migration, marriage patterns and even ancestry. A unified movement of worthy artisans struggling against bourgeois dominance, the Parisian paradigm – such an interpretation cannot be imposed upon the Midi.

Looking at the Midi as a whole, it is evident that neither the Revolution nor the anti-revolution had a natural constituency among ordinary people. Depending upon the city, the silk- or textile-workers or artisans in general can be found on either side of the political divide, and as later experience would show more clearly, so could peasants. Much depended upon the political loyalties of the various urban élites and the kinds of conflicts within trades. This is another way of saying that ordinary people could not be manipulated at will by anyone. Thus, the guardsmen on the way to the second *camp de Jalès* took the opportunity to rough up the patriots of the small towns and wreck their houses. These victims were evidently the men who had combined seigneurial judgeships, crooked legal practice and usury in the Old Regime. Sectarian differences were not the issue in these assaults. Peasant delegates in the primary assemblies in 1790 had spoken against these men when they argued against the introduction of cantons because 'they are persuaded that they are to be given three or four judges and many procurators and since they have been vexed enough, they don't want them any more'. The participants in the anti-seigneurial risings in Upper Brittany, the Limousin and Quercy-Périgord had not wanted them either. So, in a curious way, both anti-seigneurial and pro-Catholic peasants shared similar aims. The lesson for historians is to be cautious in transposing political labels which had some validity in the towns to the countryside where they could take on different meanings.

Religious Dissidence

By the turn of the year, large areas of the country had already shown their dissatisfaction with the political, fiscal and land settlement the Constituent Assembly had designed. Apart from the regions of sectarian conflict where the configuration of conflict was different, many people had gained little or nothing from the new arrangements. While their loyalties were clearly fluid at such an early date, more self-interested groups were in a position to bid for their allegiance with some hope of success. It was in this shifting situation that the parish clergy began to take the oath to the Civil Constitution of the Clergy. It was not that there was a direct relationship between the oath and earlier troubles. There appears to be no correlation either in Upper Brittany or in Quercy between oath-taking and subsequent religious troubles on the one side, and anti-seigneurial demonstrations on the other. Undoubtedly, religious questions realigned local politics in these regions in ways that are still poorly understood. But both in the Nord and parts of the west, there does appear to be a relationship between religious troubles and regions where tenants who had gained little and where they were numerous enough or powerful enough to carry their neighbours. Certainly, people tried to influence the *curé's* decision. Thus a *curé* in the Calvados claimed, 'I would have taken the oath if there had not been obstacles from my parishioners which a false zeal misleads or rather who let themselves be persuaded by the seditious speeches of some self-interested fanatics'. The municipal officers of Thieix in the Morbihan wrote, 'We consider... priests who are cowardly enough to take the oath as unworthy of our confidence'.

In these regions where the refractory had considerable support, particularly in the west and the north, the country people went to extraordinary lengths to make the life of the constitutionals miserable. People boycotted services and sacraments, chants outside the churches drowned out masses, unknown people fired shots outside the presbyteries in the middle of the night, anonymous enemies hung dead animals on the doors of their homes, there were threats to bury them alive, children hooted at them as they passed by, and so on. In many places, municipal officers resigned rather than have anything to do with them, and electors absented themselves from the primary assemblies called to choose them. Often the only people present at the installation ceremony were a handful of officials from the district, perhaps a few members of nearby Jacobin society and a corps of urban National Guards in their resplendent blue uniforms. Ceremonies like this in which the village was so scarcely represented could only dramatize the base that supported the constitutional *curé*. His supporters were outsiders and the entire community called them 'étrangers'. If the new *curé* tried to withstand the constant harassment, the National Guards could always march in to deal with troublemakers. But this only dramatized, yet again, the alien origins of the Constitutional Church. To oppose the constitutional *curé* was also to oppose the local bourgeoisie of the urban administrations, the clubs and the National Guards, men who supported a land settlement that offered little or nothing to many country people. Loyalty to the refractories was a way of demonstrating hostility to the Revolution as well.

The refractories' presence rendered the ecclesiastical settlement unworkable. The refractories had rights of access to their old churches and there were unedifying struggles over keys, ornaments, parish registers, hours of rival masses, and so on. Often refractories retired to outlying chapels where they baptized, confirmed and married parishioners loyal to them. Many of them did no more than this, but there were others who denounced the constitutional bishops and clergy, and even lay officials as heretics and schismatics. As if this was not bad enough, some claimed that the National Assembly would soon impose Protestantism. A few came close to preaching civil war.

Yet the refractories reflected opinion as much as they instigated it, for resistance to the Civil Constitution soon took on the characteristics of a mass movement. In Strasbourg, women rioted in January 1791 when a rumour got round that authorities were going to suppress parishes and close down the cathedral chapter. A few weeks later, German-speaking Catholics led by a few lawyers and small merchants organized a society based on the lay confraternities to defend religion and prevent Lutherans from taking over their churches. When adherents tried to involve the garrison, the municipality closed the society down. A month later, there was a riot in Colmar in which people shouted, 'Vive le Roi! Vive le Comte d'Artois!'

But the most dramatic examples of mass resistance took place in the west. In the summer and autumn of 1791 in the Côtes-du-Nord, Loire-Inférieure and Maine-et-Loire, there was a series of eerie torchlight processions of entire villages, with everyone barefoot, winding their way to local shrines. At the same time in the Maine-et-Loire, there were stories of the Virgin and Child appearing to the faithful in venerated oak trees at night, and of formerly simpleminded children who no longer needed food, prophesying the future of the Church. Much of this was simply an old tradition in Anjou, but authorities understood that in the changed political context it was intolerable. In what must have been the first act of revolutionary dechristianization, the deputy La Revellière-Lépeaux, on a mission to enquire into local religious troubles, had a statue of the Virgin and her chapel destroyed. But soon there were stories that She had reappeared.

On occasion, there could be far more serious violence. In January 1791 hundreds of country people around Vannes in the Morbihan became convinced that their refractory bishop was being held prisoner so they invaded the town. Troops and National Guards from Lorient soon brought the situation under control. In February, three or four hundred people tried to invade Maulevrier in the Maine-et-Loire in order to defend 'religion' and, as they said, 'destroy the district', an interesting indication of whom they blamed for their troubles. In early May at Saint-Christophe-du-Ligneron in the Vendée, a handful of sharecroppers destroyed the pews of the 'bourgeois', barricaded themselves in the church and withstood a siege by the local Jacobins and National Guard for a few days. But violence was not all on one side. In June, the women of a local patriotic society approached the prioress of the Carmelite convent just outside Nantes and demanded the nuns take the civic oath because the women knew that 'there were secret meetings at the convent which tended nothing less than to plan the slaughter of their husbands' in the National Guard. Their men, armed with sabres and pistols, arrived later and when the prioress continued to refuse, the crowd broke into the convent, destroyed some furniture and punched a few nuns.

Women were almost always prominent in demonstrations against the oath. At Aubenas in the Ardèche, for example, a general assembly of the women decided to prevent the priests from taking the oath 'to throw stones at those who replace them and then require the receiver of the district to pay the refractories'. At Vendes, in Normandy, women prevented the *curé* and the *vicaire* from taking the oath and ushered them out of the church. At Lunel, in Languedoc, a crowd of women surrounded the public crier, searched his clothes for the decree on the oath, and when they found it, tore it in pieces, burned it 'while making several demonstrations of joy and crying subversive slogans'. Many women had a particularly emotional relation to the Church. At Sommières in the Gard, for instance, the women who attempted to prevent their clerics from taking the oath were from the more economically fragile occupations, were universally illiterate, and many of them were widows or spinsters. Their attachment to the local clergy and to the parish church itself was emotional and personal. Removing these supports to their lives was a horrifying threat. For the men, religion was a pretext to carry on battles with rival groups that had begun years before. Still, both women and men had to have a refractory, not a cleric pliant to patriot authority.

Jacobins and Democrats

By mid-1791, whether it was in the form of the violent outbursts and demonstrations of the Midi, the hundreds of smaller incidents of the west, Flanders and Alsace, or the anti-seigneurial risings of the centre, opposition to the revolutionary settlement had reached extensive proportions. Yet it should not be exaggerated. In many areas of the country, where the clergy took the oath, life carried on much as before, even where, as in the Corrèze, many of them refused, there were but few incidents. This early, the situation was fluid, and whether the anti-revolution would tip into the counterrevolution was still open.

At the same time, the patriots had built up a series of organizations and acquired a consciousness that would stand them in good stead in the trying times to come. One of these organizations was the National Guard. Unlike the Jacobin clubs, these are not well known, but in the disturbances of 1790 and beyond, they were a vital arm of repression. Between 1790 and 1793, they were very successful in keeping the enemies of the Revolution off balance. In the Midi, the combined expeditions of the Guards, usually under the leadership of the Guard of Marseilles ranged far and wide to stamp out anti-revolutionaries at Arles, Avignon, and elsewhere. In a sense the march of the Marseillais against Paris in August 1792 to overthrow the monarchy was simply the most long range of the many expeditions. In the west, the Guards' activities were not as spectacular or as co-ordinated, but they took an aggressive chase after refractory priests and their supporters. After 1792, they could no longer police their localities because so many of the guardsmen volunteered for service on the frontiers or they were conscripted into the army. After, the Terror, therefore, there was almost no one available to contain the anti-terrorists, with lethal consequences for the local Jacobins.

An examination of their social origins illustrates who was willing to make these sacrifices. At Montauban, despite the formal restriction of service to active citizens, nearly three quarters of the guardsmen were petty merchants and artisans but almost all the officers who, by law, were elected, were bourgeois. The same deference in elections to the officer corps was shown at Rennes but, interestingly enough, almost all groups, except merchants and wholesalers, were underrepresented in relation to the population as a whole. This was particularly true of artisans, labourers and the former privileged orders. In a city where the *parlement*, estates and charitable institutions had contributed so much to the local economy, revolutionary militants were bound to be in a more or less isolated minority. Consequently, almost the entire Jacobin club were also members of the Guard. At the little town of Aubagne near Marseille, we know who was on the Guard because during an expedition to Arles, some of them took time out to sack a local château and so they were arrested. They consisted of the usual mix of artisans with a tilt towards the clothing trades, and a high number of peasants, and agricultural workers who had responded to the town's vigorous Jacobin club's recruitment.

At this stage, the Jacobins were spectators of local and national events but, unlike the National Guards, they had a national network of affiliated clubs which were frequently in contact with each other. The system had begun as a café society of the radical Breton deputies in 1789 and, with other like-minded deputies, had been instrumental in preparing the Night of 4 August. After the *journées* of October, it installed itself in the former Jacobin convent in Paris. Although everyone could belong if they were good patriots and could afford the stiff entrance fee, the Paris club functioned as a caucus of radical deputies under the aegis of Barnave, Duport, the Lameth brothers, and, to a lesser extent, Robespierre and Pétion.

The provincial societies had a different role. The early ones evolved out of masonic lodges or reading societies, or were founded in direct imitation of the Paris club which offered them affiliate status. Members came together to discuss events of the day. From the start, they developed an extensive correspondence network among themselves. They exchanged information, welcomed adherents and addressed the 'mother society' and the National Assembly. Since their membership fees were generally much lower than the Paris club, the potential existed for a more popular recruitment but, on the whole, their members represented the élite of local society, or at least part of that élite. Many future deputies honed their political and oratorical skills in the frequent local meetings.

Yet the influence of the clubs should not be exaggerated. Impressive as the network was, even at a very early stage, it was not a 'machine' or a prefiguration of the totalitarian parties of the future, as twentieth-century historians like Cochin and François Furet claimed. No one club, not even the Paris club, had that sort of authority over other clubs. In fact, the Paris club did not dominate the provincial societies. All the clubs were independent and the affiliations and correspondence were directed more often to other provincial clubs rather than to Paris. Their influence was not in their numbers. Their importance was that many local elected figures from municipal councillors to administrators of the district also belonged to the local club. For apprehensive outsiders, it was difficult to see a line between club activity and the implementation of policy and this is what made them sinister. Their numbers grew throughout the early stages of the Revolution, from 300 at the end of 1790, while a year later, there were 1250 of them. There were heavy concentrations in the Paris region and in the always politically passionate south-east. There were some youth branches and there were dozens of female affiliates who had the traditional role of doing good works as well as the thoroughly novel attempt to persuade their rural sisters to disown the refractory clergy.

Curiously, the greatest electoral successes of the clubs may have come in regions where electors were so alienated by the Civil Constitution of the Clergy that they refused to vote. Although it cannot be entirely attributed to local Jacobins, the most radical departments were often those where rural hostility was greatest. There was always a substantial element of artisans and tradesmen in the Jacobin clubs, in part at least because some clubs only required active citizen status, if that, to become a member.

In some of the larger cities, however, there were popular societies that emerged in response to aristocratic propaganda and the early agitation over the Civil Constitution of the Clergy. Their minimal entrance requirements attracted a great popular following. In Lyon, for example, from September 1790 onwards, there were clubs in each of the 32 sections which sent delegates to a 'central club', whose purpose was to agitate against the presence of nearby troops and to oppose counterrevolutionary propaganda, including Froment's writings. The popular societies soon boasted of a membership of three thousand, as opposed to the forty-odd in the atrophied Jacobin club. They soon attracted the notice of ambitious local politicians like the Rolands. In Bordeaux, there was a much smaller 'Patriotic Society', distinct from the Jacobins, composed almost entirely of artisans and petty merchants, almost all of them active citizens, whose purpose was to enlighten its members, and defend citizens against arbitrary acts of authority.

Although there were popular societies in other cities as well, Paris had the most flourishing movement. Sometimes neighbourhood clubs were based on the 48 section assemblies into which the city had been divided in July 1790, sometimes on the handful of fraternal societies based on sections or trades. Some affiliated themselves with the famous Cordeliers club. From its founding in April 1790, the Cordeliers and the fraternal societies, along with radical journalists like Marat and Fréron took the lead in criticizing the great and the powerful. They complained about Bailly's conduct as mayor, the accumulation of power in Lafayette's hands and the distinction between active and passive citizens. Since the institutions governing the capital were so new, conflicts of jurisdiction quickly broke out between the commune and the sections and between Lafayette's National Guard headquarters and its paid companies and the volunteer battalions in the sections over where the ultimate locus of authority lay. In terms of principle, the conflict was one between representative theories of government and doctrines of direct democracy. The Cordeliers's leaders invented, articulated and developed democratic theories which soon spread to the fraternal societies, and later to the sectional movement as a whole. The sovereignty of the section, the recall of deputies, the sections' mutual support, the right of insurrection, the right of referendum, the responsibility to prevent deputies and municipal officers from usurping popular sovereignty, and even some of the symbolism like the eye of surveillance enclosed in the masonic triangle – all the important doctrines associated with the *sans-culottisme* of the Year II – can be found in the writings and speeches of the Cordeliers' leaders and radical journalists of 1790–1.

No doubt these ideas found a ready audience among artisans and working people in the city because they articulated many aspects of their aspirations and daily experience, but men of the popular classes did not develop these ideas. Unlike the faubourg Saint-Antoine, with its heavy concentration of construction, building and furniture trades, the Théatre-Français section on the left bank where the Cordeliers was located, was home to an inordinate number of journalists, printers and book dealers. The leaders, who caucused regularly at the café Procops, were hardly ordinary working men either. Danton and Desmoulins were lawyers who had been rather indifferent to their practices in the Old Regime. Some, like the coarse Hébert, or Fréron, had been scribblers forced by printing and censorship regulations to combine semi-serious writings with pornography. For them freedom of the press created a new journalistic career although they could not abandon scurrilous journalism that quickly. There were stories that the journalist Brissot had been in the same predicament of being forced to write profitable drivel in the Old Regime, but these are almost certainly false – before the Revolution he hobnobbed with the best and the brightest, and travelled to England and America. Marat, on the other hand, was a lonely, tortured soul. He was also a failed doctor and a bankrupt. In his own mind, he was an unappreciated genius, a persecuted medical Newton, for his expertise in 'mesmerism', a doctrine about the science of manipulating invisible and undetectable fluids. Men of this sort had retained their idealism but their sufferings had envenomed their hatred of power and privilege and made them quick to denounce, in the most violent and personal terms, those in authority whose celebrity and wealth had apparently come so easily.

Few societies could boast as many creative and energetic talents as the Cordeliers but both the members of the smaller clubs and the section militants were no more plebeian in origin. The rare membership lists indicate that the genuinely committed were a mix of those in the liberal professions and officials along with a respectable proportion of more or less skilled artisans and shopkeepers. Despite the societies' democratic basis, labourers and the very poor were very rarely members, undoubtedly because few had spare time for politics. In any case, the radicals distrusted them. The destitute, the transients, the vagabonds, and so on, while deserving of the greatest sympathy, were all too easily corrupted by the rich and the aristocrats. The ideal citizen was an independent, settled, working man with a family. Thus while it is possible to find some daring schemes for a progressive income tax or price controls or general denunciations of the rich as sources of corruption or of low pay in the radical literature of 1790, the amount of space devoted to social questions in the radical press was minimal. A hatred of oppression in all its forms, however, would soon take the Cordeliers further.

By the late spring of 1791, opposition to the solutions of the Constituent Assembly had begun to develop on a wide front. The continued difficulties in collecting taxes, the refusal to pay the still legal seigneurial dues let alone the rarity of redemptions, the sectarian violence in the Midi linked to the gradual appearance of counterrevolution, the mobilization of the country people of the west against the Civil Constitution of the Clergy, the slow rise in the cost of living brought on by the still gentle inflation of the *assignat*, and the development of the club movement and the popular societies, were all serious indicators of opposition to the bourgeois liquidation of the Old Regime.

Yet, although it could not have been apparent to them, the deputies and their supporters in the provinces could be forgiven a certain complacency. The opposition was hardly unified, organizationally or ideologically, indeed much of this opposition was working at cross-purposes. The Flight to Varennes would be a further step in defining issues and into propelling the anti-revolution into the counterrevolution.

4

The Perjured King and War

Louis XVI and his family fled the Tuileries in the dead of night on 21 June 1791; he returned under escort, on the evening of the 25th, a prisoner, the fate of the dynasty in the hands of men unknown two years before. Against all odds, the adventure had nearly succeeded thanks to the brilliant planning of the Queen's friend and reputed lover, the Swedish count, Axel de Fersen. The family had made its way through secret passages in the Tuileries, leaving mounds of pillows in the beds behind, and urging the children to hush; at one point, as she was furtively crossing a courtyard to a secret carriage, Marie-Antoinette thought a torch had lit up her face to Lafayette but the general did not recognize her; there were any number of mishaps about getting out of Paris in one coach and then transferring the royal party to a secretly constructed berlin or carriage, but at last as the sun rose on an unseasonably hot day, the royal family was on its way across the flat wheat fields east of the capital. The King had always believed that the true France, the France outside Paris, loved him, so he carelessly descended from the berlin to chat with his subjects during rest stops. Some of them recognized him but none of them knew what to do. Eventually, one of them, the postmaster at Ste Menehould, did, however, and he rode on ahead where the municipality and National Guard of Varennes, in effect, took the royal family prisoner. The King could have saved himself by appealing to troops waiting nearby but, abhorring bloodshed and fearing for his family, he surrendered. As he was escorted back to Paris by special commissioners of the Constituent Assembly, he was heard to mutter, 'There is no longer a king in France'. By contrast, there was a new irritation. With none of his brother's scruples for his family and position, the comte de Provence sped to Brussels, where he added another voice, and hardly a moderate voice, to the councils of the emigration.

Perhaps Louis XVI did not even know himself what he hoped to achieve by the Flight to Varennes. Part of the plan was certainly to flee to the frontier town of Montmédy in Lorraine and put himself under the protection of the troops of the Marquis de Bouillé, the military commander of the region. There, backed by some threatening troop movements promised by the Emperor of Austria, he might be able to renegotiate the parts of the constitution he found objectionable with the National Assembly from a position of strength.

These objections to the work of the Constituent Assembly had been long-standing. As early as 15 July 1789 he drafted a letter to Charles IV of Spain (finally sent after the October Days) disclaiming everything he might be forced to do. He left behind at the Tuileries a long memorandum that mixed peevish complaints about the state of the palace on the royal family's arrival with thoughtful criticisms of the new constitution. A comparison of the memorandum with his speech at the *séance royale* is an interesting exercise since it shows the evolution of Louis's thinking over the two years of revolution. There was no longer any question of defending the prerogatives of the privileged orders. Instead, he specifically endorsed promotion by merit in the army. But he was quite consistent in his insistence on the necessity of a strong executive. He complained of the limitations of his power of appointment, dismissed the suspensive veto as practically meaningless and deplored the restrictions of his power to conduct diplomacy and war. He pointed out that the Constituent had done little to solve the financial problem and above all lamented the extreme decentralization and confusion of power at the local level, as well as the growing influence and pretensions of the Jacobin clubs. Contemporaries might have labelled the assumptions behind the memorandum 'ministerial despotism'; Bonaparte might have had a clearer idea of what the King was groping for.

The Flight to Varennes should have been a much more serious event in the Revolution than it turned out to be. In the end the politicians who dominated the Constituent Assembly were able to impose their will and not only retain the monarchy – its abolition at this point was simply too far from almost anyone's mind – but Louis XVI as monarch. Moreover, they were able to bring along the Paris Jacobin club and most of the provincial societies, and they were able to exploit the deference the vast majority of the citizen administrators in the provinces had for them. Only the Cordeliers Club and its followers in Paris thought that the punishment for the King's betrayal required a change of regime. But the Assembly mastered this challenge too in the bloody Champ de Mars Affair, and so the radical movement which had annoyed Lafayette and Bailly for over a year was effectively neutered.

But it was a fragile victory because it was so unstable. Because Louis XVI continued to play a double game, the arrangement was bound to collapse.

And it collapsed in the most spectacular fashion with Jacobin politicians edging the country to a disastrous war. In turn, this so polarized the country at home through the persecution of émigrés and refractory priests that the foreign war would have to be fought simultaneously with a civil war. The collapse of the post-Varennnes settlement nudged the anti-revolution into the counterrevolution and led to the overthrow of the monarchy itself. It might have been better to have allowed Louis and his family to escape. The most immediate consequence was abrupt decline in the popularity of the King. This had always been dependent on the general perception that Louis supported the Revolution. When the English traveller, Dr Rigby, watched the King pass from his vantage point on a balcony overlooking the rue Saint-Honoré on 17 July 1789, he was surprised at the silence of the crowd, undoubtedly suspicious of the monarch's role in the military build up of previous weeks. It was only when Louis donned the tricolour cockade on the steps of the Hôtel de Ville that the crowds erupted in joy. The October Days too, of course, were an example of the extent to which the ancient notion of the king misled by his advisors persisted in the minds of ordinary people. The King was also popular among provincials. At the federation of 1790 in Paris to celebrate the anniversary of the fall of the Bastille which was attended by thousands of provincial National Guard units, he was cheered hoarsely and, during an illness in the spring of 1791, dozens and dozens of clubs wished him well. But a great deal of that popularity and affection for his person was dependent upon the King's oath to maintain the Constitution that he swore in public before the National Guards of the nation on 14 July 1790. The flight and the fatal memorandum showed that he could no longer be trusted. As he returned to Paris through the Champs-Elyées, he was met with icy silence.

Still others blamed the Queen. In a theme that would be a major piece in the accusation against her in her trial two years later, Fréron's *Orateur du Peuple*, denounced, 'this imbecile king, this perjuring king, this wicked queen.... Execrable woman, fury of France, it's you who are the soul of this plot.'

Despite the anger in Paris, the episode did not convert the country to republicanism overnight. Only five Jacobin clubs, including Montpellier and Strasbourg and three other obscure ones, specifically demanded a republic and less than one fifth of the affiliated clubs petitioned that the King be put on trial. The overwhelming mood of the clubs and local administrations was betrayal. The King's personal popularity, always high since his coronation, never recovered, at least among patriots. With more leadership, more clubs might have swung to republicanism, but they followed the lead of the National Assembly instead.

During the immediate crisis, however, the National Assembly acted decisively, in part because many nobles and clerics, disgusted at the turn of events, had long since ceased to attend, and in part because the crisis forced the remaining factions to act together. The Lafayette-Barnave-Lameth-Duport factions put out the story that the King, the victim of evil councillors, had been kidnaped – a fiction they maintained even after the discovery of the memorandum. The Assembly suspended the King and it assumed complete legislative and executive sovereignty, forming joint committees with the ministries, ordering suspicious movements within the kingdom to be watched, sending special commissioners to the provinces, suspending the elections to the new Legislative Assembly and forbidding the export of arms and money. Although more severe proposals, such as arming the people, mobilizing the National Guard or suspending suspect officers from the army, were defeated, the Constituent's actions prefigured those of the Convention – and, for the same reason. As in any national emergency, the politicians resorted to exceptional measures.

Yet neither the capital nor the provinces waited on the Assembly for direction. In Paris, people tore down tavern signs that recalled the monarchy, pulled down a statue of Louis XVI on the Place de Grève in front of the Hôtel de Ville, forced a merchant on the rue Saint-Honoré to smash a plaster bust of the King and blacked out the words on another tavern sign, 'The Crowned Bull' on the rue de Laharpe in the Latin Quarter. Someone stuck up a poster near the Tuileries promising a reward for the return of the 'Gros Cochin [the Fatted Pig]'. A speaker at the Palais-Royal said the King ought to be brought back, exposed to public ridicule for three days, and then be escorted to the frontier and given 'a kick in the ass'. That would have been the best solution of all, as it turned out.

But there was a frightening element to the public mood as well. There were rumours of an army of aristocrats and refractory priests gathering north of the city, of sewers being mined with bombs, and of prison plots, the latest version of the fear of brigands of 1789. Citizens spontaneously closed the city gates and some small arms depots were pillaged.

In the provinces, already distressed over the activities of refractory priests and, as always, edgy over the state of the harvest, reactions were more vigorous still. Throughout the north-east, there was a panic centred on Varennes itself, as people feared an attack from Bouillé's army or an actual Austrian invasion. Almost everywhere, local authorities formed 'permanent committees' merging the administrative and military hierarchies. The Department of the Nord helped put the fortresses on the frontier in a state of readiness. Around Strasbourg, the army and National Guard secured the bridges over the Rhine. Near the frontiers, there were reports of imminent or actual invasion. Along the Pyrenees it was the Spanish; in the Nord the émigré armies dressed in black priests' costumes and wearing death's-head helmets.

Repression against the refractory priests was immediate. In Lyon, the authorities closed twenty-five churches used by the refractories; their counterparts in the Nord ordered the closure of all refractory churches in the entire department. In the Ariège, a handful of refractories was arrested trying to leave the country. In Picardy and the Lyonnais, there was a wave of château burning and some aristocrats were killed. The most famous was the murder near Sainte-Menehould of the comte de Dampierre, known as a harsh seigneur and feared as a counterrevolutionary. Almost simultaneously a very similar incident took place on the outskirts of Lyon, when the visit of some rural National Guards at the château of Guillen du Montet, who brought his habits of the captain of a slaving ship to the administration of his estates, degenerated into a siege. When shooting broke out, the seigneur fired back with bullets and a bizarre assortment of African weaponry. He finally surrendered but was stabbed and beaten to death, his body dismembered. Throughout the Maine and Lower Normandy, rural national guards searched châteaux for arms, here and there the former seigneur's pew was burned before the parish church, and on occasion, crowds of 'good citizens' sacked the château and burned old papers. In one colourful incident in the western Mayenne, the young male and female farmhands invaded the château of Cuillé, took mirrors and chandeliers, drank as much wine and cider as they could and bedecked themselves with flowers and orange tree branches.

The majority of the Assembly balked at the idea of remaking a constitution into which they had poured so much emotional energy in the previous two years. They were also convinced that republics were only suitable for small states and that a monarchy was a better defence of property and order than a republic. After all, classical precedents indicated republics could degenerate into democracies.

But these considerations required an accommodation with the King. So Barnave began a secret correspondence with Marie-Antoinette to try to reach an understanding. Publicly, the Assembly revealed its intentions by only suspending the King on 25 June, and on 15–16 July made Bouillé, who had conveniently emigrated, the scapegoat for the whole Varennes affair.

The radical movement in Paris was much more articulate and better organized than it had been in 1789, thanks to the Cordeliers and to a far lesser extent, the Jacobins. They reacted hotly to the Assembly's decision to ignore the demands that the King be dethroned or put on trial. In the Jacobins, Robespierre claimed the National Assembly had ceased to represent the people. On 22 June, the Cordeliers claimed the National Assembly had returned the French to slavery when it decreed the monarchy would be hereditary. They also declared monarchy was incompatible with liberty, that the flight itself was a *de facto* abdication and France was effectively a republic. The solution was moderate enough: ask the primary assemblies that at the very moment were choosing deputies for the new assembly to pronounce. Outside the club, opinions were more forceful. Danton claimed to a crowd in the Tuileries gardens that their leaders were traitors. Along with the fraternal societies, they began an agitation demanding the trial of the King and a referendum. But the Jacobins and the most prominent Cordeliers leaders like Danton and Desmoulins wilted once they realized the majority of the Assembly intended to re-integrate Louis into the Constitution.

Even so, the decision to make Bouillé the scapegoat was too much for many of the Cordeliers. They hastily organized series of petitions that were supposed to signed on the *autel de la patrie* on the Champ de Mars, the military parade ground and site of the anniversary celebrations of 14 July 1789. Besides calling Louis a perjurer and a traitor, one of the petitions argued that he had formally abdicated. Another demanded 'the organization of a new executive power'.

For their part, the authorities intended to have done with the incessant agitation. But their determination went back further than the Flight to Varennes. Since the radical clubs intended to use the on-going elections to the new legislative assembly to push the constitution in a more democratic direction, the Constituent restricted the right of petition. A movement across a wide variety of trades for higher wages received a sympathetic hearing in the Cordeliers press so the Assembly passed the Le Chapelier law outlawing workers' 'coalitions' on 14 June. There were also mass demonstrations against the closure of public works projects. Thus, although the petitions at the Champ de Mars were strictly political, the context in which they were signed indicated that the change to the 'new executive power' might have social consequences.

The stakes then were very high. If the agitation in Paris proved impossible to repress, there was a risk it would spread to the provinces which up to this point had been willing to defer to the Assembly, despite their anger. The most appalling incident at the Champ de Mars had nothing to do with the subsequent declaration of martial law. This involved the crowd lynching two unfortunates who had snuck under the dais to gape at the women's legs – they had brought along carpenters' tools to get a prime view. One of them could hardly escape since he had a wooden leg. So they were strung up. It shows how suspicious the crowd was, as usual.

Ideal as this pretext would have been, authority found a minor, unrelated incident in which someone had thrown stones at a National Guard patrol. Some of the crowds at the Champ de Mars were prepared to react to any circumstance since some were armed, and there had been talk among hotheads of bringing sand and pebbles to use against cavalry horses and knives to cut the harnesses. The repression, however, degenerated into a riot by the National Guard. Neither Lafayette nor Bailly deployed the red flag signifying the declaration of martial law, nor did they summon the crowd to disperse. Instead, someone in the crowd fired a shot, the National Guard panicked, let loose a fusillade and charged the petitioners. As many as fifty may have been killed; the number of wounded is unknown.

The Assembly immediately announced that it had saved society from anarchy and arrested a few foreigners to demonstrate the nefarious origins of the democrats. More to the point, at least 200 people were arrested, there were domiciliary visits at the homes and workshops of the radical leaders; other leaders like Desmoulins and Fréron disappeared; the presses of Marat's *Ami du Peuple* were confiscated and his publisher Mlle Colombe was imprisoned; Marat himself went underground; Danton fled to England; and the Cordeliers was closed until 7 August. Authorities also profited from the occasion to suppress a few royalist newspapers as well.

From the Constituent Assembly's point of view, the Champ de Mars affair stabilized the Constitution. For Parisian radicals it totally blackened Lafayette's already shaky reputation. Furthermore, the fact that the Cordeliers could get 6000 signatures for a change in the executive shows that many Parisians had been weaned from their ancestral loyalty to the monarchy. Also, there were many women making their way across the dais when the National Guard stopped the petition. Women did sign the petition in great numbers and no one among the Cordeliers leadership was bothered by this. The war changed this promising experimentation and the *sans-culotte* movement of 1793–4 became viscerally hostile to womens' issues, probably because so many women also supported refractory priests. Finally, after the Champ de Mars affair it was no longer necessary to get the crowd agitated via subsistence issues. George Rudé tried to make bread prices the motor of every Parisian *journée* throughout the Revolution. After 1791, this argument becomes much less persuasive.

The crisis did split the Jacobin club. Barnave and his friends, appalled at the flirtation with republicanism, split off to form a new club, the Feuillants, taking over half the Jacobins with them. Pétion and Robespierre, both radical deputies, campaigned successfully against the schism and eventually most of the provincial clubs that had gone with the Feuillants drifted back into the fold. A lot of this can be attributed to Robespierre's personal prestige over the network. From very early on in 1789, observers had marked him out as a man of complete honesty. People who later broke with him entirely, like Madame Roland and

Desmoulins, praised him for his probity and his truthfulness. People who saw him disagreed about how he looked. His friends spoke of his strong build and strong bearing. Others spoke of his nervousness, or of his physical ticks. Nonetheless, the political capital he had amassed from the earliest days kept the Jacobin network together.

This loss was less significant to the Feuillants than their failure to appease the King. The best they could do was restore the king's prerogative of mercy but otherwise the Assembly balked at conceding more. This hardly met the basic objections of Louis's memorandum for a stronger executive. Marie-Antoinette considered the Feuillants her dupes and, to Barnave's dismay, refused even the charade of public displays of support for the Revolution at theatre performances. Once again, the deputies showed that, however much they distrusted democracy and popular radicalism, they distrusted the King more.

Undermining the Constitution

The Feuillants thus failed in their natural constituency and they simply ebbed away. The struggles in the new Legislative Assembly were much sharper and more lethal than they had been in the Constituent Assembly. The Legislative held its first session on 1 October. All of the deputies were new because the Constituent had excluded its members from standing for election on a motion by Robespierre on 16 May. In origins, the new deputies ought to have been fairly conservative because in theory they had to meet the strict electoral qualifications. The most significant change in comparison to the Constituent Assembly was the dramatic decline in formerly privileged members, from over half in the Constituent to a little over 10 per cent in the Legislative. Over three-quarters of the new deputies had an apprenticeship at the local level as magistrates or as department or district administrators of all sorts. Many of them had dealt with the manifestations of counterrevolution in the Midi the year before, or with the continuing frustration of applying the Civil Constitution of the Clergy almost everywhere. These concerns overwhelmed a natural caution. A majority wanted to show their independence by refusing to join either Jacobin or Feuillant clubs, each of whom had close to the same number of deputies. But the King's actions drew them into increasingly radical positions.

If the deputies' opinions are hard to categorize, those of the public are even more so. Less than one quarter of the active citizens actually voted, substantially less that those who participated in the elections to the Estates-General and somewhat fewer than in the local elections of 1790. Even in Paris where there was a furious campaign in the press, turnout was only 10 per cent. The Legislative Assembly thus represented the minority of the nation that was politically active. So it did not have a mandate from the majority of the citizenry, either because already they felt the Revolution had escaped them or because they could not understand how local issues might be translated into national terms.

The elections solved none of the problems the men of the Legislative inherited. The turmoil over implementing the Civil Constitution continued; patriots, particularly in the National Guard, took matters into their own hands and attempted to ruin the refractory church as much as they could; local administrations too went beyond the law; and noble-inspired opposition became more organized both in the form of conspiracies at home, and with the establishment of 'armies' abroad, while more and more people fled the country.

The constitutional church became the church of the regime. Violence against the constitutionals also became more common as constitutionals replaced refractories during the summer of 1791 and after. Consequently, the threats, boycotts, stonings, petty harassments, beatings and nocturnal processions that had been present from the beginning also became more common. Even so, the constitutionals were often in an impossible position and many fled their charges. Only armed force could support the few who remained and their dwindling number of friends. Sometimes, impatient patriots took matters into their own hands. In the Ille-et-Vilaine, the Ardèche, the Nord, and the Sarthe, National Guards closed down churches, sacked convents, assailed supporters of the refractories, or forced refractories to flee. As the war approached, and with it greater danger for the Revolution, the guardsmen in the Sarthe justified their marauding by claiming that 'the moment of the counterrevolution was near, that the Constitution is on the point of being overthrown, that the constitutional priests are going to be chased out'.

One of the most significant contrasts between the summer of 1791 and the following autumn, winter and spring was how provincial administrations extended less and less deference to the National Assembly. In the immediate aftermath of Varennes, the willingness to defer was almost total, but the continuing crisis over the Civil Constitution tempted many provincial officials to go way beyond the law.

Repression itself was not new. The clubs had clamoured for it in the spring of 1791 and a handful of departments had petitioned for, or actually took, harsher measures against the refractories. But after Varennes, such demands became much more general. Thus between Varennes and the general amnesty of September 1791, at least twenty-one departments either petitioned for a general law exiling refractory priests or anticipated such a law by interning or exiling individuals or whole groups of refractories to various distances from their former parishes without a hearing or a trial. Many cited the influence of the confessional, especially on women, or the general conspiracy of silence to justify going beyond the law. The Rhône-et-Loire, for example, claimed that its decree of internal exile was necessary because of the progress of fanaticism, the latent 'state of insurrection' and the complicity of the municipalities. Others developed it into a general philosophy. The Sarthe adopted its decree in the name of 'the most imperious of laws, the safety of the people'. The Haute-Garonne justified its exile decrees by claiming that 'it's in vain that they claim liberty of religious opinions here; let this liberty apply only to the honest citizen who ... does not seek to propagate his principles and reconciles the exercise of his rights with respect for public order'. Naturally enough, in a case of latent civil war, one had the right to defend oneself but at the price in many cases of the due process of law. The bourgeois moderates elected in 1790 to consolidate and administer were slipping towards the mentality of the Terror. For the patriots in the towns, they were dealing with a benighted, ignorant and superstitious peasantry, with people who were too easily misled by the self-interested refractories. The solution was to get rid of the refractories. And if there was no support from Paris, locals would take that responsibility for themselves.

The problem of the clergy was easily linked in the minds of the patriots with that of the émigrés. It is only in retrospect that the émigré armies appeared so pathetic. The three separate armies that were established in 1790 and 1791, of which Condé's, based at Coblenz, was the largest, were poorly financed and poorly organized. They were also demoralized by the failure of the great powers to recognize the court of the princes. In fact, most émigrés led a penurious existence relying on hand-to-month jobs and the generosity of foreigners when they were not engaging in unseemly intrigues for commissions in the princes' armies. A small army of a few thousand in which nobody wanted to be a soldier was not much of a threat to anyone but this is not how it appeared at the time. The mass of desertions of the officers of the regular army after Varennes stunned the patriots. By the end of the year, over six thousand officers had emigrated, frustrated by two years of insubordination, disgusted that the new oath of loyalty contained no mention of the King and convinced that there was no loss of honour in emigration because the King had tried to give the example. This, of course, reinforced the impression among the patriots that the officers who remained were not to be trusted.

Civilians emigrated in great numbers too: almost the entire corps of old Regime bishops and many of the great court and parlementaire families, taking with them what appeared to be vast amounts of much-needed treasure. Could anyone doubt that such people were plotting a vengeful return?

In fact, conspiracies did exist. Calonne, who had become in effect the prime minister of the counterrevolution, hoped to cover the entire country with a network of 'coalitions' that would act as a fifth column in the event of a war. By the turn of the year the network was filling out. Active as ever, Froment had established committees in Arles, Carpentras and Avignon, had received 100,000 *livres* from the émigré court to purchase arms, and plans were unfolding to establish a redoubt at Bannes in the Jalès valley. There was another conspiracy being organized in Normandy under the comte de Oilliamson who was negotiating a plan whereby Russian soldiers would be taken up the Seine on Swedish navy vessels. There was still another plot in Brittany headed by the Marquis de La Rouerie who had established cells in most of the major towns of the old province by the spring of 1792. Local authorities never knew the details of these conspiracies, of course, but it was impossible to conceal all the recruiting and the massing of arms. The fear of internal and external conspiracy was hardly a figment of the Jacobin imagination.

Great power politics also contributed to the mounting apprehension. Artois finally persuaded Leopold II to make some show of support and by the Declaration of Pillnitz of 27 August 1791, he and Frederick-William of Prussia promised to use force to affirm 'the basis of a monarchial government equally suitable to the rights of the Sovereigns and the well-being of the French nation'. Neither country intended to act without the other powers, and since the British were indifferent and Catherine II was urging an anti-revolutionary crusade to distract the other powers while Russia grabbed more of Poland, the Declaration meant little. But such conditions were dimly perceived, particularly in the patriot press in Paris which worked itself into a frenzy over the Declaration.

An observation   As in 1789, as in the crisis following the King's flight, the end justifies the means mentality re-appeared in dealing with the internal crisis. Local officials and private citizens alike justified taking extraordinary measures that violated the text of the Declaration of Rights by claiming a national emergency existed. This mentality was present throughout patriot ranks. It was not the result of a conspiracy, nor did it grow out of the letter or the spirit of the Declaration of Rights. In fact this mentality, precisely that of the Terror, emerged in opposition to the Declaration of Rights.

The Great Treasons

If the Constitution was crumbling from below, so also did it also crumble from the top. The weak point in the post-Varennes compromise that

Barnave and his friends had crafted was a faithless King. Despite his oath, Louis XVI never believed the Constitution of 1791 could work. He swore the oath to buy time because he was dismayed at the tepid support the European powers had expressed at Pillnitz. He hoped to mediate between the National Assembly and an armed Congress of the European powers where he would express his will to a cowed nation. Whether he still endorsed a constitutional monarchy as he had at the *séance royale* and in the memo he left behind in June 1791 or whether, as his spokesman declared, he wanted a full restoration of absolute monarchy is unclear. Although the King was certainly duplicitous, these diplomatic efforts were probably not treasonous. The Queen was another matter. In her family diplomacy she vociferously solicited an armed intervention from her Austrian relatives and once war came, she betrayed French war plans to the enemy.

Yet the King's position in public opinion, at least in Paris, could not have been weaker. One engraver after another continued to pour out vile representations of the Queen, just as they had in the Old Regime, updating the cast of lovers to include Lafayette and young patriot soldiers whom the Queen debauched. Earlier still, she was accused of murdering her eldest son who died in 1789, and of attempting to poison her husband's morning coffee. After Varennes, the pamphleteers and engravers had a new target – the entire royal family. *The Family of Pigs Returned to the Stable* gives the idea. So too does another: *Fleeing by Design or the Perjurer Louis XVI*. By the spring of 1792, both the King and the Queen could be depicted as a two headed monster with cloven hooves, or the King himself as a drunken cuckold, the Queen swooning from unnatural pleasures. Needless to say, some of these depictions were unspeakably crude, like *The Two are a Pair* in which the King is shown riding a milk-laden sow but his crown is falling off.

So when some Jacobins posed the question of the King's dishonestly in his oath to the Constitution, they were on the crest of a wave. Particularly those around the journalist and now deputy, Jacques-Pierre Brissot, developed a strategy of forcing the King to show his true colours. He would be compelled to take a stand on the issues most threatening to the revolutionary settlement, namely the refractory priests and the émigrés. Part of this would involve passing measures of revolutionary defence, and another part would be to demand a war, to expose the 'great treasons', as Brissot said. War and domestic defence were related.

For Brissot and his friends, there were limitless advantages to a war. In his first speech to the Legislative Assembly, he advocated a defensive war against the German princes who were harbouring the émigrés. But war could also be a tool of liberation. Citing America as an example, he believed a free people was invincible against despots. 'What soldiers of

despotism can for any length of time withstand the soldiers of liberty?'
This was an assertion destined for a long life: free men were invincible,
only treason and conspiracy could defeat them.

He also appropriated an argument that Madame Roland, the parvenue
salon hostess, developed that armed struggle tempered the character of a
free people and purged the vices of despotism. War would test liberty,
would test whether the French were worthy of it, war would purge
depravity. Here was an echo of the pre-revolutionary assertion that
centuries of despotism had corrupted the French and that blood would
cleanse them.

The cathartic effect of war was closely linked to the notion of a
romantic crusade against the despots. As the demagogic deputy Isnard
put it, 'If, in spite of their [the French] people's might and courage, they
should be vanquished in defence of liberty, their enemies will reign only
over corpses'. Throughout his career Isnard showed a consistent fascination with macabre images. Louvet was even more extravagant:

> ...a scourge, terrible but indispensable. We shall ask for war. War! And
> instantly let France arise in arms!...With the swiftness of lightning let
> thousands of our citizen soldiers precipitate themselves upon the domains
> of feudalism. Let them stop only where servitude ends; let the palace be
> surrounded by bayonets, let the Declaration of Rights be deposited in the
> cottage.

But other groups began to see advantages in a war too. As always, the
King did not want a restoration that owed too much to the émigrés and
hoped an armed congress of the European powers would restore the
rights of the monarchy. Louis, who privately thought war would be
disastrous, nonetheless appeared before the Assembly on 14 December
to announce that war would be the consequence if the German princes
refused to disperse the émigrés. The Lafayette group in the Legislative
Assembly also converted to a war policy, because a successful war would
bring their leader to power, who would then crush the Jacobins. All of
these groups hoped a successful war would strengthen their domestic
positions. All assumed the war would be short. These assumptions would
prove to be dreadfully naïve.

The conversion of so many groups to a war policy undermined the
Feuillants and split the Jacobins. Barnave soon learned he had no significant influence on royal policy so he and the Lameth brothers quietly
withdrew from active politics. The war agitation also provoked a major
schism in the Jacobins. Robespierre thought a war was inopportune, that
the army was too disorganized and potentially disloyal, that Europeans
would not necessarily welcome the French as liberators; that America

was a unique case, and that a successful war would only increase the powers of the King and counterrevolutionary generals like Lafayette. Marat, suspicious as always, opposed the war because Marie-Antoinette so obviously wanted it. But Robespierre's faction had little influence inside the Jacobins, and almost none within the club network. Enthusiasm for the war was deliriously high among the patriots.

There were some diplomatic tensions that led up to the war too but it is hard to imagine these were decisive in anyone's mind. German princes with territories in Alsace had a grievance when the laws on seigneurial rights were applied, and there were Austrian complaints about the aggressiveness of Alsatian National Guards. Still, in normal times, diplomacy might have handled these issues. Instead, with only seven negative votes, the Legislative Assembly declared war on Austria on 20 April 1792, amid wild applause. Prussia soon joined Austria in an alliance.

Meanwhile, the Legislative Assembly did pass a number of laws that forced Louis into a lethal position. As the Assembly saw it, the principal problems facing the country were the émigrés and the refractory priests. The law of 9 November 1791 demanded the émigrés disperse before 1 January on pain of death and seizure of the revenues of their property. The law of 29 November required the refractory clergy to take a straightforward oath of loyalty to the Constitution. Refusal would entail losing their pensions, the risk of being considered suspects of revolt against the law, and the risk of harbouring of evil intentions against *la patrie*. They could also be held responsible for religious troubles in their communes. The Assembly had taken a hesitant step towards undermining due process but the law did go some way to meeting the demands of the departments which had been demanding action against the refractories. It was a law of suspects, two years before the real one.

The King vetoed these two laws and as a result revived the fortunes of the radicals in Paris for the first time since the Massacre of the Champ de Mars. Not only that, the vetoes radicalized the provinces. The local administrations and the provincial clubs were much more indignant than they had been in their protests against the Flight to Varennes. They had already allowed the Crown and the National Assembly a free pass; they would not do so again. As the Jacobins saw it, the Crown used its constitutional rights to undermine the Constitution. More ominous still, local authorities defied the veto anyway. By the end of April, forty-two departments had taken measures to exile or intern refractories, and by the end of June at least four others had done the same. The Maine-et-Loire justified its internment measures most succinctly: 'This measure is not in the law but the safety of the people is the supreme law'.

The struggle between the legislature and the executive also revived the popular movement in Paris. Thirteen sections, including the old

Cordeliers stronghold, Théâtre-Français, whose petition was presented by Desmoulins, protested against the use of the veto. Enfants-Rouges saw the law on refractory priests as a necessary measure of self-defence against 'the frightful troubles excited [by] fanaticism which are only the prelude to a counterrevolution', while Observatoire spoke of the 'unpatriotic usage of the veto by he [to] whom it was perhaps too lightly given'. Mauconseil declared that 'once the people has explained itself, the King was no longer free refuse his sanction'. This, of course, was pure Cordeliers theory. At least twenty-eight provincial clubs joined the chorus and although none echoed the Cordeliers themes that the Paris sections had, the challenge to the veto was all the same leading towards the undermining of the Constitution itself, as it had with local authorities. Indeed, the club of Pontoise declared it would ignore the veto while at least one department (Ille-et-Vilaine) imposed an oath of loyalty on refractories anyway, while two others (Finistère and Loire-Inférieure) interned priests suspected of 'incivisme'.

Defence against the internal and external enemy, the willingness to go to war defend the Revolution and protests against the veto were all linked. Sixty-six provincial clubs sent addresses to the Legislative Assembly along these lines – almost as many as had demanded the King be put on trial after Varennes. Some clubs went even further. Nantes, for example, demanded an immediate war: 'Let the warrior's trumpet give the signal to combat; around the flame of liberty, certain guarantee of victory, will gather so many unfortunate peoples who suffer under the most atrocious slavery and who will aid us give the final blows to expiring tyranny'. The National Guard volunteers of the Corrèze agreed, 'The time has come when war will no longer be the scourge of the human race. [Instead it is] the surest means of freeing oppressed peoples and of raising new altars to liberty'. Whatever else it was – and it is often asserted that the patriot war party had business connections who wanted war – a vigorous defence against internal and external enemy and, for some, a war of liberation, was also wildly popular. But it was war of a new kind, no longer for territory or commercial advantage, but for the defence of liberty which would not only undermine the Old Regime in Europe but the Constitution as well.

A Popular Mobilization

Jacobin propaganda incessantly depicted a totally unified France, yearning to defend liberty and to export its blessings. Reality was very different. 1792 witnessed a greater mobilization than anything that had been seen in 1789 and in some ways it was more dangerous. The continuing anti-seigneurial riots were more obviously politicized and the habit of grafting revolutionary slogans and symbols onto these local grievances became more widespread. There was also extensive rioting over the pressures on the food supply that the Revolution's own monetary policy had caused. Of course, subsistence riots and anti-seigneurial riots ultimately could be fitted into the Revolutionary galaxy through a policy of appeasement and repression. The disturbances in the country over the Civil Constitution could not. Neither could the risings in the West against attempts to recruit the National Guard for the war effort which broke out at the worst moment of the national peril in August.

Spectacular as they were, the subsistence riots that broke out from November 1791 onwards were the easiest to control. As always, people ascribed their food supply problems to nefarious forces working surreptitiously but there was a grim economic reality. In the first place, the *assignat* began its truly precipitate fall. From 82 per cent of its nominal value in October 1791, it fell to 60 per cent by the following June, aided by continuing emissions and massive counterfeiting. Nominal grain prices at Toulouse and elsewhere soared by 75 per cent over the same period. The result was the slow collapse of industry, which was particularly marked in places like Lyon. At the same time, the mediocre harvest of 1790 meant that reserves were lower than usual. On top of this, the revolt in the West Indies had disrupted the colonial trade. Sugar and coffee to which people in the large cities, particularly Paris, had become greatly attached, were thus in short supply.

The consequence was several waves of rioting. There was one wave of popular price-fixing in the Pas-de-Calais and in the Haute-Marne in November, and later in the market towns of the Nord in February. At the same time, poor artisans in the textile and building trades in the river ports along the Aisne and the Oise stopped barges loaded with grain and moved it to secure locations or sold it at a fixed price. In January and February in Paris, crowds of women, later joined by the men, forced grocers and wholesalers to sell sugar at a fair price. A new wave of riots then convulsed the Beauce region to the south-west and west of Paris. Thus, from late February until April, bands of pin-makers, nail-makers, spinners, weavers, day labourers, charcoal burners and so on, sometimes numbering in the thousands, marched behind their mayors who wore their sashes of office, from one market town to another. They fixed the prices not only of grain and bread but also of eggs, butter textiles, iron and wood. They also stopped grain shipments and searched the farms of wealthy peasants for hidden stores. Sometimes their leaders were forest stewards, forge-masters, master glass makers, millers and even the occasional man with legal training. Most remarkable was the participation of a dozen or so constitutional priests, of which the most famous was

Dolivier, curé of Mauchamp, whose denunciations of private property itself caused a great stir in the press and in the Legislative Assembly itself. But such ideas were less 'socialistic' than the articulation of much older traditions. The chiliastic call for a massive bloodletting that would precede the division of property by Petit-Jean, *curé* of Epineuil in the Cher, was more reminiscent of medieval notions of the end of days than of the red dawn of the future. In any case, his parishioners had the altogether practical aim of knocking down the fences of the recently enclosed village commons.

An even more impressive example of popular mobilization took place in the Midi. The obvious preparations of the counterrevolutionaries in cities like Arles and Avignon and the comings and goings of the old Jalès leadership stimulated the Jacobins, particularly in Marseille, to found daughter societies in the countryside. With mounting war fever and the concomitant fear of counterrevolution, the club movement leapt beyond the town walls so that from the spring of 1792 onwards somewhere between 50 and 90 per cent of the villages in the plains of the Ardèche, Drôme, Gard, Vaucluse, Bouches-du Rhône and Var had Jacobin societies. Within Marseille itself, the numbers attending section meetings quadrupled between the spring and the crisis of August 1792. The Marseillais also gave the example of the value of a pre-emptive strike by marching to Arles to disarm the clerical-royalist 'chiffonistes' in March. The widespread feeling that the government's unwillingness to disarm known counterrevolutionaries while the external enemy was at the gates justified citizens acting on their own.

Rural mobilization began with a small *jacquerie* in the Ardèche on 18 March which spread like brush fire with the propaganda the Jacobins were able to make out of a suspicious-looking accident in which 69 National Guards drowned near Pont Saint-Esprit on 25 March. From late March until early June, ignoring for the most part Catholic and Protestant boundaries, the movement spread south into the Gard and east into Provence and, in a second branch, west through the Cantal to the Charente and south to the Haute-Garonne emphasizing different forms along the way. There were intense fears that authorities were too indulgent towards counterrevolutionaries and everyone felt the necessity to avenge the drownings. As in earlier risings, people believed that the National Assembly had ordered the destruction of towers on châteaux, but that aristocrats and officials had suppressed them. For example, rioters accused the departmental administrators of the Ardèche of taking 'the part of the former seigneurs ... and [the rioters said that] we were opposed to their projects because we had fiefs [censives], that the department lied to them, that it printed whatever it liked at Privas [the capital] and that it suppressed a decree that ordered the demolition of the châteaux'. Insurgents set about demolishing not only towers, but roofs, moats, crests and coats-of-arms (especially those the owners had merely plastered over in hopes of better days) and removing weather vanes. They destroyed furniture, there were searches for arms and occasionally the insurgents helped themselves to the contents of the wine cellar. Rioters targeted property of known counterrevolutionaries while they spared that of 'patriotic' aristocrats. No less than twenty-five châteaux went up in flames in two days in the Gard alone, and all four châteaux belonging to the comte d'Antraigues in the Ardèche were burned. Particularly in the district of Uzès seigneurs or their agents were forced to renounce formally all titles and people made a joyous bonfire of old papers in the courtyard. National Guards of the communes around Aurillac in the Cantal marched in military order to the châteaux and planted their tricolour flags under the towers before beginning the work of demolition.

The risings in the Midi certainly showed that the hostility to the lords was still very deep but the significance of the risings and attacks on aristocrats was more long term. They produced bloody retaliation. They formed part of the very complex origins of the anti-Jacobin rising of 1793 known as 'federalism'. And they were even a part of the origins of the murder gangs that dominated so much of the Midi after 1795.

The country therefore was badly divided when it entered the war with opposition not only from counterrevolutionaries and refractory priests – this had been expected and was even desired – but also from a series of popular movements dissatisfied over the land settlement and the question of food supply.

War and Revolutionary Defence

After a violent press campaign against his 'Feuillant' ministers, Louis XVI called in Brissot's friends to the government: Roland at the Interior, Clavière at Finance, Servan at War and the military adventurer who had made himself a reputation as a patriot general in the Vendée, Dumouriez at Foreign Affairs.

From the beginning the war went badly. This belied the calculations of all those who hoped to profit from a short conflict. Claiming the army was short of supplies and seasoned officers, the generals along the northern frontier, of whom Lafayette was the most prominent, undertook desultory operations. They were forced to retire after engagements at Mons and Tournai. In a phenomenon that became deplorably common later, some interpreted the failure to win an all out victory as treason.

Setbacks were the result of conspiracy. Once the preserve of political hotheads like Marat, conspiracy theories became ubiquitous among the political élite after Varennes. Moreover, there was never just one conspiracy, there were several and they were all linked. No wonder the revolutionaries endlessly depicted the many-headed hydra of conspiracy. Thus, the deputy Basire exclaimed, 'Everywhere plots are being hatched, and we are brought continual denunciations of specific incidents which can only be linked to the grand conspiracy whose existence no one here can doubt'. Brissotins also fanned the agitation by claiming the existence of an 'Austrian Committee' that was betraying the country. Thus, the old hatred of Marie-Antoinette acquired yet another iteration, with fantastic stories of the Queen secretly leaving the Tuileries to meet conspirators at night in the Bois de Boulogne. There were also lurid accusations of a secret directory composed of the Queen, former ministers and the Austrian ambassador who were conspiring to organize a blood bath of patriots. These fantasies naturally incited dreams of revenge.

The Paris sections became increasingly alarmed, accentuating their popular character by referring to themselves as 'sans-culottes' (literally without knee breeches), and dropping 'aristocratic' forms of address like 'monsieur' in favour of the egalitarian 'citoyen'. There were several armed demonstrations before the Assembly, replete with the symbolic pikes and red caps of liberty. The patriot, or 'Girondin' ministry, riding the crest of this mounting agitation but also fearful of it, got the Assembly to pass a law on 27 May requiring the deportation of refractory priests after twenty active citizens denounced them. Another law dissolved the King's Guard and replaced it with a camp of 20,000 volunteer National Guards or 'fédérés' who were to defend the capital against invasion, check the Paris sections and protect the government from a coup by the generals, particularly Lafayette. When Louis refused to sanction either law, Roland, in a widely publicized letter to the King drafted by his wife, protested. Louis promptly sacked Roland, Servan and Clavière on 13 June and Doumouriez resigned a few days later. On the 19th, Louis formally vetoed the laws on refractory priests and on the camp of 20,000 *fédérés*. The day before, the Assembly had heard a violent letter from Lafayette denouncing the Jacobin clubs as a state within a state. Could there be any doubt that the military dictatorship so long predicted by Marat was unfolding? Such alarms redoubled the intentions of the section leaders to hold an armed demonstration on 20 June, the anniversary of the Tennis Court Oath and the Flight to Varennes. Yet the Jacobins stayed aloof and the organizers were mostly Cordeliers leaders who had been involved in the petitions of the Champ de Mars: Legendre, Rossignol and Fournier l'Américain. The *journée* of 20 June was a failure all the same. Thousands of demonstrators, many of them National Guards, poured into the Tuileries while the King, seated on a chair before a large window, donned the cap of liberty and passively listened to endless and threatening harangues laced with crude insults demanding the sanctioning of the decrees on refractory priests and the *fédérés* and for the recall of the patriot ministers. Teams of deputies flocked to the château to pacify the crowds. Finally Pétion, mayor of Paris since November, arrived and persuaded the demonstrators to disperse. Yet the King was not intimidated and advisors close to him began to plan the military defence of the Tuileries. An assault, almost certain as the foreign armies advanced, was bound to be a bloody affair.

The provinces also flooded the Assembly with addresses protesting the outrage to the King but, significantly enough, only two departments in the west (Manche and Calvados), most of whose counterparts had adopted exceptional measures against the refractory priests, joined the chorus. The local struggle against counterrevolution was weaning even the conservative lawyers on the departmental directories from their loyalty to the monarchy. In Paris, there was no repression as there had been after the Champ de Mars, possibly because such an operation would have been directed to a large extent against the Paris National Guard, an essential force given the alarming situation on the frontiers. The crowds were also demanding the implementation of laws the Assembly had passed. As always, some politicians were not averse to profiting from the violence they deplored in public.

In any case, the hostility to the sectional movement gave Lafayette a second chance. On 28 June, he appeared before the bar of the Assembly to denounce the instigators of 20 June and to demand the destruction of the Jacobins. The next day, he tried to raise the National Guard to march on the Jacobins but failed completely, a significant rebuke even from the kinds of groups which deplored 20 June, and an indication that the forces of order in the city were broadly sympathetic to the Jacobins. Lafayette's intervention also had the effect of unifying temporarily all the revolutionary forces. Brissotins and Robespierrists both condemned him in the Jacobin club while at least 22 sections, including Place-Royale and Fontaine-la-Grenelle normally thought to be 'bourgeois', denounced him as an aspiring dictator.

So too did the *fédérés*. Some of them had set out before the veto had been applied and continued the march afterwards in defiance of it. Others began to march to Paris after Louis XVI agreed on 3 July to authorize them to come to celebrate 14 July, on condition they depart for a camp at Soissons. Yet the *fédérés* were hardly mere citizen volunteers. Many of them were highly politicized. The Marseille *fédérés* had to have served in the National Guard since 1790 and members were required to have a '*certificat de civisme*' signed by the officers, many of whom were active Jacobins. The *fédérés* of Finistère were recruited by the Jacobin club of Brest. Those of the Midi had been involved in the repression of counterrevolution from 1790 onwards, while those from the west had much the same experience in propping up the constitutional *curés*. For many, the march to Paris was simply another expedition in defence of the Revolution.

As soon as they began to arrive in the capital, several battalions submitted addresses along the lines of those of the Paris sections, while on 17 July a delegation representing all the provincial battalions then in the city demanded the suspension of the King, the trial of Lafayette, a purge of aristocrats in the army and the civil administration because 'we know that without the treason of the enemies of the interior, the others were not to be feared or rather they would not exist'. The first rampart to breach was thus at home.

In the meantime, the Assembly, now more or less paralysed in its debates, took two steps that made an insurrection more likely. The first was the declaration on 11 July of 'la patrie en danger'. This ordered the departments, districts and communes into permanent session and mobilized the National Guard. Besides the electric effect of the phrase, *la patrie en danger*, it created the impression that the Revolution could be saved only by bypassing the Constitution. This was certainly how Robespierre took it when he said that in the present situation, with corruption and treason everywhere, only the people could save themselves. Mauconseil section put it more directly in demanding 'the right to forget the law to save "*la patrie*"'.

The second step was the order on 25 July that the sections go into permanent session and these responded, one after the other, by admitting passive citizens to their meetings. The revolutionaries on the Commune also used the law to create a central correspondence bureau, composed of a delegate from each section, to co-ordinate action. The initiative was passing from the *fédérés* to the Paris sections. On 1 August, the Assembly ordered the municipalities to arm every able-bodied man with a pike if he had no other weapon and, two days later, decreed that any volunteer for the army would become an active citizen. Before the national mobilization, property franchises and the Constitution itself were crumbling.

But these concessions were no longer enough. Provincials, because they faced the problems of refractory priests and counterrevolution more directly than Parisians, began to demand more radical steps. As early as 19 June, an address on behalf of the central club representing the popular societies of Lyon called Louis a perjurer, and demanded the Assembly take bold steps to seek out conspirators everywhere to 'prevent ... an insurrection which your indifference would render legitimate'. Shortly after, the municipality of Marseille denounced hereditary monarchy as a violation of the Rights of Man and on 18 July a mass petition from Angers demanded Louis's deposition. Petitions from eleven other towns demanding the trial of the King or deposition followed, while protests against the court and the use of vetoes continued to pour in from departments, towns and clubs. Meanwhile, more contingents of *fédérés* were arriving, the largest from Marseille singing the battle hymn which made them famous. They already had a national reputation for revolutionary extremism and the awesome poetry of their language: 'La liberté française est en peril: les hommes libres du Midi sont tous levés pour la défendre. Le jour de la colère du peuple est arrivé.' The mentality of inexorable struggle they brought with them joined the mounting agitation in the sections. On 3 August, mayor Pétion, representing all but one of the 48 Paris sections, appeared before the Assembly to demand the elimination of the dynasty and the calling of a National Convention.

More alarming still was the defection of the Brissotins who began to argue that the national emergency was no time to change the executive and condemned the deposition movement. In fact, the Girondin leaders, Vergniaud, Gensonné and Guadet had entered into secret negotiations with the court with a view to persuading the King to accept new patriot ministers, presumably themselves, and an unofficial council of advisors, including Pétion. Private intrigues using the popular movement to gain office, and public harangues, like those of Condorcet expressing fear of unknown consequences 'when the foreign enemy is at the gates', were certainly inept and naïve since Girondin propaganda had done so much to instil the idea of a treacherous Austrian Committee in the public mind.

Failure to act looked like calculated treason as the effects of the appalling Brunswick Manifesto began to sink in after its publication on 3 August. Issued in the name of the commander of the allied armies, the Duke of Brunswick, but in fact written by the émigrés, it promised that National Guards captured fighting would be punished as 'rebels to their King', that civilians defending their homes against troops would have their houses razed and be punished 'according to the rigour of the law of war'. It also declared all Parisians collectively responsible for the safety of the royal family. Otherwise the allies would execute 'an exemplary vengeance and forever memorable, by delivering the city of Paris to a military execution and a total subversion...' As a declaration of war on an entire city this was unprecedented, but far from intimidating the sections, it only made them bolder. Gravilliers, for example, in demanding deposition and a National Convention elected by direct universal suffrage on 5 August, took the Manifesto as proof that the King was the centre of a vast conspiracy linking foreign tyrants, émigrés, counterrevolutionary generals and corrupt politicians. Unless the Assembly saved 'la patrie', 'we will do it ourselves'.

Yet the Assembly refused deposition and proved their irretrievable corruption in the eyes of the radicals when in a roll call vote of 406 to 224 on 8 August, it defeated a motion to put Lafayette on trial. This convinced many Jacobins of the necessity of an insurrection, although Robespierre felt completely paralysed by events and the Girondins were against it.

Fall of the Monarchy and Popular Vengeance

With the Assembly defiant and the Jacobins divided, lesser known revolutionaries took the initiative. On the night of 9 August, an insurrectionary committee, many of whom were active in the Cordeliers agitation of the previous year and who had strong links with the sections and the *fédérés* – Rossignol, Robert, Hébert, etc., – installed itself at the Hôtel de Ville and overthrew the old municipality. Pétion appointed Santerre commander of the National Guard and ordered the mobilization of the Guard through their officials in the sections. Yet the Guard itself, both the battalions helping to guard the Tuileries and those in the sections, remained extremely hesitant. There were several reasons for this. The Paris National Guard had no formal links with the sections but instead was divided into sixty separate battalions theoretically responsible to general headquarters, which is usually assumed to have been pro-Lafayette, and to the Commune which had just been overthrown. As the events of 9 *thermidor* were to show two years later, the National Guard would not necessarily respond to the orders of an illegal authority. It was also in the process of being reorganized to make it more responsible to the sections. Thus, not only were lines of command exceptionally confused, so too were officers' loyalties. Also, of the major leaders of the revolt whose names are known, only a handful, Santerre and Alexandre notably, were also Guard officers. Finally, as the events of the previous week had shown, a significant minority of royalists in the sections was strong enough to overturn the petitions in favour of deposition. These considerations thus explain why the Parisian radicals put so much effort into recruiting the *fédérés* and why an alliance with them was so essential.

The overthrow of the monarchy was thus an immense gamble. Whether Parisians or provincials, the citizen soldiers who had been won to the side of insurrection faced a formidable enemy. The château was defended by no less than 4000 men, some of whom, like the Swiss regiments and bodyguards composed of aristocrats, were certain to resist. On the other side were 2000 *fédérés* and a theoretical complement of 25,000 Parisian guardsmen, who would have to assail defensive positions prepared during the previous six weeks.

In the early morning of the 10th, the King, seeking to protect his family, sought refuge in the Assembly where they were lodged in an adjoining printing room. This flight had been provoked by the defection of the palace Guard artillery companies to the insurgents. The National Guards and the mounted gendarmes fraternized with the insurgents approaching from the right bank. Meanwhile, the defences of the bridges, preventing the crossing of the forces from the left bank, collapsed. Somehow, the insurgents got into the courtyards of the château and, believing the battle over, began to fraternize. Yet some Swiss fired from the upper windows and attacked. The crowd fled, crying treason, but the Marseillais counterattacked with devastating grapeshot. Louis then ordered a cease-fire but this did not save the Swiss, some 600 of whom were massacred. Among the insurgents, about 90 *fédérés* and nearly 300 Parisians were killed or wounded. It was the most bloody *journée* of the Revolution.

The consequences of the insurrection did much to satisfy patriot demands. The Assembly's liberation of itself from the veto of the law of 27 May against refractory priests, the calling of the primary assemblies to elect a National Convention by universal suffrage and the return of the patriot ministers – Roland, Clavière, and Servan with Danton at Justice to keep the sections in line – were all in the broad spectrum of the demands made since June. So, too, was the deportation of refractory priests. On 26 August the Legislative ordered the deportation of all priests who refused a new oath to liberty and equality, unless they were over sixty and in poor health, in which case they were to be interned. Including previous clerical émigrés, about 30,000 to 40,000 priests and monks, about 40 per cent of the Old Regime corps, were scattered throughout Europe, the United States and Lower Canada. Since some regions now had so many refractories who could never be replaced, this required the laicization of the birth, marriage and death registers which now became the responsibility of the communes. Thus civil existence was defined by the state, no longer by the Church.

Yet the application of these measures introduced a new element of uncertainty. The deportation law was undoubtedly popular since local authorities had been demanding something like it for a long time. Indeed they anticipated it. On 5 August, the municipality of Lyon expelled all non-native refractories from the city and interned any others denounced by twenty active citizens. As soon as they heard of the revolution of 10 August, authorities in the Ille-et-Vilaine began rounding up priests who had refused an oath the department had designed the previous spring. Their counterparts in the Cher and Charente did much the same, while in the Doubs all refractories were arrested. As early as 1 July, authorities in the Finistère ordered internment at Brest or expulsion to Spain or

Portugal, while three weeks later, the Corrèze arrested all refractories. Other departments had already imprisoned refractories as much as six months before. Yet despite the very large number of priests who were deported, many others went into hiding, protected by a sympathetic laity. This helped nullify the law on the laicization of the vital statistics registers, for the refractories who stayed behind kept their own records or ordinary people simply refused to make the proper declarations before the mayors. Thus even a baptism could become a way of demonstrating hostility to the regime.

The hostility to the laicization of the vital statistics registers was only a small example of how measures of revolutionary defence provoked demonstrations of dissent. There were royalist risings in several regions of the west against the law of 20–2 July mobilizing the National Guard and requesting volunteers. The troubles began with the sacking of a country house belonging to an administrator of the Deux-Sèvres on 19 August and on the 22nd, a crowd estimated at 10,000, believing the enemy was in Paris 'to protect religion' invaded Châtillon-sur-Sèvre and destroyed the papers of the district and municipality. On three occasions equally large bands of peasants attacked Bressuire which had to be defended by National Guards from Poitiers, Niort and Cholet. A band of several thousand was dissipated around Carhaix in the Finistère, there was a pitched battle outside Josselin in the Morbihan and there were demonstrations demanding the release of interned refractories around La Roche-sur-Yon in the Vendée. There were anti-recruiting riots throughout the Mayenne in which insurgents shouted, 'The democrats have been masters long enough. We don't recognize the National Assembly or its laws. We'll never consent to send soldiers against the King and the priests.' One of the leaders of the Mayenne riots was a former salt-smuggler named Jean Cottereau, alias *'chouan'*, who was to give his nickname to a counterrevolutionary peasant movement more extensive than *sans-culottisme*. Cottereau had links with the conspiracy of the Marquis de La Rouerie in Brittany which was supposed to act as a fifth column once the allies reached Paris, but fortunately for the patriots local authorities discovered one of the cells in Rennes. Some good detective work rooted up other cells in the Morbihan and Loire-Inférieure and the conspiracy gradually disintegrated. The anti-recruiting riots were quickly mastered as well but it was clear that the commitments the Revolution had to ask people to make risked a powerful counter-mobilization.

The troubles in the west were handled with minimal direction from Paris because a dangerous power vacuum had opened up in the capital. Immediately after the overthrow of the monarchy, the rivalry between the Legislative Assembly and the revolutionary Commune developed into a dangerous and paralysing conflict. The suspension rather than the deposition of the King, the appointment of a governor for Louis's son, the refusal to order the arrest of Lafayette and the begrudging acceptance of a special tribunal to try those accused of treason raised questions about the Assembly's intentions. Both Assembly and Commune struggled for authority over the country and each sent out special commissioners to explain and justify the events of 10 August, those from the Assembly with wide powers to arrest suspect civilian and military authorities, which anticipated the representatives on mission of the Year II. Whatever their hesitations, the politicians also were willing to suspend civil rights, as in every national emergency.

With the national government working at cross-purposes and peasant counterrevolution spreading in the west, the situation on the frontiers seemed on the verge of collapse. Lafayette, dragging in a few civilian administrators, tried to march his army against Paris. The troops failed to support him, however, and he had to flee to Belgium on 17 August. Two days later the Prussians crossed the frontier with a small army of joyous émigrés in their train, in some consternation that they had been assigned the ignominious duty of minor siege warfare and reconnaissance, but so convinced of impending victory that already disputes had begun over who was to get which ministerial portfolios. On 23 August, the fort of Longwy surrendered, under suspicious circumstances, after a desultory bombardment. On 2 September, Parisians learned that Verdun was under siege. Danton's bullying helped keep his fellow ministers from abandoning the capital, and his magnificent speeches to the Assembly called for courage and audacity while the entire human and material resources of the nation were mobilized for war.

After Lafayette's treason and the fall of Longwy, everyone was convinced that treason was ubiquitous and the Brunswick Manifesto left no one in doubt what the consequences of defeat would be. Fear and repression therefore intensified. On 26 August, the municipality of Paris ordered the disarming of suspects and house-to-house searches for weapons. It was in this atmosphere of counterrevolution, treason and defeat that the September Massacres began. The belief in prison plots and subsequent massacre to prevent treasonous criminals from escaping to inflict who knew what atrocities was not new and not unique to Paris. In some ways it was the transference to prisoners, whether they were priests or ordinary criminals, of the fear of brigands of 1789. There had been alarming rumours at the time of Varennes too of secret plots, hidden bombs, and unscrupulous brigands. Indeed, the mentality that saw Louis XVI as the centre of a vast conspiracy, that had to be attacked before it unfolded, was the same that saw prisoners as fifth columnists only awaiting the appropriate signal from their aristocratic paymasters to break out and massacre patriots. A prison massacre, therefore, was a way of preventing the domestic and foreign plot from coalescing. Thus, for example, in June, a crowd in Dijon, including many National Guards, threw over one hundred refractory priests and nuns into prison as soon as they heard that refractories were with the Austrian troops killed on the northern frontier. A month later, a crowd at Bordeaux murdered two refractories when a rumour got around that six hundred nobles and priests were plotting to turn Saint-Malo over to the English. Priests were not the only victims. At Lyon, where an attack of Swiss and Piedmontese was expected at any moment, the municipality ordered domiciliary visits, disarming of suspects, the suppression of royalist newspapers, and the expulsion of dangerous foreigners. In the surrounding countryside, volunteers talked of cutting off the heads 'of all the aristocrats' before leaving, in order not to leave their families at the mercy of these malevolent people. In all, there were at least 34 separate incidents of lynchings and murders of priests, officials or counterrevolutionaries in the provinces before the massacres at Paris broke out, and a total of 65 between July and September. In many of them there was an air of celebration as the victims' heads were carried about on the end of pikes.

All of these elements – the fear of foreign invasion and of fifth columns, fears for defenceless civilians, the paralysis of government and the courts, and the necessity of a preventive attack – were a part of the make-up of the Parisian massacres.

The grisly slaughters began in the afternoon of 2 September and for the next five days, mobs, including National Guards and perhaps some *fédérés*, went from prison to prison and to monasteries and seminaries, killing some in cold blood. Sometimes they convened tumultuous 'trials', an unexpected but logical consequence of the Cordeliers doctrine of the sovereign people rightfully claiming to exercise justice on its own. Sometimes even, the killings occurred at night and while some murdered the prisoners, others held torches aloft. Outside the prisons passers-by heard nothing. Throughout, ordinary people and journalists insisted on how quiet Paris was. In the end, between 1100 and 1400 people, about half the prison population, were killed, nearly three-quarters of them were non-political prisoners.

A discussion   Such at any rate was the interpretation of Pierre Caron over 60 years ago. His interpretation of the September massacres with its emphasis on a pre-emptive strike that arose out of panic, has the effect, of course, of diminishing the responsibility of the perpetrators. Another look might be worth while. After all, those who were slaughtered – prostitutes, priests, teenage boys (the youngest victim was just twelve), servants, bishops, middle-aged aristocratic women like the Princesse de

Lamballe, and so on – hardly fit the profile of ruthless cut-throats who intended to stab patriots in the back. Moreover, if revolutionaries feared what prisoners would do, why not search the prisons for weapons? Why be seduced by a rumour that was after all ridiculous? How did a mere 3000 prisoners scattered in nearly a dozen prisons located all over the city, propose to co-ordinate a simultaneous break out, how did anyone imagine they would arm themselves? There were thousands and thousands of National Guardsmen and *fédérés* in Paris at the time, as opposed to a few hundred killers. Could some of these soldiers not have served the *patrie* by strengthening the security of the prisons, rather than fighting the Prussians?

Such questions come to mind after examining the experience of the little town of Aubagne, near Marseilles that had a massacre that Caron included in his catalogue, but it hardly fit. True, there were rumours earlier in the summer that 'they' were using mirrors to signal unseen ships at sea, but this turned out to be sunlight reflecting off the roof tiles of a local château. Nor were there any prisoners in Aubagne ready to escape, nor was the town anywhere near a war zone. Instead, the victim, named Jourdan, a magistrate under the Old Regime, was killed, dragged from protective custody in the town hall by a crowd that eventually killed him, because an enquiry later showed, he read pro-émigré newspapers; because, in other words, he was a political enemy.

Generalizing from the single instance of Aubagne is obviously risky, but from the small case in a small town in Provence to the big case in Paris, there are certain common features: the dereliction of duty on the part of officials and the incitement by radicals. In the capital, journalists Fréron and Marat and the vigilance committee of the Commune incited and encouraged the murders. Marat claimed all the crowd need to do was go to the Abbaye prison, seize the Swiss officers and their accomplices and put them to death by the sword; a trial was not necessary: 'it has already occurred'. It was the same attitude he took to the King's trial later. Fréron's *Orateur du Peuple* claimed that 'the first battle will occur within the walls of Paris . . . . All the royal brigands inside this unfortunate city will perish on the same day'. Roland, the Minister of Interior, declared that enemies were preparing even more evil atrocities so that any defensive measure would be justified. Danton, the Minister of Justice, repeating classic Jacobin mantra, issued a proclamation at the end of August claiming that without the interior enemy, victory would be assured. In that atmosphere, calling attention to the interior enemy or saying any response was justified, invited a reaction.

The massacres both in Paris and in the provinces were critical pivots in local municipal and national politics. In most cases, there was no prosecution of the perpetrators, or if there was, it came so late – frequently after the fall of Robespierre three years later – and involved so few people, that it was useless. Caron, for instance, cites almost no trial records in his bibliography, for the simple reason that frequently, as in Aubagne, a judicial investigation was called off. The reason for this reluctance, it is sometimes said, is that the revolutionary élites needed the support of the *sans-culottes* for the war effort. This makes a huge assumption that urban working people supported slaughter, and in any case it is largely false. Commentators at the time unthinkingly attributed the massacres to 'the people' but only small minorities were involved in the killing. In any case, the revolutionary élites needed the *country* people to support them and the decision of rural folk to support or oppose those élites derived from entirely different considerations. In the end, why politicians at the time and historians after excused atrocity is a mystery.

But the consequence of this politicized justice was that the anti-Jacobins of the Midi, and the opponents of Robespierre and Marat, concluded their enemies were out to kill them. So there was no point in appealing to a compromised and partisan judicial system. Thus, every major city that revolted against the Jacobins in the summer of 1793 – Lyon, Bordeaux, Toulon, and Marseille – and some minor ones – like Aix-en-Provence and Arles – had had a lynching in the later summer of 1792. In 1795, there was a prison massacre where Jacobins were the victims in almost every major city where there had been a prison massacre against the Jacobins' enemies in 1792. But failing a prison massacre, there was an anti-Jacobin murder gang in nearly every one of these cities and towns in 1795–7.

Moreover the massacres were a bright white light of who stood where on the political spectrum. Brissot, who was one of the few journalists in Paris to denounce the massacres at the time, must have been utterly stunned that so many politicians on the national scene like Robespierre, not only refused to engage in a debate about the massacres, they actually defended them. By that time in the autumn of 1792, Jacobin opinion, in the form of a circular to the provincial clubs, had already defined the significance of the massacres in the sense Caron gave it.

But that took some time. Giving the event a grander meaning was a process. Most of the killers in Paris and the provinces were probably motivated by vengeance. But for commentators at the time, several explanations stood alongside each other. A significant proportion of press commentary echoed Roland's opinion that a veil should be drawn over the entire incident, and nothing should be done by way of official investigation. This was the line of officials in Marseille in relation to the hanging at Aubagne: Jourdan was certainly guilty but the incident ought not to be repeated. Others excused the massacres in Paris by saying that the tribunal the Legislative Assembly had established to try traitors had moved too slowly and so the people were justified in taking the matter into their own hands. Others like Marat and Robespierre later claimed the victims were guilty anyway, that the event was a grand act of national vengeance, so what did it matter? In other words, the explanation Caron favoured, self-defence, was one of several explanations that were floated at the time.

One of the earliest newspaper articles on the subject, for example, by the Cordelier Prudhomme, says nothing about self defence. On the other hand, it justified the massacres as retaliation for the invasion for which the King was responsible. He also claimed they were a justified reprisal for Prussian atrocities, specifically because the invading Prussians cut off the ears of mayors in the north and then nailed them to their heads. But reprisal can hardly be squared with self-defence. The next issue of his newspaper, *Révolutions de Paris* (8–15 September 1792), did justify the massacres as a pre-emptive strike against co-ordinated attack but this was obviously unsatisfying because he went on to denounce the prisoners for printing false *assignats* in the prison itself (a reprise of an earlier absurd rumour) and for their 'scandalous amusements'. He did not mention self-defence at all in the provincial massacres and noted that while the killings were not done before judges, declaimed, so what, 'Heh! What importance by whom justice is done, provided it is done?'

Although the massacres were widely denounced at home and abroad, the 'septembriseurs' considered themselves patriots, their contribution as important as the assault on the Tuileries on 10 August. Indeed, Marat claimed the September Massacres were in every way as important to the progress of the Revolution as were the *journées* of 1789 and 10 August.

More decisive in fact was Kellermann's and Dumouriez's victory over the Prussians at Valmy on 20 September. With the Prussians in retreat, the successful invasion of Savoy and Nice and the occupation of the left bank of the Rhine up to Mainz the Revolution was saved. On 22 September, the Convention abolished the monarchy and proclaimed the Republic.

Revolutionary Democracy and Popular Counter-mobilization

The crisis of 1792 was national in scope. The standard, Parisian oriented historiography of the period fails to take into account the relationship between a crisis that was largely provincial in origin and scope and its temporary resolution in the capital. This national crisis involved a popular movement that was hostile to the Revolution, the anti-revolution in fact. By the summer of 1792, this had developed from a defence of the rural community against agents of outsiders like the constitutional priests, to genuine rebellion against military service and against local administrators. In some of its verbal manifestations, it was becoming the counterrevolution. The revolutionaries had two responses to this: the first was to assume that the King's veto stood in the way of self-defence. Once this was removed, their solution was, once again, to persecute and deport the refractory priests. This was a dangerously simple assumption: if one could coerce community leaders, lay opinion could no longer be corrupted. If the first level of analysis was too simple, the second came close to being delusional: the revolutionaries interpreted opposition as unified – thus the constant image of the hydra they never ceased to invoke – and the result of a conspiracy with a single source, in this case on Louis XVI and the Queen. Certainly, Louis was disloyal to his oath of office but he was hardly the head of a vast conspiracy.

It is also too easy in other words to equate the growing radicalism of the period with growing 'plebeianization' and to explain the former by the latter. The mobilization of 1792 radicalized existing revolutionaries, men who had been prominent in their regions from the beginning. Moreover, the mobilization had the betrayal of Varennes as a backdrop, but the war and the vetoes expanded the numbers of those embroiled in politics far more than anything that had occurred in 1791 or even in 1789.

But not everyone was mobilized in 1792 and not everyone was able to use what democratization there was to make their voices heard. Contemporaries were struck by the magnificent enthusiasm of Parisians throughout the crisis of August and September, as endless streams of delegations appeared before the Assembly to make patriotic gifts, as women made clothes and bandages, as volunteers went to the outskirts to make ramparts, and men, some of them without weapons even, marched to the frontiers.

But not everyone was so enthusiastic. One example is voting turnout where, in contrast to the next significant universal suffrage elections in April 1848, the degree of apathy was staggering. The turnout for the elections of August 1792 to the National Convention averaged a little better than 15 per cent, this despite the enlarging of the electorate by nearly 50 per cent by the expiring Legislative Assembly. This was a new low for a national election. There was certainly no huge disenfranchised electorate of formerly passive citizens yearning to express itself at the ballot box. Although there were many reasons why turnout varied as it did – among the highest in the country was once again the Côte-d'Or which had a long tradition of community assemblies – the miserable turnout in some areas because of the religious issue was foreboding. Voters like these had already given up on national democracy. Also, there was an interesting flip between the national and local elections of 1790 and those of 1792. In the earlier case participation was higher in the countryside than in the towns, even small ones; in the later, participation, such as it was, surged in the towns. It is tempting to say that this signifies a declining commitment on the part of rural folk, once they realized how high taxes were going to be. But this is a point that needs further research.

Furthermore, the meagre recruiting for the army due to religious troubles in Alsace, where the army was traditionally popular, was significant while the riots at recruiting meetings in the west were ominous. In this region, thousands of young men were being mobilized in the counter-revolutionary cause, made all the more sacred by the deportation of the refractory priests. The failure of the Jacobins and the Assembly to appreciate the religious issue had done much to bring this mobilization about, just as the use of the vetoes had done much to turn provincial revolutionaries into republicans. The historiography of 1792 that emphasizes a rising of the entire French people culminating in the 'revolution of equality' consistently underplays the fact that the mobilization of 'the people' evoked a powerful counter-mobilization of quite ordinary people too who were headed in exactly the opposite political direction. In the Ille-et-Vilaine the communes that contributed the fewest volunteers to the army were also those where hostility to the Civil Constitution was greatest. The revolutionaries' analysis that these troubles could be blamed solely on the refractory priests, and that the problem could be solved by deporting them, was storing up massive problems for the future.

Of course, it takes time for people to learn how voting, local affairs and national politics interact, and politicians often do things for expediency while pretending to high principle. But in broad terms, the political system from 1789 to 1792 had not been as responsive as many had hoped. Fiscal equality had not brought much relief, the seigneurial system was abolished in spite of the politicians, urban and rural consumers' standards of living were dropping with each fall in the *assignat*, the religious settlement had alienated large numbers of people in Flanders, Alsace, the Midi and the west, and demonstration by grain riot had brought some expressions of sympathy but no action beyond repression. It remained to be seen whether the exigencies of war and the bourgeoisie's near monopoly of political power could be adapted to so many conflicting popular aspirations. This was the agenda that lay before the Convention.

5

The First Year of Equality

The crimes of the tyrant have struck every eye and filled every heart with indignation. If his head does not fall promptly under the blade of the law, the brigands [and] the assassins will be able to march with head high: the most frightful disorder threatens society.... We are judges and we ought to be impassive like the divinity. The least act of weakness could spark a horrible aftermath of calamities.

'Réflexions de J. Fouché (de Nantes) sur le jugement de Louis Capet,' *Archives parlementaires*, lvii, p. 406

It was much less the monarch that I intended to strike (he was good and just) than the monarchy, [that] was incompatible with the new order of things.... [And I thought] that to overcome the crisis, we would be able to inspire enough energy in the deputies and in the mass of the people, only by exceeding every measure, only by bypassing every limit, only by compromising all the revolutionary leaders. Such was the *raison d'état* which appeared to demand from us this terrifying sacrifice. In politics, does atrocity not also offer a salutary drama?

Joseph Fouché, *Mémoires de la vie publique de M. Fouché, duc d'Ortrante...* (1819), p. 16

In the 1830s, when they were old men, a cult grew up around the surviving *conventionnels*, as men who had changed the course of European history. They were an inspiration for younger radicals, dangerous, even in their old age, but for the young, they were courageous defenders of liberty. For those who were beginning to write the history of the period, these old men acquired a simple reputation as stern, self-sacrificing patriots. Their memoirs profited from this current of opinion and so they declared themselves to be decent republicans who obeyed the rule of law. This representation of themselves was a far cry from how they were regarded at the end of their tenure in office. The electorate that cared to vote rejected them at every turn. How their ruined reputation transformed itself into a saga of heroism in their last years is another story. At the time opinion loathed them.

No matter how they were regarded, they did have an immense importance. The *conventionnels* governed France until November 1795 and, by law, assured themselves an important influence in the legislatures down to 1798, while a majority of the Directors, the executive government, had sat in the Convention. During its lifetime, the Convention attempted to master the greatest crises the Revolution faced; devised the machinery that contained the counterrevolution at home; split the coalition of foreign powers arrayed against France; and laid the groundwork for the subsequent French expansion into Europe. It was a remarkable achievement but there was a negative side that is often less appreciated. The Convention's violent methods, its failure to solve the economic and financial problems and its deliberate amputation of the club and *sans-culottes* movement left a legacy of problems that overwhelmed their successors.

They were elected by universal suffrage but this was mitigated by the system of having ordinary voters choose electors who in turn chose the actual deputies. There was a furious and violent press campaign in which opponents denounced each other in the most odious terms but this did nothing to increase the turnout, which remained poor. Even in the Paris region, the rural districts participated more than the capital itself.

In its first phase down to 2 June 1793, the history of Convention is the history of the struggle between the Girondins – the Brissotins and Rolandists of the Legislative Assembly – and the Montagnards – strongly but not exclusively based on the Paris delegation led by Robespierre, Danton and Marat – and so called because they occupied the upper benches of the Assembly to the left of the chair. Neither group was a party in the sense that they accepted a common discipline to implement an agreed programme. The ethos of the day, which equated party with faction and exalted the independence of the individual member, was too strong for that. Because of this, counts of how many deputies belonged to which group vary considerably. Much depends on how deputies are classified according to a prearranged scheme. In fact it is extremely difficult to identify who belonged to which group in a very fluid situation, because not even contemporaries knew. Marat produced a list of 102 'Girondins' but it is not at all clear what criteria he used. The Paris sections and the Commune, who more than anyone else were responsible for the later purge of the Convention on 2 June 1793, produced five lists of deputies they wanted expelled between 10 March and 1 June 1793, but only six names out of a total of 40 are common to all five lists, and nine deputies were expelled on 2 June whose names appear on none of the lists. The lists of proscribed deputies produced during the rest of the year fluctuated considerably. The common element in them is that they contain a disproportionate number of deputies who voted for a referendum on the King's fate (83 per cent in favour in the composite Parisian list as opposed to 56 per cent in the Convention as a whole, for example) but this does not mean that these splits were present from the beginning, far from it. The fate of individual deputies evolved considerably. One might class Barbaroux as an extremist for his support of the *fédérés* of Marseille in the summer of 1792 but he ended as an antiterrorist, while Fouché's views on the religious question became more and more radical over the same period. Isnard, normally thought to be a typical Girondin, was an enthusiast for war in the spring of 1792; but voted consistently against Louis XVI during the trial; introduced the legislation establishing the Committee of Public Safety; but ended up on the list of 1 June probably because of a famous speech threatening Paris with destruction if the radicals attacked the Convention.

This does not mean that all was chaos in the Convention or that voting blocs failed to emerge that acquired some consistency over time. There were three groupings within the Convention: the first was a bloc of Jacobins or Montagnards that finally came together as a more or less near majority at the time of the King's trial; the second group was known as the Girondins and even after the King's trial this group was difficult to distinguish from the third group, the supposedly moderate Plain. These two latter groups formed a sharper separation during the spring of 1793. To win, and after the execution of Louis XVI, the Montagnards seldom lost on matters of importance, they had to sway a few votes to their side. Although there were few roll call votes, the debates themselves show that members of the Plain and even the Montagnards' enemies did on occasion support Montagnard positions. Although there is not as yet a comprehensive study of the deputies of the Convention, one can imagine why the Montagnard rhetoric might have won over wavering deputies. After the Flight to Varennes, the language of conspiracy overwhelmed the political class. Many Montagnard deputies became expert at manipulating fears of conspiracy (probably because they too believed in the hidden hand of treason), at denouncing ubiquitous masked traitors, and portraying innocence seduced by the language of venomous sedition.

Yet neither set of leaders was itself united. The Montagnards were much more coherent in their voting, perhaps because they dominated the Jacobin club, particularly after Brissot's expulsion on 10 October, and so the club acted as a sort of caucus. Even so, there were important differences of opinion between Robespierre and most of his colleagues over the claim of private property to complete legal protection, with Robespierre admitting some limitations; and Marat's earthy violence embarrassed almost everyone. The Girondins were even less united, in part because their loose grouping around a number of salons, particularly Mme Roland's, was more conducive to relaxed discussion and gossip than to planning concerted action.

Most deputies, including those of the Plain, shared a number of common concerns or policies. One was an aggressive foreign policy. After Dumouriez's victory over the Austrians at Jemappes which permitted the occupation of Belgium, the Convention adopted a series of measures which were bound to expand the war: opening the Scheldt to international commerce which alienated the British and Dutch, offering 'fraternity and assistance' to oppressed peoples, annexing Savoy and bringing the Revolution to conquered territories by introducing the *assignat*, by abolishing feudalism and by sequestering noble and ecclesiastical property. The French clearly intended to use the war to destroy the entire the Old Regime of Europe and the Convention accepted the implications of implanting the Revolution abroad with little demur. Finally recognizing the inevitable fissures in international relations these expansionary measures caused, it declared war on Britain and Holland in February 1793 and on Spain in March almost unanimously. The deputies also shared a broad consensus on economic policy in that most firmly believed in private property and freedom of the grain trade. Their reaction to the popular disturbances of the winter of 1792–3 shows this well. In November–December of 1792, a series of grain riots as extensive as those of the previous spring swept over the Beauce, spreading as far south as Tours and as far west as Le Mans. From September to mid-October, a wave of château-burning rolled over Provence. Neither the Girondin nor the Montagnard deputies or journalists had much to say about these troubles except to accuse their opponents of having instigated them. Even the Cordeliers group among the Montagnards, men like Danton, Desmoulins, Fréron, Fabre d'Eglantine and so on, who had struggled against economic and political oppression in 1791, did not take up the popular cause. Indeed Robespierre, Danton, Roland and Buzot leapt over factional considerations by all agreeing on the necessity of putting them down. On a more abstract basis, Robespierre made a famous speech on 2 December recognizing limits on property rights, and Marat reiterated what he had been saying for years – that the poor had gained nothing from the Revolution – but when it came to appreciating popular aspirations the politicians did not adjust. As in the previous spring, sympathy for economic hardship took second place to more pressing political considerations.

Why was the Girondin–Montagnard Split Important?

The former chair of the French Revolution at the Sorbonne, Albert Mathiez, saw the struggle as one between patriotic Montagnards who had a clear vision of the ruthlessness required to save the country from invasion and counterrevolution, on the one hand, and the Girondins who were muddled, self-seeking careerist politicians too squeamish to save the country, on the other. The Girondins had to be eliminated from the Convention in order to create the necessary national unity to rescue the nation from its peril. Few historians are nowadays so blunt and with the decline of class interpretations of the Revolution (and Mathiez also believed the split was based upon class antagonisms), the nature of the split requires some rethinking. One avenue is to consider the division a sign of the fatal inability of the political class to come together to surmount the enemies of the Revolution. Moreover, the split had long-term consequences. When the remaining Girondins were restored to the Convention in 1795, it increased the desire among some of these survivors for a settling of accounts.

The debate had begun as a difference of opinion between Brissot and Robespierre over the desirability of an immediate war and then enlarged throughout 1792. Many new or uncommitted deputies were drawn into violent disputes arising from earlier debates in which the Montagnards had become convinced that the Girondins were unduly and stupidly tolerant of royalism and counterrevolution, and crassly ambitious for office; and in which the Girondins were convinced that their opponents would permit or encourage any massacre or any insurrection in order to institute a personal dictatorship, or to establish Parisian hegemony over the provinces. Thus, many debates in the Convention tried to shame the respective factions into accepting their role as an insignificant minority and it was often difficult to deal with the issue at hand entirely on its merits.

This was particularly clear in the case of the King's trial, which began in late December. Almost everyone was convinced of Louis's treason, but no one was able to produce any evidence for it. Even so, the Convention was not willing to accept the argument that Robespierre and Saint-Just made, that 'the people' had rendered its verdict on 10 August and that the only course was outright condemnation, without a trial. One cannot rule innocently, said the Jacobins, monarchy itself is an abomination. The deputies were too nervous about going this far but they accepted a report from their colleague, Jean-Baptiste Maihle, that gave them cover to ignore the King's immunity under the Constitution of 1791. Constitutional immunity, he said, could not apply to someone who had violated the Constitution. The deputies accepted this specious assertion. This was all the more remarkable because close to half the deputies were lawyers of one kind or another and a very large proportion of the deputies were former members of the Constituent Assembly which had enacted the Declaration of Rights and the Code of Criminal Procedure. Both were theoretically still in force but the Maihle report gave them permission to ignore their earlier handiwork.

Moreover the deputies accepted an indictment drafted by a Montagnard dominated committee that retrospectively criminalized many of Louis's political acts like the *séance royale* of 1789, the vetoes, and even the massacre of the Champ de Mars for which no had ever blamed him up to this point. The Montagnard and the Jacobin press also made a great fuss about the documents that were discovered in the *armoire de fer* that someone later found in the Tuileries, but these only proved that Louis had tried to buy influence with key deputies and that he had subsidized the royalist press. Such practices continued for a very long time afterwards in France. For all the talk about an 'Austrian Committee' that fed war plans to the enemy earlier in 1792, no one produced any evidence of treason at the trial.

Moreover, Louis was denied many of the rights that any defendant was guaranteed under the rules of criminal procedure that were adopted in 1791: he only learned the contents of the indictment when he first appeared before the bar of the Convention on 11 December; and he was denied legal council until the last minute. In fact, the trial was a reversion to the most criticized aspects of Old Regime justice, the inquisitory system and judgement without appeal.

Since the procedures were rigged to produce a single result and with no one having the nerve to protest at this judicial travesty, the outcome was no surprise: 704 deputies voted to declare Louis guilty; no one voted him innocent. In these circumstances, the proposal of some Girondins to subject the verdict to a popular referendum could be easily represented as an attempt to save the King. Although the *appelants*, as they were called, could thus flaunt their democratic credentials, the Convention agreed with Robespierre that the measure would give counterrevolutionaries an opportunity to infiltrate the primary assemblies. In plain language, he feared the chaos that might result if a popular vote should go in the King's favour. The appeal to the people lost by 421 to 290. Next, the deputies voted for death by 378 to 343. Finally, the Convention voted against a reprieve by 380 to 311. Louis XVI was guillotined on 21 January 1793. He died with great dignity. It was a little past ten in the morning.

Why Were the Trial and Execution of the King Important?

The *conventionnels* were convinced that they were living through a great moment in history, that the King's death symbolized a point of no return between an old world and a new. Many historians have agreed with them and one interpretation now in vogue sees what happened on the *Place de la Révolution* (nowadays aptly named the *Place de la Concorde*) on that cold, dull day in January 1793 as the climax of the Revolution as a whole. Once the desacralization of the monarchy had begun, once the unfortunate Damiens had plunged his pocket knife into Louis XV's fur coat nearly 40 years before in other words, it was bound to end here, before the huge and shivering crowds stamping their feet to keep warm on the snow that was now turning into ice, puffing into their hands to keep warm, before the inexorable dull noise of the drums of the army and National Guard, before the officials who successfully prevented Louis the Last from addressing his former subjects. The significance of the Revolution is regicide and parricide. Michael Walzer argued that the death of the King represented the definitive repudiation of the past and that because the nation witnessed it, the execution made the nation complicitous in the birth of the new order. But the Declaration of Rights had already repudiated the Old Regime in 1789, and since the nation was about to explode in civil war, it is obvious that many in the nation rejected the role Walzer assigned to them. Another interpretation that assigns climactic importance to the execution is the claim that the death of Louis XVI was a parricide, the sons murdering their father.

We can leave these hidden Freudian interpretations where they are, hidden. Instead, a number of things are clear. For a certain current of opinion at the time, Louis's death brought to a close the discussion about despotism and corruption that had begun in the final years of the Old Regime. For Prudhomme's *Révolutions de Paris*, the death of the 66th king, the last despot, meant that the 'blood of Louis Capet,... cleans us of the stigma of 1300 years'. So the purpose of the killing of the King was, of course, to punish him for his crimes, but also it was supposed to regenerate the French, or perhaps to re-baptize them with the blood of their monarch, to transcend the original sin of living under centuries of despotism. The death of the king was a renewal. His death, said Prudhomme, echoing both Marat and Robespierre, meant that the French could live as republicans. This day, not 22 September 1792, founded the Republic, or at least sacralized it. Soldiers, volunteers, *fédérés* from Marseilles, dipped their bayonets, their lances and their sword blades in the blood, others dipped handkerchiefs in it, still others had it sprinkled on their foreheads while someone chanted, 'Republicans, the blood of a king brings happiness'. Some said they would show this bloodied handkerchief of a relic to their grandchildren. So however much Louis as a person and as a monarch was hated at the end, his body certainly held sacral majesty, his blood was a kind a wine made real, the mark of a holy rebirth, to be sprinkled on the faithful.

Again echoing a theme of political discourse in the 1780s, Prudhomme noted that the gloominess of the day could be attributed not just to the weather, but to the women, many of whom wept over the death of the King (other newspapers reported suicides) but all this was forgivable, 'to the lighter sex who saw the glitter of the last lovely days of a brilliant court'. Women would have trouble adjusting to the 'simple and austere morals of a republic' but they would accept it once they realized they were more honored and more loved.

The death of the King also had a more practical consequence. Regicides acquired a personal interest in refusing any compromise with any form of royalism, since until very nearly the end of the era, counter-revolutionary manifestoes promised to exact retribution in kind for the King's execution. In the longer term, regicide did not found the Republic, which lasted only another eleven years. No subsequent Republic has attempted to derive any legitimacy from the King's death. The representation of the King also underwent a fundamental transformation. From the cuckold and vile traitor, from the swine, the freak, the monster, in his death he became the 'martyr-king', endlessly depicted in the nineteenth century as offering his wrenching and tearful adieux to an adoring family of sister, wife and children. In the process, he regained his humanity. Nor did the execution kill the idea of monarchy. For much of the nineteenth century, even after the introduction of universal manhood suffrage, monarchist parties were in the overwhelming majority, and the legitimists, the party of the elder Bourbons, were the largest single party. In the shorter term, the procedures and practices the Convention adopted for the trial have an uncanny resemblance to the popular, military, and revolutionary tribunals as they were operating by the end of 1793. Thus, the National Convention was the first revolutionary tribunal. As Marat expressed it just after Louis's first appearance at the bar of the Convention, 'This is not a question of an ordinary trial. We don't have to concern ourselves with the chicaneries of courts.' The execution of the King was also a victory for the Montagnards in several ways. By forcing the Convention to come out for the most uncompromising possible outcome of the King's trial – death without a referendum or a reprieve – they acquired an ascendancy which they rarely lost afterwards. The trial shook much of the anti-Montagnard opposition. The debates and the voting showed a fatal disunity among Brissot's friends with only a handful of them consistently voting in a moderate direction. Moreover, Brissot, Buzot and Vergniaud, among others, spoke rarely after the trial and the Montagnards and their supporters increasingly came to dominate the committees. The Montagnards also consolidated their political base both in Paris and in the provinces because many of the clubs and popular societies came to identify the *appelants* as either dangerous moderates or as crypto-royalists. Yet the victory was far from total. The voting in the trial had revealed for all to see a solid bloc of moderates that under certain conditions could perhaps become a majority. What made this all the more dangerous was a series of separate but simultaneous crises: the outbreak of violent counterrevolution in the west, Dumouriez's treason, and a new cycle of popular disturbances brought on by the deteriorating economy. The linkage of these disasters in the minds of the Paris radicals eventually brought the expulsion of the Girondins from the Convention.

The Crises of '93

The deposition and death of the King was supposed to solve a major problem of opposition to the Revolution. Of course it did not. Still, by the winter of 1792–3, the counterrevolution had begun to ebb. Two of the émigré armies had been dissolved for lack of money, while the third, that of the Prince de Condé, appeared to be about to share the same fate. The internal counterrevolution had virtually collapsed as well. The La Rouerie conspiracy, which was supposed to turn Brittany over to the princes, had been broken, La Rouerie was dead (from natural causes), and his subordinates were either executed, arrested, driven underground, or they had fled abroad. The only other conspiracy of significance, that of the comte de Saillans in the Midi had also disintegrated. This was an attempt to form another column based on Jalès, but as early as February 1792 associates in the Lozère rose too soon and to no purpose. Meanwhile, as the allied campaign got underway in the summer, Saillans quarrelled with Thomas Conway, the general commander of the Midi, over when to start the rising. Revolutionary authorities invested Jalès yet again, Saillans was eventually murdered and piles of compromising papers fell into the hands of the government.

Finally, the popular counterrevolution had also been checked. The deportation of the refractory priests, or their going into hiding, had reduced the number of incidents against the constitutional clergy considerably. The enforced reduction in the rivalry of the two clergies changed no one's mind, of course, but superficially at least, the countryside was quieter than it had been in nearly two years.

The expansion of the war revived the counterrevolution and drew vastly more people into it. In order to fight the impending campaign and support the war on almost every frontier, the Convention decreed the levying of 300,000 men on 24 February. This was the first time the young Republic asked the nation to make sacrifices and the result was disturbing. The response to the levy was an unprecedented wave of riots whose extent remains to be investigated but which was almost certainly greater than the subsistence and anti-seigneurial riots of the previous year. And unlike the previous troubles, these forced the Convention to take the first tentative steps towards centralizing authority and systematic repression. Some of the troubles of 1793, such as the hostility of the young men at the recruiting meetings in Besançon, Autun, Alençon and elsewhere, were probably no more than an attempt to avoid conscription. In the countryside of the west, where the young men's dislike of conscription could be easily linked to the stock of grievances accumulated over the religious issue, the risings quickly involved entire communities in Normandy, Brittany, Maine, Anjou and Poitou. Young men tore down liberty trees, burned draft lists, beat up mayors or National Guardsmen or constitutional *curés*, dug empty graves to alert officials of what might befall them, and donned white royalist cockades. North of the Loire, in the second and third weeks of March, people armed with hunting weapons and farm tools marched on the towns behind white flags demanding the abolition of the districts, which were thought to be the source of every evil from the Civil Constitution to arbitrary taxes. Near Auray, in the Morbihan, people flocked down to the beaches to welcome and celebrate a rumoured émigré landing. In Brittany, almost every district capital was attacked, and Rochefort and La Roche-Bernard in the Morbihan and Savenay and Guérande in the Loire-Inférieure fell into rebel hands. Here and there refractory priests joined the bands, but more often than not the country people sought out local nobles and demanded they take the lead.

Authorities re-established control by early April north of the Loire but south of it in the four departments which came to be known as the *Vendée militaire*, or simply 'the Vendée', where there were fewer troops and National Guards available and where communications were more difficult, government collapsed. By the end of March, in a region bounded roughly by the Loire on the north and Fontenay-le-Comte in the south, the rebels had taken all the towns and were responsible for some appalling massacres of republicans. One set of massacres, those around Machecoul in the part of the Loire-Inférieure south of the Loire, became famous and justified any number of atrocities after. All around the small town, outraged country folk slaughtered 'patriots' in groups of twenty and thirty. Worse still, once the patriots in Machecoul were captured, and therefore could no longer do any harm, they were killed anyway. This incident alone gave the republicans the means to justify a terrible reprisal later.

More immediately, Nantes, Angers and Saumur were under constant threat. By early April, the regional leaders, mostly local nobles but also priests, estate stewards and peasants as well, announced the formation of the Catholic and Royal Army with its own insignia of a cross mounted on a Sacred Heart, and sent off emissaries to seek help from the English.

Why the Vendée?

In effect, the anti-conscription riots of 1793 showed that in the west at least, the anti-revolution had become the counterrevolution. There is a limitless supply of explanations as to why this happened, but they can be reduced to an explanation at two levels. First, a social-economic level. Unlike the villages of northern France with their steep hierarchy dominated by the *coqs de village*, the basic characteristic of the west was that many tenant farmers of modest means cultivated comparatively small plots. Since they were hopelessly undercapitalized, they relied heavily upon semi-skilled labour. Conscription threatened to add to their costs of production. As indeed it did, since a decade later wages were half as high again as they had been in the early 1790s. More importantly, the abolition of feudalism and the tax hike hurt them terribly. Landlords were permitted by law to add the equivalent of the former tithe to the lease and so rents immediately rose (this would have happened anyway once the leases fell in, even without the law), and taxes themselves rose by between 20 per cent and 40 per cent. In other words, tenants saw the real cost of operating land increase without an immediate increase in productivity. Many of their landlords were the local urban bourgeoisie and many of them in turn were officials on the directories of the local districts. Thus, the cries in the urban invasions of March 1793 for the abolition of the District.

The second level was cultural and religious. There was no difference in qualifications between the refractory and the constitutional clergy but there was a difference in who backed them. Country folk in the west invariably called the constitutionals 'intruders', meaning they were perceived to be the agents of the hated districts and the urban National Guard. Refractories, by contrast, because they refused to be the instruments of outsiders, embodied the community, a community of villagers and of the faithful. The revolutionaries thought they were removing a subversive influence when they deported the refractories in August 1792; what they had done in fact, was shatter villagers' sense of a cohesive community. Only a restoration of the Old Regime could revive the community. Thus the anti-revolution became the counterrevolution.

The counterrevolution in the west was real and from the beginning, it was massive. There are some, like Patrice Gueniffey and Alain Gérard, who argue otherwise. They say that the Convention exaggerated the risings in the west out of all proportion because of the internal need of Jacobin ideology to create enemies where none existed. Thus the terrorist legislation of March–April 1793 (see below). An argument like this might have more weight if that legislation was applied in the west right away. But the various special tribunals were only generally established much later, after in fact there were some major republican victories that could have provided these courts with defendants. That did not occur until many months later. A heavy-handed repression did not stimulate the Vendée into a desperate resistance. Early Vendean victories attracted more and more followers to the royalist armies.

The risings in the west, with their demands for a return of the priests and the Old Regime and their vengeance against the bourgeois revolutionaries for the wrongs done ever since 1791, occurred almost at the same time as defeat and treason on the northern frontiers. The armies encamped in Belgium were badly paid and clothed and their poor discipline alienated the civilian population. The imposition of the *assignat* at artificially high levels and the implementation of the entire package of religious reforms completed it. Disorganized ministries and quarrelling generals and authorities on the spot and in Paris also wasted precious time that could have been better spent consolidating the victory. Dumouriez's offensive into Holland in February had to be abandoned after the Austrians drove a wedge between the French armies in Belgium and the troops fell back from Aix-la-Chapelle and Liège. On 18 March, Dumouriez was badly defeated at Neerwinden. But he made the same mistake as Lafayette the year before in trying to impose his own political solution at a time of military defeat. He ordered the restoration of plate to the Belgian churches, he closed the local Jacobin clubs, and in a letter to the Convention he blamed the War Department for the defeats. The step to treason came with the conclusion of an armistice with the Austrians, the surrender of a number of forts and the attempt to turn his army on Paris to support 'the sane part of the Convention' and to restore the Constitution of 1791, including the monarchy in the person of Louis XVII. The whole adventure collapsed ignominiously as the army failed to respond to his overtures, and Dumouriez and some of his staff had to flee to the Austrian lines under fire from his own troops.

The third major crisis was financial and economic. Dilatory payment of taxes continued to plague the government. By the end of 1792, just over half the anticipated tax revenues had been paid; over one in ten communes had not yet drawn up their tax rolls; and tax revenues constituted a diminishing fraction of expenditure. The only way the war could be financed, therefore, was by printing more *assignats*. These continued to decline in value partly because of the quantities issued and partly because of the 50 per cent decline in foreign trade. The fall also reflected the minimal investor confidence in *biens nationaux* as the prospects of the counterrevolution rose. Although the harvest of 1792 was reasonably good in northern parts of the country, and although most of the large towns subsidized the price of bread, the price of grain and other commodities shot up because of monetary inflation, and shortages became increasingly acute.

As a result, the popular movement in Paris began to concentrate on subsistence questions for the first time in over a year. In January, there was a wave of protests when the Commune proposed to raise the price of bread. On 12 February a delegation of commissioners from the forty-eight sections and some of the remaining *fédérés* denounced the principle of freedom of trade, so recently defended by all sides in the Convention, as a licence for speculators to oppress the poor. It demanded a fixed price, or 'Maximum', for grain throughout the country. Two weeks later, a delegation of washerwomen demanded the death penalty for hoarders. This hostility to absolute property rights and the demand for a controlled economy can be traced back to 1790, or even to the food riots of the Old Regime, but it was expanded more forcefully in the difficult months of 1793 by the disparate group known as the 'enragés', of which the radical priest Jacques Roux and a well-educated postal clerk, Jean Varlet, were the best-known spokesmen. Roux encouraged the riots against grocers and wholesalers that broke out in Paris on 25 and 26 February. The poor and the economically vulnerable – water-carriers, market-women, domestics, etc., – were particularly prominent and when they did not fix prices on such products as soap, sugar and candles, they simply pillaged. The Commune mobilized the National Guard as a show of force and so handled the riots easily. But the Commune itself shared the preoccupations of the rioters, if not their methods, for the next day, its procurator, Chaumette, demanded a law against hoarding, a reduction in the number of *assignats* and a programme of public works. Chaumette's justification was significant: it was the only way to attach the poor to the Revolution. It was a theme more and more Jacobins began to espouse.

These economic difficulties, as well as the civil war in the west, military defeat and treason abroad, had an obvious explanation for patriots both inside the Convention and out: they were the result of plots. The belief in conspiracy, like famine, plots, pre-dated 1789, of course but the revolutionaries politicized this way of thinking. Even deputies believed in this. One of them in 1789 spoke of the necessity to be eternally vigilant in order to uncover 'terrible but necessary truths'. After Varennes, belief in conspiracies was overwhelming. A naïve observer might see discrete facts, but they were connected with hidden webs, manipulated by a disguised master plotter. Indeed disguise, both physical and moral was the enemy. Aristocrats escaped the country dressed as peasants, their milk pails full of gold coins. Self-seeking priests took advantage of the trust of the people to inculcate ideas that sustained despotism. Royalist spies freely roamed the country. As early as 1790, Paris forbade carnival masks and during the Terror itself beards were a mark of a suspicious person.

People interpreted the crisis of 1793 through their obsession with sinister forces manipulating disparate events. But the very scale of the crisis in 1793 fuelled sensitive imaginations for some dizzying flights. Taken to its extremes, it led in the direction of Terror and justified it. In the early phases of the crisis, some of the manifestations of the plot mentality were banal enough. Thus the Montagnards, notably Robespierre, claimed counterrevolutionaries incited the subsistence rioters in February. There was a little more plausibility to the Girondins' accusation that Marat incited the riots, even though it was probably a coincidence that *L'Ami du Peuple* published a call to hang a few grocers on the very day the riots broke out. Some of these charges were simply the stuff of political debate in this period, a rhetorical device intended to offer the grossest of insults. Other conspiracy theories were more sincerely held and were more dangerous. Thus, the risings in the west were quite wrongly attributed to the La Rouerie conspiracy, or to returned émigrés. The risings were also linked to Dumouriez's treason and occasionally all of these troubles were attributed to an even deeper conspiracy, masterminded from London. Later in mid-July, the future member of the Committee of Public Safety, Billaud-Varenne, claimed each manifestation of opposition to the Convention appeared to be discrete but in reality was linked in a vast conspiracy within a conspiracy. The inner ring of conspiracy controlled the outer one, which in turn appeared to be random events from the point of view of outside observers. Fanciful as some of these notions were, they all affected the way people responded to the crisis.

The predilection to believe in conspiracies led them to the simple analysis that the economic difficulties were the fault of hoarders. Despite the petition of the section commissioners and *fédérés* demanding controlled prices, agitation in the sections and from Roux and the other *enragés* concentrated less on the question of national price controls than on securing a law against hoarders. These limited aims could not push the Convention far off its adherence to the orthodoxy of free trade – even Marat called the petition for a national maximum 'subversive of all good order'. With the politicians anyway believing the agitation was directed by sinister forces for partisan ends, pressure from the streets on subsistence questions had few chances of success.

The politicians did enact the first price controls on grain, the Maximum, on 4 May. This was unlikely to do much for Parisians because the law permitted departments to set prices on the basis of local schedules drafted in 1790. Departments that set prices high could thus divert normal grain channels from low price to high price departments. It is generally held to have been ineffective because without national price controls, inventories of stocks, and penalties for hoarding, it was too easy to evade.

If plot theories blinkered the vision of the radicals and hampered an alliance with sympathetic groups in the Convention, they did affect the measures taken to deal with the deteriorating military situation. The Convention decided to establish the Revolutionary Tribunal on 10 March to exercise summary justice in cases involving state security, because they believed that the early defeats in Belgium involved more than simply the incompetence of the generals and the Executive Council. Similarly, beliefs that traitors were everywhere lay behind the establishment of elected revolutionary committees on 21 March in each section or commune. Their original purpose was to intern foreigners and suspects without passports, but they acquired or took on considerably greater police powers over the course of the summer. Suspicion of the executive lay behind the establishment of the Committee of Public Safety on 6 April that, from the beginning, was an embryonic government. It could oversee the Executive Council and even suspend its decrees, while it was empowered to take whatever measures were necessary for internal and external defence, the only limitations being the requirement to inform the Convention of its activities and certain qualifications of its powers of arrest.

The deputies were well aware that these measures went beyond the ordinary rule of law, and as the crisis deepened they went even further. The law of 19 March, providing for the trial and execution of armed rebels within twenty-four hours without a jury or an appeal by a military commission was a direct response to the risings in the west. Scared by the scale of domestic resistance and suspicious of all the generals after Dumouriez's treason, the Convention granted increased powers to the representatives on mission. Eighty-two of these deputies had been sent to the provinces in early March to encourage recruiting for the levy of 300,000. In April, they were granted additional and almost unlimited powers over the army and the activities of the departmental administrations. In fact, many of the earlier representatives on mission had taken independent initiatives, partly because they felt that weak local administration had been responsible for the crisis in the first place, and partly that the departments on their own could not co-ordinate repression in the civil war zones. By extraordinary measures, both judicial and administrative, the central government reasserted its authority. Administrators who disobeyed could now be punished with dismissal or even arrest.

The notion that the public safety was the supreme law was hardly new. The departments had used it to justify their exceptional measures against the refractory priests and it was the rationale behind their deportation. But the extraordinary dangers and the mentality of 1793 enhanced the corollary that moderation was more dangerous to the Republic than extremism, that evil, self-serving elements had taken advantage of the muddled tolerance of those who tried to take an even-handed approach. The results of such policies were the ominous disasters of March. The deputy Fouché, who was gradually moving to an uncompromising radicalism as a result of the crisis, expressed a typical view when he blamed the risings in the west on the 'softness of the [local] administrations [which] have lost everything...By a false system of moderation and tolerance, they have betrayed their country'.

Girondins and the Crisis

This developing attitude put the Girondins in an invidious position. Ever since the King's trial, they had taken a moderate line on most issues. They were not against exceptional measures on principle. They had fought a long and successful campaign to lift the parliamentary immunity of Philippe Egalité and have him arrested; they had not opposed the law of 25 March authorizing the disarming of nobles, priests and suspects. More importantly, Lanjuinais and his Girondin friends proposed the law of 19 March which put rebels under the jurisdiction of military commissions. They had opposed the much less severe powers granted to the Revolutionary Tribunal a few days before (unlike the commissions, it had a jury). Lanjuinais later defended the idea of a forced loan on the rich when it was introduced in May. The problem for the Girondin leaders was less the principle of revolutionary government than the risk that these institutions would fall into the hands of their political enemies. That this risk was real was evident when Robespierre demanded on 14 April that Brissot be brought before the

Revolutionary Tribunal. Yet no one had initially envisaged that it would be used against deputies. The Girondin leaders' opposition to the granting of more extensive powers to the representatives on mission is also comprehensible in that most of them were Montagnards who, it was charged, used their position to spread their own propaganda and support the clubs. The Montagnards could make the same accusations. In any case, the Girondins were less hostile to the principle of increasing the powers of the representatives on mission than to a clause in the bill establishing a central committee of authorities and clubs. The clause was defeated and, when they were in power, the Montagnards banned the practice. Thus the issue of what historians call 'revolutionary government' – the right to take extraordinary measures to save the Republic – became indistinguishable from the usual faction fights.

If some Girondins drifted towards moderation because of the fear of how the exceptional institutions would be used, their attitude towards popular involvement in revolutionary defence also began to divide them from the Montagnards. It was not that the Girondins were against prosecuting the war or levying men and requisitioning supplies. Rather, they assumed that the people would accept their role passively while the Montagnards revived the policy of popular mobilization. Brissot and his friends had demanded this in near-demagogic terms the year before but in the interval popular radicals had defined them as enemies. Instead, Barère, Danton, Robespierre and Jeanbon Saint-André spoke or wrote of the necessity of an alliance with the people which would win over popular support by making economic concessions, such as subsidizing bread by a tax on the rich or selling émigré property in small lots to make it available to the poor. Such considerations were also linked to the nightmare of another Vendée. In so far as the revolutionaries had a sociology of counterrevolution, it was the belief that its origins lay in poverty and that the rich, who had abandoned the Republic, had stirred it up. Thus the sympathies for economic hardship that they had always held became harnessed to the political aim of saving the Revolution.

The special tribunals, the revolutionary committees, the special taxes, the maximum and the wide-ranging powers granted to representatives on mission were all vital elements of the Terror. Its development was a chaotic process with the Paris Commune and sections, Convention committees and ordinary deputies on the floor contributing, its various authors responding in their own way to the pressures of the March crisis. The very circumstances of its origin show that it was not intended to be a system, nor was it, since most of the legislation was applied half-heartedly, if at all. Yet the way the legislation was perceived in the provinces and the way it filtered through the particular character of local Jacobinism in some regions contributed to the very process of disintegration the Convention was trying to stop.

Federalism and Extremism

Insofar as it is possible to characterize patriot provincial opinion up until March, most of it did not take sides in the Girondin–Montagnard struggle. An overwhelming number of clubs approved of the execution of Louis XVI but this did not in itself imply acceptance of the Montagnard line. In fact, many of them spent immense amounts of energy on non-partisan activities like collecting patriotic gifts in the form of money and military equipment, and many simply deplored the unedifying and baffling faction fights in Paris. Several clubs had their own way of viewing things that cannot be characterized in Parisian terms. That of Villefranche-sur-Saône, for example, demanded the arrest of Marat, 'the vile instrument of a disastrous faction' in December 1792, while three months later it petitioned that the Republic declare food supplies to be 'national property' and distribute it free, the costs to be borne by the rich – a line far more radical than most of the proposals emanating from Paris. There were many other clubs that had earlier protested the apparent sway of Parisian 'anarchists' over the Convention but later swung behind the emergency laws. In terms of national politics, such clubs were switching from the Girondins to the Montagnards, but from their point of view they were evolving in response to the national crisis in the same way the mother society in Paris had. In any case, there were always the Montagnard deputies on mission who were eager to enlighten the provincials on the significance of the war, treasons and rebellions.

But not everyone was willing to be brought 'à la hauteur des circonstances', as the phrase went. The explanation for the rebellion against the terrorist legislation of the spring of 1793, which is known as 'federalism', has much to do with the workings of local politics and particularly with the strength and character of the local Jacobin movement. This was overlaid with intense regional rivalries, usually involving a 'federalist' department capital and one or two district administrations that remained loyal to the Convention. So it is only partially correct to describe the federalist movement as 'provincial' since Paris did retain large islands of loyalty throughout the Republic which were later used as bases for repression. In addition, though federalism certainly attracted royalists, it was not on the whole counterrevolutionary or decentralizing. The federalist manifestos proclaimed their loyalty to the indivisibility of the nation and, in most places, to the Republic. None

of the federalist manifestos adhered to the proclamation the comte de
Provence issued on 28 February when he assumed the regency. As
brother of Louis XVI and as self-styled Regent for his nephew, Louis
XVII, he promised a root and branch restoration of the Old Regime
minus undefined abuses and punishment for those who voted for the
death of his brother.

Federalists generally did not respond to this. Instead, they concentrated much more on fear of the Jacobins. One Jura federalist summed
up these fears when he claimed that the Montagnards had preached
murder and 'put peaceful citizens whose only crime is to be rich on the
index but whose fortune in truth has become their prey'. But federalism
was less an 'ism' than a cast of mind. In fact, the federalists did not even
call themselves 'federalists'. This was a Jacobin canard that unfortunately has stuck across two centuries. Insofar as it implies a philosophy
of government, a programme or even a movement that linked various
cities in unison, the term is grossly deceptive. Thus too, a great deal of
historians' efforts to link federalism, so called, with regional or provincial sentiments ought to be jettisoned as a waste of research effort.

Jacobinism defined federalism as its anti-matter and Jacobinism in
the Midi was particularly extreme. They were verbally violent to a far
greater degree than even Marat. Joseph Chalier, travelling salesman,
crazed Jacobin demagogue and the most prominent leader in Lyon,
issued a poster threatening the anti-Jacobins in lurid terms: they would
'stain with their blood the waters of the Rhône that will carry their
corpses to terrifying seas'. Ever since the local massacres of the previous
September, there had been talk of using the guillotine against merchants
who frequently refused work to militant silk-workers, or of bringing
food hoarders before a revolutionary tribunal or arresting the entire
corps of bakers because they made a vile 'dog's bread'. The Jacobin
club of the Croix-Rousse section posted in its meeting halls the names
of all those refusing to sign petitions demanding the execution of Louis
XVI. This was clearly an open invitation to intimidate moderates. In
Marseille, the club denounced indiscriminately any manifestation of
wealth, it pretended to be the arbiter of everyone's revolutionary
pedigree and it sponsored practically lawless punitive expeditions to any
real or imagined royalist disturbance within reach – in one of them, two
people were hanged at Auriol and a 4000 *livres* tax imposed on the
unfortunate village. There was also a general atmosphere of rising law-
lessness, exemplified by the five separate prison massacres that occurred
at Aix in February.

In the large cities of the Midi, then, there was not a great deal of
difference between verbal and actual violence. In the case of Toulon,
for example, the local Jacobins seized control of the municipality after

a massacre of a dozen people including some departmental administrators in the summer of 1792. Elsewhere, the moderates knew from experience that the Jacobins would stop at nothing to get their way. Every major city where federalism triumphed in the late spring of 1793, had witnessed a 'September massacre' the year before. In Bordeaux, local authorities closed the *Club National* after an ominous food riot in March 1793 because extremists had demanded a 'supplement' to the September massacres. Moreover, Jacobins not only used violence or the threat of violence to stay in power, they also corrupted the electoral process. In Lyon, for example, they jailed their opponent in the contest for the mayoralty and when he won anyway, persuaded the compliant representatives on mission to sack him. At Marseilles, the club's influence over all levels of local administration, its sponsorship of a quite illegal central committee of the revolutionary committees of the sections and the support it received from the representatives on mission terrified many fellow citizens.

Finally, the soon to be federalist cities were not content merely to implement the Convention's emergency laws. Most of them enacted their own version of the Terror. In Lyon the Central Club and the municipality formed a local Committee of Public Safety, appointed revolutionary committees composed of their own followers, created a revolutionary army, instituted a forced loan on the rich, and undertook a long campaign to obtain a revolutionary tribunal. These leaders made it clear that these measures were directed not just at distant enemies but against the internal enemy, an enemy that could include not just the aristocrats and the rich but some quite humble people as well. In Marseilles, authorities and the club instituted a revolutionary tribunal, tried to raise conscripts, levied forced loans and revolutionary taxes on the rich, disarmed all manner of suspect people and formed a special army of *sans-culottes*. Measures like these were generally illegal but the representatives on mission did nothing to stop them.

The anti-Jacobin insurrections were the consequences of these high handed and frightening measures. The Jacobins had denounced too many people, rigged too many elections, defied public opinion too often and put out of business too many employers upon whom many ordinary people depended for a living. Federalism was popular because it seemed to be a way of stopping a cabal of uncontrollable fanatics. Thus the Jacobins' self-definition as an exclusive band of revolutionary saints hardly enhanced their appeal. At Marseilles amid growing denunciations of anarchy and chaos, the city's sections began a slow moving coup against the municipality and the club in mid-May. A few weeks later, the sections established a Popular Tribunal that executed a couple of prominent Jacobins.

At Lyon, the end came when the illegally constituted revolutionary committee tried to disarm 'all suspect individuals, whether attorneys, men of law, store clerks, etc.,' and to make lists of all 'hoarders, rich capitalists and the indifferent'. Just before their downfall, the truly exalted formed a 'Society of Jacobins' which co-opted only the purest, as opposed to the Central Club, which, being composed of merely elected delegates from the neighbourhood popular societies, was potentially unreliable. This provoked howls of protest from some of the societies and the resulting fissure within the popular movement gave the moderates their chance. Chalier responded by threatening the arrest of the officials of the sections after which patriots would 'wash their hands in their blood'. On 29 May, an insurrection overthrew Jacobin control. While protesting their loyalty to the Republic and the Convention, the insurgents sent off commissioners to Bordeaux and Marseille 'to fraternize with them so that the Holy Coalition of the *gens de bien* could overawe the horde that wishes to exist only by pillage and...blood'.

The collapse of the Jacobins was greeted with fervent relief by groups well beyond the small circle of rich men whom the Convention affected to believe were behind the revolt. The Montagnards were not entirely wrong in seeing their opponents as representative of wealthy and privileged men, but they were not entirely right either, for disquieting numbers of more humble elements were federalist as well. The social composition of Jacobins and anti-Jacobins have been thoroughly analyzed in three federalist cities, Marseille, Lyon and Arles. In all three cases there was a significant over-representation of the élites among the rosters of federalists and a significant number of plebeians among the Jacobins. But the split was not at all sharp. There were also significant proportions of well off among Jacobin leaders, and significant numbers of humble working people among the supporters of the anti-Jacobins. Occupation, and presumably income, accounted for a lot of the difference between the groups but it did not account for everything. Other factors came into play too. Many of the leaders of the Jacobins in Arles known locally as 'Monnaidiers' lived on the same street, and individual neighbourhoods responded to the Jacobin appeal in their own way. Many of the anti-Jacobin 'Chiffonistes' had their own neighbourhoods too. It is just possible too that these professional and neighbourhood rivalries pre-dated the Revolution. But very little is known about this.

There is no obvious explanation of why Jacobinism in the Midi was so much more immoderate than Jacobinism in the west. Both faced an implacable enemy, mostly outside the big cities. The existence of the external enemy and its scale cannot have been the decisive factor. One clue to the difference might be that Jacobinism in the Midi arose as a result of a acrimonious struggle within the cities. The hostility of rural folk complicated the situation but did not determine urban reactions as it did in the west. The municipal law of 1789 seriously sabotaged the local oligarchies and opened the way for a democratic challenge. The élites might have weathered this, but political enlargement also brought more humble people into the arena who had their own demands to make: silk-workers at Lyon, dockers at Marseilles and Toulon, port workers along the Rhône and the more humble artisans in Arles, vineyard workers in Aubagne. Jacobins were not particularly socially conscious but they did hate the rich. That was enough to give them a constituency.

The Purge of the Girondins

One of the most important elements in federalism was the widespread refusal to make the sacrifices the Convention demanded after the crisis broke in March. The crisis also led in another direction: to the purging of the Girondins from the Convention.

Large currents of opinion among the Jacobins, Cordeliers and militants in Paris felt the Convention had to be cleansed but, initially, few felt this had to be done by force. The so-called 'insurrection' of 9–10 March which tried to expel the 'traitors' got no support from the Jacobins, the Cordeliers and the Commune, let alone from within the Convention. Instead, Varlet, Fournier l'Américain and a few other obscure agitators tried to take advantage of the first reports of the defeats in Belgium to spark a rebellion whose purpose was the punishment of traitorous generals, perfidious ministers and the elimination of the deputies who voted for 'the life of the tyrant and the appeal to the people'. Aside from arousing a single section which hurriedly retracted and a few hundred soldiers and some remaining *fédérés* and inciting them to smash the presses of Gorsas's and Brissot's newspapers, the attempt got nowhere. But the abortive *journée* was significant in that it showed that radical opinion was convinced that the Girondins shared some responsibility for the March crisis and so should be removed from the Convention. After all, the reasoning went, since a free people was invincible, only treason could defeat it. Thus the Girondins and their friends in the ministry became victims of the doctrine of the internal enemy, as others had in earlier crises.

Other sectors of radical opinion agreed with the analysis but not the solution. Before the federalists overthrew them, for example, the Jacobins, sections, clubs and municipality of Marseille, always ahead of everyone else in the nation, were among the first to demand the recall of the *appellants*. As soon as news of Dumouriez's treason filtered to an increasingly panicky opinion, section after section in Paris demanded that his accomplices, whoever they were, be tried, that traitors, wherever they were, be punished. Sometimes the conspirators were named but no one could agree on who all of them were, even though everyone was sure that the disasters had to be someone's responsibility. The movement reached a climax on 15 April when the Commune and 35 sections added various lists of deputies who would be recalled as soon as a majority of departments agreed. Dumouriez's treason also convinced the Jacobins that a purge was needed. At the club, Augustin Robespierre invited the sections to force the Convention to arrest the 'unfaithful' deputies, while Maximilien made two speeches in the Convention linking the Girondins with the rising in the Vendée and with Dumouriez's treason. This probably convinced only those who wanted to be convinced since both he and Marat had made laudatory speeches in Dumouriez's favour a month before and the Girondins were able to score a number of hits against Danton's mysterious business deals while on mission in Belgium.

The Jacobins, sections and Commune clearly hoped the *appellants* could be expelled peacefully either by a vote in the Convention or by persuading their constituents to recall them. The Girondin response made this impossible. As part of the recall campaign, the Jacobins sent out a violently worded circular to the sister societies that Marat had signed as temporary president of the club. The Girondins persuaded the Convention to lift his immunity and send him before the Revolutionary Tribunal. As an attempt to defend themselves and intimidate the Jacobins, the move was a failure since Marat was acquitted. The incident is interesting since it showed once again that no one was above using exceptional measures and institutions for partisan purposes. A more direct attack came with the formation of a Commission of Twelve that was supposed to investigate the situation of the Commune and sections. This was composed almost entirely of moderates who immediately ordered the arrest of Varlet, the *enragé*, Hébert, the popular journalist and member of the Commune, and some section leaders. But the Commune had its own defences. Since early April, municipal authorities had been meeting with commissioners of the sections to discuss problems of recruitment and taxes and these meetings became more or less regular from mid-May. Thus was born the *Comité de l'Evêché which* soon acquired an existence of its own and whose executive committee, composed of obscure radicals, planned the *journées* of 31 May–2 June.

On the 30th and 31st May, delegates from twenty-eight sections declared Paris in a state of insurrection, fused with municipal authorities to become the Central Revolutionary Committee, named Hanriot, a customs clerk, commander of the National Guard and decided to raise an army of 20,000 *sans-culottes*. Yet on the 31st, the Convention treated the petition demanding the arrest of the Girondins the way it had all the others, by passing it to the Committee of Public Safety. The Central Revolutionary Committee was not to be duped, however, and on Sunday 2 June, surrounded the Convention with Hanriot's troops and forced it to decree the arrest of twenty-nine deputies and two ministers.

Like all the Parisian *journées*, the 31 May–2 June was a military affair in which the balance of force was decisive. Like 10 August too, it was an affair in which the leading Jacobins played a secondary role. Although the Montagnards probably had some idea of what the *Comité de l'Evêché* was doing and possibly even attended some meetings, they kept their distance. On the eve of the insurrection, Robespierre made a speech of such despairing ambiguity as to disqualify him from any claims of active leadership while Danton was clearly embarrassed throughout the decisive weekend. Legalistic qualms and a realization that the provinces would likely carry out threats to protect the integrity of the Convention that they had repeated the week before explain the hesitations.

But from another point of view, the expulsion of the Girondins was not necessary because the Montagnards generally got what they wanted from the Convention. The Girondins had only been able to reverse this situation in unusual circumstances. Only 312 were present to vote on the impeachment of Marat, for example. This vote was something of a fluke since on the major issues since the King's trial, the Girondins had been in a minority. The exceptional pieces of legislation supported by Montagnard speakers rallied sufficient votes, even when the Girondins opposed them, which did not happen in every case. That the special repressive and economic legislation passed after the March crisis was not significantly altered until the following August–mid-September also suggests that there was no pent-up Montagnard frustration which could only be released by calling on outside support.

The Girondins were victims of their own moderation all the same. This can be dated from the previous summer when some of them tried to stifle the insurrection against the monarchy and when they subsequently undertook a series of demagogic attacks on Paris. Their endorsement of a referendum on the King's fate reinforced popular suspicion against them. By appearing to try to save the King, the *appellants* became victims of a mentality which had been present from the beginning of the Revolution, a mentality in which internal conspiracies were the major explanation of the nation's troubles. Once the early reverses in Belgium were known, considerations of this sort lay behind the demands from the sections both for a purge and for the Revolutionary Tribunal. As civil war and treason deepened the crisis, the movement acquired more consistency, involving the Jacobins and the Commune both of whom joined the movement after it had begun.

The purge meant little in terms of social policy, which again suggests that the notion that a handful of Girondins represented the interests of a conservative bourgeoisie that resisted popular government is either untrue or irrelevant. The Commune, the sections and the National Guard were able to impose some concessions on the Montagnards who were themselves reluctant to implement them. The Convention decreed the arrest of suspects but never defined a suspect so the decree got nowhere. It voted the establishment in principle of a revolutionary army but was able to profit from differences of opinion among the *sans-culottes* themselves over the desirability of this institution to do nothing. It also voted the sale of émigré property in small lots but local authorities were too preoccupied with other affairs to do much about this. The decision to permit villages to divide their common lands at their initiative was discussed before the purge to no one's great objection. Everyone agreed with the now familiar argument that extending ownership as widely as possible was in the Republic's interest, although in practice it tended to set poorer villagers against their neighbours. In any case it was not relevant to the *sans-culottes*. The law of 17 July that abolished feudalism outright without compensation irrespective of titles was scarcely even relevant to the peasants, although it did give legal recognition to existing practice. In all, the social consequences of 31 May–2 June were meagre. Part of the reason was that the Jacobins were preoccupied with the federalist rebellion.

The Crisis Generalized

Many departmental officials had long expressed their dismay, often fuelled by the reports of their own deputies, at the apparent influence of Paris over the Convention and at the favourable financial subsidies the Commune received merely by threatening insurrection. Addresses viewing Parisians as cruel *septembriseurs* and threats to form departmental armies to protect the deputies from them had been frequent since the Convention first met. Yet the insurrection of 31 May–2 June gave these movements a national significance they might not otherwise have had: firstly because the Paris rising broke the chain of legality and the federalists were able to make great propaganda by claiming they would adhere to all laws passed by the Convention up to the end of May, although practice proved to be considerably different; and secondly, because the fall of the Girondins widened the movement. Some sixty departments and a number of clubs protested the expulsions but the movement rarely acquired any consistency, fragmenting in a shower of retractions and very often disintegrating in the face of local hostility or indifference. Federalism in the western and eastern departments proved to be a pathetic affair. Despite the inspiration provided by the presence at Caen of a number of Girondin deputies – Barbaroux, Pétion, Buzot and Salle, among others – and despite securing General Wimpffen, commander of the Army of the Coasts of Cherbourg, as leader, a tiny army of Normans and Bretons under the Comte Joseph de Puisaye panicked when an equally poorly equipped 'Montagnard' army fired a few cannonades into the trees by their encampment at Brécourt near Pacy-sur-Eure on 13 July. Similarly the National Guards of Dôle easily defeated the departmental army of the Jura at Tassenières on 2 August in a farcical skirmish. A tiny army from Bordeaux crumbled a mere fifty kilometres from its home base. In fact, federalist leaders were remarkably naïve. The Breton and Norman departments were indulging themselves if they believed they could raise armies which they were in no position to finance or equip when the levy of 300,000 men had gone so badly throughout the west.

The federalists' incompetent leadership, their lacklustre military performance and their dwindling and patchy support gave the Convention an opportunity to seize the initiative. The publication of a constitution in June did much to undermine the federalists' position because it announced the Convention's adherence to a regime of law. The clauses of the Constitution of 1793 and the circumstances of its acceptance mattered less than the invitation it contained to rally to the Convention. The limitations on property rights, recognition of the right to work and subsistence and the right of referendum were hardly compatible with the federalists' conception of government, such as it was. The Constitution was also approved by an overwhelming majority (with the usual dismal turnout of just 30 per cent) in a hastily organized referendum, but it was immediately shelved for the duration of the war and was never, in fact, applied. Nonetheless, the Constitution was popular even in some federalist areas and in federalist Marseille, for example, people were punished for expressing approval of it. The Constitution thus added another fissure to the already rickety federalist apparatus.

The Convention also intimidated federalist authorities into surrender. On 27 July, it gave them three days to retract and when they did, as at Caen and Alençon, the pacification that followed was restrained and selective. Where there were hesitations or flickering defiance, as at Bordeaux or Lons-le-Saunier, repression was more severe but, even so, fairly limited, because the representatives on mission realized that federalism had had little popular support.

The rebellion continued, however. In Lyon, there were further arrests of Jacobins and the federalists threw down the gauntlet by executing Chalier, who immediately became a popular martyr. There were over a dozen similar executions at Marseille and authorities opened negotiations with Lord Hood, commander of the British fleet. They wanted to guarantee the free passage of food supplies. The General Committee of Toulon, which was dominated by the pre-revolutionary merchant oligarchy, set up its own tribunal. It condemned some thirty dock workers and artisans whom the tribunal convicted for participation in the local massacres of the previous year. But the General Committee in Toulon went much further than it had originally anticipated because of the desperate subsistence crisis. The representatives Fréron and Barras cut off food supplies from the land and attempted to break the lifeline by sea from Genoa and Leghorn. The Toulon authorities vainly raised the price of bread by 25 per cent, issued ration cards and began negotiations with the British to assure supplies. Hood demanded they proclaim the monarchy and so, in return for rations of sea biscuits, the federalists recognized Louis XVII. On 27–8 August, British and Spanish troops entered the town and the Mediterranean fleet fell into allied hands.

But it did not take Toulon's treason or the appointment of the royalist comte de Précy and the émigré Villeneuve as commanders of the Lyon and Marseille armies to render federalism counterrevolutionary in the eyes of the Convention. Because of the running sore of the Vendée and further deterioration on the frontiers, continued defiance could only be interpreted as treason. Despite occasional victories, the war in the Vendée was going badly. In May, the Vendeans took Bressuire, Thouars and Parthenay in the Deux-Sèvres and Fontenay in the Vendée. The royalists also acquired a greater consistency by forming a general council, and in June they took Saumur and Machecoul. This forced the evacuation of Angers, and on 24 June the Vendeans moved on Nantes. The siege was short-lived and royalists lost their general-in-chief, Cathelineau, but, even so, they destroyed General Westermann's army at Châtillon. Worse still, the republicans had fallen out among themselves with the representatives on mission quarrelling with each other and launching extravagant denunciations of the generals who naturally replied in kind. By the autumn, the war in the Vendée would be carried to the floor of the Convention and several deputies would be its victims.

Meanwhile, the nightmare of a second Vendée in the south was being realized. In the Ariège at the end of August, an attempt to round up deserters provoked a rising of six hundred people that roamed the countryside around Pamiers shouting that everyone had to declare for the Spanish and to kill or disarm the democrats and the Protestants. Or they simply cried out, 'This won't go on longer! ['Ca n'ira pas!'] Down with the nation! Long live Louis XVII whom we are going to put on the throne!' The National Guard of Mirepoix soon brought the situation under control. In the Lozère, the notary and former Constituent, Charrier, and the Allier brothers, who had been involved in Froment's conspiracies, formed a 'Christian Army of the Midi' which took Marvejols and Mende in May. Significantly, the people of both towns welcomed the small army of fifteen hundred rebels but they were soon dispersed by the timely arrival of the National Guards from several neighbouring departments and Charrier was guillotined in July. Despite this, troubles in the Lozère continued for the rest of the year. However insignificant these risings, there could be no doubt that popular royalism was spreading.

This coincided with disaster on the frontiers. After Dumouriez's treason, the Austrians crossed the frontier and laid siege to the fortresses of Condé and Valenciennes while the Prussians surrounded a French army at Mainz. The sieges might have lasted for some time but the offensive of the Vendeans in June forced the government to transfer troops to the west so that one fort after the other fell to the allies in July, amid the usual cries in Paris that the generals were traitors. Further south, the Sardinians were poised to attack Nice and the Spanish were crossing the Pyrenees.

As was predictable, the expulsion of the Girondins did nothing to contribute to the war effort. To try to reduce the number of its enemies, the government adopted a conciliatory line towards the foreign powers. As early as April, Danton persuaded the Convention virtually to negate its offer of 'fraternité et secours' to oppressed peoples. He undertook negotiations with some of the smaller states and tried to split Britain and Prussia from Austria. These moves failed because the allies were convinced of the Republic's imminent collapse. The only alternative was to fight on and the Convention showed it recognized this by putting Robespierre on the Committee of Public Safety on 27 July. On the eve of the fall of the Girondins he had written of the necessity of a single will. He had also come to see the bourgeois as the great enemy. Other Jacobins had come to similar conclusions. The Terror was about to be applied in earnest.

Yet the circumstances of that terrible summer of 1793 ensured that it would be difficult to control the application of the Terror. There was no single will and little agreement about how the Republic was to be saved. There was an equal ambiguity about the use of the instruments of repression. So long as they were used against an identifiable enemy, whether that was a foreign army or a refractory priest, the Terror could be conceived as a series of police measures. The federalist and Vendean revolts changed this in several ways. As convinced democrats, the Jacobins had always expressed sympathy with popular economic problems, even if they remained as hostile as they had always been to insurrection as a solution. Federalism and the Vendée convinced them of what the extremists had been saying for a long time that only 'the people' could save the Revolution and that 'the rich' were the enemy. Allying with the *sans-culottes* was both necessary and desirable. The tragedy of 1793 was that it dragged many ordinary people into the federalist and counterrevolutionary armies so that it was impossible to tell who the enemies really were.

The lesson was only confirmed by the murder of Marat on 13 July, in his medicinal bath, by Charlotte Corday, a noble and admirer of those Girondins who had escaped to Caen after 31 May. Her manner of approaching *L'Ami du peuple*, obtaining an interview to denounce various conspiracies, was wonderfully designed to play on one of the favorite Jacobin tropes: patriot innocence destroyed by hidden, malevolent plotters. She indeed was not what she appeared to be, she indeed carried an assassin's knife beneath her cloak.

Part of Marat's funeral ceremony consisted of displaying his medical bathtub and of exhibiting his blood soaked cloak. Eventually, his heart was suspended from the ceiling of the Cordeliers Club, and his publisher and friend, Mlle Colombe, was compared to the Virgin Mary.

Amid the lurid ceremonies of his death, there was a clear lesson: if treason and assassins were everywhere, moderation was counterrevolutionary and unremitting suspicion and vigilance were patriotic duties.

6

Terror and the
New Republican Man

I confess that in the delirium of victory I said to those who claimed he aspired to be a dictator: 'You do him much honour [but] he had neither plans nor goals, far from disposing of the future, he was dragged along, he obeyed an obsession that he could neither avoid nor master.' But then I was too close to the event to be near its history.

Fouché on Robespierre's overthrow

The 'thesis of circumstances' is a way of explaining and to a very large extent, a way of justifying, the Terror. Historians who deploy it are using a device that goes back to the Revolution itself, and that the deputies in the Convention themselves used. They argued that the peril to the nation justified emergency measures. As Robespierre argued in his speech of 25 December 1793, there was a time for constitutional government and a time for revolutionary government. In almost all of his writings on the French Revolution, François Furet tried to cast doubt on the thesis of circumstances. While he appeared to have accepted the argument that a national emergency required extraordinary measures, he was much more interested in examining the centrality of repression and even of atrocity. Furet was certainly hitting a weak point in the structure of the explanation. In its mid-twentieth century renderings, the 'thesis of circumstances' did not focus on repression much. It was enough to cite the figures of the American historian Donald Greer on the incidence of the Terror and then move on to the activities of the revolutionary government. For Marcel Reinhardt, for example, briefly holder of the chair of the French Revolution at the Sorbonne, it was possible to write a history of Paris during the Revolution in the 'New History of Paris' series, and largely ignore the Terror. In the chapter on the Terror, he mentioned the revolutionary committees only to support the thesis of *sans-culotte* power, but he did not mention what they did or how many people they arrested nor did he mention the Revolutionary Tribunal as such. For others, like Soboul, later a holder of the same chair, the theme of the period was the rise and fall of the 'popular movement'. Repression was discussed less than the struggle to achieve an egalitarian social justice.

Furet explained the Terror by reaching back to a tradition almost as old as the 'thesis of circumstances'. This was to affix everything that went wrong with the Revolution to 'ideology'. Although the term was never thoroughly defined, witnesses to the Bicentennial of the Revolution in 1989 heard a great deal about how the Terror was implicit in the Declaration of Rights; about how the Terror was 'scripted' in the events of 1789; that it was implicit in the royal vetoes because these aroused the masses; that it was implicit in the Manichean rhetoric of 1789; that there was something peculiar about the needs of Jacobin ideology that required the creation of an enemy; and so on. Each one of these formulations can be challenged but they do have a number of features in common: they largely ignore the crisis of March–April 1793 and maintain that the terrorist impulse preceded any severe crisis in the nation as a whole; they emphasize the role of ideology and culture, rather than authentic opposition in the genesis of the Terror (indeed, it is said, opposition was significant only because the Jacobins blew it out of proportion); and they argue, as Furet did, that the Terror was a utopian project that forced people into ideal forms of behaviour, and that since this demanded too much of ordinary people, compulsion was the logical result. However, according to Patrice Gueniffey, ideology did not cause the Terror but there is a common feature in the radicalization of all the great revolutions: 'a common logic of a proliferation of competing discourses about the revolution that leads inexorably, in a spiral development, to massacre'.

Clearly, the Terror was a police action but it was also more than that. For the judicial and military repression was accompanied by attempts to remake the political culture of the French. In that sense Furet and his followers have made a major contribution. But in addition to the repression and the cultural project, there was also a more or less spontaneous mobilization, known as 'dechristianization' that not only shaped the repression but also the cultural project. These three elements – repression, project, movement – also interacted in complicated ways and in ways that varied over the entire period. The consequence is that the Terror wore different faces and terrorists had different motives depending upon who and where they were. To make Robespierre and his ideas emblematic of the Terror in a line running straight from Rousseau and the classic writers to the ominous tumbrels on the *Place de la Révolution*, is far too simple. Terror sometimes worked from the top down but distances were so great that Robespierre and the Committee of Public Safety were able only to frame broad guidelines. Above all, Terror was provincial, a response to provincial crises. One of the themes of the period is how the national government tried and some-times succeeded in mastering the provincial terror.

A Strategy for Understanding the Terror

The Terror should be understood as operating along a continuum. Across the entire nation, there was no such thing as a typical terror or an untypical terror, a terror that was a police action as opposed to one sponsored by crazed fanatics. It is best to conceive of it, not as a duality, but as a range with a minimalist terror at one end and a maximalist at the other. The one was a terror where nothing much happened, the other was slaughter. The gradations between the two were very great. Although in theory every French citizen was supposed to have been a contributor to national salvation, this did not always happen, far from it. Although the rhetoric of slaughter promised unapologetic and overwhelming destruction, this did not happen either.

The Terror was supposed to affect everyone in several ways. First through the suppression of the clergy. Refractories, of course, ought to have been deported; by law, any who remained, or who returned from abroad, were to be executed immediately. The constitutionals were an-other matter and their suppression took place under quite different circumstances, but by the end of the Terror, it is unlikely there were any constitutionals practising anywhere. There was also supposed to be a revolutionary committee in every commune in the country, but again reality was often different. Instead, it is possible to imagine a terror that affected some villages and towns only through the controlled econ-omy and through the conscription of the young men for the war effort. The next stage would be dechristanization that itself had a series of gradations embedded within it. Regions that felt more than this were rare but that next stage combined all the others and moved on to repression. This too was a continuum with a repression of increasing seriousness until the final apotheosis was attained. All this varied with time and with space. Between legislative fiat and reality on the ground, there were often immense differences, but one of the factors, the most important factor in making principle describe reality was the extent of opposition the revolutionaries perceived. Where that opposition was intense, treasonous and sustained, then the maximalist terror was the order of the day. Up until spring of 1794, there never was a maximalist terror where there was no opposition. After that, the Terror may have begun to move into another stage in some places. As the revolutionary tribunals in most of the rest of the country were easing off, the Paris Revolutionary Tribunal, the Popular Commission of Orange in the Vaucluse, and the Military Commission in Bordeaux were executing people for reasons that had nothing to do with specific crimes, but with who they were or had been, or because it was necessary to make an example so innocents had to be sacrificed for the greater good. But this stage was cut short with the fall of Robespierre. For most of the time, where opposition was very dangerous to the survival of the Revolution, the response was always excessive. Repression in regions like this was never finely calibrated to the degree of opposition. This is why there were atrocities. In regions like this, there was no resisting what the Jacobins wanted to do. Elsewhere, there was some scope.

Terrorists

The men caught up in the Terror came from a wide variety of backgrounds. Some were scions of rich aristocratic families like the Chevalier d'Antonelle, originally from Arles in the Bouches-du-Rhône, former army officer, first mayor of the city, member of the jury of the Paris Revolutionary Tribunal, later conspirator and still later a famous neo-Jacobin journalist. Another would be the Marquis de Sade who spent the Terror drafting typical egalitarian *sans-culotte* manifestos as secretary of his section in Paris and at the same time sending his estate agent in Provence dunning letters demanding prompt rent payments from his tenants.

Men like these were hardly typical of the aristocracy but they were of the terrorists in the sense that they were often men whose local roots could be easily relinquished. Terrorists were often newcomers to their regions and cities, and they often had successful careers. This is important to stress because of a long counterrevolutionary historiography that has morphed into a lazy social science trope that revolutionaries were frustrated losers. They were hardly that. Instead, they were almost always artisans or professionals and generally, as in Toulouse in the Haute-Garonne or in Montbrison in the Loire, they were fairly well off. Many owned their own homes. As with the patriots in Rennes in 1788, they were better off than their neighbours. A more general study of the Jacobin clubs in over a dozen towns and cities shows that the average member after 1792 paid over one third more in taxes than non-members and that the handful of men labelled 'terrorists' later on paid nearly double the taxes of the average male. Moreover, many were not new to politics in the Year II. In the Luxembourg section of Paris, for example, eleven of the eighteen who served on the revolutionary committee paid the equivalent of ten days' labour in taxes in 1791 which put them in the top quarter of the population of the city, and although the section's fraternal society witnessed a significant influx of new members from more humble social groups in the course of 1793, the club's officers had long been active members. In the Marat section, formerly Théâtre Français, home of the Cordeliers Club and of many of the great names of the Revolution, continuity from 1790 to the Terror was the rule. The exception, an important one, was the personnel of the revolutionary committee who were mostly new men and from a lower social rank. A similar phenomenon – enlargement and plebeianization of membership that did not, however, overwhelm the more established professional and better-off artisan members – occurred in the provincial Jacobin clubs. In other words, the terrorists of 1793–4 were sometimes new men recruited from below but, depending on the time and place, were nearly as likely to have been men who had been active in local politics since 1790. The problem of explaining the Terror in terms of its personnel is how men who had always been active in neighbourhood politics became terrorists, often, in Paris, at the cost of their lives. Radical ideology does not correlate very well with greater plebianization. Men became terrorists, in other words, because of the logic of local and national politics that had been operating from the beginning.

Terrorists or Jacobins were always a minority. In the first place, they were almost always men. There had been women's clubs from the summer of 1791 onwards, about 50 in all, whose purpose was often to persuade their rural sisters to abandon 'fanaticism'. Because it was coming to distrust the politics of movement in general, the Convention banned women's clubs on 9 *brumaire* (30 October 1793), because it was not desirable to give an active part in government 'to persons [who were] more exposed to error and seduction'.

During the Terror itself, there was an explosion of new clubs raising the number to about 4250 or about one club for every seven communes. But the majority of these were very recent creations; in Upper Normandy, for instance, nearly nine out of ten clubs were founded in the Year II. About a fifth of the clubs formed since 1789 in the country as a whole had even disappeared. The clubs also witnessed a great surge in participation during the Year II that in places was very impressive. In the district of Béthune in the Nord, for example, three-quarters of the communes had a club and the smaller the commune, the greater the participation so that in some communes, the Jacobin club was more or less a new form of the village assembly. In the larger places, participation rates dropped, to between 15 and 20 per cent of the adult males in towns like Montargis in the Loiret, Tulle in the Corrèze and Limoges in the Haute-Vienne. If the womens' club at Dijon was typical, rates among women were about the same.

The same dominance by a political élite was unmistakable in Paris. There in the referendum on the Constitution of 1793, it was rare indeed for even one quarter of the population of a section to vote. In the June election, which amounted to a confirmation of Hanriot's position as commander of the National Guard, only 15,000 voted out of an electorate of approximately 165,000. Since Hanriot won by some three thousand votes, an election marked by massive malpractice showed the existence of a smaller minority of moderates whose expulsion from the sections, often through a few well-aimed chairs and fists, was only completed in September. Attendance at section assemblies was no better. Before and after the abolition of the distinction between active and passive citizens, it was rare for the turnout to elections for sectional office to exceed 10 per cent.

Militants were most influential where they dominated local institutions of the Terror, like the tribunals, the revolutionary committees, or the revolutionary armies. Their influence on national legislation is more difficult to assess. Roux and his fellow *enragés* may well have been decisive in persuading the Convention to pass a law banning hoarding of foodstuffs but generally, demands from the popular societies in Paris and from the *sans-culottes* could be ignored or delayed for a long time unless they also had the support of the Paris Jacobin club or the Commune.

The *journée* of 4–5 September 1793 illustrates the point. The initiative came from the Jacobins who had been fired up by provincial militants in town to celebrate the first anniversary of 10 August. They demanded a purge of aristocrats from the army and the establishment of a revolutionary army of militants who would roam the countryside terrorizing the rich. The club then recruited the sections of Paris to their project. On the eve of the demonstration, the Commune invited crowds upset over the food supply to join the demonstration. To underline the point, the Commune appealled to masters to close their shops for the day. On 5 September, before a huge crowd carrying banners and following some spellbinding oratory, the Convention decreed the institution of the revolutionary army, the arrest of suspects, and put 'the Terror on the order of the day'.

But the Convention was not entirely intimidated. Some demands were not met at all or were severely altered. The demands for the arrest of all nobles as suspects or their purge from the army were both ignored. The only specific task the revolutionary army was given was to assure the arrival of subsistence to Paris and other big cities. But all the petitions that demanded it envisaged a little itinerant cohort of armed *sans-culottes* equipped with its own revolutionary tribunal and guillotine. This would shock country people into disgorging their hoards and it would also exercise summary justice on the malevolent enemies of the interior. Nor did the Convention intend the revolutionary committees to have a free hand with suspects. Their members were to be paid (and hence controlled) by the government and, in Paris, they were to undergo a purge by the Commune. This was a considerable step backward from the law of 21 March which provided for their election by the assembly of the section. The Paris Commune used its new authority extensively since, of the officials in place towards the end of the year in sixteen sections, nearly 60 per cent had been appointed since 1 September. Already, the popular movement was being bureaucratized, a process that was continued by having the revolutionary committees correspond directly with the Committee of General Security by the law of 17 September and completed by subjecting them to it exclusively by the law of 14 *frimaire* (4 December 1793).

Revolutionary Government

Revolutionary government was much broader than just repression. Revolutionary government captured the totality of the nation's war effort and its efforts to subdue opposition at home and win the war abroad. If it were possible to get figures, they would no doubt show that many more men and much more money was devoted to the war than to anything else.

The *levée en masse* of 23 August also showed how what amounted a bureaucratic solution to a military crisis could be cloaked in the most stirring language. As early as August 1792, Danton had demanded a mass uprising of the entire population to expel the invader. In March 1793, there been cries from the militants in Paris that more drastic measures had to be implemented to save the country. Half the population would be mobilized and thrown at the enemy and if this did not work, the other half would then leap to the breach. On 16 August, a deputation representing all forty-eight sections of Paris petitioned for 'a spontaneous movement of a great people who will throw itself *en masse* on its enemies to exterminate them'. All along, the militants clearly envisaged a sort of vast national *journée* that would rid the country of its enemies at a stroke. But a *guerre des masses* had also been envisaged in military circles at the end of the Old Regime and it was a military engineer, military strategist, and member of the Committee of Public Safety, Lazare Carnot, who drafted the *levée en masse*. Military calculation and high rhetoric both had a role to play in revolutionary government.

In principle, the *levée en masse* mobilized the entire nation for the war. All bachelors or childless widowers between the ages of eighteen and twenty-five were conscripted, older and married men were to devote themselves to war work, women were to serve in hospitals and make clothing and tents, and old men were to rouse public opinion 'and preach hatred of kings and unity of the Republic'. Even children could make themselves useful. The entire economy was to be mobilized for the war. As Barère, another member of the Committee of Public Safety, put it, '...all the French, both sexes, all ages are called by the nation to defend liberty'.

Almost immediately authorities from the top down began organizing this new draft. Inevitably, there was a great deal of confusion between this draft and the levy of 300,000 in the spring, as well as confusion with the levy of 30,000 cavalry and the local levies that the representatives had ordered for the Vendée and elsewhere. In some places local authorities demonstrated their zeal by stretching the age limit to 40, or forcing rich men over 25 into the contingents or refusing to exempt recently married men. Authorities in some places also permitted exemptions for armament workers, millers, bakers and even actors because the theatre was 'the only school of patriotism'.

As with the levee of 300,000, the *levée en masse* was resisted. Perhaps 40 per cent of those drafted never joined their battalions, deserted *en route* or deserted even when they were in the front line. The reasons for this could vary enormously. Sometimes the resistance was politically inspired as it had been in August 1792 and March 1793. Other times, it was linked with ongoing resistance to other aspects of the Revolution. Thus in the Rhône, some draftees shouted, 'No religion, no soldiers!' At other times, the risk was simply too great. Many young men were sent to the frontiers with no other weapon than a pike or even a scythe. Supply problems were indescribable.

The economy too bent to the war effort. The principle of the *levée en masse* was total mobilization and this meant more and more draconian controls. This was because of the revolutionaries' financial strategy. They financed the war with ever increasing deficits and the only way to cover the debt was to print more *assignats*. Tax revenue itself covered a very small proportion of overall expenditure. But by the summer of 1793, the *assignat* had sunk to 40 per cent of its face value. There were two consequences to this: first, since the *assignat* was the only legal tender, each fall in its value created an incentive for producers to pay back taxes since the tax burden was not indexed. Thus real revenues for the government fell as people paid up. Second, producers, especially the big rural producers around Paris, were increasingly reluctant to market their produce, so shortages among urban consumers and the military were getting more and more severe. The armies would have to be supplied and the big cities fed some other way. The solution was controls. Mathiez and Soboul claimed that the controls were imposed from below on a reluctant bourgeois Convention in *journées* like those of 4–5 September. In reality, the *enragés* demanded laws on hoarding, not price controls. Be that as it may, controls aimed to influence distribution of agricultural produce to the armies, to Paris, and secondarily to other big cities; they did not aim at controlling production. With outstanding real tax arrears remaining terribly high, the only alternative was to regulate prices, and, where farmers resisted, to seize the produce through requisitions.

After much hesitation, the Convention decreed the General Maximum on 29 September. This limited the price of thirty-nine essential commodities to one third of what they had been in 1790 with transportation costs and wholesale and retail profits added on later, while wages could not exceed one half of their 1790 level. In some cases, this meant a reduction in wages, notably for dockyard workers in the naval ports and in Paris. Consequently, the maximum on wages was not applied until July 1794 in the capital.

This was an enormously ambitious scheme for any eighteenth-century government to undertake, and every institution of revolutionary government had a hand in enforcing the Maximum because of their determination to win the war. How effective it was is another matter. To the degree that controlled prices eroded farmers' profits, or to the degree that price controls and the falling *assignat* – the only legal tender – reduced the value of the crop, there was an incentive to sell on the black market, hoard supplies, even though hoarding was a crime, or else switch to other types of products.

Attempts to cope drew the government to greater control. In February, it produced a so-called 'revision' that was supposed to take care of the question of quality of products and to regulate distribution even more. The result was dozens of printed tables each with microscopic columns containing hundreds of figures – an administrative nightmare both for the ballooning bureaucracy that produced them, and for a baffled population which was supposed to verify them in the shops. The difficulty of translating the Maximum into the thousands of local weights and measures always offered plenty of scope for cheating. Evasion, black marketeering and bartering were common. Outside of Paris, which got preferential treatment, controls did little to alleviate hardship and may even have contributed to it. Thus government agents in Normandy reported in November 1793 that there were shortages of everything because of the Maximum. 'What is sure', they continued, 'is that there is no real shortage because the decrees have not prevented the ability of chickens to lay eggs, dried up cows, rotted fabrics and annihilated other foodstuffs and products'. Indeed, the decrees had not. Thus was born the slogan of extremists everywhere of the '*disette factice*', the artificial shortage. For them, the solution was to overawe the greedy peasants and the selfish manufacturers. In fact, they should have blamed the government.

Elsewhere, markets collapsed very quickly. At Toulouse, peasants and dealers ceased to bring grain to market in October 1793. Requisitions, grants from the central government, and what the local subsistence bureau could buy on its own account fed the city. There were constant alarms about shortages, and at one time agents had to go as far as Toulon to acquire cooking oil and soap. By the late spring of 1794, rations had dropped well below subsistence level to half a pound per person per day. Most cities introduced rationing and public bakeries as a way of handling shortages and limiting fraud. All of this was accompanied by bloodcurdling threats from the militants of what would happen to hoarders and black marketeers but the threats were rarely enforced. Although the courts punished few offenders, the revolutionary committees did intern a number of people for 'negociantisme'. By such expedients as these, local authorities did their best to keep the urban populations fed. Even Marseille, which was under a constant menace until the spring from the British navy cruising off the coasts, never faced an actual shortage.

But it is doubtful the official market could take all, or very much of the credit. By driving ordinary markets underground, the government raised real prices enormously. Depending on the product, prices in clandestine markets in Orléans rose by between 60 and 125 per cent in the year after the inauguration of the Maximum. Prices that were uncontrolled rose enormously. Even milk adulterated with water and flour was four times more expensive than pure milk had been in 1794. Butchers had to sell meat at controlled prices but buy live cattle whose price was not controlled. The result was that beef was impossible to find. Farmers either destroyed their animals and feasted on them, or else fed them grain otherwise destined for the cities.

The urban poor and the countryside paid the price for all these distortions. In cities and small towns, the government did not offer the same preferences as it did to the armies and to Paris. Folk outside these privileged regions, the vast majority of the country in other words, were compelled to make do. There economic controls did actual harm. At Montpellier, officials were recommending the slaughter of sparrows and pet dogs. As we shall see, in terms of fighting the civil war, the government wrote off huge sections of the nation in the interests of the war effort against foreign enemies. In terms of economic policy, it looks like they did the same thing. Government policy was also laying the groundwork for the economic catastrophe of late 1794. Suppliers were understandably reluctant to oblige the cities – there were reports that city dwellers waylaid peasants bringing grain, eggs and milk to Paris near Vincennes and robbed them or else paid the official price which was far below the real. Conscription too created a labour shortage that not only squeezed farmers more than ever, demands for higher wages were impossible to resist. By the spring, the representatives on mission had contrived a new category of economic crime, stigmatizing those who demanded higher wages as 'royalists and conspirators...excited by the agents of Pitt'. The Committee of Public Safety ordered their punishment but in vain.

Revolutionary Dictatorship?

Throughout the period of revolutionary government, the National Convention tried to balance two apparently contradictory principles of administration: the first one, inherited from the Constituent Assembly, showed a great deal of respect for local implementation of national laws and decrees; the second was how to combine the first principle with the necessity to co-ordinate the war effort, to make the nation behave, as Robespierre put it, as if it had a single will.

In practice the single will worked from the top down and the centralization of government could be proclaimed rapidly. On 10 October, 1793, the Convention decreed, 'The provisional government of France is revolutionary until the peace'. This meant that regular constitutional norms would be circumvented. Among the first was the separation of powers. Although the ministries of the executive branch survived, the committee system of the Convention effectively neutralized them as organs of government. Police powers too were more and more centralized beginning with the decision in September 1793 to have the revolutionary committees report to the Committee of General Security.

But the major piece of legislation in imposing the will of the Convention on the country as a whole was the law of 14 *frimaire* An II (4 December 1793). This attempted to define and co-ordinate a permissible terror and replace local initiatives with national directives. From now on departments were to have a much reduced role in local government. The districts, effectively under the control of appointed 'national agents', were to be the major unit.

Another step towards making the committees in Paris all-powerful was the passage of the *ventôse* laws (26 February, 3 March 1794). These are usually seen in a different light. The proposal to sequester the property of political enemies and use it as a basis to indemnify poor patriots has been interpreted as a maneuver to pacify the *sans-culottes* during the struggle against the factions in Paris or as a poorly conceived and inadequate measure to solve the problem of rural poverty. It was hardly that, since Saint-Just's speeches justifying the laws made it clear they were another measure to undermine the internal enemy. But the *ventôse* laws also transformed an emergency government into a dictatorship whose results would be permanent. The confiscation of the property of enemies and their perpetual banishment even after the conclusion of peace implied that revolutionary government would have lasting social consequences. The Committee of General Security was given the power to release or detain suspects after reviewing tables forwarded by local revolutionary committees. In other words, the laws introduced an administrative system of arrests and punishments whose results went far beyond the temporary deprivation of liberty envisaged by the Law of Suspects (see below on suspects).

How well the laws of *frimaire* and *ventôse* worked is another matter. They certainly produced a mountain of paper, as any researcher into the period can testify. But much of the information the national agents produced on émigrés, sale of *biens nationaux*, public opinion, and so on, is tantalizingly brief. Local bodies did begin to implement the *ventôse* laws at least in the Puy-de-Dôme and the Bouches-du-Rhône by making inventories of suspects' property and by drafting lists of the indigent. But the Terror ended quite unexpectedly and so little was done. On the other hand, the centralization of information was continuing apace. The Committee of General Security compiled a huge archive on suspects from all over the country, and the revolutionary committees became increasingly responsive to its directives. In the Bouches-du-Rhône at least, they became essential cogs in the apparatus of the Marseille Revolutionary Tribunal and of the dreaded Popular Tribunal of Orange whose mandate covered a vast swath of territory and which gathered dossiers on suspects well beyond the Vaucluse.

Dechristianization

With dechristianization, we move another step along the continuum of the Terror. More than repression even, this is where the project to regenerate humanity was experienced. It may even have succeeded in some ways in weakening the Church in the long run and in creating a situation where pastoral care was so weakened that people went their own way. But these were unintended consequences. Dechristianizers expected the entire package to effect an immediate regeneration.

Revolutionary dechristianization was a complex phenomenon that operated at several levels of sophistication and that attracted different kinds of activists. At a bare minimum, it involved stripping the churches of their valuables and economically useful materials and funnelling them into the war machine. There had been a wave of this in the crisis of 1792 and it returned in force in the autumn of 1793 with an added emphasis on iconoclasm and anti-clericalism. The churches themselves were often turned into barracks, arsenals or stables. Where there was also a formal ceremony in which statues, relics, roadside crosses and other sacred objects were burned or otherwise destroyed, dechristianization clearly went beyond the war effort. The climax of the negative side of dechristianization came with the forced or voluntary resignation of the parish priest, perhaps his renunciation of the priesthood altogether and, occasionally, his marriage to a suitable patriotic spinster, ideally a former nun. The eradication of the old religious order was accompanied by attempts to create a new one in the form of revolutionary cults, cults of Reason and the Supreme Being, the desacralization of everyday life – so thorough that it included purging the names of streets, public squares, tavern signs, cities and towns, playing cards and chess pieces of all reference to the Christian and feudal past. Parents named their children after appropriate republican heros of the past or in accordance with 'nature'. Thus in Paris, close to half the children in some quarters were named after the whole gamut of classical or mythological heros, or after revolutionary martyrs like 'Marat', or after revolutionary concepts, like 'Tyranicide'; or after nature, so that parents deployed all imaginable types of plants. They named their children 'Radish', 'Buckwheat', 'Celery', and so on. Adults even changed their names in 'debaptism' ceremonies.

The introduction of the revolutionary calendar in October 1793 by the veteran Cordelier, Fabre d'Eglantine, symbolized the anti-Christian and 'rational' nature of the entire movement. The most important date in history became the founding of the Republic on 22 September 1792. Each of the twelve months had thirty days each, with five 'sans-culottides' or public holidays tacked on to the end of each year. Each of the months was renamed to reflect the seasons (the so-called universal calendar mirrored the northern French climate all the same). Sundays and feast days were replaced by a 'week' of ten days, called a 'décade', which meant that there were only three official days of rest per month instead of four or five.

The attempt to remake all of man's references to time and place could not have been more complete. Yet, how had such a situation come about when just three years before the association of the Church and the new regime had been so intimate? The Civil Constitution of the Clergy had symbolized this, as did the Masses at the federation of 1790, the blessings of the colours of the National Guards, the *Te Deums* for the new constitution and so on. An old Catholic tradition saw dechristianization as the logical outcome of the Enlightenment, but whatever the obvious borrowing from the *philosophes* in the Year II, 'écrasez l'infâme' was meant to be a long educative process, not a wholesale destruction. An interpretation in vogue at the moment sees Old Regime 'dechristianization' as a necessary prelude for that of the Year II. Apart from the fact that the correlation has never been statistically demonstrated, it is hard to see how declines in demands for Masses after death, charitable donations and the establishment of foundations that manifested themselves in Provence, Anjou and Paris from 1750 onwards, are connected to the revolutionary cults. How does the apparent indifference of the one phenomenon connect with the profound imprint of the Catholic religiosity of the other? In any case, eighteenth-century dechristianization is measured through those wealthy enough to draw up wills, while the revolutionary variety was often the work of people of lower social groups that are under represented in the sample of wills and that other sources indicate were on the whole practicing Catholics.

This is not to deny there were no Old Regime roots. The misogynist elements of dechristianization are probably related to age-old male resentments at the priests' apparent influence over women through the confessional. Nor is this to deny that from the beginning the Revolution showed religious characteristics. The habit of dating 1789 as the 'first year of liberty', the propensity to speak of the 'Law', 'Constitution' or 'Liberty' in mystical terms, the dedication of infants to 'la patrie', the spread, especially during 1792, of revolutionary symbols such as pikes, red caps or liberty trees, tricolour cockades and so on, as well as the missionary zeal of the National Guards and *fédérés*, are only some examples. But all of this was compatible with the constitutional church. Up until 1793, the litmus test of revolutionary commitment was going to the Mass of the constitutional curés whose doctrine and liturgy were certainly Christian and Catholic, despite the disavowals of the Pope and the old bishops. Dechristianization was a break with the constitutional church first and foremost, and to explain this break is to understand much of the origins of dechristianization.

Dechristianization came about because of the failure of the constitutional church. Whatever the reasons for establishing it, the constitutional church became the church of the regime and was expected to proselytize for it. Many *curés* fulfilled this role with enthusiasm, not only through their preaching but through their activities in clubs, popular societies and the administration. In return, the authorities did everything they could to support them. The constitutional *curés* were the first line of defence against 'fanaticism', that is, against the supporters of the refractories and the popular counterrevolution, but by the summer of 1793 was not 'fanaticism' on the point of triumphing? In this sense, the constitutional church was a victim of the royalist risings, particularly those in the west.

It is possible to follow this evolution in Joseph Fouché, perhaps the most famous dechristianizing deputy of all. Whatever his private beliefs, he had spoken in 1792 of the necessity of religious sentiments and had foreseen a role for the teaching orders in the new system of public education. It was only after his mission to Nantes in March 1793, in which he helped organize the defence of the city against the 'religious fanatics' of the Vendée, and only after some rebels nearly killed him while he was returning to Paris, that he denounced the clergy wholesale. He attributed the risings to 'ignorance and fanaticism [that have become] the blind instruments of the aristocracy which work with it to annihilate the cities...' Shortly after, he advocated a system of 'public instruction inspired by the revolutionary and clearly philosophical spirit [that alone] can offset the odious influence of religion'. His caution in implementing his anti-Christian ideas can be exaggerated because he took dramatic initiatives. One of these was the 'republican baptism' of his daughter in August 1793 in Nevers. The 'female infant' was welcomed to the world in a non-religious ceremony with throaty speeches from local officials and all the pomp the National Guard band could muster. He named her 'Nièvre', after the department.

Georges Couthon, the handicapped deputy from the Puy-de-Dôme and member of the Committee of Public Safety, was a Rousseauist believer in the natural goodness of man, a deist, a believer in the afterlife and an anti-clerical, but until the autumn of 1793, he advised 'giving Philosophy the care of delivering us' from priests and Catholicism. He only proposed bypassing 'philosophy's' role in his native department, however, after a local constituency anxious 'to throw off the yoke of religious prejudice' had shown itself in October and after he was able to observe at first hand the involvement of many constitutional *curés* in the Lyon rebellion. Jacobins like Fouché and Couthon had always insisted that there was no difference in doctrine or liturgy between constitutionals and refractories so that if religion was the device by which self-interested nobles and priests manipulated popular credulity, then these machinations could be defeated by undermining religion itself. As one official around Mâcon put it, 'Since the beginning of the Revolution, the Catholic cult has been the cause of many troubles. Under the cloak of religion, the progress of civic-mindedness has been much hampered. Disastrous wars have taken place. Would it not be appropriate to authorize only the cult of the Revolution?' Or as an official around Saumur on the edge of the *Vendée militaire* reported after noting that all the priests had resigned, 'Truth is beginning to enlighten the countryside, and its lively and brilliant clarity will soon disperse the thick fog of fanaticism and error'. At Clamecy in the Nièvre, one local revolutionary was stunned at the popular following of Rogations in the spring of 1793. The Vendean rebellion, now underway for two months, had begun with similar processions, and at night as well, which made it all the more threatening since no one could recognize the enemy. This simply proved the people were ignorant and needed to be brought 'à la hauteur'. The attachment to religion of the bargemen who floated log booms down river to Paris, a group the Jacobins felt was their natural constituency, was especially alarming. Get rid of the priests and the risk of counterrevolution would vanish, they declared. As the Jacobins asserted, 'Everything is due to the people, everything is legitimate to save it from its false opinions'. Dechristianization was thus another strategy in the struggle against popular counterrevolution, just as the persecution and deportation of the refractory priests had been.

The presence of a dechristianizing representative could be vital, in part because, as with Dumont in the Oise or Couthon in the Puy-de-Dôme, they set the movement in motion, and in part because only they were powerful enough to organize it systematically over a wide area. Fouché's celebrated *arrêté* of 10 October, desacralizing cemeteries, prescribing purely secular funerals, and ordering the slogan 'Death is an eternal sleep' inscribed at the gates of every cemetery, even had a national impact. Its influence has been found at the foothills of the Pyrenees and on the plains of Picardy. One of the best examples of this influence would be the decree of 9 *germinal* (29 May) of the representative Maignet, in the Vaucluse and Bouches-du-Rhône. This labelled cemeteries 'Fields of Rest' and forbade distinctive signs around graves as an affront to equality. As opposed to Old Regime practices that imagined a community of the living and the dead, these cemeteries were sentimentalized and placed fairly far from the dwellings of the living in order to prevent lethal vapours from contaminating the community.

Aside from the patronage of some deputies, almost every sector of the revolutionary coalition was involved in the dechristianizing movement, often for its own reasons. In the Cher, the representative

Laplanche did no more than apply the laws on the clergy, but his agents, two of whom were former college professors (like Fouché), aided half-heartedly by the revolutionary committee of Bourges, were the activists. They were not very effective until the signal came from Paris in mid-*brumaire* (early November) and only then did priests begin to resign in significant numbers.

Paradoxically, former constitutional priests, often with a background in teaching in the Old Regime, showed an extravagant enthusiasm for the violent spoliation of churches. They became apostles of liberty because of their conviction that religion and the Revolution were compatible, that is, for the same reason many of them had taken the oath to the Civil Constitution. Now, in a blinding flash along their own personal roads to Damascus, they became missionaries for Reason, Liberty and Equality or Natural Religion, never ceasing to be preachers and often throwing themselves into the war effort as petty bureaucrats. Thus, to take one example among thousands, Victor Martin, former *vicaire* of Valborgne-du-Gard, resigned his functions on 15 *ventôse*, saying he had always served his country and had been a 'patriot priest' but 'To-day, seeing that I am useless to my *patrie* in the post I occupy ...I abandon it to take another...[where] I can express my love for her'.

Sometimes, these self-defrockings were part of a public ceremony. Thus at St Etienne in the Loire, one country priest at the *fête décadaire* of 10 *nivôse* (1 January, 1794), abjured the priesthood, confessed to those assembled that he had misled them and begged their forgiveness. But more imposing still was that someone had found a functioning guillotine somewhere, and rolled it to the city. Part of the ceremony consisted of decapitating kings and the pope, not forgetting the 'infamous Toulon'. After this there was public singing, dancing and feasting.

Another agent in dechristianization was the revolutionary army of Paris. In one of its forays, it stimulated acts of destruction along the entire highway from the capital to Lyon, themselves taking part in the closing of churches, ripping out crosses, destroying holy images and burning statues in Auxerre and Cluny. Other departmental armies were involved in similar incidents, but so, too, were conscripts while regular soldiers set fire to churches in the Vendée in a spirit of joyful revenge. Certain clubs were also prominent. In the Nord and Pas-de-Calais they were able to use their influence over soldiers and the local revolutionary armies to despoil and close churches and organize civic fêtes. Dechristianization was enormously popular among the activists, probably even more so than repression was. After all, activists were minor actors and more often witnesses in repression; in dechristianization, they could act out their anti-clerical and anti-Christian fantasies without much limit.

And these fantasies could be enormously imaginative. There are many cases of officers in the revolutionary armies rolling into a village, despoiling the local churches, desecrating holy objects, and uttering crude blasphemies before stunned onlookers. In another case, a local militant tried to shock his neighbours into abandoning the Church by feeding the sacred host to his horse. Or there were many cases of gangs of young men more or less spontaneously breaking everything they could inside their churches. Or parading crosses and other religious objects alongside sheep bones.

At Tulle, in the Corrèze, members of the club and munitions workers improvised their own ceremony. Unlike many of the others that followed a script borrowed from somewhere else, this one acted out a ceremony that was quite original. They symbolically buried religion and the Catholic liturgy, part of which involved them parading though the streets dressed in black, holding crosses upside down, and showing a sarcophagus, surmounted with a square sided hat onto which were stuck the ears of a donkey and a Bible.

Even in Paris, where the iconoclasm followed initiatives in the provinces and had to be given a stimulus, the enthusiasm of neighbourhood militants was enormous. Popular societies and sections gave it a life of its own. On the night of 16 *brumaire* (6 November), the deputies Bourdon, a friend of Danton, and Cloots, the friend of humanity, rousted Gobel, Bishop of Paris, from his bed and persuaded him to renounce his functions. The next day, Gobel and his vicars-general resigned their posts before the Convention. On 20 *brumaire*, Notre Dame, converted to a Temple of Reason, was the scene of a civic festival, presided over by an opera singer dressed as Liberty. This took place against the backdrop of a rising enthusiasm in the sections for the cult of martyrs of liberty, and, from the end of *brumaire*, section after section trumpeted its renunciation of Catholicism. Dechristianization was thus capable of involving most terrorists under the right circumstances. The march of a revolutionary army through a country district to seize church bells and confiscate valuable plate often encouraged village atheists to come to the fore, with murderous consequences for them when the revolutionary tide ebbed in the Year III. It could also offer great scope for individuals, as with Charles Lanteirts, national agent of the district of Ales in the Gard, whose expeditions at the head of a little column of gendarmes against 'fanatic' communes were the terror of the region. But aside from the limitless opportunities for eccentric behaviour that this period of 'anarchic terror' offered to extravagant individuals, most dechristianizing fell into one of several patterns. The apparent connection between abdications of priests and civil war zones is striking. True, there were few in the Var where Augustin Robespierre, who shared his brother's suspicions of the movement, was supervising the siege of Toulon. This once again underlines the importance of a sympathetic deputy. But the proportions in the departments around Lyon were very high, as if the representatives, popular societies, revolutionary armies and *Commission Temporaire* were trying to build a *cordon sanitaire* around the 'Ville infâme'. Further afield, in fourteen districts in Normandy for which complete information exists, almost all the constitutional clergy abdicated after the Vendean invasion of the province. These examples cast a slightly different light on the old assertion that dechristianization was a minority movement. It is true that not all revolutionaries were violent dechristianizers but such activists were quite representative of those who sponsored the Terror and became so out of fear of the counterrevolution that they attempted to combat.

It is also said that dechristianization was superficial and undoubtedly it was. The cult of martyrs of liberty scarcely survived the boring officially-sponsored cult of the Supreme Being that in turn did not survive the fall of Robespierre, while the civic fêtes of the Directory never caught on. Although the revolutionary calendar was in use until 1806, Sunday work was resisted wherever possible. But there were exceptions. In Beauvais, over half the children born in the Year II were given revolutionary names and there were few legal rectifications even in the Restoration – a reflection of political commitments being passed through the generations.

Most disastrous was the effect on the constitutional church. It is not easy to estimate how effective the abdications of the Year II were. Most of them were forced, as with Parent of Boissie-le-Bertrand in the Seine-et-Marne who wrote, 'I am a priest, I am a curé, that is, a charlatan. Until now, a charlatan in good faith...' Such typically quivering honesty raises the question of how permanent such abdications were. Many *curés* did take up their functions again and others made their peace with the refractory church in the Years III and IV. Roughly six thousand or about one in ten of the constitutionals may have married from late 1792 on. Some were executed, others were later murdered by the *chouans* of the west or the 'brigands royaux' of the Midi. In the Loire, for example, the constitutional church was just half the size after the Terror than before. The representative Javogues had ordered the arrest of the entire corps of clergy, others had resigned to become farmers, officials and small businessmen. For those who tried to resume their vocations after their release from prison, few returned to their old parishes. Large areas of the department were abandoned to a vigorous refractory church. After such travails, some were still willing to reconcile themselves to the Concordat church once Bonaparte came to power but the biases of the new bishops kept many unemployed and probably no more than one quarter of the former constitutionals became parish priests again.

At first glance, the emigration and clandestine activities ought to have saved the refractories, so that to a certain extent dechristianization had exactly the opposite effect of what was intended in that circumstances saved the 'fanatic' clergy. But not entirely. Executions, natural deaths, the inability of the seminaries to produce sufficient new priests for nearly fifteen years and a certain loss of vocation while abroad affected the refractories too.

The Concordat church was much smaller than that of the Old Regime. The number of *curés* fell by over 35 per cent, the number of *vicaires* by over 70 per cent. By 1814, there were many areas where the shortage of priests was well below what was needed for sustained pastoral work. There was a huge region around Paris, practically up to the northern frontier, east to Lorraine and south to southern Burgundy where there was an alarming shortage of priests. There was a second region in the south-west where the shortage of priests was remarkable also. One can only speculate over what this shortage meant for the laity. The first region, however, looks like the one where birth control was most widely practised, while the second was a region of popular politics that was hostile to élite tutelage in any form. What is more certain is that from 1791 when the departments took their first exile decrees against the clergy until well into the Empire, large areas of the country lived without priests. The effect could not have been negligible.

The notion that dechristianization was superficial also tends to focus attention away from the extent to which it was resisted. In some areas, this was a continuation of struggles that had begun in 1791 but resistance often spread to regions that up to this point had been fairly quiescent. The most common and the least dangerous were disturbances, often spearheaded by women, over authorities' attempts to remove church bells. But resistance became more general after the publication of the law of 12 *frimaire* (16 December) recalling earlier legislation on freedom of religion that country people naïvely interpreted as authorizing the reopening of churches. Every adult male of the commune of Plessis Biron in the Oise petitioned the Convention for the reopening of its church on 'Sundays and feast days as in the past' to no avail. When the women of Beaubourg in the Nord did the same, the revolutionary committee arrested the *vicaire* for having put them up to it. In practice, with the inevitable exceptions, the law of 12 *frimaire* was a dead letter. For roughing up a few startled Jacobins of La Ferté-Gaucher in the Seine-et-Marne on 15 December when they came to retrieve confiscated religious objects, no less than eight hundred country people were arrested and twenty were sent for trial to the Revolutionary Tribunal of

Paris. Interestingly enough, about half the accused would be classed as rural *sans-culottes*. At Cébazan in the Hérault there were only about twenty people inside the church on 20 *prairial* (29 May) to practice the official cult, while outside everyone else 'was crying that they wanted the religion that they had before'. In the Nièvre, where Fouché's dechristianization had been very thorough, resistance was dramatic. On, 6 *nivôse* (25 December), crowds of country women invaded the district headquarters at Corbigny and declared that they 'intended to exercise their religion again, that they wished to live and die for it, that they demanded right away the return of their church bells and ornaments as well as the free use of the church'. In the Sancerrois region of the Nièvre, conscripts marched from village to village forcing municipal officers to ring bells and restore crosses and emblems and compelling priests who had resigned to say Mass. This was a region that later had a *chouannerie* of its own. Again, in the commune of Entrains in the Nièvre, women demanded the re-opening of the church with the only mental weaponry they had. They blamed what had happened to them on 'idolaters and Jews', but of course, they were way behind the times. The Jacobins had, all the same, 'destroyed He who caused their grain and their grapes to ripen'.

Local militants tried to ignore the law on freedom of religious worship, in some cases successfully. The military revolutionary tribunal of the Indre-et-Loire and Loir-et-Cher, for example, condemned René Gudrin of Cussai to death for shooting at a band of outside Jacobins who came to keep the commune's church closed despite the law of 12 *frimaire*. The constitutional *vicaire* was arrested on the pretext that he was not authorized to read out the law on toleration to the public.

But in some cases, people did not resist any longer so much as try to escape. Dechristianization was such a shock to ordinary people's sense of the rightness of things, that they drew upon repertoires that were very unusual in the Christian tradition. This was no longer a demand for a return to the recent past but a yearning for an end to the unbearable present. The expression was no longer anti-Jacobin but a vault into another register of understanding. Thus, in *messidor* (June 1794), about a thousand faithful gathered in the fields outside Mortain in the Manche to hear a nocturnal Mass recited by a priest whom people believed was a direct agent of God. In the Cornouailles region of the Côtes-du-Nord, around St John the Baptist's Day (24 June), the Virgin began appearing to announce the end of the world and St Michael to warn of God's vengeance. To forestall divine wrath, crowds of barefooted people journeyed great distances to pray at local shrines and sanctuaries. Near Le Mans, the military commission executed a young Vendean woman. Very soon, the story got round that the horses sent to haul her body away could not budge it, no matter how hard they pulled. The spot became a pilgrimage site where cures occurred. Sometimes a priest was not even necessary to conduct clandestine worship. In the canton of Buxy in the Saône-et-Loire, later a stronghold of the 'Petite Eglise', people seized the churches, recited prayers 'in Latin' and laymen performed 'white Masses' in which people acted out every aspect of the regular Mass except the blessing of the host. As we shall see, women had a big role in these ceremonies. There were similar practices in the countryside. Around Auxerre, burly men with muskets guarded the churches while the faithful inside practised their own version of Mass. This region had accepted overwhelmingly the Civil Constitution and was massively non-practising in the next century but attempts to remove the priests or close the churches were a constant source of disturbance and riot throughout the Year II all the same. In the Loire in the autumn of 1794, after the Terror had ended but before anyone could absorb the significance of the event, people began to sell or give away their worldly goods. They took refuge in the woods and when they were arrested, they all said their names were 'Bonjour'. This was the surname of one of their leaders, a priest. Upon further investigation, it turned out they had decided to travel to Palestine, after having made a penance in the desert, and once in the Promised Land, they would establish the 'Republic of Jesus Christ', a land of no kings and no priests. To get there 'Moses' would part the waters. There was more than one Moses, as it turned out, and one of them was a woman, like Mary Magdalene, a former prostitute.

When they heard of it, the representatives on mission took their cue: it was a plot, it was ridiculous, it was an insult to Reason, the 'grossest illusions', and so on. And fair enough. What better example could there be of the clash between the Century of Light and this revival of a medieval heresy? Many arrests followed but in the end, no one was prosecuted. In any case, the representatives said sarcastically, Moses would do them no good; they had forgotten to apply for passports.

But there could also be no better example of the huge cultural difference between the men of the Revolution and ordinary folk. Upon thorough investigation, representatives decided that there were three priests behind this nonsense, all of whom had developed a rather disturbing theology as far back as the Old Regime. But what they did not admit was that these three had no following at all until the dechristianization. They had impressed a few gullible colleagues and a handful of nuns, but they had little or no following among the laity. Only in the Year II did the laity begin to divest themselves of their worldly goods and dream of establishing the reign of the Third Testament, the reign of Love, in the Holy Land. Even after their arrest, the uninhibited theology of these adepts evolved. By the time of Napoleon, they were dreaming of the conversion of the Jews and the gentiles, and rejecting the divinity of the Virgin Mary. One of the priests eventually fathered a son, baptised 'Israel-Elijah'. With the most fantastic background of any child ever born in France, he rejected the role of prophet that had been cast for him ('John the Precursor', the second prophet, may never have existed). He died as a successful businessman and as a colonel in the National Guard in 1866.

The drama of the story certainly overwhelms any editorial comment, but one remark might be that the escape into an utterly fantastic imaginary was a function of dechristianization. In most places, people opposed dechristianization and demanded a return to the past. Elsewhere the pain of having normal mental universes assaulted produced something more than an equal and opposite reaction. There people drew upon rare cultural models and then took them a step further, a step the official Church would never have authorized or even recognized. Ecclesiastics would have been as one with the revolutionaries that this was absurd. But then for ordinary folk, the priests were gone, only the troubled ones remained. Because France is a country where the past never disappears but only fades to the side of the stage, this cult survived until the Second World War.

The extent to which refractories practised at the height of the Terror cannot be known but a number of diocesan archives still contain the little notebooks in which some recorded baptisms and marriages. They were occasionally caught and executed, every guillotining providing an extensive martyrology for the faithful in the next century.

More than any other aspect, dechristianization was the face of the Terror for ordinary people in both town and country. Outside the civil war zones, repression did not affect large numbers of people. It was always possible to live outside the controlled economy. Hiding a few sacks of grain or disguising one's wealth from the sporadic control of amateurs in the towns was comparatively easy for a peasantry that had defrauded tax collectors for centuries. With the complicity of neighbours, it was even possible to avoid conscription. But it was impossible to avoid dechristianization and many people resented it. It is not difficult to see why. Since one aim of popular religion was an attempt to control and manipulate the caprices of an omnipresent and potentially malevolent supernatural world through ceremony and liturgy, efforts to substitute different beliefs and practices were not only meaningless, they were harmful. What could the government do faced with peasants in northern Burgundy who attributed a hailstorm that destroyed two thirds of their vines to 'the disappearance of their priests and their stone saints?' Dechristianization then shows the many diverse strands that made up the assault on Christianity, or rather on traditional religion of all sorts since rabbis and Jewish men with beards were also persecuted. Catholic writers in the nineteenth century never tired of drawing a heavy black line from the Enlightenment straight to the persecution of the Church. Unfortunately the Church they had in mind was the refractory church and they had no more use for the constitutional than the most uninhibited dechristianizer. And that is the critical issue, the constitutional church was the target of the dechristianization campaign. In that sense, this aspect of the Terror was a product of circumstance, a desire to smite the counterrevolution, to undermine it totally by suppressing its religious expression; and also to create the new republican, an individual purged of the vices and corruption of the old order. In that sense, dechristianization or the utopian project and repression might be related. The question then becomes whether the Terror as repression attempted to refashion human nature, or whether it fought counterrevolution.

7

The Language of Terror

One can try to explain the causes [of the Terror], but who has the courage to excuse it? I was a witness and when I think back on it, I am terrified by my own memories, my soul remains burdened, and my pen refuses, as it were, to describe them.

Antoine-Claire Thibaudeau, *Mémoires sur la Convention, et le Directoire* (1824), p. 44

The Terror was necessary at the time. Should we apologize for it? Not me anyway. Among those who blame us are the royalists of every colour, their hatred is in the nature of things. There are also the weak and inconsequential patriots; these people do not understand, with them every explanation is useless; besides it is not our responsibility to implant intelligence in all the moral freaks [*disgrâces*] of nature.

Marc-Antoine Baudot, *Notes historiques sur la Convention nationale, le directoire, l'empire et l'exil des votants.* (1893), p. 254–5

By early August 1793, all thoughts of a federalist offensive were out of the question. Communications between Lyon and Marseille were slowly cut throughout July, neighbouring departments that had joined the chorus against 2 June accepted the Constitution and federalism in Normandy, Brittany and Bordeaux collapsed. Within the remaining anti-Jacobin cities, the poor response to the military levies, the indecision and quarrelling among the leaders and the unwillingness, whether through remaining pro-Jacobin sentiment or simply indifference, of large pockets of the urban populations to respond to increasingly authoritarian measures, threw the intransigent federalists into desperation. Although the Marseille army did occupy Avignon, it failed to take Orange and was defeated by a small army under General Carteaux on

11 and 19 August. On the 25th Carteaux entered Marseille and many of the most compromised fled to Toulon. Detachments of the Lyon army were forced to withdraw from Saint-Etienne three days later while Montbrison was occupied on 9 September. Lyon itself took longer. Although the siege had begun on 8 August, the Convention's forces were divided because of fears of a Piedmontese attack over the Alps. The terrible bombardment did not begin for some time and the exhausted city finally surrendered on 9 October. This left Toulon, which finally succumbed on 18 December once republican forces captured the forts overlooking the city and the artillery under Captain Bonaparte could threaten the allied fleets in the port below.

There were significant victories along the northern frontiers as well. The Battle of Hondschoote on 8 September forced the British forces to lift the siege of Dunkirk and the Battle of Wattignies on 16 October forced the Austrians to lift that of Maubeuge. Although neither battle was entirely decisive, they did compel the allied armies to begin a slow retreat. By the end of the year, the Austrians and Prussians had also been pushed out of Alsace. Thus, as the respective combatants settled into their winter quarters, the Republic could carry on its internal struggles safe from the foreign enemy.

The most dangerous internal enemy, the Vendean armies, remained. After their massive defeat at Cholet in mid-October, the Vendean generals finally decided to cross the Loire to stir up Brittany, Maine and Normandy and to receive arms from the British fleet at one of the coastal ports. The crossing of perhaps 30,000 fighting men, their families, priests and noble officers was accomplished on 17 October and victories at Château-Gontier, Laval and Mayenne against a republican army one third their size were fairly easy. But communications with the British were extraordinarily difficult to maintain and at one time the Vendeans appeared to be making for Saint-Malo until they headed north again to Granville. Desperately short of ammunition, they had to break off a twenty-six-hour siege of Granville on 13–14 November. This failure was the beginning of the end. The British expedition could not be readied in time and only sailed to the coast of Normandy weeks later. Only a few hundred Bretons and Normans, who began to call themselves 'chouans', even joined the Vendeans. Now, after Granville, exhausted and defeated, the rank-and-file royalists only wanted to go home and so they were increasingly unresponsive to their leaders. But the republicans were strong enough to prevent the re-crossing of the Loire and inflicted a progressive series of defeats at Pontorson, Dol, Antrain, Angers and Le Mans on a wandering and visibly disintegrating army. The royalists had to abandon their dead and wounded, camp-followers straggled behind, food and munitions were desperately low and many were suffering from dysentery. Finally, a republican army under General Westermann smashed the Vendeans at Savenay in the Loire-Inférieure on 23 December. Thousands of royalist soldiers and civilians were killed in the battle itself or shot in subsequent mopping-up operations, thousands of others died in the forests and bogs and thousands more were jammed into makeshift prisons in nearby Nantes. The 'great war' of the Vendée, the 'war of the giants', as the local historians call it, was over. The repression could begin.

Terror

The repression of the Year II is the most notorious aspect of the period and no historian has ever been neutral on the subject. In terms of historical background, the Terror as repression was an episode of the dialectic of revolution–counterrevolution that was a theme of the entire period. Legally, there were precedents for the judicial repression of this sort that went back to the Old Regime. The prevotal courts of the old monarchy had many of the same powers as the revolutionary courts in that both could inflict capital penalties without appeal. The difference was one of scale. The prevotal courts of the Old Regime judged on a much smaller scale. These similarities between the courts continued after the fall of Robespierre. People were executed before the Terror for counterrevolution and exceptional jurisdictions were used after, most notably courts martial in the west up to the Year IV or military commissions against so-called brigands in the Midi in the Year IX. In all cases, these special courts were supposed to operate quickly and without appeal and so have a greater deterrent effect than ordinary courts. In terms of legal and institutional history, therefore, such courts were a feature throughout the period, irrespective of the rhetoric of the politicians and whether or not they were derived from the discourse of the Enlightenment.

As for the Terror *per se*, the Revolutionary Tribunal in Paris and the five others established in imitation in the provinces were most like regular courts in structure and proceedings until the law of 22 *prairial* (10 June 1794) allowed the jury to convict on the basis of moral certainty of guilt. The sixty-odd military commissions, or the dozen or so revolutionary commissions, differed only in that the military or civilian judges also acted as juries (as in the Old Regime). All gathered evidence and execution was supposed to take place within twenty-four hours of conviction. Most of the convictions took place under the law of 19 March 1793 that specified death if the accused were found armed in a counterrevolutionary assembly. Thousands of Vendeans met their deaths because of this law and its successors.

At first the exceptional jurisdictions were supposed to target specific groups of enemies. After all, the Jacobins believed popular opposition to the Revolution could not possibly be authentic or sincere. People who acted against them were obviously misled. Even Marat, for all his blood-thirstiness, demanded that the law of 19 March be applied only to leaders. Several factors contributed to breaking these caveats down. One was the rationale behind the courts themselves. From the infamous Revolutionary Tribunal in Paris to the most humble and short-lived, they were all supposed to settle scores and strike fear into the hearts of enemies. As the representative Maignet put it when requesting the establishment of the notorious Popular Commission of Orange, 'We have to terrify and the blow is frightening only so long as it falls before the eyes of those who have lived among the guilty'. In a sense, therefore, all the trials before the revolutionary tribunals were political in that they were supposed to impress the communities in which they took place with the inflexible power of the Montagnards. Punishment was supposed to be exemplary and to accomplish this aim, it had to be terrible. The infamous representative on mission at Nantes, Carrier, ordered that all those 'wearing a sign of rebellion' be killed and their property destroyed: 'let the most terrible examples frighten the rebels and those tempted to imitate them . . . . Severity alone can stop the wickedness of rebels.' Moreover, with such widely defined powers and with such extraordinary results expected of them, internal procedures protecting elementary justice in some of the courts quickly broke down. One judge on the Commission of Orange complained of another judge that he 'is worthless, absolutely worthless, at his job; sometimes his opinion is to save counter-revolutionary priests; he has to have proofs, as with the ordinary courts of the Old Regime'. Dorfeuille, president of one of the Lyons tribunals, informed the Convention of the problems of judging under chaotic conditions. 'We had neither written proofs, nor eye-witness testimony,' he said, 'Often we had to read the crime on the face of the guilty'. It is hard to believe, too, that the rapid interrogation of batches of ten, twenty and thirty people at a time at Angers, Nantes, Rennes, Lyon and elsewhere assured anything like a fair trial. But then the law itself only required establishing the presence of the accused at a counterrevolutionary assembly. Sometimes the tribunals stretched even that requirement. The commissions that operated in Brittany and Maine assumed a person was a part of the Vendean campaign beyond the Loire if that person had an address from south of the Loire and had been captured along the army's route.

On 5 *floréal* An II (24 April 1794), 21 people were tried before the Revolutionary Tribunal of Marseille. None had an attorney present, none called defence witnesses, no one asked for time to examine the evidence.

Not all the accused were tied to the same case so the judges must have had some difficulty keeping the stories straight and given the hours the court sat, each defendant would have had about 20 minutes of the court's time. The President of the court asked each witness what he had done for the Revolution, and received sad, laconic answers: 'Only what an old man, overwhelmed with infirmities can do . . . I have always been submissive to authority and I do it out of duty. I lead a very retired life.' For distributing papal bulls this man was executed. Earlier, the President, far from being impartial, accused another defendant: 'You have shown yourself to be an excellent counterrevolutionary, moderate in the moments of the Revolution, and crazed [*enragé*] in the time of the sections [that is, during the federalist revolt]. You deposed against patriots'. By early evening the day's trial was over. Everyone had been found guilty.

It is not easy to assess the performance of all the revolutionary courts. Many had a record as shocking as that of Marseille. The Commission Militaire Bignon in the Loire-Inférieure, for example, was judging 170–200 people a day at the beginning. Before it settled in Nantes, it followed the army. In three days, it condemned 660 people to death. There was not a single acquittal. It once sentenced 210 villagers from Bouguenais to death in a collective trial, and over its five month existence may have executed up to 3000 people. Often, there was no trial as such, an accused appeared, heard his or her sentence, and was marked with an F or a G, indicating whether they should be shot (*fusillé*) or guillotined. The Commission Félix in Angers condemned 658 people to death in three days in early February 1794; 465 were women.

Georges Lefebvre attempted to mitigate the appalling record of tribunals like this by insisting how many acquittals there were. There is in the archives of some of these courts a sizeable mass of paper that shows the judges and officials were trying in their own minds to weed out the innocent from the guilty. But in no civilized society is it sufficient to allow the officials of a court to make that decision in advance by consulting only with each other. Some historians have relied on this mass of paper in the tribunals' archives to claim that those who were executed probably really were guilty. Or they have claimed the tribunals interpreted the law as best they could. But there was no law that permitted the *Commission militaire* in Bordeaux to execute people who had been magistrates on the old *parlement*, no law that permitted the execution of suspects, no law that permitted the execution of businessmen for following their vocation, that is for *négociantisme*, as it was called. One wonders what law the Paris Revolutionary Tribunal used to condemn the members of the Department of Paris at the time of the Affair of the Champ de Mars, the former Farmers-General, close to forty of the magistrates in the old Parlement of Paris, and some former royal intendants. After this, would anyone claim that people who were convicted after 20 minute trials had received due process?

Not all of the courts functioned with such a shocking disregard for elementary justice even within the civil war zones. The first military commission established at Angers functioned for only two weeks because it refused to condemn enough people. Despite the impressive range of powers, two of the three revolutionary courts in the Loire showed a maddening attachment to ordinary rules of evidence while the third was active for less than a week. The revolutionary tribunal of Strasbourg punished mostly economic crimes like violations of price controls, and limited itself to fines rather than inflicting the death penalty. Since regular judges and lawyers frequently dominated revolutionary tribunals, they found it difficult to shed professional scruples overnight. This also meant that using the judicial system to overawe enemies did not always succeed – a phenomenon that must have been a good deal more common than is usually thought since only five departments were responsible for nearly 70 per cent of all death sentences, while only thirteen were responsible for 90 per cent. Not too surprisingly, these areas of heavy repression were the *Vendée militaire*, the western departments north of the Loire through which the Vendeans marched, the federalist cities of the Midi, particularly Lyon, Marseille and Toulon, and finally Paris. These regions, too, witnessed great atrocities on top of 'official' repression. The march of General Turreau's 'infernal columns' through the Vendée apart, among these atrocities were the representative Francastel's orders to shoot two thousand people without trial near Angers and the shooting of eight hundred people immediately after the fall of Toulon upon simple identification by local Jacobins. Thus the cycle of reprisal and counter reprisal that began earlier continued under the Terror. It would continue afterwards.

Moving the revolutionary apparatus could be frustrating and urging the representatives on mission to be severe was more or less continuous. For example, the representatives in Marseille were told to exercise 'the greatest severity against the traitors'. Carrier's instructions were 'to avoid softness at Nantes, that compassion would be possible only after victory'. Others were told to be severe, to not spare the guilty, that all revolutionary measures were imperative. Robespierre himself demanded 'terrible examples' against the federalist cities, against 'all the wicked who have outraged liberty'. Such admonitions were ceaseless throughout the period. The Committee of Public Safety, despite many claims that it was a force that moderated dangerous fanatics in the provinces, or that it was ignorant of atrocities, never opted for 'indulgence' as it was called at the time. The speeches of its members in the Convention and its instructions to generals and representatives in the field would certainly give the impression that the most extravagant violence was permissible.

After all, pitiless repression was the obverse of the slogan that moderation was counterrevolutionary. An examination of repression in the provinces illustrates the point.

After its fall on 9 October, Lyon became a proving ground for a whole range of radical, and *sans-culotte* ideas that were implemented only sporadically elsewhere. Couthon, who had helped direct the siege, believed that a moderate policy of repression, rather than wholesale punishment, was all that was required. The Jacobins that the federalists imprisoned were released and the club reopened. Revolutionary committees in each of the thirty-two sections were formed under the overall supervision of a city-wide surveillance committee who together were to seek out suspects and counterrevolutionaries. These in turn were to be judged and dispatched by two special tribunals. Between 12 October and 1 December, the two tribunals passed death sentences on 209 people, no small number but nothing in comparison to what was to come.

But moderation was not popular in Paris. Ever since the conspiracies in Lyon in 1790, radical circles had seen the city as infested with counterrevolutionaries, and after the conquest they were determined to set an example. Robespierre himself supported a policy of pitiless vengeance, and on 10 October Saint-Just gave a famous speech declaring there could be no quarter between the Revolution and its enemies. Two days later the Convention ordered the houses of the rich destroyed, the sequestration of the property of those same rich and the counterrevolutionaries (the income to be used to aid the poor), the change of the city's name to Ville-Affranchie (Liberated City) and the construction of a monument for posterity bearing the inscription: 'Lyon fit la guerre à la Liberté; Lyon n'est plus.' The destruction that followed thus took place within an overall framework provided by the Convention. Collot d'Herbois, a member of the Committee of Public Safety, and Fouché, both thought to be more ruthless, replaced Couthon who was recalled. Collot had been an actor and playwright who knew his stagecraft and Fouché had already considerable experience in the Nièvre with public display. They organized a dechristianization ceremony that as a single event illustrates the mawkish and sentimental religiosity of the movement as a whole. On 10 November, officials organized an elaborate ceremony that showed how much the revolutionaries plagiarized traditional Catholic modes of expression. Dorfeuille, former stage manager, now, President of the Commission of Popular Justice at Lyon, delivered Chalier's eulogy. He contrasted the impurity of Lyon, the new Sodom, with the holy Chalier, and implored the Supreme Being to pay attention to republicans who were on their knees in supplication. Chalier's body was exposed to 'public veneration', Collot reported, 'Tears flowed from every eye at the sight of the dove that accompanied and consoled him in his frightful prison and that seemed to lament before his image.' The head was shipped off to the Convention as a relic but not before an ass dressed in a bishop's mitre and staff was paraded around the square while assistants sprinkled incense. Holy objects were then smashed on Chalier's tomb. Criticism of the great and the powerful through burlesque was a very old European tradition while the use of donkeys in public ceremonies often symbolized humiliation or even death. But traditional folklore was only a temporary release and generally acted to reinforce regular authority. Despite the obvious borrowing of religious vocabulary and ceremony, Collot's staging was clearly blasphemous, not titillating, and was meant to have a far more liberating effect.

Indeed there was a great deal of theatre in the joint mission as a whole. Gruesome as it sounds, this is ultimately what lay behind the mass shootings. The *Commission Temporaire*, a body that was supposed to supplement and stimulate regular administration that became a hotbed of extremism, put it well: the object of the shootings was 'the complete and entire execution of the judgement [of the Revolutionary Commission] that will be accomplished in a manner to imprint terror without exciting pity'. Or, as Fouché and the other representatives said, 'we are sceptical of the tears of repentance, nothing can disarm our severity; indulgence is a dangerous weakness, liable to rekindle criminal hopes...devouring flames alone can express the total power of the people'. In other words, the flames were meant to cleanse, to destroy the diseased body of the city.

The shootings were also designed to alter the outlook of the Lyonnais. Collot reported that after the long siege, the population appeared indifferent to death, and the sluggish pace of the revolutionary tribunal, even at 20 capital convictions a day, was having no effect; '...the justice of the whole people...ought to crush [*foudroyer*] all its enemies simultaneously, and we are forging the thunderbolt'. Several other revolutionary officials spoke of the great effect of an immense, sudden blow against enemies.

On 14 *frimaire* (4 December), 60 people bound to a rope, before already dug graves on the meadow of Les Brotteaux, were mowed down by cannon balls and grapeshot and then finished off with musket fire. The next day, 208 met a similar fate. On the first day of the shootings women demonstrated to save their husbands and sons. For that, soldiers not only scattered them, Collot and his colleagues denounced them as having conspired against 'all of humanity'. He also claimed the women had been caught, 'disguised as men [*travesties*], armed, hidden during the night', in the representatives' hotel. Even on this great day that had been planned for weeks, a day that was supposed to echo down the centuries to express the awesome power of the Republic, people in masks lurked in order to destroy. But there were only two *mitraillades*, as they were called, because onlookers were appalled that not everyone was killed at once, that so many victims died in agony. Far from shocking the Lyonnais, far from meting out a lesson to this contaminated people, the *mitraillades* sickened them. Even so, the executions continued apace, without the recriminations between the representatives and the generals over who had bungled the great example. Of the 1667 actual victims of the representatives' Revolutionary Commission that shortly assumed responsibility from Couthon's slower courts, 935 people were shot and 732 guillotined over its 130 day existence.

Terror and social experiment were joined. Fouché imposed punitive taxes on the rich and graded their weight to political opinions; guaranteed state aid to the poor, the old and the infirm; ordered full employment for every trade; commanded the baking of a single type of bread, the *pain de l'égalité*; requisitioned surplus clothing and ordered everyone to wear wooden shoes at home. It would be interesting to know how devastating this garrison equality was to the upper classes of Lyon. Certainly, the confiscation of all the property of the condemned must have been disastrous, even if many were aristocrats whose property was outside the city. Yet there were limits. For all the bombast about blowing up or burning down buildings because the ordinary work of demolition was going too slowly, only the facades of a number of town houses, a hundred or so buildings and the fortifications were destroyed. Indeed, this aspect of the punishment was once again more theatre than anything else. In a kind of reverse ribbon cutting ceremony, some dignitaries took a few symbolic whacks with a hammer at one house that was slated for demolition because of its 'royal magnificence' but little else was done to wreck Lyon. In fact, the Jacobin municipality that was supposed to oversee the job had no money to pay demolition workers.

The attempt to intimidate the population had the opposite effect. From the Year III onwards, Lyon was the headquarters of vicious counter-terrorist murder gangs. There was a lesson too for the popular militants. The revolutionary committees of Lyon were among the most *sans-culotte* in the country, with almost all of their members shopkeepers and artisans; one third, no less, were silk weavers. But what kind of power was it to arrest neighbours when overall authority was exercised by men including the representatives, the detachments of the Paris revolutionary army and the *Commission Temporaire* who bore themselves as foreign conquerors and who distrusted even the friendly natives because after all, they had failed before the federalist onslaught and in any case, they were not 'à la hauteur?' The *sans-culottes* in Paris, too, would find the same disillusioning experience of exercising power in a dictatorship.

At first the *noyades* at Nantes appear to conform to the model Pierre Caron developed for the September massacres. This too was a series of prison massacres in which 2–4000 Vendeans may have drowned when prisoners were loaded on to old boats that were then scuttled at the mouth of the Loire. The Caron model would call attention to the over-crowded prisons at Nantes after the battle of Savenay, the British navy cruising unhindered off shore, and the army of Charette, the most wily of the Vendean generals lurking outside the town walls, an army that was still intact because Charette refused to cross the Loire with his comrades. There was always the danger the prisoners would escape, turn the city over to Charette who in turn would link up with the British. After all, the republicans knew from captured correspondence that the British would land only when the Vendeans captured a port on their own.

Attractive as such an explanation might be, it does not work. Carrier, the representative on mission whose name is so fatefully tied to the *noyades*, and the revolutionary committee, did not see themselves as acting in this context. Indeed, their motive was hardly defensive at all. Grandmaison, one of the members of the revolutionary committee, later justified the *noyades* in halting prose as

> legitimate measures and imperiously required by the circumstances... Nantes found itself confronted with the hard necessity of making a calcu-lation to sacrifice useless and criminal mouths; several drownings *[subver-sions]* were made...The shortage of subsistence, a prison insurrection had broken out, a contagious disease that threatened to spread in this city, required the representative of the people to send away 128 prison-ers...It is after this true and exact picture that the revolutionary commit-tee decided to assist in the salvation of the people of Nantes in expelling this horde of conspirators and guilty ones from its walls....

Carrier himself boasted about his activities both to the Convention and to the Committee of Public Safety. On 16 *frimaire*, he wrote, 'the priests have found their tomb in the Loire. 53 others are going to follow them'. On 2 *nivôse*, he referred to the 'miracles of the Loire that has just swallowed up 360 counterrevolutionaries from Nantes'. 'Oh, what a revolutionary torrent is the Loire'.

Carrier has the infamous reputation he has because Robespierre's enemies after the fall of the Incorruptible attempted to use Carrier's trial and execution as a way of expiating for all the atrocities in the west. But there were other atrocities elsewhere, most of which were never punished. It was said that one extremist general had ordered the shooting and drowning of 12–1500 Vendeans at Angers. The representative Fran-castel supported him without a qualm. There were *noyades* at Saumur, Ancenis, Ponts-de-Cé, Château-Gontier, and Angers. There were shoot-ings of prisoners at Savenay, Tours, Blois, Chinon, and along the road to

Orléans. The representative Lequinio reported to the Convention that he had given the order that 4–500 prisoners at Fontenay-le-Compte in the Vendée were to be shot 'without any form of trial', if the enemy was reported to be in the vicinity. He personally shot a prisoner directly in the head at Rochefort before an assembled crowd of soldiers and inmates in the prison yard because, he later claimed, this example would forestall any thoughts of a prison breakout that would hand the port over to the British. Another representative, Levasseur [de la Sarthe] ordered the shooting of prisoners when those in a convoy from Angers to Orléans tried to escape.

In short, the attitude was one of defiance and vengeance, not fear and panic. On appointing one man to preside over the Commission at Angers, the representative Francastel informed him, 'I know your principles, your republican inflexibility, your unswerving intention to purge, to bleed this Vendean generation white'. The president of the revolutionary committee of Nantes, Bachelier, later explained, 'We were all inflamed; we believed that when one acted for the people, nothing could be bad, a mistake, or a crime'. To quote General Westermann after the Battle of Savenay in December, 1793:

> The Vendée is no more. It is dead under my sabre, with its women and children. I just buried it in the swamps and the woods of Savenay. I crushed children under the hoofs of my horses, massacred women who, at least for them, will not give birth to any more brigands. I took no prisoners, I exterminated them all.... The highways are piled high with corpses. There are so many that in some places, they are piled in pyramids.... Pity is not revolutionary.

Nor were such attitudes confined to the west. After the shootings at Lyon, the terrorist Achard exulted, 'Still more heads and every day the heads fall! What delicacies you would taste,' he reported to his correspondent, 'if you had seen the day before yesterday, this national justice against 209 wicked people! What majesty! What an imposing note [*ton*]!...What a bond for the Republic!' Another of his colleagues spoke of how the guillotine restored his health. Dorfeuille, the same who gave the lugubrious eulogy for Chalier, spoke of the coming massacres on the Place des Brotteaux, as 'a great act of national vengeance...[such that] in the most far off centuries, traitors will be terrified should they imagine a revolt against the French Republic'. Collot borrowed Chalier's image of floating bodies in the Rhône: the bloody corpses of those guillotined at Lyon would drift down the river before the walls of 'the infamous Toulon', [Toulon is not at the mouth of the Rhône] he claimed, and thereby terrify the English. But the English were not really the audience for such appalling remarks, the Convention was. No one protested this post-mortem, this entirely imaginary, *noyade*. Like Chalier before them, for men like these, for Collot d'Herbois, for General Westermann and others, execution was not a regrettable punishment, a last resort; instead, it was a triumph, an ecstasy, a celebration, an elixir.

In the civil war zones, the army captured most of the defendants who appeared before the tribunals. Elsewhere, this was the responsibility of the revolutionary committees. They were supposed to have been established in every commune in the land according to the law of 21 March 1793 but few were until the passage of the Law of Suspects on 17 September 1793. Among other categories, it defined suspects as those who had shown themselves to be partisans 'of tyranny, of federalism and enemies of liberty'. Suspects were to be imprisoned or held under house arrest by the revolutionary committees. With this terrible power, the committees acquired a new lease of life, particularly after the arrival of an energetic representative on mission who was often responsible for stimulating their foundation or their reinvigorated activity. Either because the power was delegated to them, or because they took it on themselves, the committees also involved themselves in purging the administration, collecting revolutionary taxes and valuables from churches and private individuals, drafting lists of the local poor, tearing down crosses and offensive signs, searching out deserters, censoring mail, stamping passports, enforcing the Maximum, delivering 'certificats de civisme' without which no one could occupy an official post, closing churches and imposing the *décadi*, and even enforcing local police regulations like those on cheese production or gambling. In short, the committees were administrative bodies which supplemented or usurped the work of the regular organs of government, and since they had close relations with the club, which often named its own members to staff them, the committees brought to local power the uninhibited and the zealous which revolutionary government required in order to function.

The committees were undoubtedly effective instruments of revolutionary government but there were limitations on their activities. There were comparatively few of them. Local studies of the Loire and the districts of Le Mans in the Sarthe, Mâcon in the Saône-et-Loire and Saint-Pol in the Pas-de-Calais indicate a rather uneven implantation, with committees usually only in the principal centres, in larger villages along main roads or rivers or at important crossroads. The exception was Upper Normandy and Provence. In both places there were hundreds of committees, and in the Bouches-du-Rhône, most towns and villages had one. Elsewhere, the few rural committees were not very active because they were hampered, as the municipalities had been earlier, by the lack of literate talent and because country people still preferred to settle disputes among themselves. One rural committee in Normandy actually protected the refractory priest and not many cooperated in implementing price controls. The committee of Rognac in the Bouches-du-Rhône had to be goaded into making any arrests at all by a dismayed municipality and even then it released them as soon as it could. Others, like that of Istres, also in the Bouches-du-Rhône, had to cope with popular hostility, particularly from local women who wanted their menfolk left alone. Several committees in the Haute-Vienne arrested no one, and more often than not, their members held their meetings, decided there was nothing to do, signed the register and went home.

Even the urban committees showed varying degrees of zeal. That of Saint-Pol arrested 1460, Toulouse close to 1000, Dijon around 400, Nancy 334, Dax around 300, and so on. As with dechristianization, waves of arrests depended on the stimulus of a representative on mission as when Saint-Just and Le Bon ordered the arrest of all nobles and wives of suspects in the Pas-de-Calais. Since the more sincere revolutionaries were aware of the terrible power the Law of Suspects gave them, the committees and representatives often reviewed suspects' cases even before the Convention ordered this in *ventôse* (February) and so there were numerous releases throughout the period. This makes it very difficult to estimate how many suspects there were but it seems that Louis Jacob's estimate of seventy thousand is about right. If it is, it means that less than 0.5 per cent of the population was arrested as suspects. But the upper bound of this figure, and certainly the lower, revealed a substantial range. In Paris, about 10,000 people were arrested as suspects, or about 2 per cent of the population, the overwhelming majority of them from the old Third Estate. In many other places, no one was arrested as a suspect.

It was not the relatively few arrested but their essential arbitrariness and the fact there was no formal appeal against arrest that made the committees such effective agents of the Jacobin dictatorship. Who would ever have expected, for example, the arrest of one unfortunate individual at Draguignan in the Var because he was 'suspect of suspicion?' Who would ever have expected the arrest of one unfortunate woman in Clermont-Ferrand for having 'closed her window when the victories of our armies were shouted out in the street?' Or the former counsellor-clerk in the former Parlement of Bordeaux living in Limoges, who despite having done good things for the Revolution was tainted, according to the committee, with a 'triple leprosy' of an untranslatable 'aristo-clérico-rabino-cratique' background.

The committees also had a long reach. Thanks to the zeal of the committee of Saint-Pol in the Pas-de-Calais, 85 per cent of the communes in the entire district witnessed at least one arrest. This example too shows another characteristic of the committees: their urban base. In the Puy-de-Dôme, the larger the commune, the greater the proportion of the population arrested as suspects. In the more remote mountainous regions no one was arrested as a suspect even though sympathy for the refractory priests was ubiquitous. Presumably, the few local revolutionaries were wise enough not to antagonize their neighbours. Everywhere, the committees were keen dechristianizers and zealous enforcers of the Maximum. They thus became instruments of urban control over the countryside, another solution, like the National Guards earlier, to the problem of disciplining the peasantry.

For all that, the committees reflected local concerns. That of Narbonne in the Aude, for example, was so remote from national rhythms that it tried to find a confessor for the soldiers in the hospital. Nancy was so illiberal as to demand the expulsion of Jews from the Republic. Every committee tended to arrest people whom it thought backed the local version of the counterrevolution. All prisons housed their fair share of suspect nobles, wives and daughters of émigrés, nuns who refused the civic oath and so on, but in Toulouse well over two thirds of the suspects were from the two former privileged orders while at Dijon about half were. In these cities, where aristocratic power had focussed greatly on the *parlements*, the committees contributed more than any other revolutionary institution visibly to overturning the old social order. Elsewhere, however, counterrevolution wore a different mask and so the victims came from different social categories. In some districts of the Puy-de-Dôme, a suspect was someone who tried to slow or block recruitment efforts for the army. Almost all the suspects at Fontenay-le-Comte on the very edge of the *Vendée militaire* were artisans or labourers who were thought to be sympathetic to the rebels. Further away from the civil war zones, 'fanaticism' was often one of the most important reasons for arrest. Thus at Montauban in the Lot, nearly half the suspects were country people and 'complicity with the refractories' was the third largest category of those arrested. For the committee of Sainte-Foy-la-Grande in the Gironde, 'fanatics' were the second largest category, while at Sainte-Geniez-d'Olt in the Aveyron, 25 of 44 rural suspects, who comprised once again over half the total, were arrested for trying to protect a refractory priest or for insulting the constitutional. Indeed, in some country districts of the Calvados, Côtes-du-Nord, Pas-de-Calais and Nord, a suspect was automatically someone who refused to go to the Mass of the constitutional priest. In short, for all the bombast against the rich in the Year II, the committees were less instruments of the class war than new institutions for the continuation of the local struggle against counterrevolution. The Civil Constitution of the Clergy may have been a dead letter by the Year II but the struggle against its enemies continued, as, of course, it did afterwards.

Putting terror on the order of the day meant implementing a goal that was common to the Jacobin club, to those in the capital to celebrate 10 August and to various extremists. In practice, it meant putting notorious enemies on trial. Thus, Brissot and 20 other Girondins went to their deaths on 31 October before huge crowds who threw their hats in the air when the 40 minutes it took to execute them all concluded. Some of them, like Brissot, went to their deaths puzzled but certain of their innocence, while some observers said they looked like scholars. Others embraced on the scaffold. All of them cried out 'Vive la République!' Some of the later victims were simply irrelevant, like Madame du Barry, former mistress of Louis XV, dragged from a convent and executed because her corruption, according to Prudhomme, was an impediment to France's regeneration.

Still another was Marie-Antoinette who died on 16 October. Prudhomme mocked her white dress and its intended symbolism, after she abandoned her mourning clothes. He unloaded an endless stream of vitriol. He retold every ugly story about her since her arrival in the kingdom in 1770: her hatred of France, her hatred of the French people, her spying, her adultery, her debauchery, her high living, her favouritism of the Polignacs, her theft of public funds, her greed, and on and on. Her moral corruption was at the centre of every plot, at the centre of every treason with Pitt and her Austrian relatives, at the centre of every attempt to starve Paris, and of every attempt to corrupt her simple husband into imposing his veto. Even from prison, it was said, she planned to have women, or priests disguised as women, murder patriots. Yet again, the literary device in such accusations was clear: transform the naïve, like women, or the ostensive denizens of peace, like priests, into shadowy and masked assassins, transvestites and hypocrites. In this telling, and from the accusations made at the trial itself, her depravity was more emphasized than specific treasons. Some of the references to debauchery and to intrusion into political life and to dominating her husband may have been meant to evoke the steady stream of earlier denunciations of overbearing and unnatural women in the public sphere, although Prudhomme did not make the connection explicit. But his text itself also had a more direct moralizing quality about it that recalled possibly Biblical warnings of female lust, greed and treachery, qualities that seduced weak men.

Hébert's *Père Duchesne* went over much of the same material and then claimed, 'Since she reigned, she has dreamed only of murder and carnage. More than once, men have been her victims and the crimes she committed are still only rose water in comparison to those she planned...' 'In spite of you, slut,' he sneered at her, 'you have had to experience the punishment of equality, because your punishment has been as sweet as those of the other guilty.' He ended by wishing her a second death. One of the jurors of the Revolutionary Tribunal wrote to his brother that they had judged 'a ferocious beast who devoured a great part of the Republic...'

Victims of the Terror

It is impossible to say how many people died as a result of the Terror. In Paris alone, the Revolutionary Tribunal put over 4000 people on trial and pronounced death sentences on close to two-thirds of them. In 1935, Donald Greer calculated that the various revolutionary courts sentenced 16,594 people to death. He estimated that another 10–12,000 people died in prison and still another 10–12,000 people were executed without trial in the civil war zones. His outside figure was that 40,000 people may have died as a direct result of the Terror. This figure is far too low. Within the *Vendée militaire* alone, the four departments south of the Loire where most of the horrible fighting took place, some 220–250,000 inhabitants may have lost their lives. The region lost somewhere between one-fifth and one-third of its population, and as we shall see, the devastation of some villages was far worse. This raises the figure for France as a whole far above Greer's estimate but how much higher the total national figure should be revised is unknown. The experience of the *Vendée militaire* illustrates a point that can be generalized to the nation as a whole: the principal victims of the Terror were ordinary people. According to Greer, roughly 6.5 per cent of the death sentences were pronounced on the clergy, 8 per cent on the nobility, 14 per cent 'upper middle class', 10.5 per cent 'lower middle class', 31 per cent 'working class' and 28 per cent peasants. Thus nearly two-thirds of the victims of the Terror were workers and peasants. Indeed, this was true even in Paris where the percentage breakdown of victims of the Revolutionary Tribunal was about the same. Also in Paris, about one in ten of the victims were women, again with a substantial proportion of victims from ordinary people, even though one fifth of the women victims whose backgrounds are known were nobles, and a tenth were nuns, and other females of religious background. Nuns were frequently executed because they were suspected of protecting a refractory priest or for storing holy objects used for saying the mass. Sometimes, even their aged domestics were executed too.

Relative to the population as a whole, however, these figures reveal different characteristics of the Terror. Victims were disproportionately male, and disproportionately from the upper ranks of society. Nobles and clerics were over-represented by a factor of three among the victims, and the 'middle class' was over-represented as well. In the Vendée, whole communities were involved in the rebellion so that no one group was more outstanding than another. The early hopes that the repression would be selective and would target mostly leaders, however, was clearly ignored. At Lyon, where the nobles, clergy and upper bourgeoisie dominated the federalist army and civilian administrations, punishment of these groups was exceptionally severe. Of the 1734 people whose occupations are known who were executed after the re-conquest, close to half were clerics, nobles, merchants, professionals and *rentiers*, that is from the well-off non-manual minority in the largest industrial city in the country. But the Convention's vengeance, descended into the world of work as well. The luxury, highly skilled and food and drink trades, all of them well remunerated in the Old Regime and long denounced by the Jacobin Central Club before the revolt, were over represented relative to other working groups; the non-silk textile and construction groups were about even; while the near absence of silk-workers, almost all of whom were too poor to qualify as active citizens in 1790, is remarkable. The example of Lyon again illustrates the selectivity of repression and suggests that the struggle between merchants and master-weavers, which had begun a half-century before, broadened into one between the rich and the poor.

For all its ferocity, the Terror was not random. This was particularly clear from an examination of the geography of repression. Only five departments were responsible for nearly 70 per cent of all death sentences, while only thirteen were responsible for 90 per cent. These areas of heavy repression were the *Vendée militaire*, the western departments north of the Loire through which the Vendeans marched, the federalist cities of the Midi, particularly Lyon, Marseille and Toulon, and finally Paris.

Discourses on Terror

In the minds of its practitioners, the Terror had several aims, and the importance of these varied over time and with the individual. Mastering revolutionary discourse, as Fouché maintained in his memoirs, was an art that anyone could acquire. Although the vocabulary became more and more extravagant with time, there remained certain fixed repertoires that contemporaries could draw upon. One of these was 'revolutionary government', another was 'repression', and a third was 'regeneration'. There were differences of meaning within each category, and there were even contradictions. For instance everyone embraced the concept of pristine innocence and children were above all innocent, even those of enemies.

Thus Carrier established orphanages for the children of Vendeans. A variant of the discourse on repression, however, was that whole groups could be guilty so Carrier also demanded the execution, even the murder of children. Thus revolutionary discourses were fluid, and individuals could draw on aspects of them depending upon the circumstances of the moment.

One illustration of this fluidity was the definition of 'revolutionary government'. At one level, nothing could be more simple to define. After all, the classical authors, and especially Cicero, who fashioned so much of the revolutionaries' education, agreed that under threat, the government had to take drastic measures with little concern for civil liberties. Thus the demand for exceptional measures was not necessarily extremist. Charles de Lameth, Feuillant anti-Jacobin, said at the time of the Flight to Varennes, 'Moments of crisis cannot follow the rigorous forms that it is a duty to follow in a period of calm .... [Following legal forms risks] delivering the state to the enemy... Better an injustice than to lose the state.' Robespierre, in his speech of 27 December 1793, distinguished revolutionary government from constitutional government. Revolutionary government was a government of national defence operating in stormy and rapidly changing circumstances 'because it is forced ceaselessly to deploy new and speedy resources to respond to new and pressing dangers'. But there could also be variants on this definition of revolutionary government as a government of exception. Others agreed with Robespierre that revolutionary government was a single will. Thus, a delegation from Arras, creating a baffling distinction, asked the Convention whether it was 'a powerful force that directs all the passions towards a single central point or... a volcano... that only gives signs of activity in belching [*vomissant*] smoke from a devouring fire?'

But there was a partisan element to saving the state, as well. According to Billaud-Varenne, another member of the Committee of Public Safety, revolutionary government 'will be terrible for the conspirators..., daunting to the wicked, protector of the oppressed... favourable to patriots [and] beneficent to the people ....' There was nothing incompatible between revolutionary government and a continuation of the political struggle against domestic enemies and the relics of the Old Regime. According to the representative, Albitte, revolutionary government was more than just saving the state, in addition 'it destroys fanaticism at its roots, annihilates the detestable remains of royalism and feudalism... crushes counter revolutionaries, federalists and villains,... [and] eradicates poverty....'

Such an aggressive agenda for revolutionary government also meant that there could be a range of opinions about how repressive the regime needed to be. The enemy's defeat had to be total, of course, and everyone knew the struggle could never be brief. Thus the 'regenerated republican society' of Varilhes urged the Convention to assure 'the traitors, the federalists, the intriguers, the hoarders, the selfish, the indifferent and this contemptible swarm of drones who buzz around the tree of liberty...that they will find in you enemies always ready to pursue them, always ready to strike them'. There could be no mercy for the guilty. The Committee of Public Safety reprimanded Couthon for allowing flatterers to seduce him while 'you must unmask the traitors and strike them without pity'. For St Just, 'what constitutes a Republic is the total destruction of what opposes it'. For a later Couthon, having learned what was expected of him, revolutionary justice 'was not a question of giving some examples, but of exterminating all the implacable satellites of tyranny'. Collot and Fouché claimed 'the only innocents in this ignominious city are those oppressed or enchained by the assassins of the people'. That is, only Jacobins were innocent, the rest were guilty. It was a logical step to dehumanize the enemy as well. Thus the representatives Pinet, Monestier and Cavaignac claimed the Basque country was 'so corrupted that we can hope for no progress in civic mindedness so long as the present generation continues to breathe; it is terror alone, and the most terrible punishments that can contain men who are royalist in their hearts and Spaniards by religious fanaticism and personal interest'. Consequently, some villages on the frontier were evacuated, and an 'Extraordinary Commission' was established whose purpose was to intimidate the wavering population: '...terror alone can prevent the machinations and the plots against the Republic....' It moved around from Bayonne, Dax, Auch and elsewhere and in less than two months, passed death sentences on a hundred people.

This sort of language moved from demands to punish the guilty to seeing entire regions as the enemy. In that case, the rhetoric moved from punishment to massacre. In the *Vendée militaire*, the representatives Hentz and Francastel declaimed, 'We are convinced that the Vendean war will be finished only when there will no longer be a single inhabitant in this miserable land'. Carrier, speaking to the Convention after his recall, thundered, 'Let no one speak of humanity towards these ferocious Vendeans, they will all be exterminated...We cannot leave a single rebel...Their women are all monsters...Kill all the rebels without mercy!'

Revolutionaries tended to think shadowy intriguers took advantage of the people's trust and that they had seduced them or that their enemies had totally corrupted the people. Seduction required forgiveness, perhaps after some hectoring about wrongdoing. Total, irretrievable corruption required extermination or forced resettlements. Thus, Couthon concluded the inhabitants of Lyon were corrupt because the heavy air at the confluence of the Saône and the Rhône had done something to their brains. An environmental explanation of political aberrance could require extermination but for Collot d'Herbois the sensible solution was to resettle the Lyonnais throughout the land so that they might breathe the free air of the Republic. Even so, succeeding generations will never be entirely pure because a servile spirit and lack of energy are hereditary because fathers would not overcome it through education. 'It is the *mère-patrie* to deploy every means to operate the regeneration of this great number of individuals...'

It was even possible to imagine an extermination that never took place. In January 1794, the Jacobin club in Paris undertook a bizarre debate designed to question the standard distinction between the corrupt government of Pitt as opposed to the virtuous English people, groaning under the yoke of slavery. Speaker after speaker denounced the failure of the oppressed people of England [not a word about the non-English inhabitants of the British Isles] to rise up and overthrow the imbecile oppressor and tyrant George III. The reason was the corruption of the people themselves. Centuries of despotism had rendered them degenerate, an echo of a debate the French had conducted about themselves in the Old Regime. The debate spilled over into the Convention itself where Barère declared the entire English people guilty of treason against humanity, that they were a group 'foreign to humanity: they must disappear'. This was an imagined genocide. This fevered debate had a consequence: the decree of 7 *prairial* An II that ordered the army to take no English prisoners, a decree that was probably never implemented – at least Robespierre reproached hidden enemies for not having enforced it on the eve of his fall. But the debate did show the mentality of atrocity very clearly: invoke the immorality of the enemy as evil or depraved or invoke the corporeal metaphor of the enemy's body as sick, gangrened, or whatever, and any reprisal was justified.

The mentality of extermination also joined with another: that the goal of the Revolution was to regenerate. This language had been used from the beginning. As early as 1789, many speakers and pamphleteers had remarked this was the occasion to regenerate the state of France. After the reforms had been passed, there were frequent statements that the French themselves had already been regenerated.

Just as grace transcends original sin, the new man, shorn of impurity, had been born in the miraculous, violent rupture with the past in 1789. That was how the wonderful experience of 1789 had appeared to many. But there was also a pessimistic language, reminiscent of the pre-revolutionary journalist Mairobert's, that the French had been corrupted too long with centuries of barbarism and they were too mired in hopeless frivolity. With growing resistance to the Revolution, this pessimistic version began to dominate, and with it the remedy that regeneration had to be forced. Brissot had demanded war in 1791 because it would 'purge [the people] of the vices of despotism, make those who corrupt them disappear.... War alone can equalize us all and regenerate our souls.' The coupling of violence and regeneration had thus occurred early in the Revolution but Robespierre gave it a new and original twist. In his speech of 5 February 1794, he attempted to define the goals of the Revolution. Public Safety was no longer enough; instead, the Revolution's enemies were not mere insurgents but 'all the vicious, ambitious [and] greedy men.... We wish to replace... morality for selfishness... the rule of reason for the tyranny of fashion... the love of glory for the love of money....' The instruments of the revolutionary government were essential to this regeneration. As he said on 7 May, 'Enemies of the people... the Convention will never favour your perversity.... The justice of the nation... will seize with a sure hand all the perverted intriguers and will not strike a single good man.'

> The mainspring of popular government in peacetime is virtue, amid revolution it is at the same time [both] virtue and terror: virtue, without which terror is fatal; terror, without which virtue is impotent. Terror is nothing but prompt, severe, inflexible justice; it is therefore an emanation of virtue. It is less a special principle than a consequence of the general principle of democracy applied to our country's most pressing needs.

In Robespierre's mind, therefore, revolutionary government aimed at utopia.

Other actors on the national stage always had different ideas and these ideas could vary with time and place. Fouché would be one example. His mission in the Nièvre was not at all bloody. Instead, he reflected on the instrumental value of dechristianization and he presided over a number of joyless civic ceremonies dedicated to Brutus, old age and warriors. He brought these new skills to Lyon as well, but here circumstances demanded a gory repression. With the change of locale came a new selection from the revolutionary repertoire as well. Thus, the various rhetorics on revolutionary government depended upon circumstances. How rhetoric and circumstance interacted is clearly important.

The government in Paris was also determined to contain the more than life sized representatives on mission who had supervised the Terror in the provinces after the victories in the late summer and autumn. The Committee was able to exploit fissures that had opened up between these representatives and the local extreme revolutionaries. The Committee of Public Safety's special agent, the odious teenaged fanatic, Marc-Antoine Jullien, had denounced Carrier for 'oppressing patriots', an extraordinary confusion since the patriots in question were responsible for the *noyades* at Nantes. Still, compounding the confusion, he denounced the *noyades* too. He also blamed Carrier for the local revolutionary army's shooting of a handful of peasants emerging from church at Noyal-Muzillac in the Morbihan. Jullien still endorsed the proposition that the Republic should sponsor the most extreme dechristianization, in the form of razing all the churches and eliminating the entire clergy. That way, he said, in breathtaking naïveté, peasants would pay their taxes.

Jullien's denunciation probably had little effect, a lot less than Carrier's quarrel with the Nantes Jacobin club. They fell out with him because he spurned their plan to capture the Vendean general Charette, and relations deteriorated so much that he threatened them with his sword from his sickbed and Jullien had to flee the city at night.

This pattern of a quarrel among overheated revolutionaries was repeated elsewhere. A lobby of Jacobins from Lyon was in the capital steadily denouncing Collot d'Herbois and Fouché for abuses of power. A second lobby, also from Lyon, denounced the first as counterrevolutionary and for the moment the second group caught the Committee's ear. At Marseille and Toulon, Fréron and Barras had been extremist enough by anyone's standards, attributing the unexpected successes of their mission to their own 'inflexible severity', lambasting their predecessor Albitte for his repugnance for 'grandes mesures', and claiming the dockers, sailors and port workers of Toulon were as counterrevolutionary and as selfish as the wholesalers and merchants. All this undoubtedly went down rather well with native Jacobins but the two deputies went too far when they ran afoul of the officials of the Revolutionary Tribunal of Marseille whom they accused of moderation. Also, they changed the name of Marseille to 'Sans-nom', [No Name] thus apparently punishing all the inhabitants for the transgressions of the federalist cabal. The Marseille Jacobins too joined the chorus denouncing the representatives to the Convention.

In general terms then, these struggles were not so much between a Committee of Public Safety anxious to moderate the Terror and a group of extremist deputies determined to go their own way, often in defiance of the law of 14 *frimaire* or of the declarations of religious liberty – although in the cases of Javogues and Fouché there was an element of this. Rather, they were often disputes between terrorist deputies and local Jacobins whose exaggerations had done so much to bring on the federalist crisis in the first place and whose intense communalism quickly led them to resent the tutelage of outsiders. In Lyon, Fouché considered Chalier's friends so extreme and so disrespectful of authority that he closed the club. His suspicions were not entirely groundless either since they and the national agent had criticized the dreaded *Commission*

Temporaire for releasing too many suspects. Yet Robespierre took the side of the 'oppressed patriots' in the Convention on 1 *germinal* (21 March), secured orders they be hounded no longer and got Fouché recalled to explain his conduct. Earlier, the Committee implicitly rebuked Fréron and Barras for changing the name of Marseille to Sans-Nom, and when the Committee restored the original name, the message was obvious: it was siding with the local faction and against their own representatives.

Similarly, at Bordeaux Tallien and Ysabeau ran afoul of the revolutionary committee and extremists because the representatives considered their treatment of prisoners petty and abusive. They also suspended the work of the military commission for a few days in order to arrange legal assistance for the accused. When the Committee in Paris heard of this, they were outraged and quashed these measures. Tallien immediately returned to defend himself and he eventually joined those who plotted the fall of Robespierre. Then, Marc-Antoine Jullien showed up. He denounced Tallien and Ysabeau for not pursuing a policy of economic levelling directed against the merchant class and joined the extremists in making Ysabeau's mission miserable.

Thus when deputies like these returned or were recalled to Paris, the disputes were over the scope and direction of the Terror, not its principles, differences of opinion which could be lethal all the same.

The representatives on mission who replaced this earlier generation were not moderates and this clearly reflected government policy. Maignet, for example, who replaced Fréron and Barras in the Vaucluse and Bouches-du-Rhône, showed that moderation was still considered a vice. In May 1794, someone ripped out the liberty tree in the village of Bédoin in the Vaucluse and threw the cap of liberty that was on top of it into a well. For this, Maignet ordered the arrest of all the municipal officers and the entire revolutionary committee. After a trial, 63 people were condemned to death, 13 women were sentenced to incarceration until the peace and other inhabitants were dispersed elsewhere for re-settlement. 'Revolutionary flames' incinerated the village. It took three days for the burning embers to die out, to destroy the pestilence of political error, to sterilize the very spot on which the village stood. Maignet arranged for a guillotine to be transported to the site. 35 were decapitated immediately and 28 were shot, including some women and some boys.

The affair of the liberty tree was, of course, a pretext. In this case, Maignet intended to make an example of Bédoin because its revolutionary committee did not arrest enough former federalists as suspects, and because he seems to have accepted the accusation of the District of Carpentras that 'authority was despised, laws held in contempt, and

taxes financed orgies...' Why Maignet simply did not purge the committee and the municipality for this fecklessness, as he did elsewhere, is a
mystery, although it may have had something to do with his opinion that
the population of the Vaucluse was 'dangerously gangrened...', or as an
official on the Popular Tribunal of Orange later put it, the region 'is
gangrened with 36 carat aristocracy'. Moreover, the inhabitants of Bédoin were hardly intimidated. Within a few years the entire region was a
hotbed of white terrorist gangs who murdered Jacobins at will.

Government policy towards the Vendée also showed there was no
desire to moderate the Terror. The most savage declarations against the
region were not new. On 1 August 1793, the Convention had issued a
decree calling for the complete physical destruction of the Vendée, to
burn 'the woods, the copses and the undergrowth', to destroy the forests,
seize the animals and crops, and to remove noncombatants. Although the
decree was not immediately implemented, generals and representatives
on mission kept up a steady stream of demands for total destruction.
Such calls fitted in with the standard Jacobin assessment that the most
dangerous enemies were internal. But for once doctrine coincided with
strategic evaluations. Carnot, the Committee of Public Safety's principal
strategist, reckoned that France did not have the resources to continue
the campaign against the European powers beyond 1795 and that war
perpetuated internal violence within the country. The Vendean war
would have to be ended before the 1794 campaigning season started,
that is by the late spring. A strategy of drastic repression was thus
imperative and General Turreau provided it. In effect, this involved
using the army to implement the decree of 1 August, with the additional
aim of crushing the Vendeans. But Turreau was not willing to take on the
burden of massacring civilians himself. He demanded that the Committee
of Public Safety 'pronounce in advance on the fate of the women and
children I will encounter in rebel territory. If it is necessary to pass them
all by the sword, I cannot carry out such a measure without a decree that
covers my responsibilities'. The Committee replied strangely, but clearly
enough: we await 'the results before pronouncing: exterminate the brigands to the last man, there is your duty...' To underline the point, they
authorized the new representatives on mission, including one of their
own, Prieur de la Marne, 'to take whatever measures they believe necessary for public safety'.

This was a blank cheque. The representatives applied the decree of
1 August and ordered the removal of refugees from the war zone. The
aim was 'to leave only rebels in the insurgent areas who can then be easily
destroyed without confusing them with the innocent or with the good
citizens'. This was what a later generation would call a free fire zone.
These were the parameters of Turreau's infamous *colonnes infernales*.

They criss-crossed the *Vendée militaire* in the late winter–early spring of 1794. They began operations before the evacuations were completed and there were no practical instructions for the soldiers about how to distinguish patriots from counterrevolutionaries. Soldiers too had heard for more than a year that Vendeans were a *'race maudite'* so their inhibitions had been much reduced. They also knew that the Vendeans had inflicted massacres on their comrades too, including one of 800 by Charette when his forces took Noirmoutier in October. By this time the massacres at Machecoul in March 1793 had been transformed in the popular mind into ghastly atrocities. That reality was grim enough, but months later, the republicans endlessly talked about patriots being slaughtered and body parts being stuck on the end of pikes and displayed for all to see. Consequently, outraged soldiers burned or destroyed farm buildings, cottages, and churches; they pillaged animals and crops; they raped women or stabbed them to death; they bayoneted children and the old to save on gun powder; and they murdered people in their beds. The massacre at Les Lucs-sur-Boulogne in the Vendée itself is controversial, not because anyone doubts it ever occurred, but whether it occurred in one day or whether it was spread out over a longer period. Local tradition says 459 people of whom 105 were children less than seven years old were massacred on 28 February 1794. Subsequent research suggests local memory conflated events that occurred over a longer time, not that the numbers are all that inaccurate. Even so, that series of events that the telling of the tale conflated into a single event created a *lieu de mémoire*, a site of memory, a focus for local people ever since to define themselves and their history, a site impervious to historians who want to establish mere facts.

And, of course, none of this deliberate savagery worked. Before the campaign was over, troops were removed from the region to reinforce armies on the frontiers, so Turreau had too few troops to carry on with the policy of destruction. The Vendean generals, Charette and Stofflet, and their troops, survived. The war in the Vendée continued for another two years. The destruction remained for all to see for nearly another generation with destroyed houses, uncultivated fields, and deserted villages, inhabited only by wild dogs and wolves.

Was the Repression in the Vendée a Genocide?

In the mid-1980's, Reynald Sécher published two books that caused a sensation, a sensation that continued through the Bicentennial of the Revolution in 1989, and that continues to evoke powerful emotions to this day. He argued that the repression of the Vendée was a genocide and his allegation caught the historical profession entirely unawares. Up to then, historians of the wars of the west had concentrated on the events of those wars, or, for social historians, on attempting to explain the peculiarity of the west by sociological approaches into the origins of popular counterrevolution. Sécher talked about the consequences of repression. His research was so thorough, his counting of the human and material losses in the *Vendée militaire* was so detailed, that he charged the Revolution was guilty of genocide. The charge is combustible stuff because historians sympathetic to the Republic, like François Lebrun and Claude Petitfrère, have sensed, indeed stated, that the stakes could not be higher. One line of defence against Secher is to point out that earlier repressions in France and Europe were just as bad. Maybe they were, although that remains to be demonstrated. What is remarkable about the repression of the Vendée and elsewhere, is the difference in language. Repression of earlier revolts in the Old Regime spoke a very severe, even pitiless language, but it was limited to stressing the importance of punishment as such or the importance of deterrence. Nor could anyone imagine a rebirth in violence because such an idea would have been blasphemous. No one spoke of utter destruction; no one invoked medical metaphors of diseased members to justify amputation, purging, cleansing. The language of repression in the Revolution was in another key altogether. Another criticism against Sécher is to raise a political point. The very legitimacy of the Revolution itself, the principles of 1789 and even the Enlightenment are at issue. Indeed, if that were not enough, historians hostile to Sécher and his followers have declared that the motive of those who have endorsed him is to subvert the very existence of republican democracy in France. That says a lot about how historians evaluate their own importance to the polity in France, but it also shows how in France such debates among professors do capture the attention of the public since these debates have also been televised.

Another refutation, this time from Claude Mazauric, is to speak of 'the treason in wartime of the priests, the nobles and the village notables who created in 1793 a "Catholic and Royal Army" in the service of an anti-French coalition that invaded the country'. The language again is white hot and carries the careless implication that Aulard invented, that the Vendeans were not really French.

On the other side, the language of Pierre Chaunu, one of the most distinguished and prolific historians of Old Regime Europe, has, if anything, been more extreme because he has linked the repression of the Vendée to every atrocity of the twentieth century.

The term 'genocide' obviously carries a high voltage but it is equally obviously anachronistic. Since the Vendeans were not a race or an ethnic group apart, it is also inappropriate. But the word is less important than explaining the *thing* and here more needs to be done. How many were killed in the end is secondary – 180,000 or 500,000, both are large numbers, tossing them around on either side to minimize or maximize the degree of outrage is a twentieth century predilection, a reflection of a statistical age, an anachronism in the end – what needs to be understood on the republican side is the will to slaughter. Latter day sympathizers for the Vendean cause have complained quite rightly that after 1920 or so, the counterrevolution in the Revolution vanished in serious academic publications after being a major element in the nineteenth century. For one strand of academic discourse, the 'people' could not possibly be counterrevolutionary.

On the other hand, Sécher and those he inspired also do not appear to appreciate that from the republican point of view, the Vendeans were traitors. From the mid-summer of 1793, the Committee of Public Safety had solid proof, not for once of an imaginary conspiracy but of a real one, that the Vendean generals were trying to arrange for the British to land military equipment and perhaps émigré regiments and British soldiers. This was the point of the expedition to Granville in Normandy. So the motives of the republicans, usually assumed to be limited to wicked malice, or to be derived from the delirium of an intoxicating ideology, have a more concrete explanation. But was it a justification?

The republican discourse on the wars of the west was also a function of earlier political decisions. The first was the war on Europe. There simply were not enough troops and not enough logistical resources to fight a major internal insurrection and an unprecedentedly challenging external war at the same time. In effect, and this would recur for the rest of the decade, the central government wrote off devastation in the interior in order to fight the war on the frontiers. Moreover, even counting those troops deployed to the *Vendée militaire* alone, only a minority ever took the field against the Catholic and Royal Army of the west. Most were assigned coastal duty to protect against a possible British landing. Many were so under-equipped and under-supplied, they could not take the field in any case. Had the republican Army of the Coasts of La Rochelle been a lot bigger and a lot better equipped, there need never have been the necessity to invoke slaughter as a response to the insurrection.

The Politics of Terror

The Montagnards had a vision of themselves as pure and virtuous souls surrounded by debauched, self-interested flatterers who wore the mask of patriotism, but who underneath were evil counterrevolutionaries. The only defence was unrelenting suspicion and denunciation. But seeing the world in moral terms like this made it difficult to predict where and when betrayal would occur. Reverses were plots, failure was willful, disagreement was perverse, nothing was what it seemed. A friend and colleague could be suddenly exposed as a traitor who had always been associated with dark plots that had conspired against patriots from the very beginning. A traitor had always been a traitor waiting to betray his ostensible friends.

This is how to understand much of the high politics of the Terror. Underlying it all was the ever elusive 'Foreign Plot', masterminded by crooked bankers, cosmopolitan revolutionaries, and counterrevolutionary adventurers like the shady baron de Batz who had tried to rescue Louis XVI on the very day of his execution. The Foreign Plot, supposedly born of a desire to loot the assets of the bankrupt East India Company, allegedly needed corrupt politicians to achieve its goals and this initially involved some of Danton's associates. The Plot made it impossible to conduct debates on policy entirely on their merits because it raised questions of ulterior motives. This was obvious on the debates on dechristianization and on the Terror. Robespierre also believed some of the most exuberant dechristianizers were also on the Plot's payroll and that they were pushing irreligion to extremes in order to goad otherwise loyal Catholics into the arms of the counterrevolution. On 1 *frimaire* (21 November), at the Jacobins, Robespierre argued that dechristianization would only inflame religious zeal, that priests should be prosecuted only for infractions of the law and that the dechristianizers were agents of foreign powers whose purpose was to discredit the Revolution by exaggerated patriotism. The speech did nothing at all to halt the dechristianization campaign but it did signal to nervous deputies, both in the Convention and on mission, that there were limits to extremism.

The debate on repression followed a similar pattern. By the late autumn of 1793, victory on the frontiers and defeat of the internal enemy raised the question of how severe repression needed to be. Those who wanted it relaxed, known as the Indulgents, posed a legitimate issue but once again suspicion of corruption raised the question of ulterior motives. Danton, who was one of their leaders, had long been suspected of taking bribes (and then ignoring his paymaster). His friends were linked to the foreign financiers, were suspected of taking bribes to get prisoners released, and were suspected of being involved in a scam to swindle other investors, including the ubiquitous baron de Batz. At the same time, representatives on mission who were close to Danton denounced the incompetence and interference of *sans-culotte* generals in the operations against the Vendeans. At a time when radical opinion suspected the officers of deliberately losing the war and that political pedigrees were worth more than professional qualifications, this was a major challenge. Finally, Camille Desmoulins brought out the famous third number of the *Vieux Cordelier* on 25 *frimaire* (15 December). He compared the tyranny of the Caesars to the bloodletting of the present and attacked the Committee of Public Safety directly.

The Indulgents' offensive set off a furious debate and finally, their opponents overreacted. Hébert, the editor of the crude *Père Duchesne* which was very popular in Paris and in the army, and Carrier attacked the Indulgents and implicitly the government. They demanded a 'holy insurrection' not only against the Indulgents but apparently against the government. When they draped a funeral cloth over the Declaration of Rights in the Cordeliers Club – implicitly a call to insurrection – the government struck. The Hébertists went before the Revolutionary Tribunal charged with planning a military coup, to be followed by a horrible series of prison massacres and famine plots that would lead to a restoration of the monarchy. On 4 *germinal* (24 March), Hébert, his friends, and the unfortunate Cloots who was tossed into the dock to prove the foreign plot, were all guillotined. Hébert practically had to be carried from the courtroom, and he died utterly shocked and, some said, like a coward.

But this did not mean the Indulgents were safe because in Robespierre's mind both factions were the twin heads of the hydra of conspiracy: 'A few skilled stage-hands are hidden in the wings operating the machinery silently behind the scenes. At base, it is the same faction as that of the Gironde, except with different actors. Or, rather, it is still the same actors but they are now wearing different masks. But it is the same stage, and always the same drama'. A report on corruption implicated some of Danton's friends while Desmoulins continued his attacks on the governing committees. Since the Indulgents were defending people who were obviously guilty, they were guilty too. Consequently, the Committee of Public Safety arrested Danton. He was not even charged with corruption but with a whole series of political crimes: for wanting to put the duc d'Orléans on the throne, or for mocking the word 'virtue'. During the trial itself, his oratory held the audience transfixed with his demands to call witnesses until finally, the Committee of Public Safety ordered the Tribunal to cut the trial short. According to Saint-Just, speaking on behalf of the Committee of Public Safety, the very demand from the accused that the state produce witnesses was proof of their guilt. Danton and his leading associates, Desmoulins, Philippeaux, and Fabre d'Eglantine among others, were executed on 16 *germinal* (5 April). The fall of the factions was supposed to establish once and for all the governing committees' dominance of the Convention and of Paris politics. At a superficial level it did, but there were still sources of potential dissidence. Danton had many friends who survived and in any case, the question Desmoulins asked about the severity of the Terror could not be

suppressed. There were also plenty of radicals, dechristianizers, representatives on mission, and others who by now had a lurid history of revolutionary extremism. Many of them felt that their conduct in the provinces
would soon be questioned and the trials showed political error was
unforgivable.

The effects outside the Convention were more dramatic. In Paris,
sections and popular societies, ever mindful of potential traitors in their
midst, undertook an orgy of self-purgings and often tried to exclude
anyone whose revolutionary lineage could not be traced back to 1789.
After the arrests of both Hébert and Danton, the stupor, confusion, even
anger of many militants must have been tempered by the knowledge that
the two Cordeliers heros had joined the rogues' gallery of popular
politicians who, from the Duc d'Orléans and Lafayette in 1789 onwards,
had always been false patriots and secret intriguers and who were now
unmasked. In the final analysis, for all the wild talk about there being
only fifteen patriots in it or replacing it with a 'grand juge', the militants
trusted the Convention.

In the provinces, Marat's reputation in popular opinion went into
eclipse on the grounds that if Hébert was guilty, the *Ami du Peuple* must
have been too. There was a minor wave of denunciation against ultra-
revolutionaries as well. The government's assault on extremism also did
more than any of Robespierre's speeches to bring spontaneous dechristianization to a halt. After *germinal*, all the tests, numbers of priests marrying, addresses to the Convention, re-baptisms, and so on, show a dramatic
decline. As for the clubs, there were more than 2500 addresses congratu-
lating the Convention for having unmasked new conspirators against
liberty, almost all of them expressed in what was by now a totally staged,
mind-numbing language. But not everywhere. At Le Mans, where the club
was already deeply divided over strategies to fight the war in the Vendée,
the news of the drama of *germinal* provoked a reaction against the Convention itself. There were cries from the militants that politicians too long
in power considered the public trust to be their personal property and
there were shouts of 'No more viziers! No more tyrants!' For that, ten club
members went before the Revolutionary Tribunal in Paris where the
prosecution slandered their reputations with fantastic claims that they
participated in orgies and that they were drunkards. Incredibly, the jury
acquitted them but upon their return home they were re-arrested and their
ordeal ended only with the collapse of the Terror. The incident was
significant, however, because it showed how great a gap could open up
between the 'viziers' and local militants and because it resembled the kinds
of disputes between local militants and representatives on mission earlier.
Despite the appearance of conformity, therefore, there were currents here
and there that questioned the Convention.

The End of the Terror

Still, the government had evidently mastered both the Convention and public opinion. This was not the time for moderation, however. It meant to have sole control of the apparatus of repression. The law of 19 *floréal* (8 May) suppressed the provincial revolutionary tribunals and commissions outside the capital and gave exclusive jurisdiction to try counter-revolutionary crimes to the Paris Revolutionary Tribunal. The law of 22 *prairial* (10 June) deprived the accused of counsel and the right to call defence witnesses and allowed the jury to convict on the basis of moral certainty. This notorious law thus created a murder machine. It was envisaged that a good proportion of the accused were to be sent up by the six special commissions (only two were ever established) which, by Saint-Just's *ventôse* laws, were to process the dossiers of suspects. They were now to funnel unfortunate individuals, accused of the vaguest of crimes and convicted simply by administrative fiat, to a tribunal which could only acquit or punish with death. This inaugurated the Great Terror in Paris where 57 per cent of all the victims of the Revolutionary Tribunal were convicted in June and July alone, amid tales of prison plots, baron de Batz plots, and other fantasies.

The law of 22 *prairial* itself was passed because members of the Committee of Public Safety were afraid for their own lives after assassination attempts on Robespierre and Collot d'Herbois. It is an interesting commentary on the pervasive atmosphere of black suspicion that this law was seen as a solution when, in more normal times, the committee men might have hired some alert bodyguards. Worse still, the law of 22 *prairial* quietly removed the deputies' already frayed right to parliamentary immunity and, as in earlier crises in 1789 and the spring of 1793, even ordinary deputies had taken to carrying arms and sleeping at different addresses.

However, the swirling discontent might have been mastered had the governing committees not fallen out. The Committee of General Security interpreted the Committee of Public Safety's creation of its own police bureau as the beginning of a usurpation of its functions and there were rumours that the bureau was Robespierre's personal agency. Many deputies also feared that Robespierre wanted to establish a personal dictatorship.

Quarrels over religious issues further divided the politicians. On 20 *prairial* (8 June, Pentecost in the old calendar), Robespierre had the artist and deputy David stage the Festival of the Supreme Being, starring himself. At other times, such a ceremony might have been both strange and simultaneously boring, but some took it as further proof of

Robespierre's ambition, while others reckoned it might be a prefiguration of a reconciliation with Catholicism. Such fears were a link to the dechristianizing deputies who were already alarmed. Robespierre loathed deputies like Fouché because their version of dechristianization was atheistic. Then a weird incident occurred when one Catherine Théot, a self-styled 'Mère de Dieu' and harmless visionary prophesied the end of days and conflated Robespierre with the Messiah. The deputy Vadier's report on behalf of the Committee of General Security used the Théot incident as a pretext to mock religion altogether. Indirectly, this was a sarcastic jab at Robespierre's deism. It was also a high stakes challenge because Danton had been executed in part because he mocked virtue.

Robespierre also insisted on handling the Théot case personally because he thought Vadier's report minimized connections with bigger conspiracies. Thus the Committee poached on General Security's territory. At about this time, the various assassination attempts or fears of such plots seem to have paralysed him. He ceased to attend meetings of the Committee, and those who saw him at home, like Fréron and Barras, were stunned when they arrived. They had gone to his first floor apartment on the rue St Honoré to plead their case after their recall from Marseille. Robespierre said nothing, nothing at all; he totally ignored them. After several attempts to break the unnerving silence, they left. Barras recalled later that Robespierre was a frozen marble statue, that he had 'the face of an already buried corpse'. At the Convention Robespierre spoke of ghostly plots to kill him and of his own death. Such behaviour was certainly unsettling.

Events on the frontiers also made Desmoulins's question about the severity of the Terror more acute. Victory made the case for revolutionary government as an emergency government much weaker. The Battle of Fleurus on 8 *messidor* (26 June) pushed the Austrian army into full retreat and just over a week later, the armies of Pichegru and Jourdan were in Brussels and Antwerp. Carnot's strategy for the campaign of 1794 was beginning to work. At the same time, Prussia was less and less inclined to focus on the west because she feared Russian designs on Poland. But in Robespierre's mind, the purpose of the Terror was regeneration so external events were irrelevant. His self-isolation only increased suspicions against him among almost everyone. He undoubtedly planned to purge at least four deputies, including Fouché who turned to outright conspiracy soon after Robespierre persuaded the Jacobins to expel him. The practised intriguer retaliated by spreading rumours about who was next on the list of those to be purged. Right up to the last minute, however, there was a possibility of an accommodation between the two governing committees. On 4–5 *thermidor* (22–23 July), a truce involving promises to speed the reviewing of suspects' dossiers was reached. The price of reconciliation in other words was to be hundreds more executions. No one had any qualms about this but Robespierre broke the truce because he suspected the sincerity of his colleagues.

On 8 *thermidor* he appealed over their heads to the Convention. In a rambling and maudlin speech, he attacked the Indulgents. As a way of unmasking a 'criminal coalition' in the Convention, he also called for a purge of unnamed individuals in the two governing committees. That evening he received rousing support in the Jacobin club. When he repeated his speech and Billaud and Collot tried to reply, they were chased from the society with cries of, 'Les conspirateurs à la guillotine' ringing in their ears.

To save themselves, they had to turn against Robespierre and their defection showed the next day in the Convention. When Saint-Just tried to deliver what he intended to be a conciliatory speech, Tallien interrupted. Collot, who was in the chair, then allowed Billaud and Vadier to launch direct attacks on Robespierre. Each time he in turn tried to defend himself, a prearranged hubbub drowned him out. Finally, the Convention decreed the arrest of Robespierre, his brother Augustin, Couthon, Saint-Just and Le Bas, their friend on the Committee of General Security. Less than an hour later, the Commune intervened. Armed force, not parliamentary manouevres, would decide the *journée* of 9 *thermidor*.

It is common to explain the tepid support the Commune received from the sections by referring to the sapping of *sans-culotte* spontaneity since September 1793 or to the maximum on wages which was finally announced on 5 *thermidor*. Such an interpretation almost certainly overdetermines the problem. No doubt the mis-named 'popular movement' had been largely bureaucratized and its most enthusiastic elements incorporated into the army – some 23,000 men by one count; no doubt too that the maximum on wages was unpopular since its effect was to reduce wages for many trades. But the *journée* of 9 *thermidor* unfolded so quickly that it is hard to imagine how these factors could have come into play. No matter what radical opinion was, there was no time to mobilize the sections, let alone mount a serious insurrection in favour of the Robespierrists.

The outcome of the *journée* depended above all on leadership and organization. The Convention moved quickly. In the early afternoon, Barère had a proclamation printed up warning the sections against the agitation of a handful of intriguers. By 9 p.m., this was in the hands of all the sections and nineteen either refused the Commune's call to assemble or quickly drafted addresses of loyalty to the Convention. The fall of the Hébertistes in *germinal* had taught them that there were always intriguers to be unmasked and that their role in the drama was to express loyalty to the Convention. At the same time, the revolutionary committees of the sections and the sections' National Guard units, especially the artillery that had been so important on 31 May, remained loyal to the Convention. Meetings of the Commune's general assembly, the Jacobin Club and the section assemblies also took place amid near total chaos and confusion. Only the Commune began planning an armed assault on the Convention the next day. By then it was too late. The Commune's one success led directly to its undoing. Throughout the night, small units liberated the five deputies from their various places of confinement and escorted them to the Hôtel de Ville. This provoked the Convention to declare Robespierre and his colleagues, as well as the Commune, outside the law. This meant that any one of them could be executed within twenty-four hours, without trial, once a criminal or revolutionary court had simply verified his identity. The declaration of outlawry wasted the Commune's only asset. Although the response of the National Guard had been relatively poor, this still left 3400 of them to gather on the Place de Grève before the Hôtel de Ville, more than enough to undertake a serious military operation. But the outlawry decree decided many sections. As soon as they heard of it, special commissioners or officials of the revolutionary committees made their way to the Place de Grève and persuaded their detachments to go home. Seeing this, other sectional forces just drifted away. By 1.30 a.m., the Place de Grève was empty.

The Convention had triumphed. The denouement was swift and pathetic. When they heard that the section companies had vanished, the deputies in the Hôtel de Ville despaired. Le Bas killed himself with a pistol, Robespierre tried to do the same but only broke his lower jaw, Augustin threw himself from a window but survived even though he landed head first, Couthon pitched himself down a flight of stairs while trying to maneuver his wheelchair, and Hanriot, the outlawed National Guard commander, flung himself into a small courtyard where he lay undiscovered on top of a pile of manure for twelve hours. Only Saint-Just remained unperturbed, awaiting the death that had always fascinated him. Thus, when the Convention's forces, composed for the most part of companies from the sections led by the deputies Barras and Léonard Bourdon, finally invested the Hôtel de Ville around 2 a.m., there was no one to fight, only dispirited and disfigured bodies to carry off.

Later that same afternoon, 10 *thermidor*, after identification by the Revolutionary Tribunal, Robespierre, his brother and his friends were sentenced to death. They left the Conciergerie prison at 6.00 p.m. in three tumbrels. Although the journey to the *Place de la Révolution* is not long, a large jeering crowd, some of whom danced around the tumbrels, slowed the passage. Robespierre was wearing the same blue silk coat he wore when he presided over the Festival of the Supreme Being. His face was almost entirely covered in bandages, his colour was already deathly pale, his eyes were nearly shut, he had been bleeding for hours. He was the second last of the 22 to be executed.

It was 7.30 p.m.

Although no one knew it, the Terror was over.

8

Collapse and Vengeance

On the day of Robespierre's execution, Barère made a famous speech in which he assured his audience that revolutionary government would continue. This turned out to be wildly wrong. The deputies to the Convention had a natural reaction against the Great Terror but they intended to retain the most basic features of revolutionary government. After all, the reasons for implementing it in the first place had not changed as a result of 9 *thermidor*. There were still foreign invaders and there was still domestic subversion. Although the judicial system was drastically reformed, the law still permitted the establishment of exceptional jurisdictions. The laws against the refractory priests and émigrés remained in full force. The law of 14 *frimaire* on the functioning of revolutionary government that required such extensive reporting to the national government remained in place. The Law of Suspects persisted until the Convention disbanded itself at the end of the Year III. After a lot of experimentation, the controlled economy could not be avoided. Finally, despite claims that the regime endorsed religious freedom, the new law on the public exercise of religion and the regime's continuing use of public ceremonies to inculcate support for the regime, meant that many of the features of the dechristianization campaign of the Year II persevered.

At first, though, *thermidor* was, in Bronislaw Baczko's important phrase, an event in search of a meaning. What it was just after the deaths of the Robespierre cabal was very different from what it became a year later. It was very different too than what the politicians had initially intended. There were many reasons that frustrated their plan to retain a quasi-revolutionary regime. In the first place, the politicians never developed a consensus about how to deal with the Terror everyone now suddenly deplored. Nor could they agree on how far the purge of provincial terrorists should go. The anti-terrorism of some new representatives on mission produced appalling atrocities. Moreover, especially in the Midi, the newly purged local administrations returned former federalists or even émigrés to power, men who this time breathed revenge. More important was the rapid emergence of a public opinion that was thoroughly hostile to almost any notion of revolutionary government. Sometimes, this limited itself to deploring the recent excesses, or to demanding the release of suspects. On other occasions it went much further. In many of the big cities, there were gangs who attacked terrorists on the pretext that punishment was too slow or too lenient. There were also massacres of Jacobins that were often a function of a thoroughly compromised authority of anti-terrorists who did nothing to prevent or who may even have encouraged these atrocities. Worse still, the wars in the West spread to new regions and while the *chouannerie*, as it is called, was never all that militarily dangerous, it offered the British a new opportunity, which this time, they took.

The government was also too weak to master a depleted economy. By the spring of 1795, with the *assignat* on the verge of collapse and with economic controls ineffective, brigandage emerged even in the most developed parts of the country. Worse still, the food distribution network teetered on the edge of collapse and in Paris, and many other places, there were food riots. If the Year II was the year of the *sans-culottes*, the Years III–V were the years of the popular counterrevolution. For that reason alone, the Revolution itself was not over.

The thermidorean reaction began with the best of intentions of restoring the rule of law; it ended by producing an extraordinarily weak government, incapable of defending itself against counterrevolution.

The Slide to Revenge

For the ultra terrorists who overthrew the Robespierre faction and even for the moderates who ultimately profited the most from it, the Convention and the legal terrorist apparatus had to be reformed. Inside the Convention this did not amount to much. It required the re-introduction of the principle of rotation on the Committee of Public Safety and also on the Committee of General Security. By early September, most of the most compromised committee members had been retired.

The Convention also reformed the repressive apparatus, but most deputies clearly meant to retain the most basic definition of revolutionary government, that is, a government of temporary exception. Thus, the law of 22 *prairial* was repealed, and Fouquier-Tinville, the obsequious and obliging prosecutor of the Revolutionary Tribunal was removed. The

Convention made some steps towards re-introducing due process rights by requiring juries to take account of an accused person's motives and also allowing the accused to contest the evidence against them. At the same time, the Convention suppressed revolutionary committees in agglomerations smaller than 8000 people, a recognition, in most parts of the country anyway, that urban committees were already dominating their surrounding hinterlands.

The Historiography

Albert Mathiez, a truly great historian of the Revolution in its ascendant Robespierrist phase denounced these changes as opening the breach to the counterrevolution. In defence of the thermidoreans, this was clearly not the intent. Instead, the plan unquestionably was to prevent a faction from usurping control of the Convention another time – one can hardly blame men whom Robespierre had so indiscriminately targeted in his speech of 8 *thermidor* from attempting to restructure the committee system to make it more democratic and therefore less likely to be hijacked. Moreover the repressive apparatus that had just barely avoided another purge like that of the previous *germinal* also had to be restructured. What is remarkable is not how much of the apparatus of repression was jettisoned, as Mathiez believed, but how much the Convention retained. The Convention still ruled without a fundamental law, without a constitution. Without saying so, Mathiez was complaining about the premature end of the Terror. But since the Terror had ended by targeting the political class itself, and since in its extreme forms in the areas of heavy repression, it had failed, another strategy was required. The thermidoreans hoped to persuade the nation that by forgetting most of the recent past and attempting to re-introduce the rule of law, the nation could make a fresh start. That miscarried, but surely Mathiez's argument that Terror should have been prolonged was also a blind alley.

In any case, the consensus for the continuation of the Terror was no longer there. One of the most remarkable aspects of the immediate post-*thermidor* situation was the evaporation of cries for the maximalist terror, for extreme measures, for regeneration. When the Paris Revolutionary Tribunal re-convened that summer, the President, Dobsen, opened the sessions by claiming the purpose of the Tribunal was to maintain 'revolutionary government'. That is, even the most battle hardened revolutionaries only had the strength to demand the minimalist terror. If the intent was to preserve the essentials of revolutionary government, the support for that government also began to ebb. This occurred at two levels, that of the clubs and that of the institutions of exception themselves.

The clubs were the first to react to the news of the fall of Robespierre. As they had in every convulsion in Paris for over a year, they were anxious to put themselves on the right side of higher authority. Thus the obligatory addresses to the Convention expressing in the usual abject terms their undying gratitude for exposing this latest conspiracy. Thus too, the obligatory self-induced purge of people too close to the faction that had just been unmasked in Paris. But if that faction was defined as too extremist, it stood to reason that the clubs ought to re-admit those whom the extremists had so unjustly expelled just a few months before. Yet these men were unlikely to be grateful and many demanded a settling of accounts. At Nîmes anyway, the club's implosion was aided by the new representative on mission who arrived to purge the judiciary and the executive organs of extremists. These men were quite often club members too. This quite demoralized the club which began to meet less and less, until it just withered away. Elsewhere, the combination of dissension within the clubs, the desire to have so-called innocent patriots released, the pressure to conform once again to the Convention in its latest convulsion against the new intriguers, the new Caligulas, all this threw the clubs into confusion. Within weeks of hearing of the overthrow of Robespierre, some clubs like Dijon and Marseilles were expressing alarm at the new moderate turn, which, sacred ideology dictated, was the greatest of vices. But their solution was not the usual hair-raising calls for drastic measures. All they demanded was the rigorous application of the Law of Suspects. Even in their protest, they had calmed down. Still other clubs welcomed the chance to petition for the release of oppressed patriots or urged the Convention to return to the principles of 1789, but not, significantly, to those of 1793. Still other clubs, like that of Le Havre, had to suffer huzzas from the gallery. Many clubs, along with newspapers and officials, stigmatized the terrorists as 'drinkers of blood', part of 'the tail of Robespierre', 'monsters vomited forth by crime', 'offspring of the hermaphrodite race of the new Cromwell', and a zoo of 'tigers', 'hyenas', 'ourang- outangs', 'snakes', 'leopards', and so on. Often such demoralizing dissension and public opprobrium was the last act before a club either closed itself, sometimes for lack of fuel in that appallingly cold winter, or before it simply vanished from the record altogether. By *frimaire* An III (December 1794), well over 60 per cent of the clubs had held their last meeting, and most of them had disappeared well before the decree of *fructidor* An III that dissolved all the clubs.

Institutions also became less willing to take a drastic interpretation of their mandates. There was a dramatic decline in the use of repression. The number of death sentences fell suddenly from the summer of the Year II while the bloody revolutionary tribunals of the west became mere police agencies until their cases were transferred to military courts martial or the criminal courts the following winter and spring. The revolutionary committees, often against their own better judgement, began to release suspects under the widest possible interpretation of the law of 21 *messidor* (9 July 1794). This authorized the release of harvest labourers and small-town artisans, and after 29 *thermidor* (16 August) it was extended to middle-class people who had been ruined and therefore had to work with their hands. There were outside pressures demanding the release of suspects too. In Paris, for example, it came from the families of moderates who slowly began to return to the section assemblies and from the ordinary *sans-culottes* who had long resented the high-handedness of the revolutionary committees. In the provinces, the pressure sometimes came from the representatives on mission. In the Côte-d'Or, the representative Cales began releasing suspects wholesale in *vendémiaire* (October) and the last were gone the following *pluviôse* (January). In the Ille-et-Vilaine, the representative Boursault established a 'Philanthropic Commission' to review suspects' cases. He also released them outright as part of a wider policy of conciliating a disaffected countryside. At Uzès in the Gard, the municipality, still largely composed of 'terrorists', pressured the committee so successfully that of the three hundred suspects held in the local prison on 1 *thermidor* (19 July), only a handful remained three months later. With opinion moving against them and little or no support from the Committee of General Security or the representatives, the committees lost heart. Even where the terrorist personnel was retained in the post-*fructidor* reorganizations, there were very few new arrests. Like the clubs, the Law of Suspects merely withered away.

In other words, those implementing the repressive laws were themselves losing heart and another part of public opinion was demanding a relaxation.

The released suspects and the relatives and friends of the victims of the tribunals soon formed a powerful coalition demanding a settling of accounts with the terrorists. More diffuse but equally debilitating to authority was the continued resistance to dechristianization and the Convention's religious policy generally. In a phenomenon that was to be extremely common for the next five years, many country people interpreted 9 *thermidor* as a reversal of official anti-clericalism. In its overblown rhetoric, the popular society of Pernes in the Pas-de-Calais observed, 'Fanaticism whose hideous head has been crushed by the revolutionary chariot, is a monster which like Robespierre has left a tail which visibly agitates... Sundays continue to be a day of rest and solemnity such that there only lacks... the ancient and ridiculous antics of the Roman Mass'. But far from being a remnant, such manifestations became more and more common. In November 1794, the inhabitants of

Isle-sur-Serein in the Yonne forcibly reopened their church and celebrated their victory by ringing bells, lighting bonfires and chanting an improvised *Te Deum*. Around Neufchatel in the Seine-Inferièure, 'a village doctor...imitates all the superstitious ceremonies of the Catholic cult' since there were no priests to hand. Elsewhere, there were innumerable stories of priests emerging from hiding or returning from abroad to say Mass to hundreds of people, or of people forcing infirm monks newly released from prison to perform baptisms and marriages. As under the Terror, women were in the forefront of demanding the reopening of churches, harassing officials to turn over keys and urging the men to avoid the *fêtes décadaires*. Such demonstrations did not always have a direct political overtone but occasionally the link with anti-terrorism was explicit. On All Saints Day 1794, for instance, five to six thousand people went to the mass graves of the victims of the Popular Revolutionary Commission of Orange. In the event, the local committee arrested the 'poor farm worker [who]...recited the litanies of the saints' and issued a stern warning against 'the poisoned breath of fanaticism'. Stern measures of this sort were rare, however. Elsewhere, committees were more inclined than they had been just a few months earlier to leave 'fanatics' alone.

Economic Catastrophe

The comparatively sudden relaxation of political repression and the continuing protests over the Convention's religious policy showed that the alienation of town and country was still deep. Economic policy made it worse still. As in so many other areas, the problem was the trade-off the politicians of the Terror made. The financial and economic policies of the revolutionary government did much to keep the towns fed and the armies supplied but this policy could not continue indefinitely. The government continued to finance itself with further emissions of *assignats* and it did little to improve the system of tax collection. Consequently, the money supply was greater than it ever had been. The solution of printing ever more *assignats* was bound to be increasingly costly. Thus there opened up a bifurcation between the real economy and the command economy. Controlled prices in the public sector could not survive alongside the private sector because incentives to produce and sell in the latter were so much greater than in the former. The only way the controlled economy could keep going was through more and more repression. But that did not happen. Throughout the terror, very few people were convicted or arrested for economic crimes. Moreover, the more *assignats* were printed, the greater the division between the two sectors. The crack occurred in the summer of 1794, and one police report in Paris after another detailed the failure of public authority to contain defiance of the Maximum, until the police gave up altogether. In other words, the controlled economy collapsed months before the politicians had recognized its failure in law.

Moreover, so long as the government insisted on printing more and more paper, the amount of paper in private hands must have increased, since the maximum on wages was often more difficult to apply than that on prices. Conscription and the war economy probably also reduced the productive capacity of the civilian sector. After all, this was the price of mobilizing the nation for war. This situation, as well as the persistent shortages, ought to have increased the amount of black marketeering but by definition this is immeasurable.

Thus the ending of the command economy was not responsible for the collapse, as Mathiez and Lefebvre insisted. Instead, as François Crouzet argued, if the command economy had done so well, exposing it to market forces would not have revealed the blockages, shortages, inefficiencies and outright frauds that it did.

The harvest of 1794 completely overwhelmed the ability of the legal system to command economic reality. Indeed, it is doubtful whether the full blown apparatus of the Terror could have done better. After all, a marginal harvest and weak money created no incentive for producers to sell. The terrorist solution would have been increasing repression and no one had any desire for that after 9 *thermidor*.

After a most promising growing season, severe drought in the late summer destroyed much of the crop. The harvest was very poor. It was perhaps one third less than that of 1793. The conscription of young farmhands and the requisition of horses and carts for the military also delayed the gathering of the harvest. An intensely cold winter followed. Winter temperatures in Paris were the lowest for the entire century. The weather disrupted the transportation system and caused shortages that were unheard of a year before. Huge chunks of ice threatened to crush ships at Le Havre, barges carrying grain and wood were frozen in the canals, the Seine froze all the way up to Paris. The delivery of wood and much of the grain for Paris was severely interrupted. Wolves, driven out of the forests by hunger, scavenged at the outskirts of many towns.

The Convention's attempts to meet this situation were desperate and ineffective. For the rest of its existence it fiddled with free market solutions and tempered them with political control. Nor could it do more than improvise so long as the war continued. The Convention did decide to end the Maximum at the end of December but this did not mean much in itself. In reality, the Convention decreed two economies as far as food was concerned, a state controlled economy designed to help the poor and urban consumers generally; and a free market economy for everyone else. Reasonable as this might have been, the monetary situation did not recognize these boundaries, and producers preferred to sell on the free market. Uncontrolled prices shot up at a breathtaking rate. The result was that the state economy adopted increasingly severe pressures on producers and when that failed, it reduced rations in the cities. Consequently, nearly three-quarters of Parisians were dependent on the state for provisions at the beginning of the Year IV, but also their rations were being reduced from one month to the next. Already, large amounts of unspent currency, a poor harvest and no possible government commitment to reduce its expenditures were aggravating the problem of urban supply terribly. With no new sources of revenue and the state acquiring its war materials at market prices from private contractors, the only recourse was to print more *assignats*.

Even before the abolition of the Maximum, the *assignat* had fallen from 34 per cent of its 1790 value in *thermidor* to 20 per cent the following *nivôse*. After abolition, it dropped to 8 per cent in *germinal* and 4 per cent in *prairial*. At the same time, consumers and traders were bidding up prices while farmers and grain merchants were holding on to their stocks in the hope that prices would rise still higher. Bread prices on the free market in Paris rose by 1300 per cent between March and May 1795, beef more than sextupled and pork and eggs more than doubled. Overall, the cost of living climbed by over 900 per cent between 1790 and 1795.

Even so, Paris was relatively privileged because the government subsidized prices and maintained diminishing rations for the poor at the expense of cities in the hinterland. In the Nord, for example, a free market ceased to exist in the late winter of the Year III and the towns could be fed only by requisitions again because farmers insisted on payment in hard cash which had disappeared. Amiens and Abbeville in the Somme managed to feed their poor by slashing rations and cutting the subsidies on bread prices. But by spring peasant defiance had reached the point where requisitions brought in only one tenth of what they had the year before. The two cities then had to purchase grain on foreign markets but paid extortionate prices to rapacious middlemen.

The economic collapse of the Year III and the appalling cold produced indescribable misery. The number of deaths recorded at the hospital of Bicêtre in Paris climbed after *ventôse* and there were the usual stories, always a sure sign of shortage and misery, of suicides of young mothers and their children, and of people eating grass. It was said there never had been more bodies of desperate suicides pulled out of the Seine. There were also innumerable stories of mothers dying in the street, a baby attached to her breast. Whether these were urban legends or not, the number of deaths increased dramatically. The number of deaths in Paris in the Year III was half again as high as in the Year II. Deaths in Rouen in the Year III were nearly double those of a normal year, while those of the Year IV were higher still, the killer season being the spring between harvests in both years and the victims being the very old, the very young and the working poor. In effect, the country had reverted to a situation it had escaped nearly a century before, of a more or less direct correlation between prices, supplies and death rates.

As always in time of dearth, criminality born of misery also increased. In the Nord there were more and more reports of petty amounts of grain being stolen from farmers. Around Amiens there were huge bands of vagabonds roaming from farm to farm. The national agent of Mâcon reported the appearance of brigand bands in the countryside. Interestingly, the only way he could fulfil the town's grain quota was to imprison the mayors and national agents of the communes – a measure unprecedented even in the Year II. With increasing misery, inflation and brigandage, government was beginning to collapse.

Apologists for the *assignat* and for the controlled economy at the time and since have argued that monetary policy helped win the war. In fact it hampered prosecution of the war in immeasurable ways. Nominal tax revenues escalated substantially in the Years III and IV but with the fall in the *assignat*, the real value of those revenues was falling. In effect, taxpayers were taking advantage of the situation meet their obligations in devalued currency. One of the few lifelines for the government was the sale of *biens nationaux* but this was fraying day by day. Most of the Church lands had already been sold. Since it was national policy to reduce the number of émigrés, their unsold land was being returned to them. As a result of all this, the armies were poorly supplied. The penury of the Army of Italy is notorious but there were also endless reports that the soldiers of the Army of the West were without boots, uniforms or even proper food. No wonder so few could be deployed against counter-revolutionaries. No wonder too that thousands and thousands of lawless and hungry young men roamed the countryside everywhere. They calculated that poaching off their neighbours and robbing passers-by was a better way of surviving than flying to the defence of *la patrie*.

Social Basis of Counterrevolution

Dissidence in many parts of the country never went further than going to clandestine Masses and observing Sundays. As always, the anti-revolution had many gradations embedded within it. Thus, the requisitions, arrests of local officials, house-to-house searches, unprecedented rationing in the countryside, forbidding beer production to save on grain, and so on, snapped the remaining links between the big farmers and landowners and the urban revolutionaries. In the Nord, this united whole rural communities that had once been divided between rich and poor over wages, disposition of the commons, accumulation of leases and so on, against all outside authority. The result was nearly complete impunity for Belgian missionary preachers, resistance to requisitions, protection for deserters and draft dodgers, and brigandage.

But that was as far as this sort of dissidence went. Where still other regions contained substantial numbers of men who had no reason to support the land settlement, the anti-revolution slid into the counter-revolution. One example of this process was the department of the Gers which already had a long history of tithe strikes in the Old Regime and which was sharply disappointed when the Constituent Assembly decided to allow proprietors to add the equivalent of the former tithe to the leases. The peasants never accepted this and a meeting of three hundred at Mirande in July 1793 demanded half the tithe for the share-croppers. The department responded by arresting five ringleaders and issuing a stirring proclamation in patois warning the country people of false patriots and aristocrats who 'lead you like animals'. The uninhibited dechristianization of the representative on mission, Dartigoyete, could only have made matters worse. With government weakening after *thermidor*, in the Gers and elsewhere in the Midi, the result was a mounting number of demonstrations over refractory priests, church bells and conscription until the region joined the overtly royalist insurrection of the Year VII.

The sharecropping communities of the Midi tended to be pulled in several different ways because of the counterbalancing presence of masses of small proprietors and day-labourers who were often land-owners too, so the spread of popular counterrevolution was a slow and confusing process. On the other hand, the communities of the west tended to be divided more sharply between owners and tenants. The divisions between rich and poor were less noticeable than on the northern plains or in the viticultural regions. Labourers and hired hands were often tied to tenants through stable employment or kinship and the better-off tenants had a common experience of reasonable security, limited geographical mobility, and before 1789, of sharply rising rents.

The Constituent Assembly, obsessed with protecting landowners, offered no fiscal or financial relief. Instead taxes shot up dramatically. In property owning regions, the suppression of the tithe and feudal dues partially offset this because all landowners were the legal beneficiaries. On the other hand, in areas where rental arrangements prevailed, there was no possible way tenants could have gained anything. The effect of the reforms was to raise the operating cost of land dramatically. Thus a cleavage opened up between regions in the west where peasants owned their own land and where they rented it. In these latter regions, the inhabitants witnessed both higher taxes and higher rents. Indeed, from their point of view, they were indistinguishable: both raised the operating costs of land.

In regions like these, the rural élites had no incentive to support the Revolution. Moreover, there was no reason why they should do anything other than sanction the widespread revulsion against the Civil Constitution of the Clergy from going forward. Later, in March 1793, large regions of Brittany, Normandy, Maine and northern Anjou rebelled against the levy of 300,000 men and later in the year, hundreds of daring young men joined the Vendeans in their march across the Loire. When the representatives on mission arrived in the autumn and winter of the Year II to supervise the *levée en masse*, many more young men took to the woods rather than submit. There they began to organize themselves into bands to overthrow the persecutors of their religion. The result was *chouannerie* – the most extensive, persistent and durable peasant movement of the Revolution.

Chouannerie represented the armed wing of a rural community outraged at the shattering it had undergone since 1790 and nostalgic for an Old Regime in which people settled their problems on their own with little interference from government. The Civil Constitution split the ideal community and people dreamed of the day they could invert the existing order of things and expel the local republicans who had illegitimately imposed themselves.

Popular counterrevolution was therefore of a different order than that of the émigrés but the *chouans* often accepted their leadership because nobles too were a part of the ideal community and because the *chouans* knew they were weak. Above all, they lacked arms and munitions. Attempts by their leaders – Cadoudal in the Morbihan, Boishardy in the Côtes-du-Nord, Frotté in Normandy and Puisaye, the commander for all Brittany – to secure them from the incompetent British were generally failures. *Chouannerie* was therefore reduced to guerrilla tactics: murdering republican officials and constitutional priests, stopping grain convoys, forbidding the payment of rents to landowners, collecting rents on *biens nationaux* and ambushing republican patrols. Although the *chouans* were never more than loose confederations of impermanent bands, by the late summer of the Year II their tactics had brought government in the countryside to a halt. The war had also begun to spread to ten departments north of the Loire on a line west of Caen, Le Mans and Angers.

There is a persistent republican tradition that thermidorean weaknesses and incompetence were responsible for the spread of royalist insurgency. In fact, terrorist policies towards the Vendée had first re-ignited resistance and then offered no hope to rank-and-file insurgents because of the refusal of an amnesty.

One of the chronic realities of the wars of the west was the government's – any government's – inability to assign enough troops to the region to suppress the rebels. Contrary to standard Jacobin strategy, defeating the external enemy, rather than the internal, came first. During the Year II, this created the temptation to indulge in massacre. Later, the very same facts on the ground created the temptation to appease. Step by step, there was an amnesty for draft dodgers and rank-and-file *chouans*. As elsewhere, hundreds of suspects were released from prisons, representatives on mission removed priests who obeyed the laws from the lists of suspects (whatever that meant), the Convention proclaimed religious liberty once again (with many caveats), and even refractory priests could profit from the new relaxation provided they were not also émigrés. But, of course, by law, they were. One can imagine why the targets of these measures relating to the draft, to *chouan* insurrection, to religious practice and much else did not respond so enthusiastically to the thermidoreans' offer of reconciliation. The recent past apart, the law itself was totally contradictory.

Unsatisfactory as some of these divide-and-rule measures proved to be, they did produce a serious crisis of morale among the *chouan* leadership. They were also despairing of British aid, so they signed a pair of truces that applied to both sides of the Loire. Despite Mathiez's assertions to the contrary, British spies in the region concluded the truces helped the republicans rather than the royalists. The truces gave the republicans time to arrange for reinforcements while the *chouans* and Vendeans could do nothing to solve their greatest problems, the shortage of arms and powder.

Politics of Anti-Terror

The 9 *thermidor* did not in itself remove the Montagnards from power. They could claim some successes like the transfer of Marat's remains to the Pantheon, the monument to national heroes, and the expulsion of Fréron, Tallien, and the Dantonist Lecointre from the Jacobin club. On the other hand, the moderates could claim some successes too, like control of the Committee of General Security which undertook a round of arrests of petty terrorists in Paris.

What broke the political power of the Montagnards was the trial of Carrier. The necessity to put Carrier on trial was already a sign that the limitations on vengeance that Barère had expressed on 10 *thermidor* were no longer enough. The public certainly showed a limitless

fascination for the details of the death of the brute Robespierre and
pamphleteers did everything to satisfy this morbid curiosity by spinning
out more and more tales about the Incorruptible's last few months. A
device that had been used often enough against his enemies was now
turned on him. Beneath the beatific face lay the hideous visage of a
grimacing monster once the mask was ripped off. Thus too, the deputy
Merlin de Thionville summed up Robespierre's career in macabre terms:

> At first Robespierre's temperament was melancholic but finished in black
> bile. In the Constituent Assembly, his complexion was pale and leaden
> and he could not speak without shaking; in the Convention he turned
> yellow, then ashen like a corpse but a talking corpse . . .

But as fascinating as Robespierre was, Carrier met more immediate
needs. Putting him on trial for his excesses in Nantes, was, of course, a
pretext. For some, he could be made to represent all that was now
repulsive about the Terror, while saving other deputies who had done
as much. He could be a symbol of the Convention's professed desire to
restore the rule of law, but without raking up too many embarrassing
details about the past. For others, however, the trial stimulated a desire to
remedy all the wrongs the Montagnards had done. This led to a restoration of the expelled deputies and the still living Girondins and federalists. In the provinces, it also aroused passions that only the murder of the
local Montagnards could satisfy.

Those who were determined to make an example of Carrier took
advantage of the revelations of the 94 citizens of Nantes whom Carrier
had sent to the Paris Revolutionary Tribunal, in the hope, it was said,
they could be killed faster than they could be in Nantes. The 9 *thermidor*
saved them.

Their subsequent trial revealed the *noyades* in all their grisly detail.
Journalists in Paris wrote giddy stories about plots to depopulate half the
country, or about 'republican marriages', whereby young men and
women were roped together topless facing each other and tossed into
the Loire. The combination of sex and death among the young was an
irresistible theme. At the same time, there were allegations that Carrier
prowled the prisons looking for pretty girls, and returning to his abode
for orgies and gluttony. There was a story of a member of the infamous
Compagnie Marat, the local revolutionary army, who appeared at the
local club wearing a hat decorated with the ears of his victims. Finally,
there was a blizzard of pamphlets with titles like *When the Beast is in the
Trap, It Has to Be Killed*; *Off with the Head of Carrier and of all those
who Resemble Him*; and *Last Words of Carrier to Collot, Billaud, Barère
. . . and other Knights of the Guillotine*.

Both in the Convention itself and during his subsequent trial, Carrier deployed the 'thesis of circumstances'. He argued that the situation in Nantes at the end of 1793 was drastic. There was a possible siege from the Vendeans and the British were cruising off the coasts. Thus, extreme measures were necessary. The *conventionnels* and the Revolutionary Tribunal rejected the argument, even though they had already used it and many of them would use it later when they in turn were accused. They would use it later still in their memoirs. After an utter farce of a trial, Carrier went to his death on 26 *frimaire* (16 December). On the way to the *Place de la Révolution*, he stared fixedly at the crowd who cursed him and insulted him. He shook hands with his executioner before removing his coat.

But it was impossible to bury the past along with Carrier and it showed in the pamphlet literature and in the Convention and without. Even before the trial, there had been recriminations about actions while on mission and debates had begun about the legitimacy of 31 May and activities during the September massacres. Carrier's trial not only discredited repression still further but raised questions about how much the governing committees knew of the *noyades* and the atrocities of Lyon. So greatly had the atmosphere changed that on 18 *frimaire* (8 December) the Convention unanimously reinstated the seventy-eight deputies who had been imprisoned for the *journée* of 31 May–2 June. On 7 *nivôse* (27 December) it voted to impeach Barère, Billaud-Varennes, Collot d'Herbois and Vadier, the 'Four Big Guilty Ones' in the parlance of the day. Finally, on 18 *ventôse* (8 March) with only one dissenting voice, it recalled the Girondins who had participated in the federalist risings. Although the return of the proscribed deputies could be justified as a return to legality, it definitively altered the balance of forces in the Convention. Meanwhile, the Carrier trial had a fatal impact on the Jacobin network. The Jacobins' feeble attempts to defend the vigorous measures required in the Year II, if not Carrier himself who symbolized them, incited crowds to attack the Paris club. On the pretext of keeping order, the Convention closed the mother society on 22 *brumaire* An III (12 November 1794), and later forbade affiliation and collective petitions. This was a sign for many representatives on mission to close or purge the provincial clubs. They were already weakened by the post-*thermidor* confusion. Where they did not disappear on their own, the representatives usually finished them off.

The White Terror

But if the clubs generally disappeared, former club members were still around and they all shared what was by the winter of the Year III a thoroughly discredited past. Whether as former club members, former members of a local revolutionary committee, or members of the now despised revolutionary administration, they were all terribly exposed. Many simply fled the scene of their former exploits, but where they were either imprisoned or caught unawares, they were frequently killed. This was the 'White Terror'. This could mean several things at once, although it always refers to the Midi: the massacre of captive Jacobins either while they were being transferred from one prison to another or after an assault on the prison itself; or, the slaughter, one after another, of former terrorists by gangs of murderers. Whatever the form, these atrocities could not possibly have occurred without the collusion of local officials. The White Terror occurred in two waves, the first in the spring of 1795 and once again in the spring of 1797. In the first period, rabidly anti-Montagnard representatives on mission set the tone for local officials to tolerate, and even encourage, the murders of Jacobins; in the second, after the elections of the spring of 1797, selected local officials either turned a blind eye to the murders, or more likely, encouraged them. In both epochs, the local officials in question were former federalists, suspects or émigrés or all three. In other words, federalism was certainly spent by the autumn of 1793 but those who espoused its hatred of Jacobinism certainly were not.

The role of the representatives on mission was often critical. At Marseille, for example, the representatives Auguis's and Serres's policy of releasing suspects and imprisoning notorious terrorists set off a complicated struggle within the club whose president even committed suicide. Their purge of the administration, their release of scores of suspects and their closure of the club generated a massive demonstration on 5 *vendémiaire* (26 September) that snaked through the old town to the port where the representatives were lodging. Women started it and soon immense crowds of artisans and soldiers joined in, shouting pro-Montagnard slogans, sometimes in Provençal, sometimes in the usual wild and menacing language of meridional Jacobinism. The representatives labelled this a riot and so used the occasion to order many more arrests. The next step in the violent denouement at Marseille was the massacre of Jacobins imprisoned at Fort Jean on 17 *prairial* (5 June). There were many prison massacres throughout the Midi and elsewhere in the spring and summer of the Year III, at Nîmes, Aix-en-Provence (where there were five attempts that killed eight people), Bourg-en-Bresse, Lyon, St-Etienne, Lons-le-Saulnier, Montbrison, Tarascon, Aubagne, and a failed attempt at Salon. But the massacre at Marseille was probably the most bloody, and certainly among the most spectacular. Once again the complicity of authority was a necessary pre-condition. In this case, the representative Cadroy's denunciations of Jacobins were practically unbalanced and obsessed but they certainly suggested anything was permissible. Moreover, after the demonstration of 5 *vendémiaire*, representatives inflicted a thorough purge of 'Jacobins'; in other words in terms of local politics, they restored men whom the Jacobins had already persecuted. The new administrators whom Cadroy had installed lamely tried to justify themselves afterwards by claiming the prisoners had started a riot. Only the most gullible would believe this since no competent official would think of using vigilantes to repress a riot when reliable national guard and army units were to hand. The occasion for the massacre was a rising in Toulon whose purpose was to protest the massacre of 30 Jacobins in the prisons of Aix on 22 *floréal* (11 May), to protect persecuted patriots at Arles and to release those held in Marseille. The representative Isnard helped organize the defence of Marseille and urged anti-Jacobins to dig up the bones of their fathers if they could find no other weapons. A crowd of soldiers, sailors and working people from the arsenal and other workers from Toulon estimated at between 3000 and 8000 armed with cannon set out to relieve Marseille. But loyal troops and National Guards from Marseille met them outside the village of Beausset on 5 *prairial* (25 May) where 40 to 50 Toulonnais were killed and 300 were taken prisoner.

This provided the pretext to massacre Jacobin prisoners in retaliation at Fort Jean. There were probably no more than 40 killers but they were brutal, killing one person after another in their cells, then making clumsy attempts to hide the identity of the corpses by mutilating them. Others were unrecognizable because someone dragged a cannon into the prison and in blowing one cell door off, horribly burned those inside the dungeon. Somewhat fewer than a 100 'terrorists' were slaughtered. Both killers and victims shared a humble background in common, largely from various crafts, so the conflict was probably not based on class so much as status, background, and neighbourhood rivalries. Some of them were prisoners captured at Le Beausset, many others were former officials of the revolutionary committees of the small towns in the immediate region of Marseille. No one in authority in the Bouches-du-Rhône initiated an inquiry into the murders for many months afterwards, and indeed, unlike Carrier, his fellow *conventionnels* never called Cadroy to account. Some witnesses indeed claimed Cadroy arrived at Fort Jean just after the killings were finished, after he had dined well in town. Then, it was said, he ordered soldiers who had arrested some of the killers to return the weapons to the killers who then strolled out of the prison unharmed into the setting sun. One of them showed up as a killer in 1815.

Finally, on 1 *messidor* (19 June), Jacobin prisoners from Avignon, Arles and Toulon were murdered at Tarascon when a mob broke into the castle and hurled them over the dauntingly high walls into the muddy Rhône below. This was the climax of town politics that had long been divided between two competing families, a rivalry that no doubt preceded the Revolution, as similar rivalries did elsewhere. The occasion was a rumour that the armed Jacobins from Toulon were going to liberate the prisoners. A mob broke in to the castle and tossed 24 prisoners over the ramparts. Then, close to a month later, another mob from the surrounding villages broke in and threw another 23 to their deaths.

Just a month before those of Marseilles on 15–17 *floréal* (4–6 May 1795), there was a ghastly prison massacre at Lyon that illustrates the same combination of administrative incompetence, complicity and incitement that together produced an appalling disaster. Purging terrorists here after 9 *thermidor* was just the beginning of isolating former militants by disarming them, publishing their names in newspapers, and ordering them to submit to a form of house arrest. The representatives on mission, supposedly concentrating on the building subsistence crisis, ignored the threats to order. From early February, there were individual assaults and murders and there was even a newspaper, the rabid *Journal de Lyon* whose masthead called for the extermination of those who 'spill the blood of men'. The occasion for the massacre was the mob's dissatisfaction at the possibility that the trial of one terrorist would not result in execution. Finally, the grouping of so many Jacobins in a few prisons gave rise to rumours of an armed breakout followed by a generalized slaughter with multi-bladed guillotines. Like the September Massacres of 1792, the frenzy had its limits because the crowds, estimated at an unbelievable thirty thousand, allowed counterfeiters and criminals to escape while they set fire to the prisons to force the Jacobins on to the roofs where they were hacked to death. About one hundred people were killed. Some of the crowd were arrested and a trial was held before the Criminal Tribunal of the Isère in Grenoble but the amnesty of October 1795 cut the trial short and the accused were all released.

By the early summer, the round of large prison massacres ended. But the mob attacks that began before the massacres then continued for years afterwards. As early as *pluviôse* (February 1795), for example, a furious crowd at Avignon clubbed one of the judges of the infamous Orange tribunal, threw him into the Rhône and finally killed him with a harpoon. There were several cases in the Gard where the National Guard itself killed the prisoners it was escorting or on one occasion, getting out of the way when the crowd murdered prisoners on the Esplanade in Nîmes in broad daylight. There are countless examples of judges and local officials simply letting it be known when a transfer between prisons was going to take place and letting the mob do its grisly work.

Individual gangs did most of the killing. They were called 'Companies of the Sun' or 'Companies of Jesus' or both interchangeably. Because their specialty was murder, very little is known about them. At the beginning of the Year IV, the deputy Chénier claimed there were murder gangs operating in thirty towns and cities in ten departments, mostly in the southeast, although the number of such gangs was certainly higher. They had a fluctuating membership with a hard core and a fluid number on the periphery. There were about forty members in the gang of Aubagne, although as few as three could carry out a single murder. The best estimate suggests the gangs may have murdered several hundred people, far below the number executed in the same region in the Year II but enough to paralyse government altogether. Unlike the *chouans*, they rarely undertook military operations and rarely mouthed royalist slogans. Instead, they were the latest manifestation of a struggle that began before the Terror for control of the towns of the Midi. Federalism was an earlier emanation of the same phenomenon just as terrorism was the riposte to local federalism. When they expressed themselves at all, the gangs justified themselves as carrying out an anti-terrorist programme the authorities were too timid to tackle on their own. As a group of young men accused of being members of the gangs around Arles explained, 'the *septembriseurs*, the emprisoners, the hangmen of Robespierre . . . all committed murders . . . but they were included in the amnesty [of the Year IV]'. After 9 *thermidor*, they continued, 'there remained to punish the assassins who covered the surface of the Republic with blood . . . the agents of royalism . . . put in motion sentiments of vengeance by perfidious and atrocious insinuations . . . ' that the 'justice' of the Convention was not moving fast enough. But behind the rhetoric of law and order lay vengeance for all that the terrorists and the Jacobins had inflicted on them from the beginning.

Almost all the murders were premeditated. They were greatly aided by the inability of cities like Lyon and Arles to afford street lighting and so the grisly stabbings and shootings in the narrow streets of the old towns could continue anonymously, the bodies dumped quietly over the bridges into the Saône or the Rhône, or simply abandoned. These atrocities could happen in broad daylight before witnesses as well. In Lyon, five murderers stabbed a minor terrorist to death in his hospital bed where he had been taken after the same men had mugged him on the streets the day before. In Lyon too, the gangs broke into prisons before the massacres and murdered the terrorists in their cells, the frequency of this occurrence illustrating the complete breakdown of elementary government in the city. At Nîmes, a gang of men masked with balaclavas overwhelmed the prison guards one night and murdered three Jacobins in their cells. No one ever discovered who the killers were. At L'Isle in the Vaucluse, the local gang murdered a gendarme on the altar of *la patrie*. The impunity of these attacks is shown in the case of one Magnien, a printer, who, despite a military escort, was murdered by a dozen young men on horseback outside Montbrison in the Loire who then mutilated his body and repaired to a nearby inn to boast and refresh themselves.

By the end of the Year III, the few local authorities interested in doing their job often had a good idea of who the murderers were but they were powerless. Witnesses were terrified and juries almost invariably acquitted the accused. The young men thus flaunted their impunity. They took to wearing outlandish dress as uniforms, including buttons decorated with *fleurs-de-lis*. They also distributed cards inscribed with crosses or with the Virgin to young children. In Lyon, they lounged about the Hôtel du Parc on the Place des Terreaux; at Montbrison, they strutted about, their secret handshakes hardly necessary, armed with sharp-pointed canes, long swords, pistols stuffed in their pockets, stiletto knives – a favourite weapon everywhere – and long sticks known as 'juges de paix'. At Marseille, they hung about a café by the old port at the corner of the rue des Quatres Pâtissiers, baiting passers-by, forcing theatre audiences to sing the 'Réveil du Peuple', and probably murdering former militants at night. These murderers were often the same kind of people who supported the federalists in 1793. They were professionals, skilled artisans, and occasionally they worked in the food trades. Of the 19 accused of belonging to the gang at Arles, all but four were reasonably skilled artisans. The gangs of the Loire were composed of young men who were related to some of the wealthiest families of the region. They had drifted back to local politics in the Year III to offer the gangs encouragement and protection. They were almost invariably men of military age, if not actual deserters, sometimes former suspects, or even militant federalists or men whose families had been victims of the Terror by the handful. Their victims, besides being former terrorist officials, were much more likely to have been working people and artisans, constitutional priests, and professionals, including Protestants in the Gard and Lozère or Jews at Avignon.

It was only towards the end of its mandate that the Convention finally intervened to put an end to these travesties. Scared by the risings in October 1795 in Paris, it appointed the deputy Fréron to return to the Midi to restore order. Not much is known about Fréron's second mission and for contemporaries, the most memorable aspects were the sumptuous entries with floats and flowers into troubled towns like Arles. In Marseille, he was a favoured invitee to the salon hosted by Mme Bonaparte, the general's mother. The mission is controversial because his enemies accused him of being slow to go after refractory priests and émigrés and slow to purge the administration. No one really knows.

Even so, the government began placing various towns under a state of siege. Turning local administration over to the military could be effective as experience proved elsewhere but the government made a disastrous choice for the Eighth Military Division, that is the south-east. General Willot was both a knave and a simpleton. He was appointed at the end of the Year IV but he saw no reason to protect Jacobins whom he abominated, and his obsession with order was entirely one-sided. Jacobins were the enemy, no one else. So the killings could continue. Under his command, officials of the department of the Bouches-du-Rhône actually denied murder gangs existed.

Return of the Cordeliers Impulse

The Parisian risings occurred against the background of the most extensive disturbances since 1792. From the winter of the Year III onwards, there were troubles and riots in Rennes, Rouen, Amiens, Dieppe, Honfleur, Caen, Chartres, Melun and Saint-Germain-en-Laye. In the countryside, there were attacks on large farms, mills and grain convoys in the districts north of Paris along the Seine valley, and throughout the coastal regions of Flanders. As always in grain troubles, women were prominent in the disturbances, either directly or as instigators of the men. People demanded that local prices be as low as those of the controlled prices in Paris. At Rouen and Amiens, there were also cries for the return of the monarchy and elsewhere for the implementation of the Constitution of 1793 – any slogan, in other words, that would shock the authorities into action.

The Parisian risings were more complicated because they occurred in the context of the declining sectional movement. As it turned out, the sections were easy to purge. If the Marat section was typical, the revolutionary government had begun the process with purging 'hébertistes' in *germinal* An II and the 'robespierristes' could be purged in turn because there were so few of them. With moderates returning to section meetings after *thermidor*, the entire political complexion of a section could change overnight. Moreover, the end of the affair showed how much the sectional movement had depended upon the Commune and to a lessor extent upon the Cordeliers for co-ordination. With the Cordeliers gone, and nearly 90 people from the general council of the Commune executed immediately following *thermidor*, the sectional movement was in disarray.

By the autumn of 1794, the *sans-culottes* had to defend themselves too from the *jeunesse dorée*, the coiffed young vandals known for their extravagant dress, affected language and arrogant manners. Their girlfriends, often courtesans or prostitutes working out of the old Palais-Royal, wore green ribbons as a tribute to Charlotte Corday, or perhaps to the comte d'Artois. Although these thugs were not the private armies of Fréron and Tallien as was once thought, they certainly did enjoy protection from on high since many were petty civil servants and many were draft-dodgers or deserters. Nor were they a particularly important group. They did make such a nuisance of themselves that they forced the Convention to remove Marat's corpse from the Pantheon on 20 *pluviôse* (8 February 1795). Ordinarily though, their activities were simply demeaning or cowardly: destroying or defacing statues of martyrs of liberty, howling down 'Jacobin' theatre performances, beating up former terrorists, mugging militant women when they could catch them alone, and so on.

Galling as the *jeunesse dorée* was, hostility to them played a minor part in the *journées* of 12 *germinal* (1 April) and 1 *prairial* (20 May). Instead, the risings showed that many ordinary people had altered their thinking and that the anti-terrorist upsurge immediately following *thermidor* did have lasting consequences. In both cases, the cry for bread was not accompanied by the bloodcurdling threats against hoarders and speculators or demands for 'great measures' against the big farmers, dealers and millers. Some demanded the implementation of the Constitution of 1793 and thus the movement in Paris returned to its original Cordeliers roots of a general desire for direct democracy.

Indeed the 'insurrection' of 12 *germinal* was not properly a rising at all but a demonstration. The sovereign people, who were not armed, intended to read a series of petitions and addresses demanding bread and the Constitution of 1793. Representatives were then expected to implement them. This was typical Cordelier thinking. The situation got out of hand because the government did not arrange for enough guards and the immense crowds spilled over onto the floor of the Convention. After lengthy pleadings from the deputies, people went home.

As it happened, the demonstration presented an opportunity that was too good to miss. The Four Big Guilty Ones, Barère, Collot d'Herbois, Billaud-Varennes and Vadier, were ordered immediately deported to Cayenne and fourteen other Montagnards were arrested over the next few days. About 1600 'terrorists' were also disarmed.

At one level, the *journée* of *prairial* was a hunger riot, a protest against appallingly low rations which had dipped to a mere two ounces of bread during the previous month. As rations sank, as the inevitable complaints about favouritism were bandied about, as small children came close to starvation, some women reminded their neighbours that at least under the Jacobins or Robespierre, there was food. Others expressed sympathy for the King. No doubt in all these cases of extravagant talk, they may have sensed the presence of a police agent whose report is still in the archives for all of us to read.

Many of the demonstrators who descended on the Convention had the slogan 'Bread or Death!' pinned to their hats. The day began with women from the eastern quarters of the city invading shops and apartments, persuading other women and the men to join their march. Some groups marched behind young men beating drums. But unlike 12 *germinal*, there was a real attempt to employ armed force whether by suborning the artillery companies or persuading National Guard battalions to join. Once again crowds burst on to the floor of the Convention demanding bread and the Constitution of 1793. But no one among the demonstrators was willing to use their arms. After two days of confusion in which an unknown deputy was murdered, the *journée* fizzled out. Repression this time was swift. A military commission condemned 73 people to death, deportation or imprisonment. About 1700 militants were disarmed and close to 1200 were imprisoned, many without trial, whether or not they had participated in the rising. Forty Montagnards were arrested and the courts condemned six individuals to death. It was the conclusive end of the *sans-culotte* movement. After this, remaining militants were impaled on general police lists to be arrested as a matter of course whenever a regime felt jittery. Remaining militants like Babeuf in the Year IV, or others like General Malet under the Empire, or other radicals who were even more obscure during the Bourbon restoration drew the lesson that the era of insurrectionary politics was over. Their new arm was to be the secret society.

The Verona Declaration and Counterrevolutionary Strategy

By the spring of 1795, huge sections of the West were committed to out and out counterrevolution and it was spreading. The political colouration of the Midi was much more ambiguous, but even if the sponsors of the White Terror were not declared counterrevolutionaries, the effect of their activities was to undermine the Republic. With so much dissidence, a possibility was opening that might have brought conservative thermidoreans together with moderate royalists. Perhaps a restoration might have been possible, it is said, had the élites had been able to reach a compromise on the revolutionary settlement. Two things prevented this outcome. One is the purely speculative notion of whether the *chouan* and Vendean base of military royalism would ever have accepted any sort of compromise with any kind of republican. The other is whether any Bourbon Pretender would have done so. As it turned out, when the young son of Louis XVI died in the Temple prison in June 1795, his uncle, the comte de Provence, proclaimed himself Louis XVIII. His 'Verona Declaration' on ascending 'the throne' was deplorable and inept, a more reactionary document in every way than Louis XVI's *séance royale* programme of 23 June 1789. He promised a complete restoration of the 'ancient constitution' of the realm including the Church and *parlements* and promised to investigate abuses. But he never mentioned the Estates-General by name. This raised the question of whether a restoration would even be parliamentary. The promise to restore all 'stolen properties' would have alienated a huge constituency of owners of *biens nationaux* and all those who had benefited from the abolition of the tithe and seigneurial dues. The fact that the Pretender considered this a moderate document because it promised punishment only for the regicides in the Convention merely underlined his immense distance from reality. His British sponsors were appalled. Even so, the British government chose to ignore how unrealistic this was, because at this point they were not committed to a Bourbon restoration and they were prepared to negotiate with the Republic under certain circumstances. In the event, there were to be no serious concessions from the Pretender until the eve of the restoration in 1814. After the Declaration of Verona, only the Convention could defend the land settlement and civil equality. Thus, however unpopular the politicians in the Convention had become, they were the lesser evil. Moreover, the Verona Declaration committed the royalist leaders to civil war because the inflexible defence of reaction rendered any kind of meaningful regrouping of conservatives impossible. As the events of the next two years would show, it was not possible to harness the pure and constitutional royalists to the same chariot.

Within France itself, civil war in the west and in the Midi sapped the strength of the government. The Pretender encouraged this drift towards chaos. Still, the strategy Carnot had designed the year before produced some spectacular successes. Holland was occupied with ease and Dutch 'patriots' proclaimed the 'Batavian Republic', the first of the sister republics. Prussia, hoping for great things from the last partition of Poland, abandoned the coalition and by the Treaty of Bâle (5 April 1795) recognized French claims on the left bank of the Rhine in return for the neutralization of north Germany. This implied of course the permanence of the annexation of Belgium which meant that peace with Britain was problematic.

Despite the peace treaties with Prussia, Holland and Spain, the British were determined to open another front in Brittany following the collapse in Flanders. The original plan was to sponsor a landing in Brittany that would be part of an overall grand design that would involve an Austrian offensive, diversions from insurgents along the French eastern frontier, and insurrections from the *chouans* and Vendeans. None of these diversions worked out well: the Austrians remained in a stupor, the insurrections in eastern France never materialized and even in the West, the *chouans* and Vendeans failed to deliver.

The British pressed on, however, buoyed by Puisaye's and their agents' assurances that a landing would spark a vast insurrection. This never occurred either. Thus the landings at Carnac in southern Brittany of émigré regiments on 27 June 1795 had no broad support that could distract the republicans. General Hoche concentrated all available forces, some 10,000 men, against the 3000 Anglo-émigrés. Thousands of *chouans* came down to the beaches to greet their liberators as well, but very soon Hoche pushed them all into the Quiberon peninsula, sealing them off, 'as well as the rats,' as he reported. Meanwhile, quarrelling had broken out between Puisaye, the appointed commander and his supposed advisor, d'Hervilly, over who was really in charge and this fatally compromised decision making. Worse still, contrary winds held up the first of two waves of reinforcements by British soldiers. Hoche was determined to act before further reinforcements arrived, however. By a combination of shrewd tactics and guile, he captured Fort Penthièvre on 21 July thus opening the approaches to the peninsula.

Quiberon was the greatest single disaster the emigration suffered. According to the law of 25 *brumaire* An III (15 November 1794), among others, the officers and soldiers of the émigré regiments were returned émigrés and were punishable by death. Twenty-one military commissions, far more than had operated in the same region in the Year II, passed death sentences on 630 of them, including the former Bishop of Dol, while the judges affected to believe the stories of the civilians that they had been drunk or that someone had intimidated them. All but 108 of the most compromised *chouans* were also released. It was one of the bloodiest episodes of the entire Revolution and it was done using exceptional tribunals that operated without appeal, just as those of the Year II had. Moreover, no has ever claimed that revolutionary political culture lay behind the executions. Real, armed and ruthless opposition to the Republic did.

Finally, the executions created another *lieu de mémoire* that still exists: the ossuary at Auray in the Morbihan. It commemorates every leader of the Quiberon expedition except Puisaye, who simply has been blanked out, as if he never existed. This in turn is a reflection among the 'pures' who designed the monument that Puisaye was really 'England's man'. The proof of his perfidy is that he was once a member of the Constituent Assembly where all the rot had started in the first place. But if Puisaye's enemies, then and since, were fanatics, he was no moderate. When the *chouans* were finally defeated in 1796, the British shipped Puisaye and a few hundred *chouans* off to Queenston in Upper Canada, where the former general divided his time between writing his verbose memoirs and plotting how to seize this former French territory for the restored monarchy.

Constitution and the Last Insurrection in Paris

Otherwise, relative peace abroad and the victory at Quiberon allowed the politicians to concentrate on the original purpose of the Convention, drafting a constitution. As always, the drafters of the Constitution adopted a two-tier system of election. At the first level, the number of voters was about the same as the number of active citizens of 1790–1. This still made it the largest enfranchised electorate anywhere in any major country in Europe. But the direct power of choosing deputies was in the hands of men whom the voters selected. These electors had to pay taxes equivalent to 100–200 days of labour depending on the size of the locality. This was so high that many who had been electors in 1790–2 were excluded since the number of electors fell from roughly 45,000 to 30,000. It also excluded the middle-income groups who had led the revolutionary coalition from the beginning and, given the structure of wealth in the country at the end of the century, limited direct electoral power to the rich *rentier* bourgeoisie, rich tenant farmers and former nobility who were eligible, if none of their direct relatives was an émigré. By law, émigrés and refractory priests were excluded. The government had to court this relatively small group of wealthy men and it failed badly.

The nature of the electorate was a major cause of instability for the new regime. So too were the arrangements for the national government. The constitution-makers of the Year III were obsessed with preventing a dictatorship, whether from a Jacobin cabal manipulating a fickle populace or from a single individual. The solution was a rigorous separation of powers. To prevent a legislative dictatorship such as the Convention had exercised, the legislative branch was divided into two chambers, a 'Council of Five Hundred', composed of deputies older than thirty, that initiated bills and passed them after three readings, and a 'Council of Ancients', composed of 250 citizens older than forty that approved bills but could not initiate them or amend those sent up from the Five Hundred. There were no property qualifications to sit in either house. The executive branch was confined to a Directory of five members, one of whom was to retire by lot every year, the Directors themselves being chosen for all practical purposes by the Five Hundred. The Directory could neither initiate, make, or veto laws but could only suggest the legislature discuss certain matters. Although it had no control over the treasury and could not declare war, the Directory's constitutional authority to conduct diplomacy, to supervise the military, to execute the laws and to make appointments gave it an enormous power. Seven ministers were responsible to it alone as were the thousands of commissioners attached to the civilian and military wings of government. These men were supposed to supervise the execution of policy and so succeeded the representatives on mission and national agents. They also prefigured the Napoleonic prefectoral administration. The system of centralization thus continued. In practice, the commissioners acquired great power over the elected department and cantonal administrations – the districts disappeared and the communes were grouped into a single municipality per canton – because they took initiatives when elected officials did not and because they targeted the feckless or the subversive whom the Directory, quite legally, could sack. Many of these men were former Jacobins.

The Constitution of the Year III is often criticized for the strict separation of powers and for the system of elections in which one third of the Five Hundred retired each year. The British system of the 1790s got round the formal separation of powers by building royal clienteles in the legislature but the Directors could not do the same thing. The financial situation meant that any patronage was meaningless. The Directory did influence public opinion by subsidizing the press but going further would have meant reviving the clubs. Apart from anything else, the Constitution tried to shackle a recurrence of Jacobinism by forbidding clubs to affiliate or present collective petitions. The Directory could try to influence elections but its attempts to subvert the electoral process in the Year VI brought mixed results. If the Directory could not build a party in the legislature, the legislature could not alter the composition of the Directory except by waiting for one Director to retire each year and replacing him with one of their own – a slow process for an impatient legislature.

The Convention itself knew that it was unpopular and by the decrees of 5, 13 *fructidor* (22, 30 August) declared that two-thirds of the new representatives must be chosen from the corps of existing deputies, excluding sixty-seven Montagnards who had been arrested or suspended. Anyone who was eligible to vote in the 1793 referendum was invited to approve the new constitution and by a vote of 1,057,390 to 49,979 they did so. This figure may well underestimate the actual turnout, but no matter what, an estimated turnout of just 20 per cent was depressing enough. This was a decline of one-third between the plebiscites of 1793 and 1795. By the Year III, the civil war had spread so much that many primary assemblies in the west and the Midi never met at all. The law governing the plebiscite on the two-thirds decrees was so confusing that most primary assemblies just did not bother to vote on it or else they received it after they had already gone home. Some assemblies though were so outraged by this self-serving decree they re-assembled to vote against. For all these reasons, the two-thirds decrees were approved by only 205,498 to 108,754 out of a possible 6 million eligible voters. Even so, many of the negative tallies were not included in the final result. The increase in abstentions between the two plebiscites was a poor omen for representative government, rendered all the worse because local authorities often attributed it to a vague royalism or to disgust with the Convention's religious policies. Nor was the positive vote in the plebiscite an endorsement of the Republic. In the Vaucluse and undoubtedly elsewhere, the royalist counterterrorists dominated the primary assemblies and voted for the Constitution as a way of getting rid of the Convention. Most speeches in the primary assemblies showed that the electorate that did participate desired a return to regular government, internal peace and prosperity. The results of the elections to the legislature showed they thought that moderates were best able to achieve these goals. All but one of the deputies who protested on 31 May and who were recalled on 18 *frimaire* An III and all of the outlawed Girondins who were recalled on 18 *ventôse* were re-elected. Of the 511 *conventionnels* re-elected, only 157 were regicides. Of the 234 members of the 'new third', only 4 were *conventionnels* while 171 had never sat in a revolutionary legislature before. In other words, the electorate was not only anti-Montagnard but also hostile to experienced politicians in general. This was another poor omen.

From their promulgation, the two-thirds decrees raised a storm of protest that reached a climax in the insurrection of 13 *vendémiaire* An IV (5 October 1795). This was easily the strangest of all the Paris insurrections. If it was royalist, it was never avowed in the insurgents' declarations and petitions. If it was simply against the two-thirds decrees or the Convention generally, its success would have aided the royalists yet the Pretender's agents in the city disavowed it as the work of constitutional royalists. Oddly for an insurrection that is usually characterized as conservative, the sections were adept at using the language of popular sovereignty and the right of insurrection. The largest single trade category was composed of artisans and apprentices. Men who worked with their hands formed nearly one third of those arrested whose occupations are known. When partial national results were announced on 1 *vendémiaire* (23 September), a dozen sections refused to recognize them and, amid mounting disturbances involving the *jeunesse dorée* and the soldiers and campaigns in the 'anti-terrorist' press, the Lepelletier section in the heart of the financial district began an agitation to dissolve the Convention and convoke the new legislature without the two-thirds decrees. On 11 *vendémiaire* (3 October), an assembly of electors from fifteen sections, including Danton's old fief of Théatre-Français, met to protest the decrees. Later that evening, seven sections declared themselves to be in a state of insurrection. After much confusion, Barras, who had also led the Convention's forces on 9–10 *thermidor*, assumed command. Among the generals appointed to assist him was Bonaparte. Barras ordered Major Murat to seize the cannon at Les Sablons on the outskirts of the city. This proved decisive. Meanwhile, the sections' forces marched to attack the Convention. Government forces, considerably outnumbered with only 7800 men, had the advantage of cannon, and after a fruitless siege of several hours dispersed one column with grapeshot. Later, another column trying to advance from the south over the Pont Royal was similarly dispersed. By the next morning the city was in complete calm. The revolution of the 'honnêtes gens' was over.

Unlike *prairial* and Quiberon, the repression that followed was remarkably light. There were only two executions and although there was a considerable wave of arrests, hundreds were soon released. Among them or tried *in absentia* were Suard, the literary toady of the Old Regime, the abbé Morellet, the friend of the Brienne ministry of 1788, and a handful of Louis XVI's ex-bodyguards. The National Guard was put under effective control of the new general of the Army of the Interior, Bonaparte. Once a protégé of the representatives Salicetti and Augustin Robespierre at Toulon, now of Barras, the twenty-six-year-old general would soon show he was his own master. For the third time in six months, the army had saved the thermidorean Republic.

Initially, as an event in search of a meaning, *thermidor* was supposed to be about excising terror as a system of government. But those who overthrew Robespierre had no intention of abandoning revolutionary government as such. Very soon after, only a minimalist justification of revolutionary government survived; gone were maximalist definitions like regeneration or mass extermination or resettlement. Yet there also had to be a reckoning for what all agreed were crimes. Here the thermidoreans never were able to define what the boundaries of such retribution would be. For some, Carrier was a useful scapegoat, for others, the Four Big Guilty Ones. For still others the scope was far wider. For the representatives who were sent out on mission after mid-*thermidor* Year II, that scope could be very wide. While all could agree that suspects unjustly imprisoned could be released – something that even the revolutionary committees of the Year II accepted in principle – large sectors of provincial opinion wanted former terrorists not only purged and incarcerated but also punished. If the courts or the representatives on mission were hesitant or reluctant, so much the worse for them. Vigilantism, whether in the form of murder gangs or prison massacres, were the consequence. Here complicity of authority, whether it represented the national government or the former suspects who replaced the terrorists locally, was crucial.

By the winter of the Year II, government had broken down in many parts of the country. Along with the collapse of the currency, the consequence was increased vagabondage that at times slid into outright brigandage. Worse still was the emergence of an aggressive royalism, especially in the west. The *noyades* at Nantes and the march of the *colonnes infernales* had not subdued the Vendée, and local Jacobins at the time complained that these extreme measures resuscitated resistance. As troops were withdrawn to fight the summer campaign of 1794, the region watched *chouannerie* spread to huge swaths of the Republic north of the Loire. The failure of the peace treaties, the Quiberon landings which showed how deeply involved the British were in counterrevolution, the subsequent abortive attempt at an arms landing from the Ile-d'Yeu off Poitou followed by a landing from the Comte d'Artois – all of this was undertaken in the name of the Pretender whose Verona Declaration promised a total rollback to the pre-revolutionary era. For all those millions who had a stake in the Revolution's promises, this left only the new and hobbled Directory to protect the land settlement and civil equality.

It was thus understandable that the expiring Convention should have passed the draconian law of 3 *brumaire* An IV (25 October 1795) reviving the earlier penalties against the refractories and the émigrés and ordering a new round of deportations. It was understandable too that the *ex-conventionnels* used their majority in the new legislature to elect La Révellière-Lepeaux, Reubell, Le Tourneur, Barras and Carnot, all of them regicides, as Directors. Their past would be a guarantee of their future. The constitutional regime would be revolutionary, in spite of its innermost longings, because the anti-revolution and the counterrevolution would not surrender.

9

The Failure of Law

The expiring Convention did a brave thing when it established a constitutional government in the midst of a foreign war and spreading royalism and subversion at home. Moreover, the Directory, as the era is called, had some real accomplishments to its credit. Down to the end of its first phase, the coup of *fructidor* An V (September 1797), it knocked Austria out of the war and even the British were prepared to make peace. It also defeated militant royalism when it pacified the West in June 1796. After the coup of *fructidor*, it stabilized the currency at last and began to fill the government's treasury by collecting tax arrears. It also twice throttled the murder gangs, once in the autumn of 1795 and once again after the coup by purging the provincial administration of the murderers' sympathizers whose complicity allowed them to operate. It also undertook a thorough and partially successful campaign against the brigand gangs that also infested the Midi. Nonetheless, the regime failed. For all its genuine successes at home and abroad, the Directors, like almost all the political class throughout the period, believed in an aggressive foreign policy. In the end, for all the war weariness at home, the British would not tolerate this. A belligerent foreign policy had implications for the French at home. While the war was going well, troops could be released for repression at home. But the war put demands on people for sacrifices they could not, or would not, make. This showed up in tax or draft evasion. More broadly, the regime was uncompromising in its anti-clericalism, so huge amounts of opposition could be repressed but only to the point of driving it underground. The resistance to the war and the resistance to anti-clericalism in turn affected elections. Every election of the period repudiated almost all of those who had sat in the Convention and the elections of the spring of 1797 produced what looked like a near majority of deputies who voted for a relaxation of the émigré and anti-clerical laws. Many hoped this was the beginning of a Restoration via the ballot box. Three of the Directors feared exactly that and engineered one of the major convulsions of the period – the coup of 18 *fructidor* An V (4 September 1797). This saved the republican form of government but at the expense of the integrity of the legislature. Shameless manipulation of the elections of the Year VI and the crisis of the Year VII led part of the anti-directoral opposition to demand a stronger government. That opened the way for Bonaparte's dictatorship.

Administrative Collapse

In 1790, when the new constitution was forming, men by the hundreds of thousands volunteered to staff the new organs of government. Just six years later, men fled the opportunity. By the Year V, the problem of governance at the local level was almost indescribable. From the institutions of repression to the mundane organizations of government like taxing or keeping the vital statistics records, all was in appalling chaos. It is hard to imagine governments that had such a tenuous grip over their own officials and territory as the thermidorean Convention or the Directory down to *fructidor* An V.

There were several reasons for this. The price of an aggressive foreign policy was that few troops were available for repression at home. In the thirteen departments which made up most of the old province of Languedoc, there were only 4200 troops in the spring of 1796, many of the others having been drained off for the campaigns in Germany and Italy. Not one of the departments that royalist guerrillas ravaged had more than eight hundred soldiers in their garrisons. The result of leaving the departments more or less to themselves was that, unlike the prewar days, what remained of the National Guard and the gendarmerie handled most of the dissidence. Yet both of these institutions had been purged of Jacobins and many of their most enthusiastic elements had volunteered earlier for the army. Where royalists had not taken over the National Guard or where the Guard was not the Companies of the Sun or Jesus under another name, it was disorganized, apathetic and poorly armed. Like the old horsemen of the *maréchaussée* whom they succeeded, the gendarmes too were few, and large areas of the countryside remained more or less unpoliced. The scandalous state of the government's finances made this even worse. There were constant reports of gendarmes having to patrol on foot either because they had no forage or even that they had no horses. Pay was constantly in arrears and many had to take on second jobs or ask ordinary citizens for food. The picture of policeman as vagabond was equalled only by their lack of zeal, which was quite understandable since they were obviously no match for either the royalist or the criminal brigand bands. When the brigands raided the tax office at Evans in the Creuse, two gendarmes tried to save their lives by falling to their knees and crying, 'Vive Louis XVIII!'

The gendarmes might have been more zealous if the administration had supported them but conditions were dreadful here as well. Almost everywhere, the Directory's commissioners had to beg notable citizens to stand for office and on occasion even threatened them with prison if their refusal continued. Suitable candidates for office in the Côte-d'Or developed such an epidemic of medical problems and business commitments that it took four months to fill positions in the department's central administration. Apathy and the inability of the government to pay promptly even worthless stipends were only part of the problem. Politics had shown itself to be too unrewarding or too dangerous for the men who so generously assumed local office in 1790. In the Var, for instance, 105 men were department administrators between 1790 and 1795, not one of them for the entire period. At the district level, there were nearly five hundred administrators, procurators or national agents and only two served throughout. Similarly, not one of the sixty-odd individuals who served on the district of Narbonne had a continuous record of service. With the Jacobin administrators gone, this often left only the feckless, the indifferent or worst of all, former suspects and federalists to manage local affairs. Provincial officials ignored directives, protected and even encouraged murder gangs, deserters and draft-dodgers or, especially in rural areas, failed to investigate or even report assaults on constitutional *curés*, murders of owners or farmers of *biens nationaux*, muggings of former Jacobin officials and so on. Municipal officers in the countryside connived at the massive evasion of the laws on religious observance. Judges and juries were extraordinarily lax in applying the law and witnesses were intimidated either by friends of the accused or by those already acquitted so that building a case became next to impossible. Prosecutors often did not dare bring a case lest juries acquit men whom they considered guilty of strings of murders.

After the royalist victories in the local elections of the Year V, defiance had reached such a point that officials even trumpeted their attitudes. In the Lozère, where the president of the central administration no longer did any official work, and another administrator spent all his time on a private lawsuit, and where taxes were not collected and émigrés threatened buyers of *biens nationaux*, refractories had been allowed to take over all the churches including the cathedral at Mende, because, the remaining administrators claimed disingenuously, 'we do not understand by fanaticism the religious sentiment which nature has engraved so profoundly on the heart of man and which is for him . . . the inexhaustible source of the most gentle consolation'. The administrators of the canton of L'Etre in the Manche were more honest when they said that enforcing the laws on religious observance would cause an insurrection 'which could have the most disastrous consequences'. Officials in the Cantal reported that municipal officers 'are in such a state of stagnation that, out of fear of being murdered or having their properties set on fire, they do not dare denounce them [the refractory priest] or demand the execution of the law'.

Religious 'Revival'

Religious issues were both a cause and a consequence of the administrative weakness, a cause because popular insistence on religious ceremonies defied the law, and a consequence because the government rarely had enough strength to enforce the law. Although the thermidorean and directoral regimes repudiated the Terror, they did not repudiate anticlericalism or even certain aspects of dechristianization. The fundamental law governing religious observance, that of 3 *ventôse* An III (21 February 1795), permitted freedom of conscience but restricted freedom of religious expression so much that the public display of religious ceremony was forbidden. Since Catholicism especially relies greatly on collective and public rite, the law was directly at odds with huge sectors of public opinion. The state intended a heavy tutelage of the Church. Although the state would no longer pay the stipends of the constitutional clergy, churches and presbyteries remained state property. Communes could not in their collective name buy or rent a building to be used for religious purposes, nor tax their inhabitants to build one. Religious collectivities could not accept perpetual donations. Several restrictions on actual practice paralleled the desire to debilitate the Church financially. Priests could not wear their costumes in public and outdoor processions, and bell-ringing and statues, crosses and inscriptions which could be seen by the general public were all forbidden, while the *décade* was reserved for civic festivals.

The law was unenforceable. Many priests who returned from abroad or emerged from hiding never bothered to take the new oaths of submission the laws required. Nor did they remove themselves from the émigré lists, so they could still be arrested. Much religious activity therefore retained a clandestine character. The law of 3 *ventôse* itself was also bound to keep many of the faithful as alienated as they had been in the Year II. Since the parishes had often contributed a great deal towards building the churches, their confiscation could only be considered governmental theft and since popular religion contained elaborate ceremonial and liturgical aspects, the forbidding of outdoor worship also antagonized large numbers of people. The laity especially continued to defy the law. This was particularly easy in regions where geography rendered government weak. Thus in the wild and isolated mountains of the Massif Central, with its impenetrable forests, daunting gorges and impassable roads, supporters of the refractories lived almost entirely outside the apparatus of government. In this region many refractories had never been deported and conducted clandestine worship from 1792 on, moving from one safe house to another, conducting Mass in barns, private homes or simply outdoors at night. While light from the torches danced eerily over the faces of the faithful and under the tall pines above, shepherdesses kept watch, crying 'Wolves! Wolves!' if any army patrol got too near.

The constitutional church was as despised as ever. In the Lozère, the constitutional bishop claimed that he was almost alone against public opinion, while the department wrote that in the north there were cantons which were 'entirely sold to the [refractory] priests, where people are totally ignorant of the republican regime; no official does his duty; people sing publicly in the churches; processions and other ceremonies take place outdoors'. At Blesle in the Haute-Loire in the Year V, people were so anxious for religious ceremonies that they rescued two old and infirm refractories from house arrest and forced them to say Mass. In the same department, officials reported that 'several priests conspired to go in a procession according to the ancient usages to a hamlet called La Trinité, a place formerly so venerated that people came from far off to offer the priests living there offerings as considerable as they were multiplied'. There were also installation ceremonies once the priests came out of hiding or returned from abroad. The entire commune of Belpech in the Aude participated in such a ceremony with men carrying a large cross, women a smaller one, followed by the chanting priest in vestments, the rest of the inhabitants trailing behind, everyone making the tour of the parish while the church bells rang. There were similar processions at Lauzerte and Miramon in the Hérault in which people also danced the *farandole* and shouted 'Vive la République! A bas les Jacobins!'

Indeed, so many people were involved and defiance was so general that this was no longer a clandestine church. At Saint-Victurien in the Haute-Vienne, on Ascension Day 1796, 2–3000 people came from miles around and walked to a holy spot to touch the skull of a statue in the hope of innumerable cures. Throughout the Limousin, more crosses appeared at crossroads, along paths, at village squares and on private property than there had been in the Old Regime. People broke into churches to sound the bells, to mark the time of day, to ward off thunder and to re-establish community identity. At Carpentras in the Vaucluse in the Year IV, 4000 people showed up to witness a former constitutional *curé* retract his oath. When gendarmes tried to arrest a refractory who was saying Mass in a hayloft to two hundred people at Marie in the Haut-Rhin, they received no help from the municipal officer who excused himself, while his wife cried out, 'Yes, we want the Mass and we'll have it and ...know that you'll be the victim [of our religion] for everybody detests you'. Sometimes, these incidents took an utterly original form. At Maisonnais in the Creuse, near the spectacular anti-seigneurial riots of 1790, someone said of the municipal officers who enforced the law, 'that these buggers, we have them.... that the chicken is boiling and it'll soon be cooked [and] we'll eat it, that we took the nobles and soon we'll have all the bourgeois.... these wretched *messieurs* aren't capable of preventing us from ringing' the church bells.

People expressed their devotion well beyond these isolated and lonely regions. By the Year V in the Nord and Pas-de-Calais, armed peasants were guarding missionaries from Belgium or local refractories. These priests regularly said Mass in the open to hundreds, and sometimes thousands of people. In practices that were common enough throughout the country, liberty trees were torn down or defaced or replaced with calvaries. Nor was a priest always necessary. At Pecquencourt in the Nord, the women fell on the unfortunate buyer of a chapel, took the keys from him and then marched around the commune carrying a statue of the Virgin and singing vespers and litanies. In the canton of Moyaux in the Calvados, it was common for laymen to perform religious services and the lay 'priest' was a cobbler. At Sette in the Hérault, about thirty women and a few men carried a corpse from its home to the cemetery, singing funeral psalms along the way.

Clearly, the desire for religious ceremonies was very widespread and the movement should not be seen simply in terms of the government's supposed laxity towards refractory priests or returned émigrés. A priest, while desirable, was not always necessary.

Indeed, in this period, as during the Terror, the line between the defence of traditional religion and the exotic was easy to cross. The 'white Masses' or the 'blind' Masses, or the 'school masters' Masses', as they were variously called, would be the best example. In the Old Regime, the Church utterly forbade lay preaching or liturgy in almost any form. But without priests during the Revolution, the laity went from holding private meetings of devotion, which was certainly acceptable, to conducting their own version of the Mass, which traditionally was not. More remarkable still, was the participation of women in these ceremonies, a participation that in no way was traditional. For a religion that had excluded women from liturgical roles for well over a thousand years, the prominence of women in leading roles in religious practice and protest is quite remarkable. This distinction between ancestral practices and unconscious innovations is one an historian imposes to understand better what women were doing, as opposed to what they claimed to be doing. For them, certainly, no such distinction between the traditional and the unprecedented existed.

They rang bells, sang offices and vespers, and led public processions. They were almost always in the forefront of the enforced reopening of churches and almost always had a role in rescuing refractories when the gendarmes were fortunate enough to capture them. Either they fell on the hapless gendarmes themselves or they were scouts for the men who were masked and armed. In the Yonne at any rate, women were prominent in protecting the material objects related to the local church and by extension the local community. At the height of the Terror, they had opened their homes to clandestine Masses, and hid refractory priests. They spearheaded attempts to reopen churches, to prevent the confiscation of holy objects or even useful furniture, and harassed those who usurped the produce of the presbytery's gardens. Women taught morality within the family in the Old Regime and persecuted other women who violated it, but they had always needed the priests to elaborate and reinforce their authority. The removal of the clergy disoriented their role considerably and much of women's religious activity in this period aimed to restore it.

Another example of the unusual aspect that participants portrayed as a revival of tradition would be the commemoration of the graveyards of the victims of the revolutionary tribunals. We have already seen one of these, the pilgrimage to the graves of the victims of the Popular Revolutionary Commission of Orange. There are others. Outside Angers, the public proclaimed the graves of the victims of the local revolutionary commission as the 'Field of Martyrs' and the faithful visited the place until quite recently. From the beginning, local revolutionaries denounced this activity as a new fanaticism and claimed the clergy was behind it, but to no avail. Also near Angers, the story was told of a totally mysterious man from Lower Brittany whom the revolutionaries killed. Some said this man was a bishop, murdered while chanting the Mass, some said there were three bishops.

Implausible as all these stories are, they do make a serious point: the utter failure of the Jacobin and republican analysis that if only the priests could be expunged from the territory of the Republic, the natural goodness of the people would station them on the road to Reason. In fact, without priests, popular religiosity became more exotic, not less; more politically subversive, not less; and more imaginative, more creative because people were terrified that the world they knew was no more. But in invoking the past, communities created a tradition.

From composing a majority of the parish clergy in 1791, the constitutional church was in its death throes by the Year III. Its priests in the west found refuge in the towns and garrisoned *bourgs*, not daring to emerge even in daylight, otherwise the *chouans* and Vendeans would have killed them. Here, and in the centre and north of France, where dechristianization had removed them in one way or another, the parish network scarcely existed. Elsewhere, there are glimpses of individuals trying to carry on, but as often demoralized by the indifference or hostility of their parishioners. In these circumstances, the brave attempt of the abbé Grégoire, regicide bishop of the Cher, and a handful of constitutional bishops to revive the constitutional church, and with it the old ideals of a regenerated church in a Christian country, was a failure. Only thirty-two of the bishops elected in 1791 were at the head of their dioceses ten years later. Twenty-eight sees were vacant.

Although this had never been their conscious intent, the revolutionaries had shamelessly used the constitutionals and after *thermidor* trashed them. Throughout the Years III and IV, many – how many is impossible to say – *curés* made their peace with the refractory church, the humiliating retractions imposed and accepted a sign of their isolation, disillusionment and bitterness. As it turned out, a regenerated Christianity and the Revolution were incompatible. For the resurgence of religion in this period was that of the refractories. They were slowly rebuilding their parish organization from the ground up, often with the cooperation of a devoted laity. In several dioceses – Le Mans, Rouen, Le Puy and Lyon among them – the émigré bishops sent in vicars-general to reorganize the church. When they arrived from abroad, they met many refractories who were already extremely active. Many of these in turn had evaded even the searches of the revolutionary committees of the Year II. Moreover, the refractory church was for all intents and purposes a royalist church. However much some Catholic journalists and seminarians in the capital were searching for a formula that would permit an accommodation with the Republic, other clerics were totally committed to its overthrow. A majority of the émigré bishops pronounced against the oaths of submission to the Republic because they violated the 'loyalty due our legitimate sovereign' and a few equated those who took these oaths with the schismatics of 1791. One parish priest from the old diocese of Dol in Brittany judged those who took the new oath as 'scandalous, suspects, very dangerous for religion, abetters of republicanism and dishonouring their ministry by their shameful conduct'. Other priests acted on their royalist sentiments. The abbé Bernier, later one of the negotiators of the Concordat, was an important advisor to the Vendean general, Stofflet, and other priests served on the royalist councils in Brittany. In the Midi, several were actually military chiefs of the royalist brigand bands. But it was their pastoral work which was most subversive. At Champagnat in the Saône-et-Loire, the refractory preached that the Constitution was the work of 'the wicked and the impious [against] the usurpation of the property of the clergy and the émigrés...[and for the] return of the monarchy, seigneurial rights and the tithe'. In the Côtes-du-Nord, it was said that the priests 'inspired the greatest contempt for the patriots and promised heaven as a reward for those who assassinate them'. Around Orres in the Hautes-Alpes, an unidentified refractory was preaching 'to the credulous inhabitants of the countryside that the payment of taxes, [and] that the call to the young men to fly to the defence of *la patrie* are not obligatory, that religion condemns it'. At Rosières in the Haute-Loire, the abbé Bernard forbade those who followed him from 'seeing or having any relation with the schismatics, that is, the republicans'. Such anathemas had been heard earlier in 1791–2 as well, but by the Year IV (summer of 1796) they were much more common for the quite understandable reason that so many of their colleagues had gone to the scaffold. For men like these, an accommodation with the godless Republic was inconceivable.

Brigands, Bandits and Chouans

One of the consequences of the administrative collapse of the period was brigandage. Like their counterparts in the Old Regime, many of the criminal gangs reflected the distressing misery of the countryside which was aggravated terribly by the economic crisis of the Years III and IV Over one third of those indicted for their activities in the infamous *bande d'Orgères* that ravaged the Beauce joined after the Year II, men and women pushed to the edge by unemployment and near starvation, made desperate by the suppression of most public charities and the inadequacy of private philanthropy. Aside from the permanently rootless, many of them were of the same social groups which had rioted in the same region in 1792: agricultural labourers and artisans, some of whom had left a desperate situation in the towns to beg or to look for work in the countryside. Such bands could have a very wide area of operations. One band of *chauffeurs* – so called because they roasted the feet of farmers to extort money from them or to discover where the proverbial sack of coins was hidden – roamed the entire countryside between Rouen and Ghent in Belgium. Officials suspected that they used the military and gendarmerie as fences. The entire village of Bollène in the Vaucluse apparently lived from robbing travellers, and when their chief was arrested in the Year VI, two hundred of his followers disarmed the soldiers at Valréas and released him, crying, 'Vive le Roi! Victory is ours!' Nor was such village support for brigands a unique case. The frequency of reports of the murder and robbery of isolated soldiers returning home through the Alpine passes from service in Italy, and the inability of authorities to stop it, suggests a widespread complicity on the part of the local population who, of course, also protected refractory priests.

It is difficult, in fact, to distinguish criminal brigandage from royalism. Highway robbers, disguised as National Guards, took only government tax money from the stagecoach between Coutances and Saint-Lô in the Manche and left ordinary passengers alone in *messidor* An V. Their counterparts near Chantilly outside Paris dressed in green *carmagnoles*. They spoke an unintelligible slang to each other. They robbed the Paris–Amiens–Ghent stage. They also said they were part of the 'armée de Condé' and wished to 'indemnify themselves for the losses which *la nation* had forced on them'. Those who robbed the Brest–Paris coach near Mayenne were nicknamed 'Bourbon', 'Condé' and 'Artois'. Bands of young draft-dodgers who thrived in the faraway hills of the Var by robbing passing merchants and owners of *biens nationaux* called themselves 'chouans'. In the Year IX, police spies tossed a bomb into a cave in which the brigands of Aups in the Var were sleeping, killing eleven. Among the victims' effects was a 'letter dictated by Christ Himself through a wise child of seven, in golden letters and in Languedocien', promising safe delivery for pregnant women and protection against the ravages of fire, pestilence and war. Much of the 'brigandage' of this period thus turns out on closer examination to have a counterrevolutionary intent.

The distinction between genuine criminals speaking the chic argot of royalism and the 'brigands royaux' proper is not easy to make because of the habit of republican authorities of labelling all clandestine attacks on their supporters as 'brigandage'. This conflation could be deliberate. Thus, one official in the Ardèche denounced the gang around Tanargues as 'composed of ignorant beings, dragged in by fanaticism and guided by the hope of rapine, [which is] the primary motive of their atrocities'. Such claims are suspicious but there may have been something to them elsewhere. Thus, in the extreme south-east, around Nice, a smuggler approached a customs official, claimed to have threatened other officials with a stiletto knife, and bribed others to smuggle cattle over the border to Piedmont. He also said he did not want any 'Frenchmen' in his commune, predicted the defeat of the French armies and cried 'Vive l'Empereur!' that is, the Holy Roman Emperor.

Like *chouannerie*, popular royalism in the Midi had broad community support. As in the west, there are countless examples of communities forcing humiliations on local Jacobins by compelling them to replace liberty trees with calvaries or forcing them to abjure their errors by throwing them to their knees and requiring them to kiss the cross. In the commune of Clans in the Alpes-Maritimes, a band armed with stilettos, knives, carbines, led by someone with a feather in his hat, wearing a blue military uniform with epaulettes and sword in his hand, dragged one Jacobin out of his house, and in broad daylight, tied two fingers together so tight they later turned black, reproached him for pursuing conscripts and émigrés, hauled him to the edge of a ravine, but thought the better of shooting him. Instead, they extorted 25 gold *louis*. Elsewhere, women had an important role in these ceremonies restoring proper relations in the community in both the west and the Midi. In both regions, nostalgia for an idealized community dominated. As one was accused of saying, 'Were we not really happy then?...We were free then; we hunted when we wanted.'

Like the *chouans*, the 'brigands royaux' took upon themselves the responsibility for harassing, mugging or murdering local republicans who had gone too far. They were often young men of military age who had taken to the hills rather than be incorporated. Draft-dodging had begun in the Year II and the terrorist authorities could scarcely contain it. After *thermidor*, it reached amazing proportions. It was said that there were 1000 draft-dodgers in the district of Villefranche in the Rhône alone in the Year III and 5–6000 in the Vaucluse who could survive, thanks to the complicity of neighbours and municipal officers, with some ease. In the Haute-Loire, Tarn and Allier there were communes in which almost all of the young men managed to evade the draft and about one fifth and more later deserted their battalions. Neither the amnesty of 10–23 *thermidor* An III (28 July–10 August 1795) nor the recourse to military tribunals for evaders in the law of 4 *nivôse* An IV (25 December 1795) had much effect. Officials in the Landes had not arrested a single draft-evader or deserter in the Year IX despite all their efforts for the previous several months.

Attempts to round up refractory priests and draft-dodgers led to outright insurrections. At Beaupuy in the Gers a patrol of only fifteen was disarmed by a furious crowd of 1500 shouting, 'To hell with the Republic and *la nation*...We want our priests and a king!' This in turn sparked the men of Encausse, Monbrun and Cassemartin to invade L'Isle Jourdain, the departmental capital, to retrieve the church bells that had been confiscated in 1793 while bands of young men roamed the district mugging owners of *biens nationaux*. Efforts to arrest the members of these bands failed utterly. The four bands that operated around Saint-Palais in the Basses-Pyrénées specialized in the murder and pillage of former terrorist personnel. The local Basque population, who had been forcibly removed from their homes by the representatives on mission,

Cavaignac and Pinet, as part of the war effort in the Year II, strongly supported them. Of the 26 brigands eventually captured, 12 were deserters. As these examples show, the bands grew out of the counterrevolutionary sentiments of the local population and so they were grafted willingly to the wider designs of the royalist leaders. The band of the émigré Goty-Roquebrune that operated in the Haute-Garonne was a part of one of these royalist networks in the southwest. He was shot in a gun battle in *ventôse* An IV, but his men were able to survive by fleeing into the Ariège or Aude, or at worst, over the mountains into Spain.

The most nauseating of these groups was surely the *barbets* who operated in the hills above Nice. They had their own ideas about having been incorporated into *la grande nation* and to show their repugnance, they not only murdered those who collaborated with the French, they decapitated the victim. Often the head was never found again, or it was tossed into a nearby pig sty and the animals devoured it. The verbal violence of the *barbets* could be just as chilling: one named Constatin Cognoli, 'bragged on many different occasions of having murdered [*assassiné*] a considerable quantity of French soldiers, up to 150 at least . . ., and of having eaten the liver of several of them and of having eaten bread covered and soaked with the blood of another soldier'. Cognoli and his men also extorted money by threatening to bury their victims alive. Beside these atrocious individuals the heavy-smoking, gross-mannered, smallpox-ravaged Dominique Allier, leader of a band that operated in the Haute-Loire and Ardèche until his capture near Le Puy in *fructidor* An VI (August 1798) was relatively mild, although he too was a killer. He could trace his counterrevolutionary pedigree through almost every conspiracy in the Midi beginning with Froment's in 1790.

Since the brigand bands were composed of clandestine warriors, it is difficult to know much about the nature of their local support or who their members were. The geography of their operations can be known in a general way from various police reports. Thus, it was concentrated in the departments of the Rhône valley beginning around Lyon and continuing south to the Mediterranean and branching west through the Aveyron and Hérault to the mid-Pyrenees and east through the Bouches-du-Rhône, Var, Basses-Alpes and Alpes-Maritimes. Some districts were affected less than others but by now much is unknown. The social composition of the bands can be better known thanks to an analysis of some of those convicted by the special tribunals that operated over most of these regions in the Years IX and X. Thus, among the sixty charged with being members of the *bande d'Aubagne* that roamed around the town in the Bouches-du-Rhône between the Years III and IX, there were four émigrés, two priests, four in the professions, eight in the food trades; except for a single ploughman, the rest were in assorted other clothing and building trades. In other circumstances, and with the exception of the émigrés, this could have been the social composition of almost any small-town revolutionary committee of the Year II. This gang represented the urban element of the town, indeed because of complicity, it operated at the behest of the urban élite, some of whom, it was said, planned the killings in the backroom of a local café. They did not represent the surrounding countryside. The vine-dressers and frightfully poor sharecroppers were resolutely Jacobin in their politics.

But the gangs above all represented local politics because they did not conceive of themselves as being part of a broader movement. Social conditions varied and so too did those accused of being gang members. Thus, of 53 people condemned by the special tribunals in the Basses-Alpes, Bouches-du-Rhône, Var and Vaucluse whose occupations are known, 26 were peasants, only six were in non-manual occupations and the rest were scattered throughout various artisanal trades. More generally, there was a broad continuity between who supported the Jacobins and who supported their opponents. Colin Lucas's extensive survey of the breakdown of this pattern of support shows that village and town notables supported the anti-Jacobins while the relatively unskilled supported the Jacobins. But there was a very broad group of artisans who could go either way. This was the same pattern as occurred in Arles in 1792 and perhaps for the same reasons: neighbourhood, how settled a family was, how close were its ties to the community, whether one had been a member of the pre-revolutionary guilds, all counted in determining loyalties. Whatever the case, the figures do show that 'brigandage' and murder was a popular movement, dependent on refractory priests and émigré officers only to the extent that ordinary people wanted to be dominated or led. Nor was it brigandage of the rootless and criminal sort found in the *bande d'Orgères*. Where in this case only about half the mendicant brigands had been born in the region where the band operated, in the case of 53 royalist brigands where information is available, 30 were living in the same town or village where they had been born and only eight were domiciled outside their native departments. The lists of those condemned also confirm the importance of conscription. Of 43 whose ages are known, 28 would have been subject to it in 1793.

One of the reasons the Midi occupied so little of the Directory's attention was that the 'brigands royaux' were not able to accomplish much militarily. An attempt by Lamothe-Piquet's men to take Saint-Etienne in the winter of the Year IV failed. So did an attempt to take simultaneously Nîmes, Montpellier, Le Puy and Privas a few months later. But if they did little militarily they did a great deal of damage locally.

The Vendeans and the *chouans*, on the other hand, were potentially much more dangerous because of the possibility the British would be able to arm them. Several such landings of arms did take place – to Charette in December 1795 after the comte d'Artois left the Ile-d'Yeu, to Cadoudal in the Morbihan and to the *chouans* near Fougères. These shipments were disappointingly meagre to the royalists but the Directory still had to prevent the rural populations of the west from being properly armed. Failure risked repeating the nightmare of another Vendée in 1793.

To crush the west, the Directory took measures that were as drastic as any attempted in the Year II. On 7 *nivôse* (28 December), they turned the western departments over to military control, amalgamated the three armies into a single Army of the Coasts of the Ocean and entrusted command of the new army and the entire region to General Hoche. Once again, this opportunity emerged because of the peace with Spain. Veterans of this war were transferred to the west. Foreign success created the opening to tackle domestic repression. The new Army of the Coasts rose to about 100,000 men by spring of 1796, about half of whom were in the field at any one time – more men in other words than were given to General Bonaparte who began his much more famous Italian campaign at the same time. The results were almost as spectacular. With such large numbers of men, Hoche employed what was called the 'flying columns' technique of counterinsurgency whereby troops criss-crossed a designated area, pursuing band chiefs, disarming the local population and preventing bands from coalescing into important assemblies. Moreover, the troops were concentrated on particular regions so that the impression was created of an overwhelming force. The method had already shown itself brutally effective against Charette in the early autumn of 1795. He found himself hunted down, safe only in the marshes of Poitou or the most impenetrable forests, shunned by the civilian population, his irregulars slipping away and his lieutenants prudently making accommodations with republican generals. When Stofflet finally broke the peace in late January, he was only able to gather a few hundred stalwarts. He was captured and shot a month later. Charette was captured too and before execution on 9 *germinal* (29 March), he was paraded through streets of Nantes in chains like a criminal to mark the contrast with the arrogant general who had negotiated a peace among equals with the representatives just a year before.

Meanwhile, the areas north of the Loire had been stripped of troops. Yet the *chouans* were able to accomplish very little because they had so few arms and even less powder. Hundreds of them stalled before tiny garrisons of six men and were incapable of protecting properly the few landings of arms and émigré officers. They could hardly withstand the assault Hoche launched after the victories in the Vendée. Demoralized by the execution of the popular Charette and terrified of the thousands of troops marching through their areas, one by one the regional leaders began to surrender. The war in the west was over. On 2 *messidor* (16 July), the Directory decreed the Army of the Coast of the Ocean 'worthy of *la patrie*'.

Yet the west was not pacified in the sense of being won over. Instead, it was crushed. Although Hoche advocated the greatest respect for freedom of religion and was willing to make accommodations with refractories at the local level, the law forbade genuine freedom of religious expression. Nothing at all was done to mollify grievance over higher taxes, requisition of foodstuffs or security of tenure. Hoche also attempted to impose greater discipline on his troops. Yet there were too many instances of marauding for this to have been effective, and in some areas the troops' very excesses secured the *chouans*' surrender. Moreover, the Army of the Coasts of the Ocean was authorized to supply itself locally – a reflection of the inability of the Directory to support an army even within the frontiers of 'la grande nation' and a measure that obliterated the line between requisition and pillage. What good was payment for requisitions in worthless *assignats* anyway? The path was prepared for the renewal of *chouannerie* in the Year VII . . . and for the region's enduring preference for right-wing voting until the 1980s.

Victory in Italy

Hoche's victories against the Vendeans and *chouans* were a major step towards stabilizing the Republic. Yet the Directory could not really consolidate itself until it had completed the successes of the Year III against Spain, Holland and Prussia. This meant that the Austrians would have to be knocked out of the war which in turn might compel the British to come to terms. For the campaign of 1796, Carnot planned an all out sweep through southern Germany. At first, the Army of Italy was to play a diversionary role but its newly appointed commander, General Bonaparte, pestered the Directory into giving him a free hand and he was to meet General Moreau at Vienna. In the event, the Army of Italy decided the campaign. No doubt the Directors cared little about Bonaparte because the material situation of the Army of Italy constrained it to a secondary role. Under a twenty-seven-year-old general with no field experience, the Army of Italy rarely had more than 30,000 men until the end of the campaign when reinforcements from the Vendée and Brittany raised it to over 40,000. The Austrians often arrayed twice that many against Bonaparte. By contrast, the government devoted roughly 140,000 men to the German side of the campaign. Bonaparte's soldiers had no uniforms as such, pay (in *assignats*) was years in arrears, military contractors supplied inadequate food and material, and the cavalry and artillery were in lamentable shape. It resembled nothing so much as a horde, was often close to mutiny and could not be prevented from looting. The pillage of this army of liberators regularly provoked insurrections from exasperated populations.

Nonetheless, Bonaparte was determined to do great things with this depressing material. He promised his men 'honour, glory and riches' in return for their courage and endurance. By the end of April, a month after assuming command, he had knocked Piedmont out of the war, secured his flank and rear and opened the Po valley to his starving men. By taking the bridge at Lodi (7–10 May 1796), he cleared the way to Milan which was made to pay an indemnity of twenty million. Much of the countryside revolted against these exactions but the soldiers were delighted to receive half their pay in cash.

Bonaparte then turned south. The invasions of Modena, Tuscany and the northern papal states in June netted millions in cash and precious manuscripts and art. This booty was extraordinarily lucrative both for the government back in Paris and for the generals, including Bonaparte himself. When the offensives beyond the Rhine finally started, Bonaparte was able to resume the advance across the Lombard plain. The rest of the Italian campaign involved a baffling series of marches and countermarches but they all had as their object French attempts to capture the fortress of Mantua and Austrian attempts to lift the siege. The major battles, Castiglione on 5 August, Arcola on 15–17 November (where Bonaparte had to be prevented from leading his men over the bridge) and Rivoli on 15–16 January 1797, were all French successes, however, and Mantua finally fell on 2 February 1797. The Austrians thus had their backs against the Tyrol but in the meantime the Archduke Charles had driven Moreau back to the Rhine so that Bonaparte was in no position to advance through the treacherous passes to Vienna. In fact the Austrians might have taken the risk of transferring troops to Italy but fearful of an attack from Moreau and from Hoche who had replaced Jourdan, they agreed to the Preliminaries of Leoben, an armistice and the basis of the peace signed later in the year.

The Italian campaign had immense consequences for Bonaparte and consequently for the Directory. In the first place, it laid the basis of his legend. (The legend, incidentally, began with the Italian campaign, not with the ruminations of the fallen Emperor on St Helena.) The incident at Arcola, for instance, captured the imagination of dozens of sketch artists, where for dramatic effect they invariably presented the general leading his troops straight over the bridge to glittering victory. Bonaparte helped this sort of hyperbole along by the stirring bulletins of the Army of Italy and by his own newspaper, the *Courrier de l'Armée d'Italie*, where he was presented as one of those men 'whose power has no other limit than when the most sublime virtue supports an unlimited brilliance'. The apotheosis of Bonaparte as the republican, uncorrupted, stern genius came with David's famous unfinished portrait that he painted about this time. By now, the war looked eternal to the public and the quarrelling politicians appeared incapable of ending it. Here was a republican general who could.

In the second place, Bonaparte successfully invaded the civilian sphere as well. To consolidate his conquests, he organized a series of Italian republics of which the Cisalpine, based on Milan–Modena, was the most important. The Cisalpine Republic's constitution was moderate enough and, as a sign of things to come, its major positions were appointive, not elected. But the Directory would have sacrificed all the Italian conquests to secure Belgium and the Rhine frontier. Bonaparte had other ideas. He proposed the Preliminaries of Leoben himself and the Directory had to accept the *fait accompli*. With the republicans having badly lost the recent elections to resurgent royalists, it might need the Army of Italy. For his part, as he said later, after Lodi, Bonaparte knew he was a truly extraordinary man.

The Conspiracy of the Equals

The government's policy of stabilizing itself also meant an offensive against the slowly rebuilding Jacobins. The ease with which this was done shows how weak the Jacobins were and how much they underestimated the unscrupulousness of the government. Babeuf's 'Conspiracy of the Equals' provided the occasion to strike not only at a shaky conspiracy but against the democratic opposition as a whole.

François-Noël Babeuf, known as Gracchus, was a life long Cordelier in his democratic politics. His contribution was to tap into a long tradition of European utopian economics. He became an enemy of private property. His communism involved popularly elected magistrates linked together in a lateral and hierarchical national network allocating workloads, gathering produce and manufactures and distributing them on an absolutely equal basis. Babeuf would have denied the underlying bureaucratic authoritarianism of his utopia because he remained a Cordeliers democrat. By early in the Year IV, he had developed the doctrine for which he is best known, the leading role of the inner circle of the revolutionary vanguard.

For this the Directory's policies towards the clubs were directly responsible. Already persuading the masses to revolt seemed impossible but the

Directory stifled the growing club movement too. They closed the neo-Jacobin club on 8 *ventôse* An IV (27 February 1796) and then shut down several provincial counterparts. On 27 *germinal* (16 April), the government made advocacy of the Constitution of 1793 a capital crime and began purging the administration of Jacobins. This left conspiracy as the only means of opposition.

Babeuf's reaction played straight into the government's hands. He formed an 'Insurrectionary Committee' to organize the 'final' revolution, assume sole executive power for three months to handle the problems of transition and finally to implement the Constitution of 1793 and the communist utopia. Yet the conspirators only had hatred of the Directory in common. Babeuf, Buonarotti whose book established the legend of his mentor thirty years later, and Lepelletier, brother of the 'martyr of liberty', certainly shared the great ideal but others like Rossignol, the 'scourge of the Vendée' and Darthe, erstwhile prosecutor of the Revolutionary Tribunal of Arras and Cambrai, could not see beyond a mighty bloodbath of enemies of all sorts. For the Montagnards who got involved at the last moment, the insurrection would restore themselves and the revolutionary government of the Year II. The *sans-culottes* who were recruited or who were inscribed on Babeuf's lists as 'worthy of command' for the police to find could have had little idea of the ultimate purpose. Betrayed by a double agent on the eve of the rising, Babeuf and the Committee were arrested on 21 *floréal* (10 May).

There is a tendency among some Anglo-Saxon historians to minimize Babeuf's conspiracy just as there is a tendency among continental Marxists to find in it the precursor of a great tradition. The affair had quite another importance to contemporaries. The government was determined to use the conspiracy to crush Jacobin democracy once and for all. Hundreds of former militants or even hapless subscribers to Babeuf's *Tribun du Peuple* were arrested or otherwise harassed for their part in a 'monstrous conspiracy'. Since the deputy Drouet, the former Varennes postmaster who recognized Louis XVI, was part of the conspiracy and deputies could not be tried in ordinary courts, the government established a special High Court at Vendôme to hear the case against all the defendants. This was more a political decision than a constitutional one, however, because Drouet mysteriously escaped and later surfaced as a subprefect under Bonaparte. The subsequent trial did the government little good because the prosecution over reached. The press exposed all manner of sharp practices and the government could not even demonstrate the existence of the 'monstrous conspiracy' it denounced. In the end, only Babeuf mounted the guillotine, convicted, not of conspiracy but of the improvised charge of advocating the Constitution of 1793.

Misery and Monetary Collapse

One of the reasons Babeuf received the support he did was the continuing misery of the urban working population. Unlike the crisis of the Year III, the contours of the crisis of the Year IV are not well known but everything indicates that its effects were severe. The government compounded it by a truly disastrous monetary policy and alienated the rich by trying to impose a forced loan. In its defence, the Directory did inherit a chaotic currency. In June 1795, a *louis d'or* of 24 *livres* had risen to 750 in *assignats*; on 30 October to 2600; and in February 1796 to 7300. At the same time, the Convention had ordered peasants to pay half their taxes in kind or hard cash but since they received *assignats* for marketing their produce, hardly anyone did so. Some districts had troops billeted on them to collect taxes which was bound to be unfair because it was ineffective. Furthermore, prices on the free market soared astronomically and the controlled subsistence economy teetered on the verge of collapse. In Paris in the winter of the Year IV, rations had to be reduced, controlled prices raised and unpopular substitutes found. In their search for Babeuf's accomplices, the police were able to turn up dozens of former militants who had sold even their beds and sheets – usually a poor man's most valuable possessions – and who were sleeping on straw. Many of these people were able to survive somehow but thousands of others did not. Deaths in Rouen and Dieppe were far more numerous than in the Year III and higher than the average for the decade in Nancy and Strasbourg. Overall from the beginning of the crisis in 1793 to 1796 deaths in the large towns were nearly 95 per cent higher than the average of the previous decade while those in the medium sized towns were 53 per cent higher. It was probably in this period too that the urban population fell most. In 1790 there were 110,000 people living in Bordeaux; in 1806, only 92,986. In 1790 in Toulouse, 52,863; in 1814, 50,904. In 1789 in Strasbourg, 49,948; in 1805, 49,816. In 1789, more than 650,000 lived in Paris; in 1806, 580,609. Deaths were one part of the explanation but the large cities also suffered from a net emigration. Fewer people entered, more left. This was a reflection of the near collapse of these urban economies. The departure of nobles and priests counted for something but probably more important was the soaring cost of living, the diminished opportunities for jobs and the collapse of charitable institutions.

The government's attempts to deal with the catastrophe were a monumental failure. Since its own revenues were almost worthless when it received any at all, it tried to increase them and reduce the number of *assignats* in circulation by imposing a forced loan on the rich on

19 *frimaire* An IV (10 December 1795). It hoped to raise 600 million in
cash but the administrative chaos was so great and charges of political
bias in assessments so loud that the attempt had to be abandoned in the
summer of the Year IV. The forced loan was also intended to be a prelude
to retiring the *assignat* but the new 'mandats territoriaux', created on 28
ventôse An IV (18 March 1796) were grossly overvalued relative to the
assignat. They too began to depreciate rapidly, so much so that *biens
nationaux* could be acquired at only two and three times their annual
rental value. A month after their emission in March 1796, the *mandats*
were worth 20 per cent of their face value; by July, less than 5 per cent.
Until the government decided to accept only cash for *biens nationaux*
months later, anyone with money could legally strip the state of its one
valuable asset. The Directory finally recognized the failure of its policy by
demonetizing the *mandats* on 16 *pluviôse* (4 February 1797). Of course,
this did nothing to improve its financial situation, and following the
elections of *germinal* An V it faced a vigorous royalist minority in the
legislature determined to wreck any financial reform the Directory proposed. In short, financial policy, by threatening the rich, once again gave
the counterrevolution an opening. It was one to which its leaders and
backers were moving anyway.

Spies, Subversion, a New Coup

The pacification of the west and Bonaparte's continuing victories forced
the royalists, émigrés and the British to emphasize another aspect of their
strategy, subversion of the Directory from within. There was nothing
new in this. The centre of all the webs was William Wickham, ostensibly
British minister to Berne, but in reality spymaster. Wickham had already
tried the military option of encouraging an Austrian invasion and finan-
cing murder gangs in the interior but these came to naught. Both he and
the émigrés expended enormous energy trying to subvert the army. The
target was General Pichegru who succumbed in the autumn of 1795
to the blandishments of the Prince de Condé and to British gold because
of the deplorable state of his army, the demands of a greedy mistress and
the pleasures of high living for himself. Pichegru's reasons for treason
were so light-headed and the man so timid that the royalists could
scarcely get him to do anything despite vast efforts and money. When
the Directory removed him from his command in March 1796 for failing
to carry out offensives, his effectiveness evaporated. By mid-1796, it was
obvious that an equivocating general, stifled insurrections, low-grade
assassinations and unrealized invasions were hardly the stuff of counterrevolution. Consequently, Wickham and the British reoriented their

efforts towards getting royalist sympathizers elected to the legislature. This threw them on to the royalist spy organization, known as the *Agence de Paris*, which had pretended for years to have conduits to deputies who were secret monarchists. In fact, most of the Agency's reports were gathered from the newspapers or from the street gossip by a half-dozen 'spies' who mostly hated each other. The reports in turn were doctored with fantastic stories by the Agency's foreign head, the comte d'Antraigues, who passed the quasi-fabrications on to foreign governments. With Antraigues, one enters the murky underbelly of fanatical royalism beside which the Pretender's intransigence and Condé's refusal to deal with constitutionalists until they repented appeared moderate. A melancholic bisexual, before the Revolution, he detested Marie-Antoinette and loathed Calonne. His friendship with Rousseau and his attacks on ministerial despotism in the name of provincial rights gave him a reputation as a patriot in 1789 but for Antraigues the ideal polity was dominance by the provincial squirearchy. As soon as he emigrated his dark obsessions overwhelmed him. He specifically aimed to be the Marat of the counterrevolution, was convinced that Jacobinism was part of a vast Orléanist plot and welcomed the execution of Louis XVI because it undermined the moderates. With a mentality like this, the arrest of many of the leading members of the Agency in January 1797 was something of a blessing in disguise.

The strategy of subverting the Directory from within also brought the British into contact with the Philanthropic Institutes and with the moderate deputies around d'André. The Institutes were front organizations active mostly in the south-west. Their public face was charity while the real purpose was securing a restoration of the monarchy. Wickham was so impressed with their potential that he allocated at least £10,000 to them; more, in other words, than the Directory itself spent on subverting the elections of the Year VI. There were claims that there were Institutes in 58 to 70 departments in the summer of the Year V, although this was surely too high. D'André, who had been elected to represent the nobility of Provence in the Estates-General, was the major link between Wickham, the Institutes, the Pretender's court at Verona and the moderate deputies centred around the Clichy club.

No one can be certain how many *clichyens* there were since they included sincere advocates of the rule of law under the Republic, men for whom a restoration was a possible but not necessary option, former Feuillants and Fayettists, constitutional monarchists and outright reactionaries. D'André himself wanted no more than improvements to the Constitution of 1791 but eschewed theoretical debates to concentrate on welding the reactionaries to the constitutionalists of various hues. His great problem was Louis XVIII who remained stubbornly wedded to the Verona Declaration. Although the Pretender finally issued a proclamation on the eve of the elections promising clemency and moderation, there was no backing down and no assurances for the owners of *biens nationaux*. Some of his followers even hoped the restored *parlements* would quash any amnesty and the vast settling of accounts could begin. Undoubtedly because they were so fundamentally at odds, the royalist campaign in the spring of the Year V was vague and shrill: peace at almost any price, promises of prosperity, denunciations of anti-clericalism, financial policy and of Jacobinism. The Directory retaliated by publishing lurid details from the trials of the *Agence de Paris* and of Babeuf but to little effect.

A negative strategy was good politics for the royalists since the electorate continued to reject the men of the Convention as it had in the Year IV. Of 216 *conventionnels* up for election in *germinal* An V (March 1797), only 11 were returned and the proportion of regicides in the new legislature dropped to less than one in five. Of the 260 seats being contested, royalists of one sort or another won 180 bringing their total strength in the Five Hundred and the Ancients to roughly 330, a sizeable enough group to swing a wavering centre to their side on some issues. Wickham was naturally exultant and credited d'André but it is doubtful whether the royalists were correct in seeing a vast electoral wave rolling in their direction. As usual, turnout was very low: 10.6 per cent in the Meurthe, less than 10 per cent in the Eure-et-Loir, 22 per cent in the Côtes-du-Nord, 25 per cent in the Côte-d'Or, 28 per cent in the Sarthe, while Toulouse at 71 per cent appears to have been genuinely exceptional. Nationally, less than a quarter of those eligible actually voted, and this decline would continue until the Year VII. Furthermore, there was no correlation between the reported existence of a Philanthropic Institute and departmental election results. The results themselves were hardly a guide to national opinion. Rather, they showed an anti-political attitude on the part of the rich secondary electors. Aside from the wholesale rejection of *conventionnels* as such, nearly half the deputies in the legislature of the Year V had never sat in a national legislature before and of the rightists, roughly two thirds were newcomers. Among these were General Willot – who had protected the counterterrorist murder gangs in Marseille – Pichegru and Imbert-Colomès. It was a particular electorate that was profoundly alienated as well. The northern, wealthy, populous and urban departments returned the greatest proportion of royalists. These same regions also had been the most progressive in their *cahiers* of 1789. Thus the Directory had clearly lost the support of the wealthy landowners, *rentiers* and bourgeois. The regime floated in a social vacuum, hated by the élites whose favour it so desperately wanted, yet spurning any attempts to revive the politics of movement.

The results of the election of *germinal* An V were a huge opportunity for the royalists. They could also have exploited divisions among the Directors who squabbled over big things and small. But they also faced a major dilemma. They did not have the votes to restore the monarchy as such and any moves they took in that direction were bound to arouse suspicions among the moderates that this was their ultimate aim. After all, by this stage in the Revolution softness on the issue of refractory priests and émigrés was a very bad sign and denigrating victory abroad was a public relations disaster. Yet the *clichyens* did tip their hand. The Five Hundred relaxed the laws substantially on the émigrés and then in stages abolished the restrictions on refractory priests. They were now subject only to a weak oath to obey the laws. The result was not only a new round of complaints from the provinces about these enemies of the Revolution emerging in large numbers, it also set off the second round of white terrorist murders.

In addition, there were exceptionally mean-spirited speeches and vicious press attacks on Bonaparte's successes in Italy. These only resulted in lusty proclamations of loyalty to the Directory and the Republic from the officers and soldiers of the Armies of Italy and Sambre-et-Meuse. Creeping royalism at home convinced many in the military that the army was the last bastion of pure republicanism and virtually invited them to intervene in politics. The legislature also stalled on any financial reform. Without the loot General Bonaparte was shipping back from Italy, the Directory would have been bankrupt. That in turn might have tempted the Austrians to break off the peace negotiations. These were ominous developments but when Antraigues and his huge archive were captured at Trieste in July, the links of a vast conspiracy, this time quite genuine, were exposed. General Bonaparte forwarded a mass of correspondence and interrogations to Paris, after carefully editing out all references to the royalists' attempts to recruit him. Mysteriously he then let Antraigues escape. After further investigations, the extent of Pichegru's treason and Wickham's involvement in internal subversion with the deputies was reasonably clear. It was enough to bring Barras on to the side of Reubell and La Révellière. The 'triumvirate' which was to dominate the national scene until the spring of the Year VII took an increasingly aggressive attitude towards the Councils. They ordered troops from Hoche's Army of Sambre-et-Meuse to Paris. This was a violation of the Constitution which forbade the presence of troops within the perimeter of Paris. A simultaneous reshuffling of ministers in a more republican direction was a slap in the face to the moderate constitutionalists who were urging the appointment of ministers more to their liking. The royalist deputies were morose but in the end did nothing.

D'André and the royalists could see the Directors were preparing to defend themselves. The royalists too began to prepare for a military confrontation. There were attempts to subvert the Paris National Guard and most importantly, dozens of *chouan* officers began slipping into the capital. But the Directors acted first.

The blow fell on the hopelessly divided *clichyens* on the morning of 18 *fructidor* (4 September 1797) and continued to roll through the country for the next six months. The triumvirate purged the two other Directors, Carnot and Barthélemy, and ordered the deportation of 53 deputies. It annulled the elections in 49 departments, arrested 32 journalists and banned 42 Parisian and provincial newspapers. The purge reached out into the provincial administrations as well. These had long tolerated all manner of questionable disturbances. During the summer as the legislature debated the anti-clerical laws, the country people of the Midi who believed that full freedom of worship was imminent demonstrated massively in favour of the refractories and attacked buyers of *biens nationaux* and republicans generally. The brigand bands and murder gangs were extraordinarily active. It is no wonder that republicans felt that cries in the legislature for a return to legality were merely pretexts for violent counterrevolution. Local administrations that permitted these activities were purged far more systematically than in the Year II. In the Sarthe, 599 of 807 elected officials were replaced; in the Pas-de-Calais, 73 of 87 cantonal municipalities were purged; in the Haute-Loire, all six judges in the civil court, and 22 of 34 cantonal commissioners were dismissed and 29 of 34 municipalities purged. Of 509 municipalities in the fairly peaceful central and western regions of the country covering 10 departments, 241 were reorganized or purged. To judge from the rare studies on the new terror of the Year VI, such a massive upheaval often brought local Jacobins back to power, but if the Eure-et-Loir and Var were at all typical, these men often had considerable administrative experience dating back to the early Revolution as well. The 'Second Directory', as it is called, was clearly trying to bureaucratize local administration without being dependent on the clubs. Bonaparte's Consulate merely consolidated the process.

The new terror tended to limit itself to the government machine and to well-defined groups. The law of 19 *fructidor* An V (5 September 1797), wrested from a stupefied legislature, reinstated penalties against émigrés and refractory priests. It also imposed a new oath of 'hatred to royalty' on the clergy and officials. About 1400 French priests were ordered deported to Guyana by purely administrative fiat, without a trial (a *lettre de cachet*, in other words), but since the British controlled the seas, most were held in great hardship on the islands of Ré and Oléron. Nearly 200 died in captivity. Acting on Sieyès's suggestion, the deputy Boulay de la Meurthe also got the legislature to deprive all ex-nobles of their citizenship. In legal terms, the Third Estate became the nation and in combination with the electoral law, the bourgeois revolution reached its apogee. Never was the bourgeoisie less interested in playing the role the politicians wanted to assign to it. The law was virtually ignored.

The government now took a ruthless attitude towards issues of public order. By the time of Bonaparte's coup in November 1799, over 200 villages, towns and cities were under a state of siege, that is, turned over to the military authorities. This included Lyon, Marseilles, Toulon, Nice and others. The government also made entire communities responsible for the transgressions of individual members or for failing to defend itself against brigands and *chouans*. The consequence could be fines and billeting. Very large numbers of communities were punished in this way. Finally, justice was militarized for certain kinds of offences. Military commissions got jurisdiction over returned émigrés and refractory priests. Once the court determined an accused's guilt, the sentence was to be carried out within twenty-four hours. Usually, the military authorities, like the representatives on mission during the Terror, made sure the execution was accomplished before as many locals as possible. Although these courts inflicted comparatively few death penalties – 275, while deporting 117 others – it included some serious offenders, like Dominique Allier and the Marquis de Surville, both brigand chiefs, the comte de Rochecotte, a *chouan* chief, as well as one Jean-Joseph Glatier, priest, armed robber, fence, accompanied by three bodyguards. His clandestine masses in which he admitted preaching the restoration of the monarchy complemented his day job. Finally, the military courts were assigned jurisdiction over brigandage, and other forms of robbery, like robbery at night. Thus among the victims of these courts were not only *chouans*, but sheep stealers, burglars, and cattle rustlers.

These measures were a startling departure from the early hopes that the Constitution of the Year III would restore the rule of law. The exceptional jurisdictions in some ways were a revival of the spirit of the Terror although the fructidorian military commissions were far more discriminating in their choice of targets than their earlier counterparts. They also represented a reversion to the practices of Old Regime summary courts, with the difference that sentences could be appealed. Appeals, however, were processed in less than a week. Nonetheless, such measures were brutally effective and all indications are that brigandage in whatever form did decline. The restoration of order was relative of course. In the west, the calm hardly meant acquiescence. Cadoudal, who had become *de facto* commander of the *chouan* bands, was trying to put his men on a war footing. He had even gone so far as to order the refractory priests still in hiding not to marry young 'conscripts'.

Despite the obvious collapse of the Constitution of the Year III, the Directory could govern without a hostile legislature. With a lull in the fighting abroad and a semblance of peace at home, the Second Directory, quickly at its full complement with the addition of Merlin de Douai and François de Neufchâteau, was able to undertake some vital reforms that for once had a permanent effect.

The most important was the reform of finances. In effect, the Directory repudiated about two-thirds of the national debt. It established a new set of indirect taxes. This was the beginning of the abandoning of the Constituent Assembly's reliance on direct taxes. At first, this reconfiguration was hesitant, but during Bonaparte's Consulate and Empire, the government returned to Old Regime practices of relying heavily for its revenue on indirect taxes. Fiscal policy traversed regimes, in other words, and this was no more true than in the government's attitudes to tax arrears.

The Second Directory felt strong enough to begin a thorough collection of delinquent debts. This activity continued into the Consulate and Empire. It is rarely appreciated how aggressive the state became in collecting taxes after 1798. There was an amnesty for almost any offence committed during the Revolution: for political offences, for counterrevolution, for murder, for terrorism, for emigration, for refusing oaths of loyalty, for draft-dodging, and much else, but never for tax evasion. Although large parts of the country took a tax holiday during the more chaotic phases of the Revolution in the early and mid-1790s, the Directory and the Consulate bore down hard on tax evaders, extracting both current obligations and arrears. Indeed, the great nineteenth-century historian of the Revolution, Alexis de Tocqueville, would have appreciated the fundamental logic of state-building whereby the Directory collected the outstanding taxes of the absolute monarchy of Louis XVI. Shortly after the coup, the Finance Ministry produced a document that showed that the country still owed a huge amount of back taxes, roughly 40 per cent of what the government demanded and some of these arrears dated back to the 1780s. Unjust as everyone felt Old Regime taxes to have been in 1789, no one in government circles in 1798 would have dreamed of forgiving these arrears. By the Year X, arrears had been reduced to nearly zero.

This ruthless and aggressive fiscal policy could hardly have done the regime much good among the taxpaying and landowning bourgeoisie. The introduction of conscription could hardly have done it any good among the common people. In the military sphere, the Jourdan law of 19 *fructidor* An VI (5 September 1798) annually registered all the young men aged twenty, known as a class. They drew ballots to see who would actually depart, and, although Bonaparte later reintroduced the appalling practice of allowing the rich to buy exemption, replacement was not allowed.

The restoration of law and order and of public finances were conditional upon establishing peace abroad. With peace on the continent, an opportunity opened up to stabilize the regime, yet a renewal of war risked once again the government's having to ask large sectors of the population to make sacrifices that they had always resisted. Yet in the immediate aftermath of the coup, prospects were good. The Treaty of Campo Formio of 26 *vendémiaire* An VI (18 October 1797) with Austria, which Bonaparte negotiated in defiance of the Directors who owed him too much, recognized the huge French gains since 1794. It shamelessly handed over Venice to the Austrians and with it a base for the campaign of 1799, but left the French dominant in northern Italy. It also achieved Austrian recognition for the annexation of Belgium and the left bank of the Rhine, an even greater success.

The Directory broke off peace negotiations with the British that had begun at Lille because they knew enough of British machinations in the elections of the Year V. That left Britain as an enemy but not a very threatening one, since without continental allies, the British could harass shipping and take colonies but not threaten the continent. Yet the settlement of 1797 came apart in less than two years because the Directors, like the political class generally, believed an aggressive foreign policy was in the French national interest. The idea of liberating oppressed people still mattered, or at least it did to the public, and so the Directory derived legitimacy from foreign conquest. An aggressive foreign policy also permitted the imposition of economic controls on recent conquests while various treaties with the satellite republics carried the war against the British in another way by requiring a boycott. Finally, foreign conquest allowed generals, contractors, ministers, and any number of shady characters to build immense personal fortunes. One example is irresistible: after failing in a scam to sell pigs at inflated prices, Fouché amassed a huge fortune in the thoroughly disreputable business of army contracting in Italy.

Despite the peace, therefore, the Directory continued its push to dominate new areas. One of these was Switzerland. They found this attractive for strategic reasons because it would give the French more control over mountain passes to Italy, and also because the reputedly huge treasury of the city of Berne was there for the taking. And of course, there was the great satisfaction of punishing the Swiss for giving refuge to Wickham. Consequently, a conveniently timed series of insurrections sponsored by Swiss patriots gave the French the pretext they needed. Thus the French annexed Geneva and established the 'République hélvetique'. Another region the French eventually dominated was Rome. Although few in official circles pushed for it, insurrections within the Papal States made it impossible for the French not to intervene on the side of patriots. The result was the Roman Republic, and of course, much personal profit for corrupt agents. The new republic was turned over to willing puppets. One dishonest company of war contractors succeeded another and the Directory itself had 640 cartons of paintings, books, manuscripts and jewellery looted from the Vatican shipped to Paris.

Such aggressiveness was bad enough but the Egyptian expedition began the process of forming the Second Coalition, and with it the collapse of the Directory itself.

The Egyptian expedition was a way of attacking the British since it was impossible to mount an invasion of Britain directly. This would assure France of her share of the expected break-up of the Turkish Empire, restore commercial domination of the eastern Mediterranean, and above all threaten some British trade routes to India, inspire the restive Indian princes to revolt and provide a base for an expedition to India through the Red Sea. A successful blow against the British would also restrain Austria and Russia both of whom were alarmed at the continued French expansion after Campo Formio.

The Egyptian expedition was a disappointment that was nearly a disaster. Bad luck and bad weather prevented Nelson from sighting the French transports at sea and thus from capturing a prize of incalculable value. Consequently Bonaparte easily captured Malta and landed peacefully near Alexandria on 1 July. Three weeks later, he crushed the Mamelukes at the Battle of the Pyramids and the French occupied Cairo the next day. On 1 August, however, Nelson finally found the French fleet at anchor at Aboukir Bay and raking it with a devastating crossfire, destroyed or captured eleven of the thirteen ships of the line. However much Bonaparte tried to evade the blame for not ordering the fleet out of Egyptian waters, and however much his strange aping of Moslem customs has distracted subsequent biographers, the fact was that an army of 30,000 men, many of them veterans of the Army of Italy, were now totally isolated, without hope of relief or rescue.

The repercussions in Europe were immense. Turkey declared war on France on 9 September. The Kingdom of Naples, egged on by the Austrians and British, and believing the sister republics vulnerable, occupied Rome on 27 November. The half-mad Tsar Paul, self-styled protector of the Knights of Malta, and intolerably vexed at the reception given to Polish 'patriots' in Paris, declared war on 23 December. For allowing Russian troops transit rights on its territory, France declared war on Austria the following March. The French response also was to occupy most of the rest of Italy. Another sister republic was established based in Naples, the Parthenopean, Tuscany was occupied, and Piedmont annexed following a rigged referendum. Even the Pope was taken prisoner and he was packed off to Valence where he died in August.

Political Instability

One can imagine that with the Great Powers, Britain, Austria, and Russia, as well as their minor allies threatening the country, a situation was arising much like that facing Napoleonic France in 1814. The difference between 1814 and 1798–99, of course, is that in the twilight of the Empire, the regime was stable and no one rose against it. Post-*fructidor* France was far from secure. In the first place, the coup itself created immense problems for the Directory. Not only would one third of the seats in the Five Hundred have to be renewed in the Year VI, so too would the purged deputies of *fructidor* have to be replaced. That is, three fifths of the seats would be contested. The Directory would have to take the matter in hand. After all, no one could trust the electorate. The new Director, Merlin de Douai, became the effective election manager for the government. Amid a shrill press campaign highlighting its self proclaimed moderation, the government attempted to buy influence with the electorate. A tiny sum was spent, however, far less than the British had spent the year before. At the same time, the government moved against the Jacobins, thought to be the natural beneficiaries of the previous year's coup. The government closed down so-called constitutional circles, suppressed newspapers, and extended the state of siege to new cities. While the Parisian circles appeared innocuous enough, advocating an essentially Cordeliers programme of democratization and progressive taxes, their provincial counterparts, especially in royalist areas, espoused the usual formulas of persecution of superstition, and denunciation of refractory priests as 'ferocious animals'. In any case, the Jacobin press thought 9 *thermidor* was a tragedy and sympathized with Babeuf. Finally, many Jacobins who were prominent in the Year VI had a terrorist past, as *sans-culotte* generals, judges on revolutionary tribunals or zealous representatives on mission. Neither the government nor the electorate trusted them; nor was there any reason they should have, given the absence of any serious reflection from the Jacobin camp on the recent past.

As usual, the turnout was dismal but Jacobins were the principal beneficiaries despite all of Merlin's efforts. Many electoral assemblies had divided, however, often with government encouragement. The 'scissions' as they were called, had to be decided and the law of 22 *floréal* An VI (11 May 1798) determined the issue. It deprived 127 newly elected deputies of their seats, 83 of whom are thought to have been Jacobins. As Ballieul, the deputy of the legislative commission applying the relevant enabling law reported, elections that produced a 'bad result' would be annulled and divisions that 'were only the product of caprice and cabal'

would also be rejected. Hardy, one of the more unrestrained anti-Montagnards of 1793, put it even more baldly: 'If a scoundrel presents himself
here as a deputy, you have the right to repel him; for it is a question not
only of the electoral mechanism but of its results'.

The new coup inaugurated a policy of eliminating all opposition. The
press law of 19 *fructidor* was renewed and shortly afterwards twelve
conservative newspapers were suppressed while the *Journal des hommes
libres*, the influential Jacobin newspaper, underwent half a dozen bans
and name-changes by the end of the year. The constitutional circles
withered away when they were not forcibly shut down, too dispirited
to offer any more than perfunctory protests. The Directory also promised
rewards for those who denounced returned émigrés and it organized domiciliary visits in Paris. As an antidote to Catholicism, it also
tightened the laws on the use of the revolutionary calendar and observance of the *décadi*. François de Neufchâteau, Minister of the Interior,
prescribed the ceremonies of the *culte décadaire* in a famous circular
whereby local officials read new laws to the assembled citizens, recounted military successes and celebrated civil marriages while everyone
listened to patriotic hymns sung by school children.

Still another election loomed in the spring of the Year VII. Almost
everywhere, turnout in the primary assemblies reached record lows. After
all, if the government was going to alter the results, there was no point in
voting. Even so, the electors continued their policy of rejecting experienced politicians and the Directory's candidates. Less than one fifth of the
legislators of the Year VII had sat in a national assembly before the Year
IV, and of the 187 recommended candidates only a little over one third
were elected. Contemporaries interpreted the results as a Jacobin victory.
There is some truth in this even though only 21 Jacobins 'floréalized' the
year before were re-elected. But the elections are better conceived as a
rejection of the existing ruling group and of the triumvirate in particular.

Nonetheless, the deputies were determined to reassert themselves.
They first elected Sieyès to replace a departing Director. This was significant because Sieyès was already thinking of new constitutional arrangements that would reinforce the executive. As the campaign abroad heated
up, with the loss of Italy and the threat of a Russian invasion through
Switzerland, cries went up looking for a scapegoat. Standard Jacobin
ideology as always blamed the internal enemy for external defeat and
this time opinion fixed on certain members of the Directory. No one
blamed an overly aggressive foreign policy; instead, cries arose to seek
out corrupt army contractors, sleazy financiers and politicians on the
take. First one Director, Treilhard, was hounded from office and he took
the umbrella, as was said later, out of the Luxembourg where the Directors sat, and proudly strode into the morning sun. Then it was the turn of

two other Directors, La Révellière and Merlin to resign on 30 *prairial* An VII (18 June 1799), under threat of investigations of corruption, and the intervention of the military, if they failed to resign. The coup of 30 *prairial* was a huge tactical success for the neo-Jacobins but it was short lived, a summer lightening. Soon the ministries began to fill up with Jacobin appointees, the press and pamphleteers had not been so active in years, clubs in over two dozen provincial towns coughed into life, and above all in Paris a neo-Jacobin club claimed 250 deputies and 3000 members. There were some legislative successes as well. On 9 *messidor* An VII (27 June 1799) Jourdan persuaded the Five Hundred to call up simultaneously the five classes of conscripts specified in his earlier law. The same day, the legislature passed a forced loan to help finance Jourdan's conscripts. In reality, this was a politicized progressive income tax, exempting those with an annual income of less than 300 *livres*, rapidly doubling the incidence on incomes between 300 and 4000 *livres*, taking as much as three quarters of the annual revenue of the very wealthy and authorizing the total confiscation of purely 'speculative' fortunes. The tax also singled out the regime's enemies, nobles who could be classed above a category their wealth justified; and speculators who could be taxed at whatever level officials wanted.

Finally, they passed the infamous 'Law of Hostages' on 24 *messidor* (12 July). This was more radical than even the Law of Suspects of 1793, because not only could the regime imprison relatives of political enemies – this had happened in the Year II – it could deport them.

All this was stirring stuff, proof at last that the government would strike out pitilessly at its enemies. Unfortunately, it did not work out that way. In theory, conscription ought to have produced 402,000 young men but in fact only 248,000, or about 60 per cent, ever joined the colours. In some departments, draft-dodging reached breathtaking proportions. In the Ariège, for example, only 11 of 1319 young men joined their regiments, the rest never appearing at all or else stealing away at night from the columns marching to the rallying centres. Nor was the Ariège unique. Along the northern frontier extending into Normandy, in Gascony to the Spanish frontier, throughout the Massif Central and finally along a band stretching through Lyon from the Alps to the Hérault, there was considerable resistance. As in 1793 and the Year III, many of the young men took to the forests and mountains to join the brigand bands or the *chouan* diehards. They were encouraged too by counterrevolutionaries and refractory priests so that the reappearance of the royalist bands in the interior was certainly linked to the application of conscription. Aside from simple resistance in a country not yet habituated to conscription, the reason the government could do so little to combat 'the spirit of subordination nourished by fanaticism' as one official put it, lay with the elected municipalities. Fathers and employers saw no advantage in seeing the young men depart and they were as dilatory at drawing up the lists of eligible conscripts as they were apathetic about searching out draft-evaders. The post-*fructidor* departments which were a good deal more zealous could do little with an inadequate gendarmerie and no funds to equip conscripts.

The forced loan and the Law of Hostages failed in similar ways for similar reasons. The press claimed the rich bribed the tax juries who were in any case amateurs too poor to be subject to the tax. Evasion and arbitrariness were evidently rife and there were innumerable stories of workshops closing because of the tax. By the time of the *brumaire* coup, only about 10 million of the estimated 100 million *livres* had been gathered. Overall taxes in the last three months of the Year VII were down by one third over the corresponding period of the previous year because of the lack of business confidence and a depression.

The Law of Hostages ended by alienating large sectors of opinion. Sieyès's Directory was slow to list which departments were considered to be in a 'state of trouble' and there was considerable infighting among the ministries over the law's application. Fouché, now Minister of Police, was sceptical the law would do any good and in the end the law was only authorized in a number of western departments.

Meanwhile, implementation was far from easy. Some commissioners were hostile to it because they feared it would ignite resistance but even enthusiasts for it had to rely on the inept and often hostile municipalities to suggest names. In the Sarthe, there were only 22 'hostages', most of them women or ageing ex-nobles. Experience in the Vendée, Morbihan and Ille-et-Vilaine was almost identical. Officials in the Ardèche scorned the law and said a military commission would do more good.

As in 1793, conscription was a recruiting device for anti-revolutionaries and in the west, for the *chouans* who had never surren-dered. They began to find recruits once again and to organize them into tighter units. As in 1791–3, measures of rigour against perceived internal enemies provoked a bloody response.

Meanwhile, the Jacobin offensive in Paris began to falter. The former terrorists were weeded out of the ministries before they even had time to get settled. The club itself was tossed out of the riding school where it met on 8 *thermidor* (26 July) and finally closed three weeks later, a warning to the Jacobins not to pursue their campaign for the indictment of the deposed Directors and possibly a move to reassure the financiers with whom the government concluded a loan on the same day the club was closed. Five days later and after a vigorous anti-Jacobin speech by Sieyès, the Five Hundred rejected the indictment of the Directors by a narrow majority of three. The Jacobin press replied by accusing Barras and Sieyès of royalism and treason to the foreign enemy and there were certainly many clubbists in the provinces and local officials who believed the central government to be hopelessly corrupt.

More Royalist Risings

Although the Directory's ruthless use of military commissions, declarations of states of siege, vigorous patrolling, purging complicitous officials and so on, was very effective, there remained a low level resistance. The declaration of a state of siege itself could provoke panic. For example, when Bonaparte toured the little village of Auriol near Marseilles in October 1797, he reported that the young men had taken to the surrounding hills, probably in fear of having to join the army; even the purged municipal officers and the disgraced *commissaire* found refuge there 'pell-mell with the émigrés, the cut-throats and the draft dodgers'. Indeed, they had much to fear from the newly installed Jacobins whom they had persecuted and murdered for the previous three years.

Convulsions in Paris therefore did not necessarily have the consequences their authors intended. An even better example of this was how the coups of the Directory in Paris were perceived by some in the provinces. No matter what the sense of the coup, many provincials hoped it would presage a restoration of religion. In the mountains of the Ardèche, 'the refractories celebrated religious offices with as much solemnity as before 18 *fructidor*. The processions of Ascension and Fête-Dieu have attracted an extraordinary following...' At Is-sur-Tille in the Côte-d'Or, the inhabitants broke the windows of the former presbytery and ripped up the trees in the garden because, they said, the new owner was responsible for a thunderstorm that had harmed the crops. When soldiers tried to disperse Sunday worshippers at Ecommoy in the Sarthe, they provoked a riot that quickly swelled to 800 people. Elsewhere, there was a wave of attacks on liberty trees and harassment of officials. Even in Paris, several churches were reported to be overflowing, mainly with women, and priests were appearing in public in clerical dress.

Royalist conspirators could orchestrate these sentiments and the deteriorating situation abroad in the summer of 1799 gave them new energy for their machinations. As always, however, conspiracies over a broad territory were hard to co-ordinate. Communications among the various cells, which this time stretched from Lyon to Toulouse, were difficult to co-ordinate. Communications with the Princes were nearly impossible. Arms smuggling from Spain proved to be difficult too, bands of malcontents could not be easily incorporated into the cells, and of course – this always happened – royalist leaders fell out with each other.

Nonetheless, circumstances were very favourable for an insurrection in the south-west that summer. There were only 30 line troops in the entire Haute-Garonne and a mere 539 National Guards in the Ariège. Even so, the insurrection began too soon. This can be blamed on the misplaced zeal of Rougé, former republican general turned royalist, and the pressure of his men, many of whom were conscripts due to leave shortly for the frontiers. Rougé's troops came pouring out of the hills of the Ariège on 19 *thermidor* (6 August), ten days ahead of schedule, shouting 'We're going to kill all the Huguenots' children, then their mothers, then their fathers, to be rid of them at last!' Many insurgents heard Mass before going into battle. The news of Rougé's rising set off major insurrections in the Gers and Ariège and minor ones in the Hérault, Lot-et-Garonne, Basses-Pyrénées and Aude so that as many as 32,000 rebels may have been involved. But all of this was to no avail. Although Rougé picked up support in the Haute-Garonne and as many as 16,000 royalists besieged Toulouse, the republicans counterattacked and, at Montréjeau on 3 *fructidor* (20 August), inflicted a devastating defeat. About 2000 rebels were killed, another 2000 in mopping-up operations and 1100 prisoners were taken. Although the government soon released many on the grounds that they were misled or drunk, hundreds languished in prison for months afterwards. Nonetheless, given the scale of the rising, the repression was light, perhaps because no evidence of treason showed up. There were only 15 executions and 27 other sorts of punishments. Significantly enough, many of the rebels were small farmers and labourers from the Garonne valley where bourgeois land holdings and acquisitions of *biens nationaux* were extensive. As always, for all its ability to appeal to nostalgia and anti-Protestantism, royalism in the Midi drew on material frustrations as well.

Bonaparte and Brumaire

Royalist morale was as high as it was before Montréjeau because of the continuing success of the allied advance. After the midsummer reconsideration, the new allied plan was to direct a four pronged advance through Provence, the Jura and Alsace with Austrian and Russian troops while an Anglo-Russian force would land in North Holland. The allies had one sole success. They halted a French advance at Novi on 28 *thermidor* (15 August) and Joubert was killed, shot through the heart as he was leading his soldiers. This could have left Provence open to the Austrians but cautious as ever they contented themselves with a few desultory sieges. Meanwhile, Masséna inflicted a heavy defeat on the Russians and Austrians at Zurich on 25 September. This also spelled the end of the

Anglo-Russian expedition in North Holland. This had landed on 27 August but it could do little in a difficult countryside of dykes and canals. The initially outnumbered French troops under Brune also fought a steady defensive war. On 18 October an armistice was signed that permitted a humiliating allied withdrawal in return for the release of eight thousand prisoners of war held in England.

By the end of the campaigning season, the Directory was out of any serious danger from royalism at home or invasion from abroad. Because of the lull, the politically ambitious could settle scores.

Amidst vicious quarrelling between the now defeated Jacobins and the aggressive Sieyès, the general who would inter the Directory landed at Fréjus on 17 *vendémiaire* (9 October). Sieyès had long planned to replace the Constitution of the Year III with one that would strengthen the executive. The Jacobins had been convinced for years that the Directors were in the pay of speculators, jobbers, and army contractors. The electorate itself, when it bothered to vote at all, showed its repugnance for the political class. Sieyès's plan was to cast a general as a fig leaf, presumably to profit from the widespread perception that the army alone was the remaining bastion of republican virtues. The first choice though, Jourdan, got killed at Novi. Moreau, once an idealistic law student during the long ago disturbances in Rennes in 1789 and now an equally decent soldier, declined to let himself be associated with overthrowing the Constitution. Bonaparte had no scruples about betraying the Constitution. He had also abandoned his army in the Levant when the English gave him old newspapers that related the poor performance of French arms in the spring of 1799. Of course, Sieyès hoped to have a general who would be passive. Bonaparte's reception as he made his way north ought to have given the conspirators pause. Almost as soon as he landed, authorities in the Var printed up an improvised proclamation to commemorate his arrival in Toulon:

> Let the Republic live forever
> She is imperishable
> It's on the 17 vendémiare An VIII that the genius of Liberty landed on our coasts
> The hero of Italy
> The brave, immortal Bonaparte

Although it did not rhyme in French either, the doggerel did capture the essence of what everyone else would say about the providential hero in the next few weeks: republicanism, liberty and military victory converged upon a unique man. Jacobins in the Five Hundred celebrated him as the sword of victory, peace and the author of the 'political regeneration' of Italy. The *Ennemi des tyrans* claimed his return confounded those 'who wished to surrender the territory of the Republic in a humiliating peace'. The moderate *Messager du Soir* claimed his arrival 'could change something of the system of violence which has been established for some time... Bonaparte has proved that it is possible to ally victory to moderation and patriotism to humanity'. According to the police, the public saw his return as 'an omen for the success of our armies, as a guarantee of prompt and striking victories...' His reception was everywhere ecstatic, just as it would be in 1815. Peasants in the foothills of the Alps flocked to see him and escort him along his way, just as they would do again in 1815. People in Lyon crowded around his hotel trying to catch a glimpse. Actors quickly improvised a play entitled *Le Héros du Retour*. Part of this extraordinary reception was the hope that Bonaparte's unexpected return would finish off the foreign coalition. The normally staid *Moniteur*, kicked over the traces and reported that the news of his landing interrupted theatre performances in Paris and that the audience broke into spontaneous applause. 'Victory,' it continued, 'which always accompanies Bonaparte, outran him this time and he arrives to deliver the final blows to the already expiring coalition'. This delirium about his arrival attached the *élan* of 1792 to the man of Toulon in 1793, to the man of *vendémiaire* in the Year IV, to the victor in Italy and to the author of the Treaty of Campo Formio. When he finally arrived in Paris, audiences disrupted theatre performance so much that he had to leave early; when he visited the Directors, people crowded around to see him, to touch him. Those who came to gawk at him were entrusting to him the revolutionary spirit that brought 'liberty' to Europe once and would do it again. The roots of the revolutionary upsurge after the return from Elba were here too, because for all the despotism and disappointed hopes of the next 15 years, many retained the faith that he personified the Revolution.

He was not welcomed because he was a military man; he was welcomed because he could decide the crusade of liberty that had begun in 1792. For although Frenchmen certainly wanted peace in 1799, the constant linking of Bonaparte with military success showed that large sectors of opinion had lost none of their martial ardour. Most sinister of all, Bonaparte was popular in the army not only because of his successes but because officers and men had felt for years that civil society had let them down, that they were the last bastion of true revolutionary principles and that they might be obliged to regenerate the nation as a whole.

But Bonaparte not only had a popular following, he had personal contacts among the intellectual and political élites. Fellow members of the Institute admired him greatly. As the spiritual descendants of the Encyclopaedists of the Old Regime, these scientists, engineers and writers dreamed of an efficient government of talents, a government that would be liberal without being accountable, where their expertise would be appreciated without having to endure the tawdry politics of representative government. So he seduced the intellectuals just as he had seduced much of the nation because he promised them power. One of his few public appearances before the coup was an address to them on the possibilities of a Suez canal and on Egyptian antiquities. Bonaparte was always able to dazzle some of the best minds in the country. The link with the Institute was also a link with the Sieyès faction and this was reinforced by his brothers. Joseph had kept his brother's name before salon society throughout the summer. Lucien had played a prominent role against the Directors on 30 *prairial*, and had proved himself one of the most able anti-Jacobin speakers in the Five Hundred. Already, he was cooperating with Sieyès before his famous brother's arrival in Paris.

The anti-Directoral coalition was thus already quite large and extensive. Within the legislature, it was composed of newcomers and moderates. Of the sixty-odd known legislators who supported the coup, about half entered national politics only under the Directory and, while most of the others had served in the Convention, only seven were regicides. Of the 19 surviving members of the Committees of Public Safety and General Security of the Year II, less than one third ever served the Consulate or Empire, despite the spectacular exceptions of Jeanbon Saint-André, Carnot and David. Of the 38 principal Jacobin speakers between 30 *prairial* and the coup, 24 never rallied. Thus the regime's claim to have reconciled the factions turns out to have been, as usual, a half-truth. In practice, the regime was more anti-Jacobin than not.

What drew the conspirators together was the conviction that the Constitution of the Year III had to be replaced by another that gave more authority to the executive. They were so confident that they felt they could do it with an appearance of legality and a minimum of force. The conspiracy unfolded in the early morning of 18 *brumaire* An VIII (9 November 1799) with the convocation of sympathetic members of the Elders. They were then informed of a terrifying Jacobin plot and voted two decrees, one transferring the entire legislature to Saint-Cloud just outside of Paris for the next day, where it would presumably deliberate on the nation's peril in safety, the other appointing Bonaparte commander of the Paris military district. The Directory itself collapsed. Barras resigned while Moreau and his troops held Directors Gohier and Moulin under protective custody in the Luxembourg.

The plan came apart the next day, however. When the Councils met at Saint-Cloud, the Five Hundred realized the Jacobin plot was a hoax and immediately took an oath to defend the Constitution, a constitution which, of course, many of them had violated on 18 *fructidor* and 22 *floréal.* With the Elders wavering, Bonaparte tried to retrieve the situation by addressing the deputies. He was no public speaker and when he appeared before the Five Hundred, there were cries of 'Down with the tyrant!' and 'Outlaw him!' In the melee, he was jostled. Bonaparte's bumbling intervention thus failed. While he beat a strategic retreat under Murat's protection, Lucien, who was president of the Five Hundred, addressed the Councils' guards outside claiming the jostling incident was an assassination attempt, imploring them to disperse the 'représentants du poignard' inside and swearing he would stab his own brother if he ever betrayed liberty. This proved decisive. With the regular soldiers under Murat menacing them from behind, the guards cleared out the deputies. That night, a rump of both houses established a provisional Consulate of Sieyès, Roger Ducos and Bonaparte. They also established two commissions composed of their own members that would design a new constitution. Finally, they deprived 62 members of the Five Hundred of their seats. Like every other coup of the period, it had to have a purge.

Why the Constitution Failed

The Constitution of the Year III disintegrated amidst deception and false hopes on the part of the conspirators and a hypocritical oath on the part of the Five Hundred. No doubt this clumsy instrument had to go sooner or later because, like the Constitution of 1791, it contained no device for resolving an urgent clash between the executive and the legislature. Force remained. In that sense the failure of the Constitution was the fault of those who drafted it. But the problem can be taken deeper still. Throughout the French Revolution, there was a huge disconnect between the political class and large sectors of the population. From a very early stage, as early as 1791, certain currents of opinion – Catholic, anti-Protestant, pro-aristocratic – simply could not be represented in any national legislature. It was illegitimate, worthy only of scorn and repression. Thus, what historians often carelessly take to be national opinion when they examine election results or analyse petitions and addresses, was already an opinion that was being expressed within a narrow, and an increasingly narrowing band. True, much of counterrevolutionary opinion, however it is defined, was not very elegant, attractive or articulate. But the fact is that ugly as it was, it did not count. Nor, in any realistic sense could it be represented, given the counterrevolutionary agenda.

But it was impossible for the revolutionaries to draw the line there. The history of the period, as every beginning student knows, is the bewildering labelling of former fast friends in one year as out and out counter-revolutionaries in the next, along with the allegation that they had always been so. This tendency is captured in an illustration in one of Jean-Clément Martin's books (*Contre-révolution, révolution et nation en France: 1789–1799* [1998]) that shows the definition of the counter-revolution as the Jacobins saw it. By the climax of the Year II, the counterrevolution included almost the entire French nation and it was opposed by an impossibly narrow group of true believers. Put another way, the political classes had a script for the nation to follow, and frequently the nation did. When it did not, the consequence was a major convulsion because the political nation would not adjust. In effect, all of the major convulsions of the period can be traced to the fact that the politicians elected in 1789 and after refused to accept the verdicts of elections. Where it suited a majority in the Constituent Assembly, the wishes expressed in the *cahiers de doléances* were ignored. The over-throw of the monarchy in 1792 was also the overthrow of a duly elected Legislative Assembly. As for the Convention, expulsion of political en-emies was routine down to the end. The thermidoreans followed suit with the 'two-thirds decree', with the purges of 18 *fructidor* and 22 *floréal* and with trying to rig the elections of the Year VI and Year VII. In their own minds, ignoring or defying the electorate was justified by the higher necessity of fighting off counterrevolution or the extremism which would lead to the same thing.

In short, the Constitution of the Year III failed because it could not accommodate Jacobin and especially royalist opinion. Where these two 'tails' became too threatening, the Directors attacked them. After 18 *fructidor*, only a very imperfect representative government survived. The consequence was a dwindling interest in voting at all. After all, why vote, when the government was going to ignore the result? Probably more young men dodged the draft than voted in the Year VII. Another conse-quence was a steady repudiation of *conventionnels* and regicides in the legislature and a consistent preference for new men, untested at the national level.

Bonaparte had to face the same fractured polity as his predecessors did. His solution was at the cost of political liberty of any sort, and eventually of the Republic itself.

10

Citizens into Subjects

It is easy to think that with the arrival of Bonaparte, all was different and all was successful. On the contrary, the regime faced the same problems the Directory did, a precariously unstable situation on the frontiers, and domestic subversion at home. Certain responses were the same. The regime had no more use for Jacobins than did the departed Directors. Its policies to royalists, however, were much more imaginative. Insurrectionary royalism was still to be crushed at all costs, but the regime also intended to undermine the royalists' bases of support. This meant reconciling the émigrés to the regime and above all reaching an accommodation with the Catholic Church. There were continuities on other fronts as well. The strategy of repression using states of siege and military courts against banditry, *chouans* and the 'brigands royaux' continued. The Second Directory's first steps in reforming money and public finance absorbed a great deal of the new government's energy but there was no departure from the course the Directory had set. Jourdan's law on recruitments was tightened to make desertion or draft dodging much more painful but otherwise, the new system remained intact.

Bonaparte and Government

One of the differences was Bonaparte's personality. He was indeed a man of relentless, untiring energy. He could work eighteen hours at a stretch, sleep at will, keep half a dozen secretaries busy, absorb vast amounts of information and distil it into crisp formulae and never allow one problem or decision to intrude upon another. He learned quickly. At first he knew little about government and so listened unperturbed to all sorts of unpleasant advice or criticism (so long as it was in private), but as he learned more and became enamoured of his own ability, he did more on his own. For all that, it is doubtful whether the quality of government declined as he became more despotic. It is doubtful too whether his own powers of organization, intuition and boundless energy ever left him. After all, he was only 44 when he fell.

He had few fixed ideas and no principles. He considered himself enlightened but his deism did not prevent him from reconciling with the Church and his progressivism from re-establishing slavery in the colonies that the Convention had abolished in the Year II. He abhorred demagoguery but his use of it in 1814 on the return from Elba was inspired and poetic. Although he was the most successful general of his day, he was not a violent man. Violence was a means to an end and if he had to murder the duc d'Enghien as a way of avoiding greater violence or deport Jacobins without trial, he could do so without regret. If he could cajole or manipulate his enemies into submission, he would do that too.

Although it was extraordinarily weak at first, the government signalled that it intended to be its own master. On 22 *brumaire* (13 November), the Law of Hostages was repealed and Bonaparte made a great sensation by going to the Temple prison to receive the released hostages himself. The forced loan was replaced by a modest surtax on existing taxes on the 28th. Four days later, Bonaparte met with a party of leading bankers, promising them a government of social defence and order, although they loaned the government only a fraction of what he asked for. Unlike every other coup of the period, no purge followed. Bonaparte prevented the ever narrow-minded Sieyès from deporting hundreds of Jacobins. The incident also showed right away who the dominant personality in government was. The government also lifted the legal penalties on the relatives of émigrés – the first step towards closing the émigré list altogether. As Bonaparte said so often in this period, he meant his government to be one of reconciliation.

He also meant that government to be strong. The Constitution of the Year VIII established an extraordinarily sharp separation of powers, even among the legislative and executive branches of government, and a significant reduction of the role of elections. Thus there was to be a bicameral legislature. The Tribunate of 100 members would discuss government bills but could not vote on them, after which the Legislative Body of 300 would vote on bills but could not discuss them. Before promulgation, a bill would then be examined by a Senate of 60 members for its constitutionality. None of these bodies was elected directly. Instead, the Senate was to choose the members of the Tribunate and Legislative Body from a national list of 6000 'notabilities'. In a bizarre and complicated arrangement, all adult males in a 'communal arrondissement', irrespective of wealth, would elect a tenth of their number to a communal list. The communal notables' could elect a tenth of their number to a departmental list and departmental notables another tenth to form the national list. In Sieyès's convoluted reasoning, this evaded the weakness of democracy or of any representative system, of governors being inherently incapable of exercising sufficient power over the governed. As he put it, 'Confidence from below, authority from above'.

Originally, Sieyès intended a 'Grand Elector' to choose legislators and officials from these lists and executive power to be exercised by two Consuls, one for foreign affairs, the other for internal. But Bonaparte, whether he feared being appointed 'Grand Elector' or not, as is often said (he called the position 'a fatted pig'), had no intention of seeing government paralysed by an excessive balance among its institutions. He wanted a government that was above all effective and, not surprisingly, drew upon a military model for it. Thus Sieyès was intimidated into accepting the demise of the 'Grand Elector', and the appointment of Bonaparte as First Consul for ten years. The two other Consuls, Cambacérès and Lebrun, were both able men, but by law had only advisory powers, after which, as Article 42 of the Constitution said, 'the decision of the First Consul shall suffice'. This clause put the entire executive authority of government in the hands of an immensely able, indefatigable and restless man. At a stroke, Bonaparte acquired staggering powers of appointment in the local, national, military and civil spheres of government. In no sense were the Consuls or the ministers responsible to the legislature. Instead, they had control of budgetary proposals which would be passed as an annual financial law, and the right to initiate legislation, while the First Consul alone could propose amendments, not the legislature. In all of this, he would be aided by another of Sieyès's ideas, a Council of State. This remarkable body, which still exists, soon attracted some of the most able men in the country. It prepared bills, often after considerable investigation and internal debate, and its members took turns defending them before the Tribunate and Legislative Body. It also acquired the powers of an administrative tribunal. As experience would show, Bonaparte's powers of appointment, his constitutional position and his own and his colleagues' abilities reduced the powers of the legislature still further.

As in 1793 and in the Year III, the Constitution was submitted to a plebiscite. The result was hardly an unqualified vote of confidence from the nation. About 1.5 million voted in favour, about 1500 against. The electoral apathy of the nation had not changed. About 400,000 more voted in the Year VIII than in the Year III but the turnout was still

400,000 fewer than in 1793. In fact, the process of depoliticization of the nation, and especially the cities, continued. From 50–60,000 voters in 1793–Year III, the turnout in Paris fell to 32,000, that is to 23 per cent of those eligible to vote. There were 2500 signatures on an anti-royalist petition in Marseille in the Year IV, 1200 voters in the Year VIII. Nearly 40 per cent voted in the elections of the Year VII in Toulouse, only 20 per cent in the plebiscite.

In fact, however, the plebiscite was made to look like a ringing national approbation of *brumaire* by a colossal fraud. Lucien Bonaparte, now Minister of the Interior, possibly with his brother's knowledge, had officials add between 8000 and 14,000 affirmative voters to each department's total with the result that the number of voters nationally was about double. The navy voted under very dubious conditions while the soldiers' votes were simply invented out of thin air since the army did not vote at all. Until very recently, both contemporaries and historians believed the officially announced results: 3,011,007 yes, 1562 no.

Continuing Disintegration

But fraud was not going to solve the problems of this extraordinarily fragile regime. Many officials remained loyal to the Directory and practised a prudent *attentisme*. The departments of the Pas-de-Calais and Pyrénées-Orientales refused to publish the decrees of 19 *brumaire* while the administration of the Jura tried to raise its own little army. Throughout the Midi, departments held the central government at arm's length and avoided making commitments as much as they could. The Jacobins were divided and dispirited and did little. This was probably wise, if unheroic, since the coup encouraged anti-Jacobin sentiments, and here and there prominent clubbists were mugged or meeting halls forcibly closed down. In wide areas of the country, the coup was once again perceived as anti-Jacobin and therefore many expected greater religious freedom. Priests in Alsace and along the Pyrenees advised their parishioners to accept the Constitution for this reason but in the civil war zones of the west, where the priests had long ago given up on the Republic, the royalist laity did not vote.

Brigands and bands of draft-dodgers continued to dominate the countryside in many regions. On the eve of the coup, for example, royalist brigands, men 'habituated to crime' backed by 2500 deserters and encouraged by defeats on the frontiers, had taken the field again in the Vaucluse, attacking gendarmes, robbing a tax officer and ripping open the chest of a married priest. There were murders of officials and raids on tax offices in the Ardèche, Maine-et-Loire and

Bouches-du-Rhône, and threats against the owners and farmers of *biens nationaux* followed by arson in the Hérault and Lot. Ex-nobles were trying to recruit a royalist army in the forests of the Seine-Inférieure, 'cavaliers royaux' were roaming the countryside around Amiens and Abbeville in the Somme. Bands of brigands calling themselves the 'Armée rouge', probably in imitation of British soldiers, were trying to recruit draft-dodgers in the Indre-et-Loire. The situation was hardly any better after the coup. With authority in disarray and the military preparing for the spring campaign, it was possibly even worse. There were only two hundred soldiers in the Gard, five hundred in the Ardèche, recuperating from wounds and so poorly supplied, according to General Ferino, that they became 'the most impure' in the army, themselves a cause of 'brigandage and murder and an impediment to the direction of the present government'. Their ill-disciplined reprisals on innkeepers and farmers suspected of harbouring brigands simply added to the prevailing chaos. In fact, their desperate blows were powerless. In the first six months of the Year VIII in the Vaucluse alone, the brigands murdered 79 people while the number of victims in the Year VIII in the Drôme was higher than it had been for the entire White Terror before *fructidor*. In one particularly ghastly incident in the Bouches-du-Rhône, they murdered the daughter of an official while her neighbours continued working in the fields. Officials' homes were burned in the Aveyron, there was a pitched battle with the National Guards of Pertuis in the Vaucluse, an invasion of Joyeuse in the Ardèche where the brigands disarmed the garrison and robbed tax offices, further robberies of the tax offices at Saint-Esprit in the Gard and Gamas in the Allier, as well as a hold-up of the Toulouse–Bordeaux stagecoach. A riot at Auterrive in the Haute-Garonne in which five hundred people liberated three recently arrested draft-dodgers showed that little had changed.

It would be another year before popular royalism in the Midi was brought under control, but the Consulate did have a quick success against the *chouans*. They should have risen at the same time as their counterparts in the south-west in the summer, but the usual lack of direction from the princes and the fatal decision to postpone the insurrection until the harvest meant that the last of the royalist insurrections of the Year VII was fatally isolated. The second *chouannerie* began well enough. On 22 *vendémiaire* (14 October) Bourmont's men surprised Le Mans and this provided the signal for similar occupations of Nantes, Saint-Brieuc, La Roche-Bernard, Redon and Locminé. Even the attacks of 1793 had not been so successful. But the *chouans* were not strong enough to hold these towns while Cadoudal failed to take Vannes and Frotté and d'Autichamp failed in Normandy and southern Anjou. Unable to exploit initial successes, the *chouans* were much less numerous because conscription, which had helped them so much in the first war was not applied in the Year VII in the west. As always, they were short of powder. The allied defeats on the frontiers and the abrogation of the Law of Hostages after the coup also sapped morale so that they agreed to an armistice with General Hédouville on 2 *frimaire* (23 November). The *chouans* also hoped, as did many émigrés, including the Pretender for that matter, that Bonaparte would restore the monarchy.

Spurning Reconciliation

Bonaparte soon disillusioned royalist agents on the subject of a restoration. In fact, he meant to undercut royalist popular support by making concessions on the religious issue. One edict rapidly followed another: permitting Sunday worship, returning churches that had not been sold to the communes, replacing the 'Hatred of Royalty' oath of 1797 with a bland one on loyalty to the Constitution, limiting the use of the revolutionary calendar to officialdom, abolishing the anniversary celebrations of the execution of Louis XVI, and limiting the regime's festivals to 14 July and 22 September. The government also rescinded the laws depriving relatives of émigrés and former nobles of their civic rights. This was followed by a whole series of individual measures of reconciliation. These measures gave some force to the words of the famous proclamation of 24 *frimaire* (15 December) presenting the Constitution to the nation: 'Citizens, the Revolution is established upon the principles which began it: It is ended'.

The country was not so sure. Proclamations could not stop people from carrying on their local struggles. In January 1800, a crowd convoked by the nocturnal ringing of bells by a carpenter invaded the church at Flogny in the Yonne, tossed the busts of national heroes into a joyous bonfire, restored statues of saints, chanted 'Down with the Republic, Vive le Roi, no more laws!' and hung a dog wearing a tricolour sash on the end of a ladder. Elsewhere in the Yonne, people started quietly working on the *décade* again and covering the statues of liberty with a cloth during Sunday worship. At Caen, there were funeral processions in the streets 'with all the signs and pomp of the Catholic cult' while there were rumours in the rural Seine and the Lot that religious toleration merely presaged the destruction of all republican institutions. It was now routine that there was yet another rash of destruction of liberty trees and republican emblems. Needless to say, the only priests who could be counted on to take the oath to the Constitution were the constitutionals. Few refractories bothered, many emerged from hiding or returned in droves from abroad. Nor were they much tamed. In the Morvan region of the Nièvre, seven of them preached against conscription and paying taxes. Another told the 'ignorant and coarse' peasants of Saurnt in the Ariège that the Revolution was a divine punishment 'for the sins of the people' and predicted 'the time when everything would return to good order'. Much of this sort of preaching was clearly welcome. A 'popular insurrection' installed the refractories in the church at La Canourgue in the Lozère where they proceeded to demand the return of *biens nationaux* and to reinstitute the Old Regime fees for baptisms and funerals. At Doziene in the Loire, a crowd of 'furies' interrupted a funeral service being conducted by a constitutional and dragged him out by the hair. Clerics who preached sedition or who refused the new oath were sought out by the gendarmerie and wherever possible imprisoned. Many could be forgiven for believing the regime had not changed substantially.

Just as many refractories returned because they interpreted *brumaire* as anti-Jacobin, so did many laymen. 'They are returning with all the trust and candour of innocence,' one official reported from the Bas-Rhin. Although the Constitution maintained the émigré laws in all their force, the returnees were scarcely molested because the government had decided to move away from the laws altogether. On 25 *pluviôse* (3 March), a decree of the Council of State closed the list from 4 *nivôse* (25 December) and Bonaparte established a commission to speed the removal of names from the general list. Magnanimous as this was intended to be, past experience suggested that it was still a risk.

Centralization and the Rule of Experts

The government meant to minimize the risk and bring the country under tighter control by reorganizing the basis of local government. The great ideal of 1790 that locally elected citizens would participate in the execution of laws had long ago also broken down under impossible pressures. The law of 28 *pluviôse* An VIII (7 February 1800) implicitly recognized the failure of citizen participation in local government and instead turned over all its operations in each department to a prefect. He was to be appointed by the First Consul and responsible only to the Minister of the Interior. Except in the Seine where police was under its own prefect, he was to supervise all aspects of local government including police, communal affairs, hospitals, roads, forests, *biens nationaux*, communal finances, public works, conscription, payment of taxes and so on. Below and subordinate to the prefect were subprefects in charge of a new unit called an *arrondissement*.

These officials had no independent authority and were merely the prefect's executors. The municipal cantons of the Directory were replaced with the communes of 1790 administered by a mayor and council. Municipal councils were severely controlled by the superior organs of government. The prefect nominated the mayors in communities with less than five thousand people and could suspend or sack their mayors or councillors. In larger communes, the central government exercised this right directly. As with the national government, the ability of citizens to influence government through elections was much reduced. Each department or *arrondissement* had a council composed of notable citizens who were appointed at first and later elected but their functions were purely advisory and generally were limited to allocating the distribution of taxes among the *arrondissements* and communes.

Tocqueville rightly celebrated the institution of the prefects as completing the centralization of the Bourbons, a centralization which has scarcely altered to the present day. Yet the institution was a radical break with revolutionary practice. The commissioners of the Constituent and Legislative Assemblies and the representatives on mission of the Year II had limited terms of reference and, along with the commissioners of the Directory, they were supposed to cooperate with elected local bodies, even though practice often differed. While co-optation of experienced administrators became more of a habit after *fructidor*, the prefects differed essentially in that they were rarely local men and their careers entirely depended on the central government. This administrative reorganization had social consequences too. The lawyers who ran the departments and districts in 1790 and the country notaries who ran the municipal cantons after the Year III were often shunted into the department or *arrondissement* councils, replaced by men of a different and sometimes higher social standing. Of the initial appointments, roughly half were lawyers and/or politicians while nearly one quarter were recruited from the military or civilian administration. Nearly one quarter were nobles and the return of so many to local administration was probably a real innovation. Certainly the prefects' substantial salaries, between 8000 and 24,000 francs in addition to generous allowances, raised them well above the incomes of all but the wealthiest of the former administrators. Bonaparte's respect for expertise and social éclat thus showed itself from the beginning.

The regime showed its preference for experts in the fiscal sphere as well. Gaudin, who remained Minister of Finances until 1814, secured the passage of the law of 3 *frimaire* An VIII (24 November 1799) which turned over the collection of direct taxes in each department to a special directory. Its members and the local tax collectors were not bureaucrats in the modern sense, since they received a percentage of the taxes collected, posted bonds to assure their honesty and were often ordinary private businessmen and financiers in their other activities. This crusty Old Regime method of tax collecting was deliberate. Gaudin said in his memoirs that he modelled the collection of the *contribution foncière* on the *vingtième* of the Old Regime. It also worked. For the first time ever, the bulk of the taxes of the Year IX were collected in the year they were assigned.

The curious overlapping of private and public also showed in the organization of the Bank of France established on 24 *pluviôse* An VIII (13 February 1800). Among other things, it was to discount promissory notes held by tax collectors, make loans to the treasury and receive and manage some government assets. Yet it also issued 30,000 shares of 1000 francs each to the public, and the shareholders elected fifteen of their number, called 'regents' to the bank's governing council. As the regime became more authoritarian, so too did the organization of the bank. In 1803, the 200 biggest shareholders alone could elect regents. The Bank of France operated in the stratosphere of high finance since the denomination of its notes had to exceed 500 francs.

More relevant to ordinary people was the law of 7 *germinal* An XI (28 March 1803) which established the so-called 'franc de germinal'. This regulated the silver content of the franc, fixed the value of silver to gold and set the denominations of the coins in circulation. Even so, ordinary people continued to use ancient and/or foreign coins along with the new and to ignore the decimal system of money for another couple of generations.

Eclectic and utilitarian in the recruitment of personnel, the Consulate also affected to ignore the political past of its servants. This appears to have been reasonably true in the case of the Council of State. Of the forty appointments in the Year VIII, nine were former *conventionnels* while ten had been imprisoned in the Year II. There was even a handful of federalists and veterans of the émigré armies who rallied to the regime. The reaction against professional politicians, which also manifested itself in the initial appointments to the prefectoral corps, showed here as well. Only 23 had been deputies and of the 112 appointments down to 1814, only 41 had sat in the revolutionary legislatures, many of them, like the prefects, coming to national politics for the first time after the Year IV. Again, like the prefects, they were chosen less for their political background than for their expertise in legal, financial, educational or administrative areas which they had acquired in the Old Regime or revolutionary bureaucracies.

By contrast, the appointments to the various branches of the legislature reflected the desire to reward the *brumaire* coalition. Sieyès was especially influential in drawing up the list of the first twenty-nine senators who were to co-opt the rest. Bonaparte limited himself to vetoing men he felt were too young or radical. The first senators were conservative former deputies and ministers, members of the Institute, businessmen and military officers. From the beginning, lustre outweighed political or legal acumen and this in turn was to propel the Constitution towards dictatorship. The Senate chose the members of the Legislative Body and Tribunate largely from the world of politics. Less than one in ten of the legislators had never held a national post before, although the trend against regicides that had begun under the Directory continued. Only twelve of the members of the Legislative Body and a handful of tribunes and senators were regicides. The same was true in the Council of State, incidentally, where only six initial appointments were regicides. Whatever institution the Consulate established, it could largely do without overly prominent Jacobins.

Defeating the External and Internal Enemies

The *brumaire* coalition was riddled with factions based on personalities, quarrels over strategy and attitudes to the First Consul. What held it together was the conviction that the Directory had been too weak to defend the post-thermidorean property settlement from Jacobinism and popular royalism. In itself, the coup had done nothing to stave off these threats and none of the reforms in local government, finance and the Civil Code, which was already in the process of being drafted, could have any effect unless the war and internal subversion could be mastered.

Bonaparte realized from the beginning that there was an intimate connection between external and internal threats to the Republic. Right after the coup, he had launched peace feelers to the allies but was rebuffed. As the spring and summer campaign of 1799 had gone fairly well for the allies, they saw no reason to respond. Since a spring campaign was certain, Bonaparte was determined to finish off the internal enemy partly to convince foreign opinion of the solidity of his government and partly because he needed the troops to fulfil the plan of campaign. Measures were taken to reorganize the gendarmerie and two special military commissions were established in the Rhône valley and the southwest to give summary justice to the 'brigands royaux'. Appropriately, Fouché, the Minister of Police, was the spokesman for the harsher measures against internal dissidence. 'Clemency is a virtue,' he told local officials in language reminiscent of the Year II, 'but weakness is a vice...a crime when it is applied at the expense of the public security'.

Bonaparte judged military commissions useless against the *chouans*. A new commander, Brune, with significant reinforcements, took over the Army of the West. Bonaparte ordered Brune to abandon the towns to their own defences, shoot captured rebels without trial, and burn the most intransigent communes to the ground. The whole region was put under martial law. It is doubtful, however, whether measures worthy of the Year II were applied extensively, for the *chouan* bands were desperately short of powder. One by one, the bands on both sides of the Loire began to surrender, their spectacular seizures of the towns earlier now completely nullified. Frotté and his staff in Normandy were arrested and later shot in spite of a promise of safe conduct to the local negotiations issued by republican officers. The procedure was indescribably shabby but Bonaparte, who undoubtedly knew most of the details and who wanted an example, was exultant. Although the *chouan* die-hards gave trouble for some time, *chouannerie* was defeated yet again, a victim of poor co-ordination among the leaders and with the British and the émigrés; and fatally weakened against a regular army with greater fire power. And Bonaparte had accomplished it by applying the old Jacobin formula of defeating the internal enemy first. Even as martial law was lifted on 1 *floréal* (21 April 1800), veterans of the western campaigns were marching to join a special Army of Reserve centred on Dijon. Two weeks later, the First Consul left Paris to take them to Italy to defeat the foreigner.

The campaign was very nearly a disaster. Bonaparte moved the Army of Reserve through the Swiss Alpine passes, a surprise thrust into the Austrian rear immortalized in another of David's famous paintings, although in fact the First Consul travelled by donkey through the treacherous St Bernard Pass with his troops hauling artillery by hand over the snow and ice. By 13 *prairial* (2 June) he was in Milan but, despite a heroic resistance, Masséna was finally compelled to surrender Genoa two days later. Nor did Bonaparte anticipate the Austrian attack when it came at the village of Marengo near Alessandria on the morning of 25 *prairial* (14 June). With all his reserves desperately committed, it was only the arrival of fresh troops under Desaix that turned an apparent disaster into a stunning victory. The Battle of Marengo led to the French reoccupation of Piedmont and Lombardy and, along with Moreau's belated occupation of Ulm and Munich, to a truce with the Austrians. The talks which followed were abortive, however. When hostilities began again, Moreau resumed the drive on Vienna. On 3 December, he smashed the Austrians at Hohenlinden. This produced the Peace of Lunéville (8 February 1801) whose terms were essentially those of Campo Formio, so that the French restored their dominance over northern Italy and the left bank of the Rhine.

The foreign victories had immense consequences on the internal political situation. Marengo, for all that the Italian campaign was a gambler's throw, consolidated Bonaparte's prestige at home. It put an end to the intrigues of the politicians around Sieyès who were disgruntled at the amount of power the First Consul had already acquired. Without a victory, he might not have survived. The public was overjoyed. The prefects reported spontaneous illuminations in Paris, Strasbourg, Lyon and Bordeaux. The peace with victory that so many had desired the previous autumn appeared to be imminent.

Some of the victorious troops were quickly assigned to repression of brigandage in the Midi and to mopping up the remnants of *chouannerie* in the west. The British, who had given Cadoudal considerable sums of money to put his die-hards in the Morbihan on a permanent footing, now told him to postpone an insurrection indefinitely. They also stopped payments to Condé's army of émigrés and it had to disperse.

If the British were withdrawing support for royalist military operations, the government meant to shut them down altogether. In February 1801, no less than two hundred newly established brigades of gendarmes were scattered throughout the western departments. A series of amnesties proclaimed in the summer of the Year VIII in the Midi brought a mixed response, however, and the royalist murders, robberies and pillaging continued much as before. Authorities were able to make some gradual progress. Some of the prefects, notably those of the Drôme and Var, organized a system of spies which produced some spectacular catches. Mayors were able to inform military authorities which private citizens could be reliably armed. Within months of its foundation, therefore, the new administrative system was contributing effectively to the repression of popular royalism. Most decisive was the use of troops. With large numbers released from the Italian theatre, commanders were able to make use of the flying columns technique which had proved so effective in the west in the Year IV. From the late autumn, there were more and more reports of brigand bands being arrested or dispersed, fleeing their mountain hideouts, profiting from the amnesty on condition they denounce their comrades, of collective defections or even killing their own intransigent chiefs. The government managed to wrest the law of 18 *pluviôse* An IX (7 February 1801), from a legislature belatedly sensitive to civil rights, which was to try brigands by special judicial commissions without juries or possibility of appeal. At least two hundred brigands were shot by these commissions in the Midi and possibly as many in the west, not to mention hundreds of others killed in countless skirmishes.

The establishment of a special National Guard unit at Marseille composed entirely of outsiders reduced vengeance killings in the city to

about one every six months. The government's vigorous show of force
encouraged the brigands' enemies, many of them undoubtedly local
'patriots' or terrorists, to take a stand, and in the Var, for example, no
less than seventy-four communes were described as being 'in a state of
insurrection against the brigands'. There were seventy-nine assassinations in the Vaucluse in the Year VIII, but only nine the next year.
There was not a single incident of brigandage in the once-infested
Basses-Alpes in the first six months of the Year IX. Even the refractory
priests were intimidated and it was said many of them were too afraid
to excommunicate the buyers of *biens nationaux*.

More Conspiracies

Repression showed the limits of the government's trumpeted policy of
moderation and reconciliation. Its increasing success and the consolidation of the regime after Marengo and Hohenlinden drove the true believers and the die-hards, both Jacobin and royalist, into conspiracy. The
extremist Jacobins attracted an array of insurrectionary veterans, former
deputies, exasperated artists and Italian revolutionaries. In the cafés and
backrooms it was difficult to distinguish their intoxicating talk about
convoking the primary assemblies and imposing the Constitution of
1793, from genuine plots to kill the tyrant. All of their plots, to stab the
First Consul at the Opera, or blow him up as he rode by on the street,
were nipped in the bud. Fouché's informers were able to report most of
the extremists' activities but they were less successful in penetrating the
royalist organizations. These too plotted kidnappings and explosions
and just failed to assassinate Bonaparte himself on 3 *nivôse* An IX (24
December 1800). The 'affair of the rue Nicaise' was another element in
driving the regime to dictatorship. It was the work of several of Cadoudal's most trusted associates, particularly Picot de Limœlan alias Beaumont, whose curriculum vitae in conspiracy stretched back to the La
Rouerie affair in Brittany in 1791, and Saint-Régent alias Pierrot who
was a former *chouan* commander in the Ille-et-Vilaine. When the
'machine infernale' exploded with shards of glass and bits of iron on
the rue Nicaise on the evening of 3 *nivôse* (24 December), somewhere
between 39 and 78 people were killed or horribly injured. Bonaparte,
who was on his way to the Opéra, was unharmed because the fuse had
been lit too late. Saint-Régent and his domestic who turned him in were
captured two months later and executed. Most of the important conspirators remained at large, prepared for another try.

The 'affair of the rue Nicaise' propelled a shocked political nation
into giving Bonaparte still more authority. At first everyone except

Fouché was convinced that the outrage was the work of Jacobins. Bonaparte led the way denouncing 'anarchists', 'septembriseurs', men of blood', 'the hundred or so *misérables* who have slandered liberty by the crimes they have committed in its name' and so on. Two days later, he saw advantages in the situation. He told the Council of State, 'The action of the special tribunal would be too slow, too limited. A more striking vengeance is necessary for such an atrocious crime, a vengeance as rapid as lightning.... We must profit from the occasion to purge them from the Republic...' 'A great example' against the chiefs would also dissolve the party, persuade 'workers' to return to work and 'attach the intermediate class to the Republic'. It was decided therefore to deport to the Seychelles and Cayenne 129 'Jacobins' culled from a prearranged list. All of them were quite minor people in the movement, although they all had a past. There were also officers the revolutionary army, officials of revolutionary committees, Parisians who had been with Fouché at Lyon who knew too much and Lyonnais whom Fouché knew all too well after the quarrels during the mission. The deportations were not the first exceptional measures the Consulate had taken against political enemies – shooting suspected *chouans* without trial came earlier – but it was the first that directly associated the brumarians in what was certainly an illegal measure against innocent men. This illegality in turn established a precedent which permitted subsequent violations of the Constitution.

The regime's institutions promised support. The Tribunate vowed in advance to accept a statute, whatever it might be, that went beyond the law on murder. Despite considerable qualms, the Council of State was unanimous in supporting a mass deportation. The Senate declared the act constitutional on 15 *nivôse* (5 January 1801). This was the first *senatus consultum*, a device later used to subvert the Constitution altogether. As Bonaparte was aware, it made the brumarians his accomplices.

There was perhaps a twinge of conscience when Fouché finally proved the royalists were responsible for the affair. No one rescinded the deportation order. In the end, they all accepted Bonaparte's logic that the deportees were guilty for what they had been, not for what they had done. As he expressed it, 'in the absence of legal proofs it [the government] cannot proceed against these individuals. We transport them for their share in the September Massacres, the crime of 31 May, the Babeuf Conspiracy, and all that has happened since.' Cambacérès concurred, 'It would be misleading to speak of the crime of 3 *nivôse* as being the motive for this measure, which is one of general utility'. But even this was not true either, although no one acknowledged it. They deported the Jacobins because they could, they deported men who long since had ceased to be a threat to anyone, men whom even the Directory had scarcely bothered to harass. Although no one said so, they did it to demonstrate that the state had reasserted itself.

Peace, Concordat...

Talleyrand, the Foreign Minister, supported a dramatic measure against the Jacobins because it would demonstrate the government's strength to the foreign powers. It certainly reduced still further the ability of the British to interfere in French affairs. Their diplomatic positions had deteriorated when the Scandinavians, the Prussians and the Russians closed the Baltic to British shipping. Despite dramatic successes with their Turkish allies in the Near East against the army Bonaparte had left behind, and despite a sudden Russian *volte face* towards the British, the British political class had become war weary.

So despite these successes, the British continued peace negotiations. The talks resulted in the Peace of Amiens of 25 March 1802. France was to keep her continental conquests, although Great Britain did not recognize the sister republics. Of all the conquests in the Mediterranean, the Caribbean and the Indian Ocean, Britain was to keep only Ceylon and Trinidad. Malta would be restored to the Knights of St John as soon as the Order was strong enough to defend its fortifications.

Neither side was entirely satisfied. The British were disappointed that there was no commercial treaty and Bonaparte considered the Peace of Amiens a device to curtail British economic and political influence. Still, Bonaparte's prestige within France was immense. As many had hoped, he brought peace with victory.

This prestige gave him the opportunity to negotiate the Concordat. He had determined to challenge the received wisdom of the previous decade that the clergy was the most ferocious enemy. The reasons were entirely practical. As he explained to his advisor Rœderer at Malmaison in August 1800, religion had its uses: 'How can there be order in the state without religion? Society cannot exist without inequality of fortunes and inequality of fortunes cannot exist without religion. When a man is dying of hunger beside another who is stuffing himself, he cannot accept this difference if there is not an authority who tells him: "God wishes it so..."' Social and political utility were inseparable. He told Thibaudeau, 'A religion is necessary for the people...Fifty émigré bishops paid by England lead the French clergy today. It is necessary to destroy their influence. The authority of the Pope is necessary for that...' An accommodation with Rome would thus contribute to the pacification of the west and help assuage the religious discontent in the conquered territories and sister republics.

Yet if Bonaparte meant to co-opt the clergy, Thibaudeau realized that the clergy's hostility would mean a 'war to the knife between them and the Revolution forever'. But persecutions were incapable of mastering popular counterrevolution. Bonaparte had an alternative: a 'good discipline and an effective police,' as he put it. This was essential. From the beginning the revolutionaries had concluded that the only way to assure the loyalty of the laity was to persuade or persecute the clergy. Bonaparte's solution was to co-opt the clergy, and stifle their freedom of expression through a 'good police'. Although there were many continuities between the Revolution and the Bonaparte solution in other spheres, this was a major break, one that easily overwhelmed the other continuities. But a reconciliation with the Church required greater authoritarianism.

The papacy, for its part, was willing to go far. The saintly Pius VII was appalled at Bonaparte's demand for the simultaneous resignation of all the Old Regime bishops. He tried to save them for as long as possible. It was Louis XVIII's clumsy attempts to prevent an accommodation that finally convinced the papacy of the truth of Bonaparte's point that the émigré bishops were erecting the interests of the monarchy above those of religion. In the end, the papacy wanted a reconciliation, at the price of the bishops, of the ecclesiastical property sequestered in 1789 and even a declaration of Catholicism as the state religion. Instead, the Pope had to settle for a declaration of Catholicism as the religion of the majority of the French. He would even have to accept the constitutional bishops. Pius demanded they accept the condemnations of his predecessor but Bonaparte refused to accept even this mild form of retraction. The abbé Bernier, one time advisor to Vendean generals, now a negotiator of the Concordat, assured Cardinal Consalvi, his Vatican counterpart, that the constitutional bishops had retracted when in fact they never did. As experience would show, this was only one of several deceptions practised on the papacy. But there was also justification in the papacy's hope that the Concordat was a mere beginning for the restoration of the Church.

... and Dictatorship

The Concordat provided the occasion for a sharp deterioration in the government's relations with the politicians. Already victory abroad and the beginnings of order at home left the politicians free to grumble about whether the government had become too authoritarian. Yet

Bonaparte interpreted all public manifestations of opposition as subversive. In his view, his relation with the nation was special. He stigmatized opposition orators in the Tribunate like Constant, Chenier and Daunou as 'ideologues' and 'metaphysicians'. Reacting to opposition to a bill (which was passed) which set time limits on debate, he said that the government aimed 'to destroy the spirit of faction'; to govern through parties was to become dependent on them, 'I am national'. Almost as soon as opposition appeared, all but thirteen newspapers in Paris were suppressed and this was later reduced to nine. Like so many of his contemporaries, he was incapable of conceiving of a loyal opposition or of politics as a process of reconciling interests through compromise. Like the Montagnards and the Second Directory too, his solution to the problem of faction was to eliminate it in the name of national unity. He described opponents to the special tribunals bill as 'vermin that have got under my skin . . . They need not think that I will let myself be attacked like Louis XVI. I won't stand for it'. Thus when the legislature reconvened in November 1801, it was difficult to disentangle the politicians' anxieties over the government's authoritarianism from their objections to specific government proposals. Probably they were not sure themselves but Bonaparte had clearly misjudged their temper if he expected them to applaud unquestioningly the restoration of order at home and peace abroad.

Everyone expected the crisis to come over the Concordat but Bonaparte delayed sending this and other bills to the legislature. At first, he seems to have been willing to live with this stalemate but since the Constitution required the renewal of one fifth of the membership of the legislature in the Year X, he soon saw an opportunity to rid himself of his most galling opponents. The Constitution was silent on how the renewals were to proceed. Most assumed it would be by lot. Instead, Bonaparte delegated to Cambacérès, the Second Consul, the shoddy business of cooperating with the Senate in designating which four-fifths of the Tribunes were to stay. The majority of senators, however queasy they were, seem to have gone along for no better reason than to end the legislative stalemate and out of fear that they were forestalling something worse. Thus in March 1802 they eliminated the same men they had appointed two years before. Among the eighty were the 'ideologues', Constant, Chénier, Daunou and Ginguené as well as friends of Sieyès and anticipated opponents of the Concordat.

With most opposition eliminated, Bonaparte secured the passage of a number of controversial measures that imposed his sense of hierarchy on the nation. The Legislative Body accepted the Concordat and the accompanying Organic Articles on 8 April 1802. A *senatus consultum* of 26 April granted an amnesty to all but about a thousand émigrés, provided they took an oath of loyalty to the Constitution. This meant that they had to accept the sale of *biens nationaux* as definite. Although the government returned all unsold property except forests to them, they had to remain under police surveillance and controlled residence for ten years. The government was hardly caving in to counterrevolutionaries. The Legion of Honour was created on 19 May. As we shall see, this reflected the increasing militarization of national life. The government tightened its control over the Bank of France and re-established slavery in the colonies. Finally, the passage of the Treaty of Amiens by the Senate on 6 May provided the pretext for a further and decisive subversion of the Constitution. As a token of gratitude, the senators proposed to re-elect Bonaparte for an additional period of ten years. The Council of State, with only a few members absenting themselves in protest, then drafted a proposal for a plebiscite asking the nation whether Bonaparte should be made Consul for Life. The Legislative Body approved, as did the Tribunate which presented its approbation in a particularly grovelling address.

The plebiscite was approved by a vote of 3,568,855 to 9074. While no one knows whether these results were altered as they were in the Year VIII, the votes of the soldiers and sailors was certainly manipulated, and the votes of at least one department – Seine-Inférieure – were 'corrected'. Also, the vote was hardly anonymous. As in the Year VIII, voters had to sign their names in a public register and some may have feared reprisals. Officials in the Ministry of the Interior certainly marked down any prefect who failed to engineer the expected turnout and the expected vote. Local officials were easily exposed to intimidation as were priests, many of whom were seeking appointments. And if the official results were honest, the turnout of roughly 47 per cent (within the boundaries of 1815) was by far the largest of the period. In the Côte-d'Or entire communes voted unanimously. Some women voted too and there were questions about the consent that illiterates could have given. In the end, it is hard to assess what the vote meant. It was the highest turnout of the revolutionary era, and the vote in favour was huge. On the other hand, a majority of eligible voters did not endorse the Life Consulate, despite Bonaparte's real achievements.

Yet there were reasons why a large yes vote could be expected and indeed the rise in participation between the Year VIII and the Year X, once the frauds are eliminated, shows a significant rise in enthusiasm for public life. With the return of peace, taxes were marginally lower than they had been in 1791. The demands for conscripts were dramatically lower than they had been in the Year VII. Only 150,000 men were called up in the classes of the Years VIII through X, as opposed to the 200,000 in the class of the Year VI alone under the Directory. With large numbers of soldiers demobilized, the families of the young could be grateful. Finally, the Concordat restored freedom of religious expression, the only kind of freedom large numbers of Frenchmen had shown they cared about, under a clergy who were not obviously the tools of others. Paradoxically, the establishment of a dictatorship meant less government for most people. Before the results of the plebiscite were even known, the Constitution of the Year X was drafted and later promulgated on 16 *thermidor* (3 August 1802). Combined with two other *senatus consulta* of 30 August and 20 December, this effectively organized the dictatorship. Bonaparte became Consul for Life with the ability to nominate his successor. The independence of the Senate, whose record was supine enough, was further reduced since the First Consul could nominate up to forty members. With fourteen vacancies still available, he could control the majority. In cooperation with the Senate, he could name the other eighty members nominated by departmental electoral colleges. These were new bodies which replaced Sieyès's excessively complicated and much-criticized indirect electoral lists. Instead, citizens chose members of electoral colleges from the list of the six hundred most heavily taxed men in the department. Since election to the college was also for life, the citizenry's participation in the institutions of the nation was an illusion. So too was that of the notables in the colleges since the First Consul could make up to twenty life appointments to the colleges from the list of the thirty most heavily taxed as well as choose the presidents of the colleges.

The Legislative Body no longer ratified treaties of peace or alliance which the First Consul alone negotiated, and the Tribunate, already divided into three permanent sections after the purge, had its membership reduced to fifty. Neither had to meet regularly. In theory, the Senate still had some feeble powers of appointment over these bodies but the senators were given considerable reason to be cooperative by the creation of 'senatoreries' in each appeal court jurisdiction, that is a domain that offered sizeable revenues to the favoured few who received them. Senators could also hold other lucrative government jobs so there was an additional incentive to be docile. If the original idea of a fief was a grant of land or revenue in return for state service, a 'senatorerie' was a fief. There was thus considerable irony in Bonaparte's constitutional oath 'to oppose the return of feudal institutions'. In fact, the Constitution meant nothing to him. 'The belief that a sheet of paper can be of any value unless it is supported by force has been one of the cardinal mistakes of the Revolution'. 'A constitution,' he said, 'ought to be made so that it does not impede the action of government and force it to violate it.... [A constitution's] development is always subordinated to men and circumstances.'

The Process of Dictatorship

In order to understand how 'men and circumstances' had brought the dictatorship about, it is necessary to question some of the persistent myths about Bonaparte's rise to power. One of these is that the Consulate was a military dictatorship. The army was critical, of course, in *brumaire*, at Marengo and Hohenlinden and for defeating the *chouans* and 'brigands royaux'. But the army as such did not take power in *brumaire* or afterwards. There was no marked infusion of military personnel into civilian institutions. If anything, the army was an obstacle on the road to dictatorship since envious generals retained the same limited views of politics they had held under the Directory. The police kept abreast of officers who muttered about 'the tyrant' and in the worst case, units of the Army of the Rhine and the Army of Italy whose hostility was annoying were shipped off to repress the rising of former slaves in Saint-Domingo, where they were never heard from again.

Bonaparte himself claimed that 'France would never submit to a military government.... Any attempt of that kind is bound to fail, and to ruin the man who makes it. It is not as a General that I am governing France; it is because the nation believes that I possess the civil qualities [earlier defined as "foresight, power of calculation, administrative ability, ready wit, eloquence"... and above all knowledge of men] which go to make a ruler'. The dictatorship was thus the work of civilians but this can be misunderstood too. Bonapartist historians constantly claim that a grateful nation, sick of disorder and bloodshed, turned to a saviour. There is some truth in this. The joyous reception upon the return from Egypt and the plebiscites, however fraudulent or poorly administered they were, attest to a genuine popularity among some people. Yet the plebiscites played almost no role in establishing the dictatorship. Popular attitudes to the regime contributed to the dictatorship in so far as they were basically apathetic. The Concordat had much the same effect on Catholic and royalist opinion. With the return of the old priests and wide freedom of religious expression, there was no need to challenge the government. To borrow an expression of Tocqueville's, repression and co-optation removed the 'intermediary institutions' of popular opinion and action and so made government effective for the first time in nearly a decade. Although the basis of Bonaparte's dictatorship was his constitutional right to pack assemblies, he never had to use it to secure the regime. After the purge of the Year X, the Legislative Body never again rejected a government bill and opposition in the Tribunate was trivial until its unlamented abolition in

August 1807. The Senate was supposed to safeguard the constitutional rights of the citizens. Over the period until 1814, it considered just 585 petitions from those who considered themselves unjustly imprisoned. They secured a few releases but if the Ministry of Police dropped a quiet word, so much worse for the prisoner. The most famous of these prisoners was the Marquis de Sade.

These toadies gave everything the government asked of it until the senators tried to save themselves in the catastrophe of 1814. In short, Bonaparte did not usurp power, it was given to him by a fairly narrow political class who, strictly speaking, represented nobody because they had all appointed each other. This was because, like the Directory before them, the brumarians fundamentally distrusted elections and parliamentary government. When Thibaudeau proposed a return to this system upon the conclusion of peace, his fellow councillors of state shuffled in embarrassed silence. Lanjuinais, whose whole career can be understood as a defence of parliamentary government, was the only senator to oppose the Constitution of the Year X. Indeed, the distrust of assemblies was so great that Cambacérès considered even the Council of State as a potential impediment to administration.

This attitude in turn was a function of the sense of the fragility of the achievements of the Consulate. 'Hardly any institutions,' wrote Roederer in 1802, 'nor yet any formed or rooted habits'. As the councillor Defermon said regarding the settlement with the clergy who were still perceived as potentially hostile, 'All that will go very well so long as the Consul lives. The day after his death, we will all have to emigrate.' To men like this, the surrender to someone who was prepared to use power crudely, even brutally, was necessary since the country was only recently pacified, the Concordat's prospects of success were not yet certain and the peace had only been achieved through conquests in Italy and along the Rhine. This is what the Council of State meant when it approved the plebiscite on the Consulate for Life claiming that 'stability alone can avoid war and permit the enjoyment of the advantages of peace'. It was also an argument derived from the thesis of circumstances. Once it had been deployed to justify Terror, now it was being used to justify personal dictatorship.

Conspiracy and Empire

No one in governing circles was inhibited about exploiting an advantageous peace to the fullest and this in turn led to a new war with Britain. The dictatorship applied an aggressive tariff against products of British origin, and signalled an equally aggressive attitude to British interests in the Caribbean. Developments on the continent aggravated these commercial quarrels. Bonaparte's refusal to evacuate Holland, the annexation of Piedmont, the Act of Mediation of 19 February 1803 which left the Helvetic Republic with only a fig leaf of independence, and renewed intrigues in Egypt and the Middle East generally with the implicit threat to India, encouraged all those in England who had doubted the wisdom of peace in the first place. The British press, still in its most licentious epoch, pilloried the dictator mercilessly and Bonaparte, who understood the value of propaganda better than the rulers of his time, was enraged when the government refused to curb it. Such belligerence in Europe, the Near East and America determined the British to hold on to Malta, which was an explicit violation of the Treaty of Amiens. None of the other great powers was satisfied with French conduct either. Neither Prussia nor Austria was content with the new territorial settlement in Germany and the Hapsburgs risked losing a great deal of prestige since the settlement gave a majority in the Imperial electoral college to Protestants. Russia too was anxious about French designs on Turkey. Thus more essential issues underlay the agonizing negotiations over Malta: commercial supremacy over the oceans, Mediterranean hegemony and the European balance of power.

The renewal of hostilities led directly to Bonaparte's assumption of a crown. Ever since 1792, war had divided the nation but for once this did not happen. When the British began seizing French merchantmen, shortly after breaking diplomatic relations on 2 May 1803, a controlled press and the absence of political outlets created the impression of a unified national indignation at the piracy of the hereditary enemy. Public opinion, such as it was, thus rallied round the government of the invincible general.

More importantly, the royalists' attempts to break the apparent consensus strengthened the dictatorship even further, as such efforts always had. This involved an ambitious conspiracy to kidnap the First Consul or failing that, kill him, as soon as a prince, presumably the comte d'Artois, arrived in France. Cadoudal and an élite company of *chouans* would slip into Paris from England to take charge of that operation. Pichegru would secure at least the neutrality of the army by approaching Moreau whom Bonaparte greatly resented for the victory at Hohenlinden. How much responsibility the British government shared in this plot has never been settled satisfactorily but it is hard to imagine the royalists arranged all their finances and maritime transport on their own.

In any case, there was never much chance of the plot succeeding. Despite Cadoudal's waiting in Paris for five months completely unknown to the police, no prince ever materialized. Moreau, if he promised Pichegru anything – which is not clear – refused to lend himself to a conspiracy aimed at restoring Louis XVIII. Eventually, the police captured a minor royalist agent who confessed after having his fingers crushed under a musket hammer. In February–March 1804, Moreau, Cadoudal and Pichegru were arrested, along with dozens of other agents and *chouans*.

Although a hopeless failure, the Cadoudal plot had momentous consequences. Bonaparte decided that the prince in question was the duc d'Enghien, grandson of the Prince de Condé, who was residing in Baden. The unfortunate young man was kidnapped, dragged back to Paris and shot within hours of his arrival after a farcical appearance before a military tribunal. Although Enghien was captured on neutral territory and no connection with the Cadoudal plot was ever proven, Bonaparte never regretted the murder. It may have stunned his admirers then and since, it may have made him a regicide after a fashion, but it worked. It was the end of the cycle of royalist assassination plots. The same brutally opportunistic cast of mind operated with Moreau. His eventual banishment was a further warning to the other 'Jacobin' generals that plots of any sort were futile. Even the mysterious suicide of Pichegru, found in his cell apparently having somehow garrotted himself, showed sceptics how unscrupulous the regime was prepared to be. Cadoudal died a martyr to royalist hagiographers but that was all. His plot seemed to show that only Bonaparte stood between a restoration and the preservation of what remained of the revolutionary achievement. It was a conclusion which the British government was already well primed to take in its own way after the rupture of the Treaty of Amiens. The ministry was now committed wholly to the Bourbons because only their restoration could also restore peace and the balance of power on the continent. The overthrow of Bonaparte's regime and the destruction of the conquests in 1814 were implicit in the events of 1804.

Most of the significance of this was lost in the spectacular elevation of Bonaparte to the imperial crown on 18 May 1804. The dictator's entourage, particularly Fouché, adopted the entirely specious argument that only the hereditary principle would eliminate assassination attempts. Everyone – the Tribunate, the Legislative Body, the Senate, the Council of State and ministry – acquiesced with even less maneuvering than that which preceded the Life Consulate. Speakers in these non-elected bodies claimed representative institutions would be preserved and that the Revolution of 1789 had not been hostile to monarchy. This presumed, of course, the monarchy of 1789 even resembled the dictatorship of 1804. Everyone also hoped to advance himself in the regime. After all, if no one of note even resigned after the Enghien

Affair – the decision to kidnap was collective at which a large number of ministers, councillors and senators were present – no one could be expected to protest the reintroduction of an institution many had sworn to die opposing. In the Tribunate, only Carnot, a man of principle in lost causes, voted against and promptly resigned. The nation dutifully voted in favour by 3,572,329 to 2569 even though the new constitution had already been adopted, so this plebiscite was an afterthought. At least one councillor of state supported the Empire because he reasoned his income could not have been higher in any other regime; because he might have to return to pleading cases if the regime failed; because others had gone along with it; and because, of course, deep down, Bonaparte was a liberal constitutionalist. Everyone knew that.

'The government of the Republic is confined to a hereditary emperor,' it declared, and the Emperor was to take an oath to respect 'equality of rights, civil and political liberty [and] the irrevocability of the sales of *biens nationaux*'. Aside from organizing a court with pompous medieval titles and permitting the childless Napoleon to name his successor, government institutions changed little. Any possibility of opposition from the Senate was forestalled by permitting the Emperor to appoint an unlimited number of senators.

The revolutionary era began with men hoping they could place limits on the actions of an arbitrary government. It ended with some of the very same men creating a government far more arbitrary and despotic than the monarchy of the Old Regime had ever been. Thus Napoleon's frequent claim that he found the crown in the gutter is only a typical half-truth. The political and intellectual élite picked it up first and embossed it for him in the interests of national stability. But even while Napoleon crowned himself at a gaudy ceremony presided over by Pius VII at Notre Dame on 2 December 1804, the development of the war was showing what a costly and calamitous risk the surrender to a dictator was proving to be.

11

Napoleon and Thirty Million Frenchmen

In 1802 Napoleon said that the aim of his reforms was to create institutions which would act as 'masses of granite' binding the nation together. The statement reflects how far the brumarians had travelled from the preoccupations of the Constituent Assembly which also thought of itself as reconstructing a nation out of chaos. Instead of a society based upon the free exercise of property and limiting the state by defining political and civil liberty, the men of the Consulate and Empire wanted to create a society based on order and hierarchy. Protecting property was as important to them as to the Constituents but the despotism they established ended by favouring the rich and heaping honours upon the wealthy and the exceptionally talented. Since the regime was at war from 1803 onwards, military values and military notions of hierarchy seeped into the system of rewards and honours, and even to a certain extent into religious and family life. The Consulate and Empire was not so much a military despotism, however, as a bureaucratic and professional machine that encountered remarkably little opposition. As the war dragged on, it became more arbitrary and more demanding. It is a measure of the success of the construction of the 'masses of granite' that it could be toppled only by the foreign invasion.

Honours and Titles

If a society can be characterized by the kinds of activities and people it rewards, then the Consulate and especially the Empire were military societies. This tendency showed itself from the beginning in the institution of the Legion of Honour founded in May 1802. Despite protests in the Tribunate that it was a violation of the principle of equality, the practice of recognizing civic contributions was not new. The Conquerors of the Bastille were a special unit, with their own uniform and a lifetime pension. But with its internal hierarchy of grand officers, commandants, officers and legionnaires, and its combative oath of defence of the Republic, the Legion of Honour did resemble several of the military orders of the Old Regime. Once its members received decorations and a new oath shortly after the declaration of the Empire, the resemblance was even closer. The difference was that no one was excluded on the basis of religion or birth. But it was military merit that counted. Of the 38,000-odd creations between 1802 and 1814, only 4000 went to civilians, most of them to high officials.

The Legion of Honour was the first step towards the recreation of an aristocracy. There were others: the creation of *senatoreries* and of princely titles for the imperial families, and the resuscitation of the honorific title of 'marshal' for outstanding generals. Finally, Napoleon created imperial titles in March 1808, because, he said, he wanted to fuse the old and new elites and because he wished to forestall the restoration of the Old Regime nobility. None of the cluster of associations that once defined the old nobility in law and practice – legal privilege exemptions, reserved office, venality, seigneuries, and so on – were revived with the new nobility. Only imperial titles were recognized, Old Regime titles were not. The Emperor, not office, was the source of titles and the sole criterion was state service. The most distinctive criterion was that the holder of an imperial title had to be a man of defined wealth. Dukes, counts, barons and knights had to have revenues appropriate to their title which was defined on a sliding scale. Money in itself did not imply a title since only a few businessmen and financiers, including only a minority of the Regents of the Bank of France, were ever ennobled. Instead, the imperial nobility practised an ideal of the Old Regime in that status determined wealth. Men whose personal fortunes were unimpressive received grants of property from the imperial domain or a share of the tribute from the conquered territories, and this in turn allowed them to build up substantial fortunes on their own account. Thus Marshal Davout, the descendant of an old but modest family of Burgundian nobles, acquired an annual income of close to 1.2 million francs, over three quarters of it derived from lands and revenues in Poland, Germany and Italy. Ney, the son of a barrelmaker, acquired a similarly fantastic fortune, equally dependent upon foreign sources. The spectacle of wealthy generals was not particularly new since Ney, Leclerc and Murat, among others, bought magnificent châteaux and their dependencies in the later Directory and early Consulate with money that was almost certainly derived from accepting 'gifts' from conquered towns and territories. Napoleon transformed the practice of accepting personal tribute into an extravagant system of largesse. This generosity towards the marshals and their dependence on foreign sources of revenue gave them a direct material interest in maintaining the frontiers of the Empire at their greatest possible extent. However war-weary they are said to have become in 1814, it is no wonder that none of them 'betrayed' the Empire until the military situation was hopeless.

The acquisition of an imperial title became in effect another honour marking a distinguished career. Napoleon created 3263 nobles between 1808 and 1814, the great bulk of them, understandably enough, in the first three years. Since state service in this period was above all military, it is not surprising that nearly 60 per cent were officers, the grade of the title neatly corresponding to the holder's military rank. The others were divided between the upper ranks of the civil service (councillors of state, prefects, bishops, etc., accounting for 22 per cent) and notables (senators, members of electoral colleges and mayors, accounting for 17 per cent). Service in the arts or culture or in economic life was scarcely rewarded at all. In social terms, the imperial nobility was drawn overwhelmingly from the old Third Estate. Only 22 per cent were from the Old Regime nobility while 20 per cent were from the popular classes and 58 per cent were bourgeois. Not, however, from the supposedly frustrated office-holding families of 1789 but from the more modest milieux of minor officialdom, law, medicine and petty industry. The recognized social élite of the country, therefore, had been drastically shaken and there was some truth in the regime's claim that it was open to men of energy and talent.

To acquire its talent in the future, the regime once again had recourse to a military model. The law of 11 *floréal* An X (1 May 1802) replaced the decentralized secondary schools of the Directory with 'lycées' of which there were only forty-five, that is fewer than one for every two departments. They implemented an eighteenth-century continental idea that the state should educate its future officials. 2500 scholarships were even set aside for the sons of officers and civil servants. Both teachers and students were subject to a strict military discipline. Both wore uniforms, those of the teachers indicating their rank, both were subject to a graded series of punishments for violation of rules, the boys participated in military exercises for an hour a day and were subject to discipline by their older or brighter peers who were given military titles. The curriculum was actually narrower than that of the 'central schools' of the Directory since the *lycées* eliminated the study of modern languages to concentrate on Latin and mathematics. An arid environment and unexciting curriculum may have alienated some parents. The lack of religious education certainly did. Despite close state supervision and the fact that they were taxed, other secondary schools established by municipalities or the 'Frères des écoles chrétiennes', the Old Regime teaching order revived in 1802, attracted many more boys than the *lycées* did.

Napoleon allowed both girls' and primary education to languish since in his view women had no other destiny than marriage and there was no advantage to the state in educating the masses. Yet it was in these areas that some of the greater strides of the period were made. Whether it was through the restored religious orders who taught both boys and girls, by itinerant schoolmasters, by teachers hired on an occasional basis by the communes or by village savants, popular literacy continued to increase throughout the revolutionary and imperial epochs.

The Crisis of the Concordat

In fact, the Empire meant to control popular opinions, not educate them, and its primary instrument was the Concordat and its accompanying police regulations. The Concordat recognized the right of the government to regulate the public exercise of religion and this provided the justification for the Organic Articles published on 18 *germinal* An X (8 April 1802). This was an extremely detailed law that restrained considerably the powers of the papacy in France. Despite protests from Rome, the government revived a number of measures taken from the old monarchy and added a few of its own. It gave the Church an almost military hierarchy. The publication of papal bulls, the convocation of national councils, the establishment of cathedral chapters and seminaries, and the creation of new parishes were all subject to government approval. The duties of archbishops, bishops and parish priests such as maintaining the faith, pay scales, residence, visitations, clerical garb and certain career requirements, were all specified. Diocesan and parish boundaries were fixed while below the bishops there were three thousand or so *curés*, ideally one per canton, who in turn were to supervise 'desservants' in the 'succursales' or communes. *Desservants* alone could be removed by the bishops and initially they were unpaid. The clergy was also required to denounce all crimes, subversive or otherwise, to the police, as they had been expected to do in the Old Regime. The government also required them to preach obedience to the state, particularly to the conscription laws, a tendency reinforced by the publication of the *Imperial Catechism* in 1806. The Feast of the Assumption, 15 August, was even followed the next day by the celebration of Saint-Napoléon, once the story of this obscure martyr was unearthed.

The reconstruction of the Church was a long process that continued well beyond 1815. Portalis, the first Minister of Religion, intended to strike a reasonably fair balance between the former refractory and constitutional clergies, but in fact the application of the Concordat tended to benefit the refractory more. Thus a document that gave the state an enormous authority over the Church could be evaded and stretched in practice to suit the perceptions and biases of the refractory clergy. Bonaparte led the way by appointing twelve former constitutionals and sixteen refractories to the new episcopate and promoting thirty-one refractories and only one constitutional. In the dioceses, overt discrimination and circumstances combined to keep the constitutionals out. In the Bouches-du-Rhône, for example, less than one quarter of the *curés* and less than one third of the *desservants* were former constitutionals. In the diocese of Rouen, headed by the brother of the Second Consul, a little over one in ten of the *curés* and one in five of the *succursales* went to constitutionals. Of twenty-seven appointments to *curés* in the diocese between 1806 and 1818, only one went to a constitutional. In some regions of the country, the dislike for constitutionals was so great that even their parishes were suppressed on the pretext that they were too small. In the diocese of Limoges, the bishop did everything he could to whittle down the number of constitutionals he had to appoint, including forcing them to serve an apprenticeship as a *vicaire* because, he said, 'I have decided to neutralize all the constitutionals by placing them among the Catholics'.

But such discrimination was only partly a question of bias against men the bishops considered schismatics. In the Mâconnais, 80 per cent of the *curés* had taken the oath but refractories received 35 per cent of the parishes in 1802 because so many constitutionals had retracted after the Terror. In the Charente where former constitutionals and refractories were evenly balanced, pastoral care suffered greatly because there were so few ordinations during the Revolution and the Old Regime clergy just died off. Consequently, in 1815, well over half the parishes had no priests at all. In the Morbihan, there were simply not enough constitutionals left as loss of vocation, dechristianization, marriage and the *chouans* had thinned their ranks considerably. In the diocese of Quimper, the bishop's policy was to appoint priests to their former parishes whether they were former constitutionals or not, but since the deportations of 1792 and 1797 had kept the corps of refractories better intact, four of five *curés* went to them. Throughout the west, a generally hostile laity often refused to accept constitutionals and noisily demonstrated against them, much as they had ten years before. Even the appointment of a constitutional bishop did not achieve the equity Portalis desired. Monseigneur Belmas in the Nord had to accept a generally refractory clergy because refusal of the oath had been very high in 1791. He had also to endure an unedifying campaign against him from his subordinates until the prefect forbade all discussion of the past. The prefects intervened weakly to protect the constitutionals, if at all. Their usefulness to government had long since passed.

The Concordat was close to a restoration of the refractory church. Civil authority often tolerated violation of its spirit. So long as the clergy did not preach sedition – and few did even in 1814 – the Consulate and Empire had co-opted a major source of popular discontent. In the first appointments, the prefects simply insisted that those rare priests who had served actively in the royalist armies should not be given places. The bishops usually concurred because such men were too independent and often too violent. The prefects tolerated much in other spheres. Although it was strictly illegal, they ignored the humiliating retractions that were forced on the constitutionals in the dioceses of Aix, Bayeux, Bordeaux, Limoges, Nancy, Rennes and elsewhere. They also tolerated ceremonies 'cleansing' parish churches that had been 'sullied' by the Mass of constitutionals and they ignored collective re-baptisms and remarriages. Bishops were eventually able to impose outdoor religious festivities.

Much of the Old Regime public presence of the Church returned too. The government permitted the return of the religious orders, at first those dedicated to teaching and hospitals, and ended by subsidizing foreign missions. Although the network of religious orders was nowhere near as dense as it had been before the Revolution, it was beginning to fill out. For the female orders especially, the growth would be spectacular so that by the middle of the so-called secular nineteenth century, there were more sisters in holy orders than there had been even in the Middle Ages.

The amount of money the government devoted to religious affairs mounted. *Desservants* received a modest salary in 1804 because communes proved exceptionally niggardly in supporting them and, until the break with the Pope in 1809, seminarians were exempted from military service. Within a decade, poor-relief institutions were largely rechristianized and the period witnessed the beginning, or rather the revival, of paternalistic conceptions of poor-relief that were to continue in ever more elaborate forms for the next half-century. In Montpellier, for example, nursing sisters ensured that the hospital routine was governed by the traditional liturgy and calendar, the bishop chaired the hospital board and priests and pious laymen organized much private charity. When the Bourbons returned in 1814, the Church had gone far in restoring its influence over public life and even in regaining some of its former independence.

None of this was accomplished painlessly and there remained serious problems at the pastoral level. Revolutionary dechristianization had wrought such havoc in the Marne that only one third of the priests could be restored to their former parishes; 40 parishes had no priest at all as late as the Year XIII and since there had been so few ordinations in the 1790s, nearly 40 per cent of the parish clergy were aged over sixty. In the diocese of Rouen, the figure was 30 per cent, and in 1815 nearly half the parish clergy in the country was over sixty. In the Vendée, where the executions, drownings, massacres and deportations had been terrible, only a little over half the Old Regime clergy was available for service in 1801 and of these, over a third died in the next ten years and were only slowly replaced. In the nearby Vienne, nearly half the secular clergy had died or had disappeared without trace in 1801. The problem of ageing and replacement was as severe as it was because in most parts of the country the newly established seminaries did not graduate enough priests – some parishes in the Var had to make do with Italian priests until the 1820s – but even where they did, as in the exceptional diocese of Vannes, it was accomplished at the price of an increasing ruralization which was not new, and an increasing plebeianization which, on the whole, was.

A more rural and modest recruitment did not necessarily reflect on the Concordat clergy's abilities or the quality of pastoral care but it was certainty one of the roots of the anti-urban, anti-liberal attitudes that turned the nineteenth-century church in on itself. Consider the attitude of the students in the seminary at Vannes to the better-off bourgeois, all the more remarkable since the town was one of the most backward in the country: they disdained 'the luxury and wealth of the cities which they could not share . . . and the success of the young gentlemen who, enriched by a better upbringing, stole the prizes and applause from them in every class in society . . . '

The crisis of clerical recruitment may even have aided the revival of forms of popular piety in the sense that the shortage of priests made controlling these forms more difficult. Assertions from the clerical and government élite that the people were indifferent to religion on the eve of the Concordat have to be treated sceptically. The councillor of state, Français de Nantes, observed, for example, that 'Avignon and Aix are the only towns where the priests have a great influence. There is no question of it at Marseille, and at Toulon, there is no priest and there are no services of any sort'. But lack of priests or clerical influence did not mean that popular piety had died out, far from it. Further, the popular assertions of the previous decade made it certain the ordinary folk would have a voice in how the Concordat would work out.

Among the first lay organizations to be revived were the parish and trade confraternities and funeral societies, authorized or not, and with them an old debate among authorities about institutions that too easily escaped official control. Nothing could better illustrate the government's desire to regulate what it could not suppress than the subprefect of Tarascon's opinion that confraternities should be contained within the archbishop's surveillance because they limited 'libertinage', added to 'the majesty of the cult' and gave 'a very great ascendancy to the priests'.

But it was not always possible to channel popular religious feelings. Priests who boycotted pilgrimages to local shrines or feasts of patron saints because they usually degenerated into mass drinking bouts often had to restrain a quiet rage as the celebrations took place anyway. Country people showed a great deal of nostalgia for feast days suppressed under the Concordat. In the Côte-d'Or, a region not noted for its fervour, peasants 'daring to take the place of the curés... filled the functions of the priesthood in the most scandalous manner... recited the prayers of the Mass [and] sang vespers...' to celebrate Nativity in 1807. In the Limousin, the faithful brought out relics like fragments of the true cross or statues of saints they had rescued just before the dechristianizers moved in. Diocesan authority wanted to have this material authenticated but often public opinion insisted. No doubt this was because the local clergy sympathized, as they did when the saints of one parish were exposed as they always had been every seven years. As a result, a child recovered his speech and the use of his legs. The *curé* reported his dilemma: support popular opinion that believed in the miracle and that urged him to authenticate it, or risk the derision of the local sceptics. There was little lay or religious authorities could do about such powerful currents of popular opinion because ordinary folk had passed through the previous decade often without clerical care and had learned to insist. Some beliefs the clergy never supported either before or after the Revolution just had to be tolerated, for example, the elaborate cult of the dead in Lower Brittany where people left biscuits out for drowned sailors at All Saints or warmed rocks, thought to be anchors for lost souls, in bonfires on St John the Baptist's day.

If the Concordat unleashed a burst of popular religious sentiments thus giving people a freedom of expression under an authoritarian government that they had not enjoyed before, there were still signs at the individual level of a mutation in religious feeling. At Montpellier and no doubt elsewhere, for example, bequests to traditional charities and requests for Masses for the souls of the departed continued the slow decline that had begun over a half-century before. Whatever this means – a decline in religious sentiment as such, the transformation of the baroque and ostentatious ceremonies of old into a more private faith or a growing conviction that family members would care for the needs of the dead – at the very least, a different form of religious expression was emerging. More significant perhaps was the decline in the national birth rate, an indication that at least among men, a quiet defiance of traditional Catholic teaching on the family and reproduction was spreading. Knowledge and use of 'evil secrets' was not new but the revolutionary decades appear to have marked a decisive step.

Family, Law and Property

There is a genre of historical writing that knows no bounds when writing about women and the French Revolution. The aftermath of the Revolution is, apparently, quite bad. Women were confined to a ghetto, it is said, or worse still, to a gulag. Needless to say, this is all false. Extravagant language masks quite a different mundane reality. The lawyers who drafted the Civil Code defined the legal status of women with assumptions that are totally unacceptable nowadays but that had a certain logic at the time. Not only were women considered to be in a separate sphere from men, not only were they confidently considered to possess a common frivolity and child-like incapacity for adult life, it was also assumed they had to be protected. Thus in the formation of a marriage contract, a husband had the usufruct of his wife's portion, but he could not alienate it in any way. The property was hers but both her property and his had the tremendous advantage of being pooled to support their credit. This was essential for young couples undertaking the lease of a farm. The bond they could post together assured landlords and permitted the couple to undertake a lifetime of work together. If the husband predeceased the wife, the widow could take on the farm in her own right, with full rights to the family's assets, or do so in association with one of her sons.

The Civil Code also recognized the right to divorce, although this must have been a mixed blessing. Divorce had been legalized in 1792, and almost any imaginable grounds were permitted, including simple incompatibility. There was a flood of divorce petitions, overwhelmingly from women who had been deserted. After this initial flurry, divorce remained quite rare. The Civil Code eliminated desertion as a basis, but recognized adultery, cruelty and imprisonment as grounds, plenty of scope in other words, to stretch family situations to conform to the law. Furthermore, instead of the emphasis of the revolutionary period on reconciliation through *ad hoc* family and neighbourhood councils which unfortunately had never been an entire success, the Code introduced an appalling double standard. The husband could obtain a divorce for his wife's adultery but the wife could only do so if the husband brought his mistress into the household. A husband could even have his adulterous wife imprisoned for up to two years. In fact, such things were unusual because divorce, whatever the method of obtaining it, became very rare. In Rouen, for example, divorces averaged 161 per year under the Convention, 71 under the Directory and 8 per year during the Empire. At Lyon, there were 88 divorces a year until the Year IV, 64 a year until the Year XI and just 7 a year under the Civil Code until 1816 when divorce was abolished. A majority of plaintiffs were women, and the skilled artisans and the liberal professions were over-represented among those seeking a divorce while the unskilled, the bourgeoisie and the former nobility were under-represented.

There were also few constraints over the disposition of private property, which, after all, was the ideal of all the revolutionary assemblies. Contracts always favoured men of property. Thus tenants had no legal security on the land they farmed beyond the stipulations of the lease, their personal property could be seized for arrears and they could be imprisoned. But the text of the law did not describe reality on the ground. All over northern France tenants stayed on the land for generations, and if they did not, it was because they were seeking even better opportunities. In the Midi, however, where research on this question has scarcely begun, any reasonable security of tenure may well have been imaginary.

As for the sphere of urban work, the law of 22 *germinal* An XI (12 April 1803) forbade attempts on the part of employers and employees to undertake actions in restraint of trade by conspiracies to lower salaries or by strikes to raise them, but provided much more severe penalties for workers than for employers. Workers were also obliged to carry a 'livret' or passbook to be held by the employer in which the details of the employee's work record were kept. The *livret* thus helped ensure a working man's docility.

The Civil Code also increased the theoretical freedom of testators to dispose of their property. Where the Convention required an absolutely equal division of property among heirs, the Code permitted a testator to reserve anywhere between one quarter and one half of the property, depending upon the number of heirs, for a single heir. Thus the Code permitted a preference for eldest sons and the partial maintenance of family holdings. On the other hand, this could weaken the position of widows who had no legal claim to her deceased husband's property. In Montauban and no doubt in many other places, testators overrode the Code in this respect and frequently gave half or even the entire usufruct to the widow. Thus the couple survived the death of a partner. Only with the death of each party could the property be distributed to heirs. Equal division among heirs was the rule. Most parents followed the law but from the beginning some families like artisans, shopkeepers, and small landowners, faced ruin if the property were divided equally. So they invoked portions of the Code that permitted preference or even circumvented the law itself. In fact, very old practices that privilege one heir over another survive to this day. It requires dispossessed heirs to choose not to exercise their legal rights and to do so generation after generation. Thus in one region of present-day Auvergne, testamentary practices among landowning farmers privilege youngest sons. Older sons and daughters accept this because of heavy moral pressure to keep the family patrimony intact and because fathers establish sons as café owners in Paris or finance daughters' advanced education. And this route, of course, might be the better investment for the older children.

Nineteenth-century commentators were convinced that the Code was responsible for breaking up family holdings. But they were oversimplifying a complex situation. Critics like Tocqueville repeated endlessly that the Civil Code was grinding the land of France into dust. This was misleading since several Old Regime provincial codes (e.g., Normandy, Anjou) had permitted equal division. In fact, the pulverization of land the critics of equal division deplored did not happen, and it has not happened. France was and remains a country of big and small landowners, as Marc Bloch said it was in the Old Regime.

Thus on many issues, tenants' security, widowed women's property, and equal inheritance, the Civil Code failed definitively to reshape the behaviour of the French. The law could not override family conceptions of property and the rights of its members.

How the Empire was Ruled: Conscription and Taxation

The Consulate and Empire established themselves by force but they did not always rule that way. On matters of conscription for instance, the government imposed itself on the nation through a combination of intimidation, guile and incentives. Throughout the revolutionary years, conscription and resistance to it had been one of the many elements linking popular royalism, *chouannerie*, brigandage and simple disobedience. The Consulate inherited all of these problems following the war crisis of the Year VII and the near failure of the levies of that year. It naturally used the same methods the Convention and Directory had to try to bring draft-dodging under control: patrols by the gendarmerie, encouraging denunciations, billeting troops on recalcitrant communes and sending mobile columns of soldiers on rapid searches through forests, wastelands and mountains.

In themselves, these methods would not have been any more successful than in the past without several other steps. Prefects were given far more authority than mayors in raising conscripts because the mayors were too often tempted to favour their sons, or those of important constituents, or simply defraud the government by providing physically unhealthy draftees. By law, the government made the communes responsible for their draft-dodgers and required them to provide substitutes for successful evaders. Other laws made it illegal for an evader to inherit property; fines were levied on evaders' families; those who gave evaders shelter were prosecuted; and in the most spectacular revival of an Old Regime bad habit, the wealthiest taxpayers in a commune would have to pay for the cost of billeting in the home of an evader's family; finally, the government resorted to using flying columns of soldiers who blasted through a region looking for draft dodgers. Eventually, all this wore the country down.

The government also took account of economic resources and regional attitudes to military service, and asked more of the frontier departments of the east and often considerably less from the west, the Midi and the annexed territories of the Rhineland. Thus in the Year IX, it demanded one conscript for every 860 people in the Haut-Rhin, one per 4930 in the Finistère, one per 1204 in the Lozère and one per 2208 in the four Rhine departments. Greater centralization, making prefects' careers depend upon fulfilling their departments' quotas, greater co-ordination between the prefects and the military authorities, assigning officers in each department to oversee conscription and offering cash rewards were among the administrative measures taken to secure obedience.

The Concordat also helped in immeasurable ways since the clergy was expected to preach obedience to conscription from the beginning. One sign of the success of the Concordat was in the west, which met its deliberately reduced quotas without serious trouble when conscription was applied to the region in the Year XII for the first time since 1793. Above all, the Consulate demanded far less of the country than either the Montagnard Convention or the Directory had. Military victory, the destruction of the royalist bands that conscription had helped produce and that in turn protected draft-dodgers, as well as the Concordat, permitted the government to align its administrative capacity to raise troops with the nation's willingness to submit. Draft-dodging remained a problem for the Empire because not even a dictatorship could transcend certain geographical facts and political attitudes. In the Hautes-Pyrénées where escaping over treacherous sheep-tracks and smugglers' trails to Spain was fairly easy for knowledgeable locals, 40 per cent of the conscripts evaded as late as 1809. In the Puy-de-Dôme, the prefect felt that it simply was not worth the effort to send gendarmes into the mountains to pursue the families of draft-dodgers when whole villages decamped with their meagre belongings to hideouts higher up. The scale of the government's demands was yet another element. After the amnesty of 1810, there were only 1250 deserters and draft-dodgers being sought in the Puy-de-Dôme from all the classes from 1806 onwards, but the next year there were another 1500. Even so, this did not approach the 4000 who evaded the call-up of the Year VII.

This example suggests that administrative capacity was crucial. Punishment for evaders thus appears to have become much more certain. As the administrative machinery tightened, the number of condemnations declined. Between the Years XII and XIII, punishments inflicted in the once brigandage-ridden Department of the Loire fell from 1597 to 836, in the Haute-Loire from 1066 to 562 and in the troubled Nord from 1270 to 501. The link with brigandage had been virtually broken. In 1809, there were a mere 18 stagecoach robberies in the entire Empire, in 1810, only 11; in 1809, 168 murders, in 1810, only 167.

Thus the administration was able to ensure departments met their quotas. For instance, anti-conscription sentiments in Côtes-du-Nord produced *chouannerie* but after 1807 the department met all of its quotas down to the end of the Empire. So too did the Var and the Nord where religious troubles, anti-conscription and brigandage had gone hand in hand in the 1790s. Political factors among the population as a whole remained important down to the end. There were only 19 draft-dodgers in the nine separate levies in 'revolutionary' Finistère between 1809 and 1813, while the 'chouan' Morbihan next door had 900 in the five of 1813. In the levy of 1814, which was a disaster nationally, Finistère not only met its quota but provided 350 volunteers. In general terms, it would appear that well into 1813 resistance to conscription was less than it had been under the Consulate, let alone the Directory. It was only with the massive levies of over one million men following the catastrophe in Russia that officials became genuinely alarmed. By then, the conscription service was overwhelmed by the demands placed on it, national morale sagged, especially after the Battle of Leipzig in October 1813, and public opinion was shocked by the government's attempt to conscript married men or men who were the sole support of their families. Until then, the administration was strong enough and intimidating enough to prevent conscripts from voting with their feet, no matter what their inner feelings.

The contrasts with the revolutionary years were dramatic. The three major forced levies of the 1790s – February and August 1793 and the Year VII – all produced less than half the number of conscripts expected. Throughout the Consulate and up to 1808, well over 90 per cent of the young men actually joined their regiments.

No one accepted conscription with enthusiasm and evasion remained a problem to the end. In the west and the Massif Central, for example, young men carried talismans to recruiting centres to protect themselves from drawing the wrong number. Parents gave their sons charms against death in battle. Self-mutilation, destruction or falsification of records, marrying aged widows to become the sole support of a family and bribery of officials and doctors were commonplace down to 1814. But this merely shifted the burden to the less cunning for at no point during the Empire was anything like a majority of those eligible actually conscripted. For all the devastation of his wars, Napoleon conscripted about two million men between 1800 and 1814 or about 7 per cent of the total population; by contrast, the Third Republic conscripted four times as many between 1914 and 1919, or about 20 percent of the population.

Aside from taxation which affected everyone, conscription was the most important institution linking state and nation. Its administration illustrates much about the attitudes of the men in power to their fellow countrymen. It was grossly unequal, thus demonstrating that the loss of equality accompanied the loss of liberty. Differentiating conscription demands by region may have shown an empirical good sense but it was still the case that the Ile-de-France was expected to surrender five young men for every one from Brittany. Such a flagrant regional inequality diminished over time as the regime became stronger and more informed about the demographic profile of each department but it never altered the opportunity for a rich man to pay someone to replace him. This particularly vicious amendment to the Jourdan law was passed in the first legislative session of the Consulate by the Tribunate and Legislative Body. All of these men been appointed and they would never have to face direct popular election. Such was the result of Sieyès's constitution exercising authority from above.

Bonaparte himself considered replacement a natural consequence of economic inequality. Thus 5–10 per cent of the conscripts managed to buy themselves out. That the poor had to be greatly tempted is suggested by the extraordinarily high price of a replacement – it rose from 1900 francs to 3600 francs in the Côte-d'Or between 1805 and 1811; that is, from more than six to more than nine times the annual income of an unskilled labourer. In other parts of France, the cost of a replacement could be well over 8000 francs by 1810. This meant that only the very rich could escape their duty. Conscription discriminated against the poor in informal ways as well. Among the wealthy families of Upper Normandy, there was a remarkably high number of merchants' sons who managed to get themselves places in such exempted professions as ships' carpenters. In fact, the authorities had to hush up a scandal involving more than two hundred families who had bribed exemptions of one sort or another lest it create an unfortunate impression among the common people.

Such partiality undoubtedly contributed to the increasing hostility to conscription that manifested itself as the regime collapsed in 1814. The same result occurred with taxation. With the renewal of war in 1804, the government jumped to imposing to indirect taxes, in other words it raised the burden on consumers and the poor. Although the Directory revived these Old Regime devices, most notably the *octroi* (in effect tariffs on certain goods entering towns and cities), the Empire expanded them greatly. In the Year XII, the government regrouped taxes on tobacco, playing cards, coach seats and hallmarks into the *droits réunis* and extended them to alcoholic beverages. Thus the regime once again reverted to Old Regime habits.

Indirect taxes were cheap to collect, but the regime also deliberately undertook a programme to reduce taxes on landowners. The reason was that they paid a disproportionate amount. This was probably true, since the Constituent Assembly believed direct taxes were more transparent and therefore political authorities would be rendered more accountable to taxpayers. Needless to say, this was an entirely reasonable position for a representative government to take, indeed daring, since career politicians abhor this kind of accountability. It was entirely unreasonable for a dictatorship because such regimes do not want to engage in a dialogue with important taxpayers through parliamentary institutions about fiscal burdens under any circumstances. Masking the tax burden was quite consistent with the downgrading of the importance of the legislature. Indeed, in the Consulate and Empire, the two occurred simultaneously. The best principle of taxation, according to Napoleon's minister, was a veiled tax that everyone had to pay on an indispensable object, although no one knew they were paying it.

Thus there were 11 reductions in the incidence of the land tax between 1798 and 1820, while the ratio of direct to indirect taxes reverted to Old Regime proportions. This was a shift from producers back to consumers. For urban workers, the incidence of such taxes was not only great, they also had to bear a huge number of incidental fees on water, burials, stamps, and so on. By the end of the period, no less than 2000 municipalities were collecting an *octroi*, so tempting had the determination to collect indirect taxes become. In 1806, the state re-established taxes on salt which recalled the *gabelle* of the Old Regime, raised postal rates (which varied by distance at that time) by 50 per cent, and finally, in 1810, re-established the state's tobacco monopoly. Sycophantic politicians in the Tribunate actually denied any of this was a reversion to Old Regime practices, because, they said, the Empire was a regime of liberty so no resemblance could possibly exist. Thus does a dictatorship render men stupid, or more likely, servile. The prospect of public hostility mattered little to Napoleon. As First Consul, he had rejected indirect taxes; as Emperor, he thundered, 'Don't I have my gendarmes, my prefects, my priests? If there is a rising, I'll have five or six rebels hanged and the rest will bend.'

The importance of these shifts was immense. The Consulate pursued the Second Directory's policy of collecting every possible outstanding tax. At the same time, the reconfiguration of the incidence of taxation was blunting any popular opposition to taxes as well. The result was twofold: when the war began again, the Empire was awash with money from old arrears, and thus the thrust for universal dominion could be financed; before, that is, the burden was once again shifted to the conquered peoples, mainly to the Germans and the Italians. Second, as the demands of the Empire increased as the burdens of war increased, the system of stealth taxation blunted popular opposition. And, of course, as Bonaparte said in another context, a good police helped.

Were People Better Off?

The answer is they probably were, not because of revolutionary legislation as such, but at least in part because of the unintended effects of government decisions. Before illustrating the point however, it is important to realize that there was no straight line of prosperity from 1789 to the Empire. The inflation of the currency for much of the 1790s caused enormous hardship. Inflation was a kind of tax on consumers and an outright confiscation for those who saved, or for those living on a fixed income. Many widows in already tight circumstances must have suffered terribly. Decreed prices and requisitions were another tax, this time on producers and since they were unevenly applied, there were arbitrary also. So the country had to climb out of an economic trough at the end of the 1790s. The return to hard currency was the beginning of this process. On the other hand, for labourers the economic effects of conscription were beneficial. The various drafts, whether the voluntary ones of 1792, the *levée* of 300,000 of February 1793, the *levée en masse* of the following August, or the drafts under the Jourdan law of 1798, did not capture a large percentage of those eligible. But they tried to incorporate the most robust and the healthiest. That was always a minority of young men since the number of fit young men in the countryside had always been quite small. (Army returns that date from the 1820s show that many young French men were short – thus malnourished as infants – and often debilitated). The consequence was to drive wage rates of permanent farmhands or casual labourers high. Although there was great regional variation, wages of farm labourers rose between 1790 and the early nineteenth century by 75 per cent.

The situation for non-agricultural workers was more mixed. The dislocation of the Revolution and the breakdown of markets ruined many rural industries. This coincided with a structural change in the textile industries, as cotton continued to displace older fabrics like silk and wool. In and around St-Quentin in the Nord, there had been 12–14,000 looms before the Revolution; in 1802, no more than 3000; the female spinners, in much reduced numbers, were earning half the wages they got in 1790; and exports to Eastern Europe and to America were down to zero. Regions like this continued a slow reversion to agriculture which, although prosperous, did not need as many people so population dropped. Lyon and Nîmes, their hinterlands and Piedmont were hit very hard since the price of silk fell by 97 per cent. Consequently, wages in the textile industries overall dropped by 40 per cent. In part, this crisis was due to the wars and the blockades, whose effects were exceptionally serious after the traditional Spanish market was cut off, and partly it was due to the increased popularity of cotton.

Behind the high protective wall, the cotton industry grew at a breathtaking pace throughout the region bounded by Ghent, Rouen, Paris and the northern and eastern frontiers. The population of Mulhouse, for example, grew by over 40 per cent between 1800 and 1810 thanks to cotton and calico printing. The number of cotton-spinning firms in Paris doubled between 1803 and 1806, tripled between 1806 and 1808 and nearly doubled again to 57 between 1808 and 1811. In 1807, there were 12,270 cotton workers in Paris, 7900 of whom worked for the giant Richard-Lenoir firm whose revenues were 24 million francs in 1810. But much of this was a forced and unstable growth due to war. The British blockade raised the price of raw cotton to levels considerably higher than those in London, sudden shortages threw the manufacturers into disarray and, understandably in the circumstances, the industry was plagued by shortages of skilled workers, speculation and undercapitalization. Richard-Lenoir could only survive the crisis of 1811 with government loans, and when the frontiers were thrown open in 1814 the industry nearly collapsed.

Nonetheless, the economy of Paris and many provincial cities revived. With the restoration of a court, Paris soon found its old vocation as a world centre of the luxury trades, particularly fashions, jewellery, clocks, porcelains and fine furniture. Thus in part, the revival of Paris industry was due to government, from the largesse it distributed to its functionaries and clients, itself partly financed from tribute from abroad. Parisian workers were especially fortunate. The daily wage of a navvy rose by 72 per cent, of a carpenter by 55 per cent, painters by over 60 per cent, and so on. The structure of manufacturing in the provincial centres followed a similar pattern. The economic growth that occurred within these old structures was real enough, however. One estimate puts production 50 per cent higher in 1810 than in the 1790s and while this seems high, there was a modest prosperity.

Using a Labroussian technique of comparing wages with price risings would seem to confirm a real gain. Grain prices fluctuated enormously during the revolutionary and imperial epochs because there were so many poor harvests: in 1788, 1792, 1794, 1795, 1800–2, 1807 and

1811–13. At Rouen, rye prices, a better proxy for popular standards of living, were above the average for the 1785–1815 period nearly half the time. Thus, high wages were needed to cope with this unprecedented series of bad years. Overall, gains for urban workers may well have been quite modest since they also had to pay higher rents. Also, since a large portion of the tax burden was being shifted to them, the gain might have been more modest still. One sign would be the calorie intake. The daily calorie intake of Parisians was not much different in 1820 than it had been in 1790, and most of those calories came from bread, very little, if any, from meat. The number of cattle sold on the market at Poissy remained more or less steady.

By the time of the Empire, the countryside was picking up the thread of an agricultural revolution that had begun before the Revolution, but that had been seriously delayed. The rise in taxes more than offset the abolition of feudal dues and of the tithe in most places. Where taxes rose the most, rents flattened out, but where the tax rise for some reason had not been all that great, rents soared. The ultimate beneficiary of the abolition of feudal dues was the state itself, since the tax rise represented a lost opportunity cost for landlords. Either way, whether it was a tax rise or a rent rise, tenants supported the new rise in the cost of operating land. At first, one might think that tenants were badly mauled during the revolutionary decade, what with rising farm wages, rising taxes or rising rents. But the situation was more complicated than that.

Most historians assume the landlord–tenant relationship was a zero sum game, that the income of each party was dependent upon depriving the other. Thus historians favourable to the Revolution want to argue that the legislative arrangements of the period actually transferred income to the peasantry. Unfortunately, the situation on the ground is a lot harder to characterize. Tenants did have a hard time in the 1790s, but outside the war zones where requisitioning must have been devastating, they could cope. Interestingly, they had the hardest time, not in the early 1790s but after 1798, when the Directory returned to hard currency. Families that had not paid their taxes or rents in ages now found themselves presented with bills from the fisc for long standing arrears. Since landlords were legally responsible for their tenants' taxes, they bore down, collecting not only tax liabilities, but also outstanding rents. Worse still, former feudal lords dug around their archives and found that their former 'vassals' still owed arrears dating back to the Old Regime. They insisted upon payment. Thus years after the seigneurial regime ceased to have any legal validity, former feudal lords inflicted a 'seigneurial reaction', a seigneurial reaction in thin air. The overall result was that among the tenants of the hospitals of Le Mans and Gonesse anyway (hospitals were important landowners and so historians use their records as proxies for the land market as a whole), tenants were hard pressed to pay, and often they did not pay for many years. In other words, the period of highest political turmoil did not coincide with the years of financial stress.

Nonetheless, this inability to pay for many years after 1798 did not result in expulsion which remained very rare. Landlords of large farms preferred to retain their tenants as much as they could because tenants' managerial skills, their capital and their credit were irreplaceable. Paradoxically, a high turnover of tenants, as around Chartres during the revolutionary and imperial epochs, was a function of other tenants willing to bid up rents, confident they could make a go of a farm in an area that was being pulled more and more into the Paris orbit. Thus once tenants got over the difficulties of the return to hard currency, they could resume the extraordinary growth that had begun in the mid-years of the reign of Louis XV. At least around Paris, they invested more and more in animal husbandry, the very thing their English critics, Keyder and O'Brien, accuse them of not doing. The specifics of this investment was in sheep and their efforts at cross-breeding Spanish merino sheep with local strains was so successful, they forced other regions, like Le Mans, to abandon sheep raising altogether in favour of cattle. Ascertaining tenants' patterns of investment is not easy, but what landlords did is more accessible. In northern France anyway, landlord investment may have always been quite high but until the eve of the Revolution, it was limited to maintaining the estate. Afterwards, as urban demand accelerated, first the hospitals in Rouen, then their counterparts in Le Mans and Chartres, began to construct an increasingly large number of new granges, stables, pens, and so on. This was very likely at the demand of tenants who insisted on these buildings to shelter their larger herds.

In short, the Empire witnessed the resumption of an agricultural revolution that had begun earlier, that the 1790s had interrupted, but that continued with the return to domestic tranquillity. The Revolution's contribution to this was nil because it did not release any new sources of income that could be re-invested in animals or equipment. But productivity did increase. Although the sample size is still small, the ability of tenants to capture these productivity increases was also improving. Throughout the Old Regime and until the early Empire, landlords seized all productivity increases for themselves every time they renewed a lease, as they always had. After that, productivity increases moved so fast that landlords could not keep up. From 1810, or so onwards, those who worked the land, tenants and wage labourers, were the most important beneficiaries of productivity increases.

The result was again a continuation of the demographic revolution that had also begun before 1789. The population of France rose from approximately 28 million people in 1790 to approximately 31 million in 1820. This apparently modest increase masked a dramatic shift in demographic patterns. Young men and women had reacted to such 'Malthusian' pressures in the past by marrying later in life. The classical result was fewer legitimate births that in turn reduced family size. So a higher marriage age and fewer children imposed a return to an equilibrium. But the timeless patterns of yesteryear did not recur this time. On the eve of the Revolution, the age at first marriage for women began slowly to drop while the decline for men was dramatic because many hoped to avoid conscription. Another 'Malthusian' reaction, but utterly forbidden, was to adopt birth control. Some couples had begun to practise this before the Revolution in parts of Normandy, Languedoc and the Ile-de-France, but after 1790, it had become general and national. Depending upon region, the number of births per married woman fell between 13 per cent and 28 per cent between mid-century and the Restoration. No one is certain why birth control spread so rapidly but it may be related to the relaxation of traditional family morality. Interestingly, the regions where it was practised most were those with a high proportion of constitutional priests. This suggests that the destruction of the constitutional clergy from 1793 onwards, and the difficulty of staffing the Concordant church in these regions, led to a relaxation of clerical discipline and with it a more independent attitude to family planning.

In any case, if the number of births per family fell, infant and child mortality fell even more from the 1780s onwards so that life expectancy rose dramatically. And the rise in life expectancy must have been unprecedented. From the reign of Louis XVI until that of Louis XVIII, that is forty years, life expectancy for women and men jumped from 28 years to 38–39. For life expectancy to rise by a third over two generations, something dramatic must have happened. The obvious explanation is something about the Revolution itself. The rise in wages because of conscription must have done a great deal to help the rural poor. Apart from this it is hard to imagine how any legislative change that ostensibly re-arranged rural incomes could account for the rise in life expectancies.

So why did the population rise over the period? It could be that the price of this rise was a decline in living standards, as Michel Morineau argued for the Old Regime. But that is unlikely. It is also unlikely the Revolution re-distributed income, as many others, including Peter Jones and Paul Spagnoli, argued. What may well explain the rise in population that occurred without a shock to living standards was a rise in agricultural productivity that eventually found its way into the pockets of those who worked the land. This gave them the ability to look after their children better. The legislators of the Revolution never intended to do this, nor did they ever set as a national goal to raise living standards. Much of what the politicians did, including the war of liberation, then of conquest, killed a huge number of young men, the able bodied, robust labour force necessary to achieve the agricultural revolution. The French people themselves did what they did to improve their lot.

Considerations of productivity put the evaluation of who gained land during the period in a different light. Again, if access to, and ownership of, land is considered a zero sum game, the outcome of the revolutionary epoch for peasants is rather pessimistic. In the Nord, for example, the share of peasant property rose from 30 per cent to 42 per cent but that of the bourgeoisie rose from 16 per cent to 28.5 per cent, each group an unequal victor over a despoiled church and weakened nobility. Peasants did better in the region around Chartres since their share rose from an average of 33.6 per cent in eight villages in 1790 to 44.6 per cent in 1820 whereas the share of the bourgeoisie rose from 26.4 per cent to only 29.6 per cent. But demographic pressures had raised the number of proprietors overall by 30 per cent over the same period. The peasant majority had to make do with the lion's share of the property of less than 5 hectares whereas the urban minority came close to monopolizing the holdings larger than 10 hectares.

Such a process was very old. The formation of large holdings by clearing and purchase and the pulverizing of the peasant remainder had begun in the sixteenth century at Lattes in the Hérault. By 1677, the number of estates greater than 40 hectares had doubled and the average size had increased from 66 hectares to 84 hectares. In 1820, there were 15 such estates, averaging 125 hectares. The nearby village of Mangulo had 8 estates larger than 100 hectares occupying 37 per cent of the surface in 1770; by 1820, there were 16 large estates occupying considerably more. In other words, even for the owner-occupying peasantry, the abolition of the various feudal levies had done little to provide the extra margin of security necessary to preserve their holdings for the next generation.

But the issue was not how much land peasant owner occupiers possessed before the Revolution and after. The question is what use they could make of it and no one has ever investigated this issue. One can imagine a situation of a peasantry newly enriched with land from a political upheaval, literally ruining their gains because they had no credit, no tools, no animals with which to sustain or improve their windfall. This would drag national production figures down. As best one can tell, this worst case scenario did not happen in France because small property owners were just that – small. They simply did not have enough land to make a significant impact on production, either before or after the Revolution.

The Notables, a Powerless Elite

What kind of élite emerged from the Revolution? The question is vital because historians have found the significance of the entire period in the altered nature of the élite. According to classical historiography of which Lefebvre was the last great exponent, a thrusting, ambitious bourgeoisie hurled aside a privileged aristocracy in 1789, and, after a momentary challenge in the Year II, eventually consolidated its power under the Empire. Recent research on both the Old Regime and Revolution has shaken the classic view considerably. If the argument about a rising bourgeoisie does not explain the origins of the Revolution, neither does it explain the aftermath.

The Empire itself called its rich the 'notables' and the term aptly describes those at the top of the social heap. The notables included businessmen and financiers but overwhelmingly, they were a group of landed proprietors and professionals. In other words the post-revolutionary élite was not particularly different than the pre-revolutionary élite.

Moreover, nobles were an important component of the notables. Estimating how much the Old Regime nobility lost in the Revolution is far from easy. The most spectacular destructions, execution and emigration, affected only a minority. The typical noble response to the Revolution was to become inconspicuous and await better days. One example would be Berset d'Hauterive, a minor noble near Laval in the Mayenne who remained outside of politics throughout the period. He was arrested as a suspect in the Year II and he was harassed by the *chouans* later. But he welcomed the coup of *fructidor* An V because it would restore order in the countryside. The suppression of tax exemptions did not hurt him, although higher taxes did, but only a little. He had some compensation from much higher rents and he continued to collect 'my tithe', as he put it, as a separate item in his accounts until well into the Empire. Other nobles were not so fortunate. In some regions like the Sarthe, they had reconstituted their estates by 1830 while in others like the Nord and the Eure-et-Loir, they lost between a fifth and a third of their land. Nonetheless, all of them could increase their incomes by raising rents. So how much income declined, if at all, for many is a subject very much worthy of more research.

Above all, nobles were rich. A survey of the 1000 biggest landowners in the country in the Year XI shows that 33.9 per cent were former nobles. Even the Parisian nobility which was certainly hard hit, managed to survive. In 1749, in the Marais quarter, nobles comprised one third of those whose marriage contracts were over 50,000 *livres*, over half of those over 100,000 and all of the millionaires. Although the *parlementaire* nobility still comprised one third of the notables in 1809 in the same district, their fortunes were commonly in the 15,000 francs to 20,000 francs range. It is doubtful whether any could have financed the fabulous marriage contracts of their ancestors since their fortunes, heavily invested in state bonds before the Revolution, had been ruined as much by the inflation and bankruptcies as by executions and confiscations. Still, nobles were a wealthy group, even if they had to share the top drawer with non-titled *rentiers*, officials and bankers. In the rich and dynamic First Arrondissement, they comprised 81.2 per cent of those with landed revenues over 60,000 francs, 36 per cent of those between 10,000 francs and 50,000 francs and 36.8 per cent of those with less than 10,000 francs. Moreover, their share of private wealth was disproportionately large. In the Paris of 1820, they filed 1.4 per cent of the wills for 18.2 per cent of the value and among the largest fortunes, 40 per cent of the wills for 70 per cent of the value. As late as 1840, 10 of the 15 wealthiest men in the country were descended from Old Regime nobles. Once again the pattern of fortunes in Paris mirrored that of the nation. The lists of imperial notables indicate that former nobles comprised between one sixth and one quarter of the 600 most highly taxed, and their share was exceptionally large. Among the 30 most highly taxed in most departments, about two-thirds were Old Regime nobles. As in the Old Regime, aristocrats were the wealthiest single class. What had gone irrevocably for the old aristocracy were the partial fiscal immunities and the virtual occupational monopolies they had enjoyed under the old monarchy. Nor were they or the notables in general a ruling class in any meaningful sense because the despotism dominated them and used them as a pool of talent. The government did not defer to them as such. Their influence was above all local and they were massively inter-related. In the Allier, for instance, about two dozen civic-minded families, continuously allying to each other through marriages to produce intricate family trees, emerged in 1790 to produce prefects, deputies, bureaucrats, local councillors and mayors in lush variety for the next hundred years. Curiously, only the Jacobins of the 1790s produced no prominent descendants.

Among the important institutions of state, notability was allied with 'capacité'. This was the ideal the ruling class had of itself down to the 1870s. Of Napoleon's ministers, for example, about one third were ex-nobles, all, except Talleyrand, of fairly minor extraction. The rest derived from professional or military families. Among the generals, the percentage of former nobles steadily fell from 26.6 on 1 April 1802 to 20.1 on 1 April 1814, which refutes the frequently repeated comment that Napoleon increasingly favoured nobles. Nor is it likely that he reconciled the counterrevolutionary aristocracy to his regime. Some 1353 generals served the Empire but only eight had fought in the émigré armies. It is also a cliché of the period that every soldier had a marshal's baton in his haversack. This is true enough in the cases of Ney and Gouvion Saint-Cyr who were born to very modest families or of Lannes, Brune and Suchet who rose from the voluntary and conscripted levies of 1791–3. The overwhelming proportion of generals, however, were born to commercial, civil service or military families who had already destined their sons to military careers before the Revolution.

Moreover, Napoleon's generals were the beneficiaries of a very rapid promotion. In 1805, a very large proportion of them were, like the Emperor, men in their thirties; while the generals of the Revolution were significantly older. They were also very brave. Almost all of Napoleon's marshals had been wounded in battle, sometimes more than once, sometimes severely. Only the Emperor had never been wounded but there was no doubting his courage either.

The career pattern among the prefects was almost identical: no 'noble reaction' as such, recruitment mostly from bourgeois families, increasingly professional training, promotion following further experience, and close supervision by superiors. By the time one reached the upper echelons of the state apparatus, the civil and military personnel of the Empire were energetic professionals.

The Mechanics of Repression and Opposition

Linking the old and new élites, bureaucratizing the administration, rewarding friends and loyal officials, currying the rich, making the principle of subordination a feature of every institution, mobilizing the young into the military were all characteristics of Napoleonic government. So was repression. As the war made increasing demands on the country and the administration became more professional, the regime became more dictatorial. Representative institutions counted for next to nothing. The Legislative Body met for only seventeen days in 1811. There was no session at all in 1812 and the first meeting of 1813 was notable only for the Emperor's brave speech and the grant of more money following the catastrophe in Russia.

The enfeebled state of quasi-representative institutions was even more evident in the provinces. If the Côtes-du-Nord was at all typical, the sessions of the general councils became more perfunctory from 1807 onwards, declining to a mere three days in both 1812 and 1813, just long enough to vote an address of loyalty to the Emperor. Outside the government apparatus, there was no legal forum for opposition. The Paris press, cut to thirteen then to nine newspapers in 1800, was further reduced to four in 1811. From 1805, a system of prior censorship evolved and the government taxed newspaper profits heavily. Napoleon regularly dictated articles himself or told his ministers or editors what to write. From 1807, the provincial press had to take all its political articles from the official *Moniteur* and after 1810, there was to be only one newspaper per department. Prefects tried their hands as journalists and the result was predictably boring and misleading. Writers too were subject to prior censorship and for those who felt they could get along with the regime, like Bernardin de Saint-Pierre, Monge or Sismondi, there were handsome pensions. For those who could not, like Mme de Staël, Necker's daughter, there was police harassment, seizure of works and eventually enforced residence outside Paris. Finally, in addition to the continuing bureaucratization of government, the manipulation of public opinion, the system of rewards and exile for friends and enemies, the government introduced a system of administrative arrest in 1810 and designated prisons where internees could be held indefinitely without trial. Most of the prisoners were royalists, not former members of the by now broken Jacobin movement. The practice was not new and while there were comparatively few such prisoners, at least by modern standards of despotic imprisonment – 810 in 1811, 289 in 1812 of whom 106 were political, 640 in 1814 of whom 320 were political – there were still far more than those held by *lettre de cachet* in 1789. Interestingly, of the 304 listed in one roster, 25 were in state prison at the request of their families, a perfect reversion to how *lettres de cachet* were mostly used at the end of the Old Regime.

The regime was still arbitrary, if bureaucratic. The Minister of Police once justified the imprisonment without charge of one thief because 'if he has escaped justice, it is only because of lack of material proof'. So he was imprisoned on the basis of moral certainty of guilt. The regime also used the device of internal exile to punish enemies. This completely escaped any judicial control. Of course, the Senatorial Commission on Individual Liberty took a narrow view of the law and stayed out of such cases. This allowed any high official like a prefect or the minister of police to order the exile to another residence within France of any one they pleased. This too was a revival of an Old Regime practice. There may have been about a thousand of these people at any one time, troublemakers, clerics of the Petite Eglise (see below), and various ne'er-do-wells. Although such practices could cause genuine hardship, Cardinal Broglie, exiled to Beaune for his support of the Pope (see below), hardly suffered. Local clerics flocked to meet him and 'the caste of former nobles' feted him. 'The only thing with which he might justly be reproached,' reported the mayor, 'was spending too much time in high society'.

There was always opposition to the Empire, from elements in the Church after 1809, from royalists, from some of the common people and from malcontents in the military, but it is doubtful whether that opposition was growing or was even very effective in undermining the 'masses of granite'. An examination of the sources and strength of opposition illustrates a great deal about how the imperial administration worked.

One of the tests of how strong the regime felt itself to be was how it handled the breach with the papacy. This was a crisis that did not have the consequences that might have been expected because Napoleon was able to divide the prelates and eventually to intimidate Pius VII himself into submission. The crisis began with the annexation of Rome and the papal states in 1809, ostensibly to bring these territories more firmly into the Continental System but ultimately because the self-proclaimed successor to Charlemagne and the Caesars could not resist possessing the ancient imperial capital. The Pope was arrested and interned in the northern Italian town of Savona. Pius excommunicated Napoleon and refused to invest bishops. On learning of the excommunication decree, Napoleon dismissed the Pope as a 'raving madman' and claimed that Pius had excommunicated himself. This was very nearly true. Pius was moved to Fontainebleau in June 1812 and six months later, Napoleon, turning on his usual charm, got the old man to agree that a metropolitan could confer canonical institution under certain circumstances. Napoleon immediately published this as a 'Concordat'. The Pope's dissent was swept aside, he remained interned and cardinals who supported him were arrested. Only the defeat of 1814 averted the papacy's becoming an appendage of the Ministry of Religion.

The long quarrel with the Pope undoubtedly shocked Catholic opinion in regions directly outside French control, particularly in Spain, where it hardened opinion still more against the irreligious usurper. Within imperial France itself, the consequences were considerably muted. There was some wild talk about a revival of the persecutions of the Year II and a few funeral orations for Louis XVI. There were some arrests in the Belgian departments because some priests refused to recognize the bishop; there were also some arrests in the Kingdom of Italy but very few. The Church remained outside the dispute. Catechisms continued to refer to military service as a sacred duty and bishops preached that desertion was against religion. Right up to the end, the Church sustained the regime.

But the quarrels with the Pope did contribute towards giving a new direction to royalism. Of course, royalism never died out. As late as 1808, the police uprooted a vast network of safe houses, courier-drops and hideouts in Brittany which served to inform the British of naval dispositions in Lorient and Brest. This was run by the same spy service that had informed the British of the activities of the *chouans*. All the spies were émigrés. After the police uprooted this remnant, genuine royalist activity, as opposed to a bucolic nostalgia, risked dying out. Ferdinand de Berthier, a son of the intendant of Paris who had been murdered in 1789, took it upon himself to recast remaining royalist sentiment. His prayers told him that his only sign would be success and, undaunted by this rather Calvinist mark of religious favour, he founded yet another royalist secret society known as the 'Chevaliers de la Foi'. As a group, the Chevaliers are more interesting for their quixotic romanticism and what they reveal about royalist mentalities than for their political impact. Formed in 1809, the Chevaliers were no ordinary secret society. With its cells called *bannières* under the direction of a *sénéchal*, it reflected both a reviving sense of medieval chivalry and the flourishing anti-freemasonry of royalist circles. Indeed the abbé Barruel, whose celebrated history of the Revolution explained the collapse of the Old Regime as a masonic plot, was an organizational consultant. The Chevaliers were arranged in circles with only the inner group knowing the true royalist purposes while the front organizations masqueraded as public charities. Like the continental free masons, there were also the same heady array of secret handshakes, signs and menacing oaths as candidates were inducted from one organizational ring and one level of knowledge to the next. The Chevaliers soon claimed to have *bannières* in most of the cities and regions of the country. The claim may well be true but, as their blundering efforts in the crisis of 1814 showed, they were not a significant military organization. Theirs was a salon royalism that served to keep the memory of the Bourbons and the better days of the Old Regime alive among the squirearchy, little more.

Insofar as there was a popular movement during the Empire that was also dissident, it was the Petite Eglise, the 'church', whose members refused to recognize the Concordat. The numbers involved even in its strongholds were never very large: perhaps 2000 lay followers in Rouen, perhaps as many in Lyon, at least 20,000 in Poitou whereby by far the most of the followers lived, and much smaller numbers of adepts in pockets of Brittany, Normandy and the Midi.

But the influence of the Petite Eglise cannot be measured in numbers alone for it was held in great respect by many laymen who normally went to the Mass of the Concordat clergy. This was because of the extraordinary clerics who refused the oath to the Concordat and the compromises it involved, and because in many ways the Petite Eglise continued the forms of popular religious dissidence that had shown themselves under the Directory or earlier. The best example of this would be the Béguins or 'Bleus' of the Forez in the Loire. Some of their preachers began announcing the arrival of the Messiah and of his prophet Elijah in 1792. As we have seen, some were arrested attempting to journey to the Holy Land in 1794. The refusal of Concordat Catholicism was all of a piece with their belief that the Church was the Prostitute of the Apocalypse, that the Mass was an abomination and that there was only one sacrament, baptism.

Some of the individual priests certainly showed uncommon courage. Charles Barbedette, *curé* of Grand-Luc in the Deux-Sèvres, for example, refused all of the oaths of the 1790s, was never captured and never emigrated. He also evaded the imperial police because after a decade's experience, he was an expert at disguising himself. The abbé Grangeard, former *curé* of Souligné-sous-Vallon in the Sarthe, had been deported to Jersey but returned in 1801 to preach for the next twelve years until his arrest. For years, he celebrated clandestine Mass at dawn in haylofts, private rooms and barns to followers who often considered him a 'real' priest and a martyr. Clerics like this spoke to a laity that had not reconciled itself to the changes in legal status of the Church. Their followers retained the popular hostility to the sales of *biens nationaux*, to the constitutional clergy who were now incorporated into the Concordat church, to the abolition of many of the Old Regime parishes and above all to the suppression of the innumerable feast days that had traditionally marked the passage of the year. Popular religiosity had always laid great emphasis on liturgy and ceremony as a way of controlling the unknown and the supernatural so that a strong nostalgia for 'true' religion persisted.

The Petite Eglise also shared another characteristic of popular mentalities: a taste for prophecy. Sometimes this was the work of laymen. In the Hautes-Alpes, a man known by no other name than 'Louis' who claimed to know the esoteric languages of Latin and English and to have visited the New World, despised Napoleon so much he refused to handle the coinage. He predicted all manner of catastrophes including the fall of the usurper from 1812 on. In 1819, a certain Fleuriel from Alençon appeared in the Sarthe to announce that he was the angel of life come to combat Bonaparte, the angel of death, along with his minions, the king and the heretic pope. The world would end in flames in two years when Bonaparte returned from Elba. Much to the distress of the Petite Eglise clergy, their congregations were very sympathetic to such predictions but the priests often prophesied too, especially about conscription. The abbé Grangeard regularly predicted that all the young men without exception would be conscripted, while in the Deux-Sèvres the areas of greatest resistance to conscription were those with the highest numbers of adherents to the Petite Eglise. This undoubtedly explains why the government found what would otherwise have been a movement of harmless millenarianism and hopeless nostalgia so threatening. Arrests of dissident priests usually coincided with renewed military efforts.

In the final analysis, however, the Petite Eglise was no threat. According to the prefect of the Seine-Inférieure, its followers were 'widows, men without education, illiterates...the most miserable class of the people...' This was not quite true, for among the laymen arrested in one of the periodic sweeps in Rouen were three flannel manufacturers and an apprentice printer, but the prefect was right enough to lay the emphasis on the poor and the powerless. Women were much more attracted to the Petite Eglise than men, and in the Auvergne the audience was almost entirely female. The prefect of the Deux-Sèvres claimed that it was only dangerous in his department because there were so many 'sharecroppers, small tenants and poor peasants who rent their land. The police have much less leverage over this class of men than over proprietors whose interests keep them obedient because they have something to lose.' The Petite Eglise was also weak because there was no national organization, no bishops and no seminaries. It was a concoction of local movements, as indicated by the bewildering variety of local names for them: 'illuminés' in Gascony, 'purs' in Languedoc, 'élus' in Perche, 'enfarinés' in Rouergue (so called because followers wore long hair whitened with flour), and so on. The Petite Eglise is significant for its great tenacity. The last 'Louiset' around Fougères in the Ille-et-Vilaine only died in 1970 and there still is a little community of 'Blancs' near Charolles in the Saône-et-Loire that has lived without priests now for a over a century and a half.

With such popular and clerical dissidence as there was easily contained and with the politicians in the Legislative Body and Senate supine, the only potential threat to the regime was from the army. The general who took it upon himself to play this role was Claude-François Malet. Strictly speaking, neither of the Malet conspiracies was military since none of the officers involved had an active command. Indeed, Malet's first conspiracy in 1808 was something of an accident, since he was only in Paris because he was awaiting a hearing on charges that he was running illegal gambling casinos while stationed in Italy. He contacted a little circle of extremists and dreamers remaining from the Year II and together they hit on the old solution of a dictatorship that would prepare the country for a return to the Republic. The idea was to throw the government into disarray while Napoleon was at the Spanish front by means of a false *senatus consultum*. This document would announce the deposition of the Emperor. The conspirators would form a provisional government. As always, however, word leaked out and the conspiracy dissolved. The police took Malet so lightly that he was imprisoned only as a mildly dangerous crank. Once Malet got himself transferred to a hospital prison where security was extremely lax, he began to plan the second conspiracy. His means were essentially the same, except Malet hit upon the crafty device of claiming in the fake *senatus consultum* that Napoleon had been killed in Russia. Escaping from the hospital prison on the morning of 23 October 1812, with two other cashiered generals who were completely taken in, Malet managed to bamboozle the commander of the National Guard at the Popincourt armoury. His men then tossed Pasquier, the Prefect of Police, and Savary, Minister of Police, into La Force prison (thus Savary's enduring nickname, Duc de la Force). Comte Frochot, prefect of the Seine, was also relieved of his post. All three of the highest officials in the Empire had been completely duped. It was only when Malet personally tried to use the counterfeit *senatus consultum* to take over the military police headquarters that a sceptical officer had an aide-de-camp grab him from behind and arrest him in turn. The whole adventure was over by 10 a.m.

The conspiracy, ludicrous as it was, nonetheless revealed much about the Empire and the opposition to it. Malet himself had no fixed ideas. He appears to have wanted to reintroduce the Constitution of the Year VIII which had done nothing to impede the tyranny he so deplored and there may have been an understanding with the Chevaliers de la Foi to recall the primary assemblies and let the Republic and the monarchy fight it out at the ballot box. The abbé Lafon, who drew up the inevitable proclamation deposing tyranny, was a member of the society, albeit a renegade. In other words, opposition to the Empire was small and originated from extremists. Even so, the government in 1812 was frightened. A secret military commission condemned fourteen men to death either as conspirators or for failing to do their duty, that is, for taking Malet seriously. The higher gullible officials were spared after one of Napoleon's interminable fits of temper but as the Emperor was quick to realize, almost no one reasoned that the *senatus consultum* had to have been fake because if he was dead, it should have proclaimed a regency for the King of Rome. Few, in short, had much loyalty to the Bonaparte dynasty. The affair also showed a weakness in the bureaucracy. Malet got as far as he did with his suborned National Guards because the military never informed the civil police of its movements in the capital. Although this was soon made good, it is doubtful whether anyone could have done anything about the combination of numbing credulity and habits of passive obedience that made the affair possible. After all, the existence of the dictatorship depended on such an outlook.

12

The Failure of Empire

With the largest population in western Europe by far, with roughly 40 per cent of the men in the full vigour of adulthood, with the economy making a decent recovery from the disasters of the previous decade and with the state subject to a single will as it never had been in the Year II, France was well poised to support the great military adventures of the next few years.

How to be Victorious

For all his incredible attention to detail in planning a campaign, Napoleon also realized that the ultimate aim of speed, flexibility and surprise was to dazzle and defeat the enemy on the battlefield and to demoralize his political superiors into capitulation. The ideal Napoleonic battle was to manipulate the enemy into an unfavourable position through maneuver and deception, force him to commit his main forces and reserve to the main battle and then undertake an enveloping attack with uncommitted or reserve troops on the flank or rear. Such a surprise attack either would produce a devastating effect on morale or force him to weaken his main battle line. Either way, the enemy's own impulsiveness began the process by which even a smaller French army could defeat the enemy's forces one by one. With the exceptions of Eylau and Auerstadt, the battles of Marengo, Ulm, Austerlitz, Jena, Friedland and Wagram thus produced enemy casualties at least three times greater than those of the French. Where the enemy refused to be enticed, as at Borodino and Leipzig, the result was a draw or even a numerical loss.

The ability to carry out an offensive war depended on certain qualities of the ordinary soldier which Napoleon inherited and developed from the

Revolution. Many republican historians deny this, claiming that the imperial army was increasingly cut off from the nation. It was not. The *Grande Armée* of 1805 was still composed of a sizeable majority of recent conscripts. Only one quarter were veterans of the revolutionary wars, roughly the same proportion of veterans, in other words, as were present at Valmy in 1792. Nor were training methods much different – a week's training at home base and a march to the front of 50–60 days to get in shape and receive equipment along the way. Most of the training was received from veterans on the battlefield. The imperial soldier too shared many of the same qualities as his revolutionary predecessors: self-reliance and unending sacrifice. Since the soldier was assumed to be an upright citizen, he could be trusted to fend for himself without deserting, while the other European armies, composed of every conceivable ne'er-do-well including criminals and prisoners of war, had to be kept well supplied by expensive and lumbering baggage trains. The French soldiers thus travelled light with a week's rations at the most and their superiors were willing to pay the price of an alienated invaded population. When Napoleon was compelled to adopt an extensive supply system for the 1812 campaign in Russia his army too proved to be almost as cumbersome as those of his enemies.

Victory and the Grand Empire

The Anglo-French war languished for over two years with neither side being able to harm the other much. Napoleon sold the Louisiana territory to the Americans for 80 million francs in the hopes of embroiling them with the British. It did indeed light the fuse which provoked the American attack on Upper and Lower Canada but only in 1812. In the meantime England had no continental allies as in previous wars. So she was limited to controlling the Channel approaches. For his part, Napoleon assembled a huge army christened the 'Army of England' around Boulogne and constructed hundreds of flat-bottomed boats and transports in the harbours from Antwerp to Le Havre. But both naval and diplomatic developments postponed the invasion of Britain. The naval development was the catastrophe of Trafalgar. On 21 October, 1805, off Cape Trafalgar, Nelson trapped and split the combined French and Spanish fleets. Of thirty-three ships of the line, only nine escaped. Trafalgar not only closed the Channel-crossing option for good, it made possible subsequent British operations in Holland, Spain, Portugal and Naples. Without it, it is doubtful whether the 'Spanish ulcer' would have bled quite so much.

Meanwhile, the same aggressive exploitation of the peace which had so alarmed the English also alienated the continental powers. This was hardly an inevitable result. However much Napoleon was hated in European aristocratic circles as a revolutionary parvenu and spiller of royal blood, none of the powers initially was inclined or able to offer much beyond token resistance. Austria was exhausted by her mauling in the 1799–1801 war, Prussia was kept in breathless anticipation by waving French-occupied Hanover before her, and Russia was a potential rival with England in the Baltic and Mediterranean. Of the great power courts, only the Russian went into mourning over the murder of the duc d'Enghien. (The embarrassing Gustave IV of Sweden ostentatiously adopted the young prince's dog and paraded it through the smaller German courts.) But when Napoleon refused to respect the neutrality of many Italian and German states, Tsar Alexander of Russia concluded an alliance with England. In the treaty signed in April 1805, Pitt promised generous subsidies and both agreed to work for a restoration of the frontiers of 1791 and of the Bourbons. In short, the British were committed to inflicting a more thorough defeat on France and imposing a more drastic alteration of her government than they had been ten years earlier. The proclamation of the Empire finally goaded Austria into the alliance. The assumption of the title 'Emperor', the coronation in the presence of the Pope and crowning himself King of Italy at Milan in May 1805 showed the Hapsburgs that Napoleon meant to claim a Roman, Carolingian and Hohenstaufen legacy they considered their own. Unlike the rickety Holy Roman Empire, this was a claim to universal dominion which could be enforced. Thus the War of the Third Coalition was no more a defence of France's 'natural frontiers' than any of the other wars of the period, although the great historian Sorel claimed otherwise.

At the end of August, well before Trafalgar but while there was still a campaigning season, Napoleon wheeled the Army of England to the Rhine and the upper Danube. On 20 October, a converging maneuver surrounded the Austrian general Mack at Ulm who surrendered 30,000 men in addition to 30,000 who had already been captured, as well as 60 guns. But there were still the Russians, the main Austrian force slowly retreating from Italy and the Tyrol and the possibility Prussia would join the allies. Napoleon, therefore, chased after the Russians but Kutusov refused to give battle, retreating to more secure lines of communication and to reinforcements in Poland and Silesia. The *Grande Armée* was also close to exhaustion because of the unrelenting marches, the miserable sleet and cold and short supplies. The more it extended itself the more it risked being caught between the Russians in the north and the Austrians from the Tyrol in the south. But by purposely feigning weakness while calling up troops under Bernadotte and Davout from near Vienna, Napoleon tempted the emperors Alexander and Francis to attack. On 2 December on the anniversary of his coronation, Napoleon achieved one of his most decisive victories at the Battle of Austerlitz. The Austrians and Russians suffered 15,000 casualties, lost 12,000 prisoners and 180 guns while the French suffered perhaps 9000 casualties. Ulm and Austerlitz shattered the Third Coalition.

The campaign of 1805 produced the Grand Empire, a series of institutions, territorial rearrangements and shufflings of sovereigns dependent on Napoleon alone. It was designed to reflect the new power relations following the victories, to reward family and favourites, and to reorganize European resources for the war against England. Thus, the Grand Empire was bound to carry the possibility of renewed conflict so long as England remained undefeated. This was shown from the beginning in the treatment of Prussia. Napoleon knew that Frederick William had intended to defect to the allies as soon as France's defeat was certain, so although the Treaty of Schonbrunn of 24 February 1806 did give her Hanover, she was forced to cede other territories. As if possession of Hanover was not enough to embroil her with the English, she was also forced to close her ports to British commerce. Austria fared even worse. By the Treaty of Pressburg of 26 December 1805, she lost Venetia to the Kingdom of Italy and other German territories to Bavaria and Wurttemberg which became kingdoms in their own right. Later, on 12 July 1806, the Holy Roman Empire ceased to exist, replaced by the Confederation of the Rhine. Napoleon's brother Louis became King of Holland, a move to spread largesse within the family and to tighten economic warfare against the British. As it had been under the Directory, Italy especially became a source of private profit. Principalities and dukedoms were showered upon favourites and marshals. Another brother, Joseph, became King of Naples after a short invasion and even his rapacious sisters received little territories.

Prussia was first to react. The British reacted to the occupation of Hanover and the closure of the Baltic ports by declaring war and seizing hundreds of Prussian merchant ships in British harbours. Her officials then revealed that Napoleon intended to return Hanover to George III in a proposed peace settlement. Napoleon also refused to satisfy Prussian ambitions for a North German Confederation of her own. All this was enough to encourage the war party at the Prussian court and preparations began in August. Despite its respectable size of 171,000, however, the Prussian army and its allies had not been modernized since the death of Frederick the Great. With no thought of awaiting Russian reinforcements and with a hopelessly confused and shifting campaign strategy, the Prussians stumbled into disaster. On 14 October 1806, Napoleon engaged the Prussian flank at Jena inflicting 10,000 casualties for 5000 of his own, while on the same day Davout withstood the main Prussian assaults at nearby Auerstadt, killing 10,000 as against 7000. In addition to the casualties, the two battles netted 25,000 prisoners and 200 guns. Nor was this all. The relentless and rapid pursuit accounted for at least another 100,000 prisoners and 1500 cannon as one fortress after another capitulated. The Prussian army had ceased to exist.

Yet the now weary *Grande Armée* could have no respite. The Prussian court, particularly influenced by Queen Louise, refused to sue for peace because there was still the promise of salvation from Russia. Austria too might intervene and so long as England was available to finance future coalitions, Napoleon's overall position was risky. England and Russia would have to be defeated.

To handle the first, Napoleon issued the Berlin Decrees in November 1806 blockading all commerce with Britain. The 'Continental System' was not new; the Directory had tried a blockade in 1799 and the Consulate and early Empire had tried to choke off British trade too. Despite the limited success of these measures, the Berlin Decrees were intended to be much more systematic, their ultimate aim being to ruin the British economy and its government's finances. Yet, since trade flowed around and through artificial barriers, Napoleon was drawn to increasingly strong measures and new conquests.

Circumstances also required that Russia be defeated as quickly as possible and so the *Grande Armée* pushed on into Poland, Murat occupying Warsaw on 28 November. The French arrival stimulated nationalist feelings among the aristocracy and bourgeoisie but there was never any question of restoring Polish independence, let alone freeing the serfs. Napoleon raised many hopes with his praise of the Polish nation and so raised many Polish battalions, but behind the backs of her leaders he was usually contemptuous, willing to sacrifice the Poles for future relations with the partitioning powers. More immediately, the advance against the retreating Russians slowed because of the appalling roads, winter rains, and food and clothing shortages. With discipline breaking down, Napoleon contemplated wintering along the line of the Vistula but the Russian maneuvers and counterattacks tempted him into another knock-out blow. Yet he probably did not intend to give battle at Eylau on 8 February 1807 where the Russian artillery raked the French and only Murat's resplendent and daring cavalry charge saved the day. It was a severe check, Napoleon losing perhaps 25,000 men, the Russians and a Prussian remnant, 15,000, many of the wounded on both sides suffering horribly until they froze to death, their blood spreading over the falling snow. The Russians retreated, however, while the French used the rest of the winter to re-equip and to integrate reinforcements. At last, on 14 June, the anniversary of Marengo, as he repeated to his refreshed troops, he achieved the great victory he had sought so long against the Russians. At the Battle of Friedland, he inflicted losses on the enemy nearly three times his own. Four days later, Tsar Alexander asked for an armistice. On 25 June, the two emperors met on a covered barge decorated with their eagles on the Niemen River near Tilsit. For the next few days, Napoleon and Alexander privately settled the fate of Europe, each convinced his own charms and blandishments had seduced the other. On 7 July, their ministers signed the Treaty of Tilsit. Two days later, a separate treaty was signed with Prussia whose King, Frederick William, had been kept waiting in supplication at a nearby village. The treaties arranged yet another German settlement. The Confederation of the Rhine, already greatly enlarged after its initial proclamation, acquired a new member, the Kingdom of Westphalia, under younger brother Jerome, composed of parts of Hanover, some formerly Prussian territories and some central German states. Prussia, who lost half her population, was reduced to four small provinces, ceding all of her territory west of the Elbe, most of her Polish lands to a newly created Grand Duchy of Warsaw with the King of Saxony as ruler, and Danzig which became a free city under French occupation. Prussia would remain occupied until she paid a massive indemnity. She also agreed to join the Continental System. Alexander agreed to do the same and to influence Denmark and Sweden to follow. Undoubtedly, Alexander thought of this as little more than a revival of his father's anti-British League of Armed Neutrality of 1801, a device to extend Russian influence in the Baltic since the agreements also recognized Finland as his sphere, whereas Napoleon thought it made Russia part of his 'system'. The war in 1812 thus grew out of this original misunderstanding. For his part, Napoleon abandoned Turkey to Russia who agreed to remove her garrisons from the Ionian Isles and Dalmatia, although, in fact, he had no intention of permitting Turkey to be dismembered totally. If he was not willing to concede the eastern Mediterranean to the British, why should he to the Russians? Finally, there was an understanding that Portugal would close its ports to the British. As with the Treaties of Lunéville and Amiens, the Tilsit agreements laid the basis for the next wars.

It had been almost two years since the *Grande Armée* had plunged from Boulogne to the Danube. France herself was now composed of 110 departments and her influence and vassal states stretched from the Straits of Gibraltar to the Baltic, from the Atlantic to the Niemen. It had been achieved with dizzying speed, with the courage and patience of the thousands of ordinary soldiers and officers of the *Grande Armée* and with a centralized command system subject to a single will that had managed to defeat its enemies one by one. There was a heavy price to pay, of course. In the six major battles alone, over the two years, the *Grande Armée* had lost nearly 65,000 men out of an effective original strength of about 210,000. The losses were made good by calling up the classes of 1806 and 1807 early, and the class of 1808 no less than eighteen months before its time. Switzerland, Holland, Spain, Poland and Italy were also asked to contribute so that the strength of the army was perhaps 600,000, two thirds of whom were stationed between the Rhine and the Niemen. The effect of the Grand Empire was to Europeanize the *Grande Armée*. Although the demands for conscripts from France were nearly triple what they had been under the Consulate, the country appears to have accepted the situation well enough. Nor was the fiscal burden very great since most of the war had been financed from tribute, Germany alone contributing 560 million francs. The army itself was overwhelmed with loot of all sorts, the Prussian fortresses alone providing enormous stores, equipment, artillery and horses. A period of consolidation was necessary.

The Grand Empire Unravels

So long as the war with England continued, however, the Continental System had to be regulated, refined and expanded. For those countries already within it, this meant increasing resentment among the conquered and for those outside, the threat of conquest. Resistance to expansion also inspired resistance among those already conquered. This gave the English another opportunity to subsidize continental allies. There was a straight logic, therefore, between the rising of the Portuguese and the Spanish, English intervention in the Iberian peninsula and the new war with Austria. The settlement following that war also contributed to the growing alienation of Russia. At a more minor level, the invasion of the papal states and arrest of the Pope, intended, among other things, to bring all Italy into the system, not only inflamed the Spanish rebels and Catholic Europe generally, but contributed directly to the renewal of conspiracy at home. Napoleon could have prevented the forging of many of the links in this logical chain but his increasing penchant for forceful solutions, which had always been present and which his very strength after Tilsit made quite understandable, resulted in the unravelling of the Grand Empire.

Although most of the continent joined the economic boycott after Tilsit, Portugal refused because so much of her trade was with England. Such defiance was intolerable. Napoleon secured transit rights through Spain by the Treaty of Fontainebleau of 27 October 1807. Although the French army under Junot found the march difficult, as it always did in poor countries where there was little to forage, it was never put to the test because the Portuguese royal family fled to Brazil. Junot took Lisbon without a fight on 30 November.

At the same time, Napoleon typically stretched his treaty rights to the point of beginning to occupy Spain as well. Sensing a great opportunity to regenerate Spain, Napoleon summoned the royal family to Bayonne where he intimidated Charles IV into surrendering his crown outright. The Bourbons were promptly interned, the crown handed to Joseph, Naples to Murat. Meanwhile, the departure of Ferdinand, Charles's heir, sparked a rising in Madrid on 2 May 1808. Although Murat hanged many of its leaders, the Spanish rebellion had begun.

The Spanish rising was quite unlike those the French had encountered in the Tyrol and Calabria or in their own Vendée fifteen years earlier. True, there was a strong religious element which was understandable in a country whose ostentatious and lush Christianity contrasted so much with the austerity of the Concordat. But the social forces were far more complex than the intemperate preachings of fanatical monks on a superstitious peasantry which was how the French characterized this revolt. There was plenty of that but these same peasants profoundly distrusted the 'rich' as potential collaborators; urban working people in Castile and elsewhere attacked officials who collaborated; and students donned red cockades. The juntas which sprang up all over the country in the summer of 1808 comprised the most diverse elements: cranky aristocrats, reactionaries and conservatives who joined only to keep order, idealistic middle-class professionals who hoped to impose a constitution on the absolute monarchy, and so on. All too could focus on Ferdinand as the prince whom they mistakenly believed could realize their conflicting hopes. When he left for Bayonne, many hopes departed with him. But the juntas could scarcely agree on how this was to be done, nor did the provincial juntas show much inclination to help each other in military operations.

Even though the Portuguese also rose and even though much of the regular Spanish army went over to the rebels, there was so much bickering among the juntas, so much provincial feeling and so many conflicting social forces that the French could have dealt with the rebels piecemeal. The major difference, however, was British intervention. British agents worked hard to force the juntas to work together and funnelled large quantities of arms and money to them. This was not substantially different from the policy they had pursued towards the Vendeans and *chouans* in the 1790s, but with the Spanish rebellion they finally realized the potential of exploiting internal subversion and landed an army of 30,000 under Wellington on 1 August 1808. Until the winter of 1812, Wellington conducted an essentially defensive war using Portugal as a base where his troops could be supplied by sea and so the war was inconclusive. But the British and their allies pinned down forces of the *Grande Armée* that rarely numbered less than 200,000 men and inflicted casualties which averaged about 40,000 per year. In a short stay at the end of 1808, Napoleon himself could not force a result. In fact, he had to hurry back to Paris to prepare for a new war. The Spanish rebellion had inspired the Austrians to take the field again.

Dealing with the Spanish rebellion required securing the eastern flank which meant appeasing Tsar Alexander. The meeting of the two emperors at Erfurt in September 1808 was a moderate diplomatic success for both sides even though relations had clearly cooled since Tilsit. Neither had been able to agree on the details of a plan to dismember the Ottoman Empire and the Tsar had to settle for a reduction of Prussian reparations, not the complete evacuation he wanted. But Napoleon only wanted to stall Alexander long enough to transfer much of the *Grande Armée* from Germany to Spain. With his usual makeshift diplomacy, Napoleon did achieve this, although it was ominous that Russia refused to intervene to stop Austrian rearmament. Thus it was Russia's *de facto* neutrality which made the war of 1809 possible while Austria's war made it impossible to finish off Spain.

Once again the inadequacies of his enemies played into Napoleon's hands. With only English money and some incomplete military reforms, the Austrian court whipped itself into a war fever without bothering to search for allies. The Austrians were certainly encouraged by the amount of popular support they had. Once the war began, peasants in the Austrian and Italian Tyrol, fearful of increased taxes and conscription, rose in the name of religion. Among the enemies were Bavarian and French officials, soldiers and the 'rich'. Once again, a popular movement was anti-French and counterrevolutionary.

Napoleon took the field with the usual improvizations: calling up the classes of 1809 and 1810 early and mobilizing troops from the Confederation of the Rhine, Holland, Italy and the Grand Duchy of Warsaw. This gave him roughly 300,000 men. It is doubtful, however, whether the international character of the army was as important in explaining the Emperor's difficulties as the Archduke Charles's inherent caution which saved him from falling into the typical Napoleonic traps. Thus Charles was able to inflict a serious check on Napoleon at Essling on 21 May where Lannes was killed, even though the Austrians had to evacuate Vienna. Napoleon did defeat him at the Battle of Wagram on 5–6 July but the French suffered too many casualties to undertake a pursuit and much of the Austrian army was able to retreat intact. In the end, however, neither Prussia nor Russia would help so Austria had to submit. By a new Treaty of Schonbrunn of 14 October, she had to pay out 75 million and surrender the area around Salzburg to Bavaria, Istria to the Grand Empire and Galicia to the Grand Duchy and Russia. The most significant aspect of the treaty was that it continued the alienation of Russia since

Alexander hoped for more of Galicia and perhaps even a predominant influence in Poland. Napoleon's divorce of Josephine and remarriage to an Austrian princess, Marie-Louise, had the same effect. Alexander probably had no intention of allowing a Russian princess to marry Napoleon but he was certainly miffed when Napoleon abruptly broke off the talks and announced his engagement to Marie-Louise. Thus the birth of the long-desired heir, the King of Rome, on 20 March 1811, took place amidst new threats of war, and so did nothing to consolidate the regime.

Developments in the Continental System completed the break. The British replied to the Berlin Decrees of 1806 by issuing a series of Orders in Council restricting neutral shipping to the continent, forbidding some products altogether and subjecting merchantmen on the high seas to search. Napoleon retaliated by issuing the Milan Decrees of November–December 1807 declaring neutral shipping which complied with the Orders in Council to be lawful prizes. These measures certainly hurt the British economy particularly when the American government, outraged at the violation of freedom of the seas, imposed an embargo of its own. Manufacturing, cotton and shipping interests in the United States did not submit to the embargo for long, however, and by 1809–10 Anglo-American trade had resumed its former levels. Meanwhile, Britain found new trading partners in the Levant and, with the weakening ties between Spain and her South American colonies after 1804, began developing a commercial empire in Latin America which flourished for another century. By 1809–10, Britain had so frustrated the Continental System that overall exports of coal, iron and cotton production were at near-record highs. Problems remained, of course. The beginning of the independence movements in Latin America after 1808 disrupted trade, the quality of relations with the United States plummeted after 1810, the import of wood supplies from Lower Canada for the merchant navy could not compensate for the closure of Baltic sources and the country still had to import a significant amount of its grain despite land clearings and investments in livestock and leguminous crops which far surpassed the improvements of the previous century.

British success was thus one of the pressures which induced Napoleon to modify the Continental System. A series of decrees permitting import licences, imposing heavy tariffs, and severe measures against contraband had a severe effect on the British economy. Without the war in Russia, Britain's prospects were certainly bleak. This, however, was the problem. As in 1805, measures designed to weaken Britain had serious repercussions on the continent too. The offensive against contraband in 1810 led to the annexation of Holland and the Hanseatic towns which were major sources of smuggling into Germany. The consequent absorption of the

Grand Duchy of Oldenburg whose Grand Duke was the Tsar's brother-in-law was a further slight to the Russians. Alexander could not understand why licences permitted some French merchants to trade with Britain while Russia could not. With the Russian economy in trouble and the big landowners complaining, Alexander finally retaliated in December 1810 by imposing heavy duties on imported luxury goods, which were mainly French, and by opening his ports to neutral and British shipping. The tightening of the economic war on Britain thus blew Russia out of the Continental System. Finally, Russia interpreted the Swedes' invitation to Marshal Bernadotte to become their Crown Prince in May 1811 as a hostile act, even though within a year Sweden proved she was no French puppet.

The purpose of Napoleon's attack on Russia was to bring her back into the Continental System. The issue too was the maintenance of French hegemony in Europe. If the Russians challenged it successfully, Prussia and Austria could be expected to spin out of the French alliance altogether. In the event, the maintenance of the Bonaparte dynasty was also at risk.

The Disaster

Napoleon was well aware of the staggering problems of mounting a Russian invasion. With the exception of parts of Spain, the French armies normally supplied themselves locally which would be impossible in the poorly developed and sparsely populated plains of western Russia. To operate in such an unprecedentedly vast theatre, Napoleon estimated he would need 600,000 men who would have to be equipped and supplied over long distances and poor roads, so that one of the largest armies Europe had seen in centuries would have to bring its own supplies with it. Consequently a year-long effort was put into organizing transport battalions and when the *Grande Armée* finally crossed into Russia, it resembled a small kingdom of soldiers with their attendant corps of bakers, cooks, shoemakers and tailors. Even the exact timing of the invasion was affected by the problem of supply – it was expected that by June the cavalry and transport horses and oxen would be able to acquire some supplies locally. But the *Grande Armée* was no longer the army of the *Grande Nation*. No less than a dozen nationalities from throughout the Empire were represented in its ranks. No European army had been so heterogeneously composed since the Crusades and it was almost as difficult to command. The Prussian and Austrian contingents were potentially unreliable: brother Jerome, King of Wesphalia, commanding 70,000 Germans proved to be obstinate and incompetent;

stepson Eugène de Beauharnais, Viceroy of Italy, commanding 80,000 Bavarians and Italians was just adequate; several marshals refused direct orders or proved unable to take initiatives; and Napoleon himself was inexplicably indecisive and lethargic at critical moments.

Because it was the Napoleonic style and because of the problem of supply, Napoleon needed a quick victory. But the Russian generals refused to give battle, possibly because Napoleon's reputation intimidated them, possibly because they stumbled upon the winning strategy of surrendering space to gain time. On three occasions between the crossing of the Niemen on 28 June and the capture of Smolensk on 17 August, Napoleon was almost able to maneuver one or the other of the two Russian corps into an encircling trap but each time they escaped. By then, the campaign had already gone well over Napoleon's estimate of a mere twenty-four days. Consequently, supplies began to run short and discipline began to waver. Hot weather fatigued the troops, rains delayed transport convoys, the sick and wounded suffered horribly since medical services had been inadequately prepared, thousands of horses died because of fatigue or green fodder. By mid-August, the central army group commanded by Napoleon may have lost as many as 100,000 men from active service and a further 60,000 were lost by early October. This increasingly desperate situation certainly affected French tactics at the Battle of Borodino on 7 September. When Kutusov finally ceded to court and public opinion and made a stand, he faced an army which Napoleon himself estimated was too weak and depleted to execute Marshal Davout's proposal of an encircling maneuver around the Russian left. The battle thus consisted of an endless series of brutal frontal assaults and even though the Russian losses were immense, the main corps were able to withdraw, greatly tattered but intact, while the French losses were so great that no serious pursuit could be undertaken.

Borodino left the road open to Moscow, however, which the French entered on 14 September. As far as Napoleon was concerned, the war was over, since he had captured the enemy's ancient capital. But Alexander, whose sense of betrayal was by now boundless, rebuffed all peace feelers. Nor was there any reason why he should accept them. Napoleon offered no concessions and while the French situation weakened daily, the Russian was improving. The French had made no appeal to the serfs; instead, all levels of the Russian population had from the beginning worked themselves to a furore of hatred of the irreligious invader. Thousands of young men flocked to the national colours much as their French counterparts had in 1792. The Russian position was consequently improving while the French was greatly overextended. More and more troops had to be detached from active service for garrison duty and to protect the stretched lines of communication. Napoleon wasted a month in Moscow waiting for Alexander to come to his senses, as he saw it, even though the Russians' failed attempt to burn the holy city as they retreated ought to have convinced him of his enemy's determination. When he finally realized the Tsar would not negotiate he decided on a retreat, possibly intending to go only as far as Smolensk for the winter.

But a number of circumstances forced a ragged and calamitous retreat into Germany. At first, the weather remained reasonably good; more disastrous was the decision to take the same road the *Grande Armée* had already traversed. Since the two enemy armies had already devastated the region, there were few supplies to scour, supply dumps were too far west and necessities too difficult to move over the poor and muddy roads. Men were numbed at the horrible sight of the decomposing bodies of their comrades on former battlefields or of the wounded who had been sent ahead but who had died because their escorts abandoned them. No one, not even Napoleon who was normally so cool under fire, dared face up to the disaster. He deluded himself that it would be possible to winter in Russia. His officers refused to abandon some artillery which the horses were too weak to haul only to abandon all of it when the horses died. Thousands of transport and cavalry horses were also slaughtered for food and the army's retreat was lit by the fires of abandoned baggage and munitions wagons. Starving men abandoned their guns and struggled along behind their more disciplined colleagues. The harassment from mounted Cossacks and civilian partisans also caused great damage. The weather began to close in almost as soon as the army reached Smolensk in November and all thoughts of wintering there had to be abandoned. There were far fewer stores than expected and the Russians had destroyed much-needed relief troops further west. With lines of communication severely threatened, Napoleon had to continue the retreat, made all the more desperate by the Russian capture of the supply depot at Minsk. The *Grande Armée* had to fight its way westward and in one particularly murderous engagement while crossing the Berezina river, it may have lost 20–30,000 troops. By the time it staggered into Poland and Prussia in January, it had lost 570,000 men, 370,000 through death in battle, sickness or frost and another 200,000 taken prisoner. The French had also lost over 200,000 trained horses and over 80 per cent of their artillery. The Russians' losses were almost as great so no headlong pursuit was possible, but their prospects took a decided turn for the better when the generals of Napoleon's Prussian and Austrian contingents, Yorck and Schwartzenburg, signed armistices with them, each treaty a prelude to their own sovereign's defection to the Anglo-Russian alliance.

Defeat and Abdication

Meanwhile, Napoleon had left his marshals to conduct the last stages of the retreat and returned, on 18 December, to Paris – where the catastrophe was quite misleadingly blamed on the weather – partly to put out his own version of events and partly to raise new armies. Amazingly enough, many of the losses in Russia were made good. By a whole series of expedients – calling up the classes of 1813 and 1814 in advance of their normal times, combing through those between 1808 and 1810 for more able-bodied men, conscripting National Guards, transferring naval gunners into the artillery and mounted gendarmes into the cavalry, removing regiments from Spain, and so on – an army growing to over half a million men was constituted. The country was also transformed into a vast arsenal to make uniforms, guns and cannon. Inevitably, there was a makeshift quality about these efforts. Young men arrived at rallying centres to find inadequate food or shelter or too few uniforms and the new armies were inexperienced, poorly trained and overly weighted with the young or with ageing veterans. But clearly a prefectoral corps and conscript organization which could put nearly 300,000 men into the field within four months of the Emperor's return, however haphazard their training and equipping had been, had suffered no perceptible decline from the disaster in Russia.

The campaign of 1813 showed that battle ardour too remained high among recent conscripts and the remaining soldiers. Yet the military odds against the Empire were mounting. Prussia defected to the allies in March. The shortage of horses and trained cavalrymen, the most devastating loss of the Russian campaign, prevented the French from following up on initial successes against the Prussians and Russians.

Consequently, the combatants signed an unexpected armistice on 2 June. Probably neither side was sincere in its public protestations of a desire for a general peace since the allies put forth the impossibly high demands of a restoration of the pre-1805 German territorial arrangements and the restoration to Prussia of her pre-Jena frontiers. At the Congress of Prague, Napoleon played for time and tried to prevent Austria from joining the alliance by offering a few trivial slices of territory. But the interlude benefited the allies far more than the French whose resources were stretched to the limit. First Sweden then Austria joined the coalition against Napoleon so that when the fighting resumed again in mid-August, the allies were able to put close to a million well-equipped and fresh soldiers against the weary French.

The effects were to show almost immediately. While Napoleon was able to inflict a serious defeat on the allies at Dresden (26–27 August),

separate detachments on special missions under Marshals Oudinot, Van-
darme and Macdonald were badly mauled. It was not possible, therefore,
to envelop the allied armies and deal with each piecemeal as in 1805–6.
Thus individual battles were not likely to bring the enemy to heel and
produce the spectacular political results of Napoleon's earlier career. The
best he could do was not lose. At the Battle of Leipzig (18–19 October),
the so-called Battle of the Nations (more 'nations' fought in Russia the
previous year), for example, the French were able to fight the allies to a
draw with about equal numbers of casualties on both sides but were
forced to retreat in the face of advancing allied reinforcements. This
forced a withdrawal to the Rhine which in turn produced great dividends
for the allies. The King of Bavaria defected on the eve of the battle,
Saxony was subsequently occupied and its king, Napoleon's only
German ally, was made a prisoner of war, while one by one the German
princelings prudently switched sides. Furthermore, the entry of Austria
into the war had opened a new front in Italy which pinned down
Eugène's forces. The situation in Italy was rendered all the more difficult
by Murat's defection in January, while in Spain, Wellington and his allies
were advancing towards the Pyrenees against the French armies which
had been depleted to reinforce the army in Germany.

   As the vice tightened, Napoleon responded with a flurry of diplomatic
activity and a renewed attempt to plumb the depths of French resources.
Among the main combatants, there was a confused round of negotiations
at Frankfurt in which the astonished allies had to withdraw an offer of a
general peace on the basis of France's 'frontiers of 1792' after Napoleon
accepted it. Once again, neither side was sincere. Much of allied diplomacy was directed towards painting Napoleon as warmonger to both
French and European public opinion and it is certain that the British,
who were the paymasters of the coalition, would not have accepted the
annexation of Belgium which the phrase 'frontiers of 1792' could have
implied. Napoleon, for his part, probably only wanted to spin out negotiations while he organized yet another army for the approaching campaign.

   Napoleon was also facing considerable pressures at home for peace
which manifested themselves in the Senate and Legislative Body which
met towards the end of the year. Both were allowed to examine diplomatic
documents to evaluate Napoleon's claim that he had done all he could to
secure peace and while the Senate reported favourably – of course – an
unpublished report presented by Lame, an unknown Bordeaux lawyer,
argued that Napoleon had needlessly delayed replying to the allies and that
a truly national effort against the impending invasion was only possible so
long as Napoleon respected liberty, property and free institutions. This
was too much and the Legislative Body was promptly dissolved. The
Emperor would appeal to the nation directly.

For once, the nation's response was poor. In a crudely cynical move, the government tried to revive the sentiments of 1793 by ordering a *levée en masse* and sent out *commissaires* to whip up patriotic fervour and supervise the prefects' efforts to conscript more men and resources. Bonapartist and patriotic historians have consistently misunderstood this phase of the decline for they lay the blame for the failure of the *levée en masse* on the *commissaires* whose twenty-year average age difference over the representatives on mission of the Year II is supposed to have made them lacklustre and uninspiring. Yet the unspoken assumption behind this interpretation, that ardent Frenchmen only desired to be given a lead which was not forthcoming, masks a very real difference from the circumstances of 1793.

In 1814, France alone had lost about 562,500 soldiers through death, going missing in action or being taken prisoners of war. Overall, the Napoleonic wars cost her roughly 916,000 men. For the age cohort born between 1790 and 1795, this represented a loss rate of 38 per cent which is 14 per cent higher than the casualties inflicted on the generation of 1891–95 in the First World War, generally thought to be France's most devastating war.

With the tribute from the conquered territories lost, France was expected to finance the war entirely from her own resources at a time when large sectors of the economy were unable to do so. The land tax was raised by 30 per cent, and then by another 50 per cent, personal taxes by 50 per cent and then by 100 per cent and the various indirect taxes at rates varying between 10 per cent and 100 per cent. Even before this immense gouging, taxes of all sorts in the Côtes-du-Nord, and undoubtedly elsewhere, had risen by 42 per cent between the Year IX and 1813, more, in other words, than most incomes had. It is no wonder that as political control slackened, with the allied advance, the country underwent a fiscal rebellion. Nor was there time to raise, equip and train a new army. From the beginning, recruiting ran into difficulties. Culling the classes of 1808–14 once again brought an excess of 24,000 men because of enthusiastic volunteers in some of the old revolutionary areas, but the call-up of the class of 1815 was not pursued with vigour and the levy of another 300,000 men from all the classes between 1800 and 1814 ran into enormous difficulties. The administrative system could scarcely keep track of individuals in the shower of levies, classes that had already been called up two and three times were resentful and many deserted. All the old tactics of garrisoning gendarmes and reprisals against families were deployed with mediocre results. In the west, the old link between conscription and violence was reforged as bands of deserters robbed stagecoaches and tax offices. At the end of January 1814, only 63,000 of the levy of 300,000 had been enrolled. Nor were there any weapons, since many of the arsenals in Germany were cut off by the allied advance. Altogether, it was estimated that 700,000 muskets had been lost in the previous two years. Finally, there were no reserves. At the cavalry depot at Versailles, for instance, there were only 7100 men available for service out of a theoretical complement of 18,600 and there were only 3600 horses.

The *levée en masse* of 1814 then failed because the imperial government had already accomplished much of what the Committee of Public Safety was trying to do in 1793. But the invaders of 1814 were very different from those of the previous generation. In 1793, the Austrians had restored as much of the Old Regime as they could along the occupied northern frontier, including the *parlements* and the tithe; in 1814, the allies proclaimed that their only enemy was Napoleon, not the French people. Not only did they not repeat the mistake of the Brunswick Manifesto, they did not even proclaim the restoration of the Bourbons as a war aim. This was not because of a wily instinct for propaganda but because there was no consensus about the shape of postwar French government. The British were convinced that only a Bourbon government could secure a lasting peace but were not willing to impose Louis XVIII; Tsar Alexander spoke vaguely about consulting the French nation on its future; Metternich, the Austrian minister, could see advantages in a regency under Marie-Louise, a Hapsburg princess after all, so that France could be used as a counterweight in the coming dispute over Poland; and the stolid Prussians were prepared to follow an Austrian lead. More than anything else, it was Napoleon's stubborn insistence on fighting to the end against all odds which brought down the Bonaparte dynasty.

That he would not have the time to reconstitute and train his armies ought to have been clear to Napoleon once the allies decided on a winter campaign. In the event, the defensive line of the Rhine was easily breached and the allies poured into France from several points. From then on, a defeat was inevitable for however brilliant and successful Napoleon was in the half-dozen or so engagements and battles in which he took personal command, he had lost the ability to control the overall strategic situation. As late as February, the allies offered the French representative, Coulaincourt, at negotiations at Châtillon-sur-Seine, the prewar frontiers of 1792 while Napoleon held out for the 'natural frontiers', that is, the Rhine. The failure of these talks produced the Treaty of Chaumont (1 March) whereby the allies, lubricated by considerable British subsidies, promised each other not to conclude a separate peace and to continue the war for twenty years if necessary. They gave Napoleon an ultimatum of a cease-fire and a settlement on the basis of the 1791 frontiers, which he, gambler to the last, rejected.

Meanwhile, the vice was closing. By mid-March, the allies were in control of large areas of French territory on a line from Lyon to Nancy, and in the southwest Anglo-Spanish forces were threatening Bayonne and Toulouse. On 12 March, Lynch, mayor of Bordeaux who had been recruited into the Chevaliers de la Foi the year before and who was aided by conspirators, some of whom had been involved in the insurrection of the Year VII, turned over Bordeaux to Wellington. Bordeaux's noisy proclamation of the Bourbons was designed to convince the sceptical allies that there really was popular support for the former ruling house and no doubt it helped but, as always, military events were decisive. After the Battle of Arcis (20–21 March), Napoleon was forced to withdraw eastwards to the fortresses near the Marne, which exposed Paris to an allied attack.

In the event the capital surrendered. Characteristically, Napoleon was convinced he could fight on but almost no one else was. In Bonapartist historiography, this phase comprised the series of weaknesses and betrayals which brought the Empire down but these events are better conceived as the struggle for the nature of the successor regime. Napoleon's position was extremely weak. In the immediate vicinity of the fighting, he was outnumbered by well over two to one, not counting other troops available to the allies on short notice. Paris was also in no position to withstand a long siege. The only fortification was the incomplete octroi wall, good enough to protect against cavalry raids but useless against artillery. The only men capable of handling the city's artillery were the coastguards and polytechnic students since the naval gunners had been sent to the front. The only experienced troops were a handful of Young Guards and gendarmes. The National Guard, which had been revived only in January, soon reached an impressive number of 40,000 on paper but many were armed only with ancient hunting muskets and 3000 were armed only with pikes. Overall then, the city's forces were no match for the 145,000 allied troops rapidly massing near the northern and western barriers. Accordingly, brother Joseph, lieutenant-general of the Empire, authorized Marshal Marmont to open talks with the allied generals and then he, Marie-Louise, the King of Rome and some members of the government left the city. The next day, 31 March, Marmont arranged an armistice which permitted the withdrawal of his army to the south of Paris. A few hours later, 'the Cossacks', as Parisians called most allied troops, entered the city.

The marshals too finally lost their fighting spirit. In a celebrated interview at Fontainebleau, Ney, speaking for the four other marshals present, told Napoleon that the soldiers would no longer fight, a statement which was manifestly untrue since the ordinary soldiers with the Emperor were enthusiastically clamouring to march to relieve Paris. It was an ominous portent for the future. But Ney undoubtedly spoke for his colleagues.

Napoleon had to give up. At allied insistence, he abdicated both for himself and his successors on 6 April 1814.

The First Restoration

When the allied armies occupied Paris, they issued a declaration under the name of the Austrian commander-in-chief, Schwartzenburg, refusing to deal with Napoleon or any member of his family and inviting the Senate to form a provisional government. For the first time in public at any rate, the allies proclaimed the overthrow of the Empire as one of their aims. This made a restoration of the Bourbons inevitable. There had to be a new constitution. This was the work of the Senate which contributed five of its number to the provisional government and twenty members to a constitutional commission. That is, the body which took responsibility for deposing Napoleon on 2 April was composed of men from the old revolutionary legislatures, the dignitaries of the Empire, imperial officials, officers and the like. The conceptions of government of all these men reflected their backgrounds as revolutionary and Napoleonic politicians and officials. There would be a bicameral legislature responsible for consenting to taxes, an independent judiciary, equality of opportunity, an amnesty for all political opinions, freedom of religion and the press, fiscal and legal equality, irrevocable guarantees for owners of *biens nationaux*, and recognition of both the Old Regime and imperial nobilities. Although this was changed later, it was even said that Louis XVIII was 'called' to the throne by 'the French people', in other words, the nation, not the king, was sovereign. Strangely, many members of the Senate who drafted this document were from the annexed territories that were eventually split off from France itself. In a sense, therefore, the Charter was a European document, imposed upon the French without so much as a referendum to endorse it. All the other constitutions, except that of 1791, had been placed before the electorate. It should not be surprising that the 'Charter' resembled the Constitution of 1791. The self-appointed constitutional committee literally had a copy available to consult.

If the 'men of 1789' were to triumph, it was essential to get Louis XVI's brothers to accept the Charter. In the event, it was forced on them. When the comte d'Artois arrived in Paris in early April in the uniform of the National Guard no less, the Senate was extremely reluctant to recognize his title of lieutenant-general until he accepted the Charter. Tsar Alexander also insisted that he recognize it. Thus the emergence of a parliamentary regime in France depended upon a completely unelected body and upon the most despotic of the European monarchs. With nowhere to turn, Artois conceded. As long ago as 1805, his brother the

Pretender had interred the Declaration of Verona which had promised an integral restoration of the Old Regime. Instead, the Pretender accepted the existing judicial, military and administrative structure but said nothing about a legislature with powers over taxation. Another declaration issued from his English residence at Hartwell on 1 February 1813 reiterated these points and expressed the hope that the issue of *biens nationaux* could be settled by 'transactions' among the present and former owners. Privately, he disliked the notion of the state paying Protestant ministers.

In the circumstances of 1814 he too would have to bend and, recognizing reality with none of Artois's bad grace, he waited until the eve of his entry to Paris to publish the Declaration of Saint Ouen on 3 May which accepted the principles of the Senate's project but not the actual document. A new commission set to work on a new charter which differed from the old only in that the Senate was replaced with a Chamber of Peers nominated by the king, the 'senatoreries' were abolished, and the most restricted franchise of the entire period was adopted for the Chamber of Deputies. This put electoral power overwhelmingly in the hands of big landowners. Finally, the preamble to the Charter did not recognize national sovereignty; instead the Charter was said to be 'granted' by the king. Thus were planted the seeds of the revolution of 1830.

The fact that the Restoration was effected the way it was ensured that it would not be counterrevolutionary. None of the elements of opposition to the Empire – the clergy, the malcontents in the army, the intelligentsia or the royalists of the Chevaliers de la Foi – played a crucial role. Nor had the out-and-out reactionaries. In 1790, Artois and the émigrés had planned to effect the counterrevolution by a combination of military conspiracy and popular insurrection. Yet in 1814, the officers had remained loyal almost to the last and many of the troops were Bonapartist. In fact there had been no great royalist upsurge. Even the royalists of Bordeaux were probably a minority. At its most optimistic, the little royalist Bordelais army never numbered more than 800 in a city of 70,000. Elsewhere, violent royalism was rare. The Chevaliers de la Foi tried to seize Rodez but the leaders called it off when only 200 'knights' showed up. There was a royalist riot at Marseille on 14 April in which Provençal-speaking crowds vainly attacked the prefecture. This showed that popular royalism still existed but such disturbances were almost unique. Even the old *Vendée militaire* and the *chouans* north of the Loire had not risen, an indication of just how effective the imperial government's policy of disarming the west had been. Instead, the young men had responded by trying to avoid conscription, and by the spring there were signs of a general breakdown of law and order as brigand bands roamed the countryside. But this was only a pale shadow of the great days of 1793.

There were even pro-Bonapartist demonstrations. Peasants in Lorraine, goaded beyond endurance by requisition or outright pillage, formed partisan units. One of them was actually led by a parish priest whose men showed considerable skill in guerrilla attacks. There are numerous examples of country people killing allied stragglers or observation troops, or picking up muskets from allied dead on the battlefield and turning them over to imperial soldiers or coming forward to help troops move heavy cannon through the muddy roads of Champagne. In mid-April, soldiers stationed in Clermont-Ferrand countered the prefect's reading of the deposition decree with cries of 'Vive l'Empereur!', while a crowd of cavalrymen led by junior officers broke down the door of the cathedral to harass a priest who had unfurled the white flag of the Bourbons. In the countryside of Auvergne, there were rumours that a restoration presaged the re-imposition of the tithe and feudal dues, while later that summer in a few communes peasants paraded an effigy of the king on an ass. In Strasbourg, soldiers almost rebelled when they were told to wear the royalist white cockade. Almost everywhere there was a general refusal to pay taxes, and in some places there were anti-fiscal rebellions. In the Haute-Garonne, Gironde, Vendée, Seine-Inférieure, Pas-de-Calais and at Marseille, Rennes, Cahors, Châlon-sur-Sâone and Limoges, officials of the *droits réunis* and the octroi were attacked and their registers burned. Royalist agents and a proclamation of the Prince de Condé had led people to believe that those taxes would be abolished or much reduced. In some regions like Anjou, people acted on this propaganda, reasoning that since the war was over no taxes at all were necessary – a remarkable example of the survival of medieval notions of fiscality. When Louis XVIII maintained the *droits réunis*, disappointment was sharp.

    Given time, the restored Bourbons might have been able to assuage these fears, but from the top down experience soon showed that reconciling the servants and loyalists of the imperial and royalist regimes would be far from easy. As major instruments in overthrowing Napoleon, the senators did exceptionally well. Only 37 of the French senators were excluded from the 155-member Chamber of Peers, 12 because they were *conventionnels*, while 84 were included, each with a magnificent pension of 36,000 francs. To the end, they had known how to look after themselves. The continuity of personnel among the upper courts was also great but other institutions suffered more. Since it was so closely identified with the Emperor, it is not surprising that 40 per cent of the members of the Council of State were eliminated. There was no thoroughgoing purge of the prefectoral corps but 28 of 87 were fired outright because they had been revolutionaries or imperialist zealots, while of the 36 new appointments which the first Restoration made, one third were former émigrés. The number of nobles in the corps as a whole nearly doubled – a significant indication of whom the regime thought its friends were. Much of this was to be expected and the purges were not very great in comparison to those of the previous twenty-five years, but the voluble courtiers around the comte d'Artois let it be known that this was only the beginning of a vast settling of accounts. Intelligent and indolent, Louis XVIII could not muzzle his dim and impetuous brother.

A careless historiography usually blames the Bourbons themselves and the utterances of careless ministers for what happened next. This is far too simple. Whatever gaffes various ministers committed, public opinion did not turn against the First Restoration overnight. Instead, opinion remained totally loyal to the Emperor.

In the constitutional scheme of things, the common people counted for nothing so nothing was done to wean them from the shock of Napoleon's defeat. Thus the Emperor retained much of his popularity well after his abdication. The old Napoleonic bric-à-brac – playing cards, medallions, statuettes, broadsheets, dinner plates, and so on – continued to circulate with the addition of mawkish engravings of the Emperor confining the King of Rome to the care of the National Guard who supposedly represented the French people. Enterprising printers put out other drawings depicting a sleeping eagle with the caption, '*He* will return!' Prisoners of war returned with a grudge. Those who returned from the ghastly hulks of English prison ships were looking for revenge. Prisoners from Germany, whom the allies had overrun, knew they had not been defeated. Soldiers like these would welcome a second chance.

Indeed, there were rumours from the beginning of the Restoration that he already had returned or had escaped to raise an army in Turkey. The docks in the lower courts were jammed with unfortunate individuals being prosecuted for having shouted 'Vive l'Empereur!' within earshot of a gendarme. During the Second Restoration especially, there were many who predicted that his third coming would be a prelude to the end of days or that he returned secretly and spoke only to those who really believed or to innocent children.

Many simply refused to believe the Emperor had gone. Many believed that somehow Napoleon had been betrayed. Even defeat did not convince soldiers from Spain who marched through the streets of Grenoble shouting 'Vive l'Empereur! Vive Le Roi de Rome!'

The Hundred Days

The insensitivity of the Bourbons to Napoleon's continuing popularity among the common people and the army created a fantastic opportunity. For a time, it appeared as if the old gambler would content himself with his fate. The Treaty of Fontainebleau gave Napoleon the island of Elba off the coast of Tuscany and certain Italian states to Marie-Louise. The powers also lived up to their policy of maintaining that Napoleon was the only enemy and the Treaty of Paris limited France to her Old Regime frontiers with significant adjustments. But fissures that had always existed in the anti-Napoleonic coalition, particularly over the disposition of Poland, quickly manifested themselves. The allies also refused all contacts between Napoleon and his son who was to lead a pariah's existence at the Hapsburg court until his sad death in 1832. Finally, the Bourbons refused the pension they were bound by treaty to pay. So as Napoleon busied himself with organizing his Lilliputian army and navy and throwing himself with characteristic energy into organizing public works of all sorts on Elba, his agents were able to report the division among the allies and the bad faith of the Bourbons. Most promising of all were stories of the massive discontent in the army and among the common people.

Adventurer to the last, he escaped, eluding a small British naval squadron and landing on the French coast near Cannes on 1 March 1815 with a mere 1100 men. On 20 March, he was in Paris. As he had predicted, he had reconquered his kingdom without firing a shot. Louis XVIII had fled to Ghent. Soldiers had thrown down their arms at the sight of him. Ney melted, despite his promise to bring him back to Paris in an iron cage, partly because his troops had begun to defect to the Emperor and partly because the old magic had mesmerized him too. It was symbolized by the poetic proclamations printed up on Elba and rapidly distributed: 'The eagle, with the national colours, will fly from steeple to steeple until it reaches the towers of Notre Dame.' Many of his old officials were ecstatic. His former postmaster, the comte Lavallette, met him amidst a tumultuous crowd on the steps of the Tuileries: '... he walked up slowly, his eyes closed and his hands outstretched, as a blind man walks, and showing his happiness by his smile alone'. On 12 June, Napoleon set out for Waterloo. The adventure was over.

The sudden flash of the Hundred Days lit up the many faces of France as they had been for the previous twenty-five years. Not only did the episode show the Empire's trumpeted claim to have united Frenchmen to have been utterly hollow, it nearly ignited the dialectic of revolution and counterrevolution of the 1790s. It also showed that Napoleon had been assimilated into ancient peasant beliefs of a just king protecting the people against a vexatious nobility. When that protection was removed, the result was panic. Thus as early as April 1814, officials in the Corrèze reported the anxieties of the countryside that the Restoration meant the revival of tithes and seigneurial dues. During the Hundred Days, peasants in the mountains of the Cantal were saying 'Eh bien, if Bonaparte returns, we are certain not to pay the tithe and dues', while in the Puy-de-Dôme, peasants 'were overjoyed to be subjected no longer to the nobles who are already beginning to regard them as their vassals'. In the Tarn, the country people regarded his return 'as a grace from heaven which has saved them from oppression'. In the Nièvre, one former constitutional priest even denounced the pretensions of 'the noble caste'. In all of these assertions, it was less a question of fear of returned émigrés since the vast majority had returned home over a decade earlier, than the fear of a rapacious nobility once the government ceased to control them.

Thus, the Napoleonic myth in the countryside showed how ancient beliefs of royalty tinged with divinity could become revolutionary in the appropriate circumstances. Napoleon's very presence thus stimulated revolution. When his army approached Grenoble on the night of 6 March, it was accompanied by at least 2000 peasants bearing torches to light the way and laying pine boughs before his horse. There were some who reminded him that 'liberty' had begun in these lonely mountains – they were referring to the agreement at Vizille in 1788. His proximity set off a revolt among the soldiers and working people of Grenoble and the commanding officer had to flee. Much the same happened at Lyon. The La Guillotière quarter where many silk-weavers lived was particularly over-joyed and some shouted, 'A bas les prêtres! Mort aux royalistes!' Similar anti-clerical and anti-royalist slogans were heard at Besançon, Bar-le-Duc, Rennes, Saumur and Strasbourg. Insurrections broke out in most of the Burgundian towns along the route while thousands lined the highway to celebrate his passage, sing the Marseillaise and plant liberty trees. Further afield, in the Corrèze, peasants removed the 'seigneurial' pew from a parish church and burnt it on the public square just as their ancestors had in 1790. In the Isère, at least four châteaux were attacked by rural National Guards and a crowd of unruly Guards murdered the mayor of La Sône, who was also a silk manufacturer, because he tried to prevent them from raising the tricolour. Earlier, the inhabitants of the same commune, shouting anti-royalist slogans, and had attacked the employees of the *droits réunis*.

The Hundred Days revived anti-seigneurial, anti-clerical and anti-fiscal sentiments among the common people. It also revived Jacobinism among the small-town bourgeoisie. In Burgundy. Brittany, Dauphiné, the Lyonnais, Languedoc and elsewhere, 'patriots' formed 'federations' to 'defend liberty', 'maintain the rights of man menaced by the hereditary nobility. . . ' and to 'terrify traitors, confound plots and vanquish the counterrevolution'. There was a good deal of talk about immobilizing the interior enemy, about the danger of moderation, and about the necessity of 'grandes mesures de salut public'. No more than in 1793 were the men who uttered these chilling statements wide-eyed individuals on the margin of society. As earlier, they were often provincial officials, small-town lawyers and ordinary working people. In Paris, the social composition of the 'fédérés' was much the same.

Napoleon must have been astonished at the extent of revolutionary feeling his return evoked. The two Elba proclamations he wrote himself appealed to the glory of the army, blamed his defeat in 1814 on the betrayal of Marshals Marmont and Augereau and claimed the throne in the name of a plebiscitary monarchy born of the Revolution. He scarcely alluded to social problems and to fears of the old privileged classes. Although he soon adjusted his language to suit the situation, as when he referred to himself in one speech as the 'father of the poor', his profound aversion to terrorism and disorder and the necessity to appease the broadest possible current of opinion, pushed him in a liberal direction. This was symbolized by the appointment of Carnot to the Interior. More importantly, he induced his old political enemy, Benjamin Constant, to draft a new constitution, called the 'Additional Act to the Constitutions of the Empire'. Aside from raising the electorate from 15,000 to 100,000 for the new lower house and instituting a more liberal press law, the 'Additional Act' was remarkably similar to the Bourbon Charter. No matter who reigned, France would be a constitutional, parliamentary monarchy. It goes without saying that neither liberal-royalist nor liberal-imperialist trusted their respective monarchs. The political situation in the spring of 1815 showed that he could not act without the support of the liberal bourgeoisie and the common people, that is, the major elements in the old revolutionary coalition.

The results of the plebiscite on the Additional Act show this clearly. It was approved by 1,552,942 to 5740 with exceptionally large majorities in a broad band stretching from Lorraine south-westwards to the Charentes, that is in regions where the Revolution had always had strong support. In Paris, nearly half the positive votes came from officials, and in the provinces support came overwhelmingly from mayors and notaries who voted in far greater proportion than their fellow citizens. Just one in five of the electors bothered to vote, with most of the large towns showing only half as much interest as the surrounding countryside. Insofar as it is possible to generalize about a plebiscite with such a low turnout, Napoleon had lost significant support compared to the plebiscite of the Year X but Bonapartism was already showing its ability to appeal to the rural masses.

Contemporaries were quick to notice the parallels between the Hundred Days and the Revolution. As in the 1790s, a revolutionary upsurge evoked an equally powerful response of popular counterrevolution. In the west, the leaders from the great days of the Vendée or their descendants, d'Autichamp, Sapinaud, La Roche Jacquelin, etc., prepared to organize another explosion under the duc de Bourbon. Their prospects were hardly encouraging. As always, they quarrelled about the timing of the rebellion, the men lacked arms, the gendarmerie stopped powder from getting into their hands and the *fédérés* in the towns and villages were mobilizing in their turn. The leaders were so demoralized that the duc de Bourbon, who soon left the country, asked for terms from the imperial authorities. The men were less discouraged, however. Soon, the *chouans* in Brittany and Normandy, some of whom were beginning their third campaign, were roaming the countryside undertaking the familiar ambushes of troops, molesting mayors and buyers of *biens nationaux* and trying to besiege the towns. Although the western departments were exempted from the hated conscription which had so fuelled rural discontent in earlier risings, the government still had to leave 20,000 badly needed troops in the region to contain the situation. The 'internal enemy' therefore, aided the 'external enemy' at Waterloo.

The royalist response in the Midi was much more vicious. Lynch and his friends got a meagre response from the National Guard of Bordeaux and none at all from the garrison so that their small army soon capitulated. Headquarters, at Toulouse under the baron de Vitrolles, quickly collapsed too, but elsewhere the overall commander, the duc d'Angoulême, did manage to recruit large numbers of rural volunteers, called *miquelets*, from the Gard, Ardèche, Aveyron, Lozère and Haute-Loire. But the untrained *miquelets* and the single royalist regiment moving on Lyon were no match for the Bonapartist army especially since it was rapidly being reinforced by enthusiastic volunteers from the National Guards of the Saône-et-Loire, Ain, Côte-d'Or, Jura and Haute-Saône.

Consequently, Angoulême capitulated at La Pallud on 8 April. Unfortunately, the *miquelets* had been responsible for all sorts of excesses on their way to battle: killing Bonapartist prisoners, molesting Protestants who were overjoyed at Napoleon's return, raiding tax offices or pillaging the rich. As they returned home, there were numerous reprisals. In one particularly ugly incident in the Protestant village of Arpaillargues, they were fired on, a few were killed, the women, it was said, finishing them off with scissors and stripping and mutilating the bodies. After Waterloo, the response to this and other outrages was another round of the bloody White Terror in which hundreds of Protestants, *fédérés* and Bonapartists were assaulted or killed.

The legacy of the Hundred Days that most struck the generation of younger romantic writers was the image of the lonely figure stalking the rock of St Helena. For many ordinary Frenchmen there was another, of bloody violence and civil war.

Conclusion:
Towards a Future Democracy

In 1790, the French Revolution had achieved its goal. It had defeated despotism and it had defeated privilege. This rupture was also definitive. A return to the Old Regime was simply out of the question.

The Constituent Assembly had created a civil society so powerful that it overwhelmed the state. Aside from the military, there was almost no bureaucracy as such. Instead government everywhere was in the hands of amateurs, paid only with small expense accounts and meagre stipends. They were also elected, theoretically responsible to the king but practically to the Constituent Assembly, its committees and the ministries. But the only tie that really held them in place was their sense of civic loyalty, their idealism and their willingness to sacrifice their time for the sake of the greater good. At the beginning anyway, the new citizens were willing to do so, indeed, over a million of them were willing to volunteer to assist the national regeneration.

The contrast with the Napoleonic regime could not have been greater. The Empire recognized the electoral principle only for the most minor offices, the village and small town municipalities. Otherwise the most important offices in the state, the judiciary, the legislative, the executive, and the military were all appointive. Moreover, there was a huge transformation of the social composition of the governing bodies between the era of the Constituent Assembly and the Napoleonic era. At the level of the department and the district, the overwhelming victors in the elections of 1790 were the small town lawyers.

For the Napoleonic regime, the outcome was more complex. Those at the top of the social heap were the notables, an officially recognized group of rich landowners and officials, many of whom were former Old Regime nobles. But it did not rule in any meaningful sense. Instead, they were a powerless élite that contributed talent to the regime, but had no voice in its own right.

A state that was almost constantly at war, that drew on military models for most of its institutions, that aggressively demanded obedience from its citizens on matters of prompt payment of taxes and obeying the conscription laws was not what anyone anticipated in the spring of 1789. Tocqueville argued that there was a tension between liberty and equality, that the French demanded more and more equality and therefore lost liberty. In fact, as an empirical reality, in surrendering most of the liberties outlined in the Declaration of the Rights of Man, the French lost equality under the Empire too. That is, the one liberty that remained, the only one a decade's experience had shown the French cared about, freedom of religious expression, had to be balanced against the new inequalities. The men of 1789 had tried to make citizenship an equal burden. But the fact that the rich could buy their sons out of military service and that the increasingly regressive tax system put burdens on the poor, and especially the urban poor, gave the lie to that. For a long time after the Empire, citizenship was not an equal burden.

And this is where it ended, not with the Terror but with the dictatorship. The legacy of the Empire was huge. As everyone knows, the creative period of the Consulate established institutions and legal codes that survive to this day, not only in France but abroad. At the level of popular political culture, much of the dictatorship survived too. The legacy of the Empire was popular Bonapartism, not republican democracy. One can pore over the police and judicial archives of the Restoration endlessly and find no trace of the radicalism of the Year II; or if one does, it is a shadow, not even the Cordeliers version of direct democracy, that one finds. Whatever the version, it was overwhelmingly grafted onto the name of the fallen Emperor. The legacy of the Revolution was a popular political culture that celebrated the hatred of priests, nobles, and the rich that was also indissolubly associated with Napoleon, the Napoleon of the Hundred Days. The result was the election of the nephew as President of the Second Republic on 10 December 1848.

But that is not what academic historians want to talk about. Instead, they want to debate the relationship between the Revolution and the Terror. Classical historiography wanted to divide the two, to insist upon a sharp division between the 'good' revolution of 1789–91 and the 'bad' revolution of 1792–4. Or else, as with many others, like Alphonse Aulard, they say that the excesses of the Revolution came from extreme provocation, from forces external to the Revolution itself. The Terror was a necessary act of self-defence. How external it was in Aulard's mind has to be appreciated because for him the Vendeans and the *chouans* were not really French, they were for all intents and purposes British agents, forces of the armies arrayed against republican France. Subsequent chairs of the French Revolution at the Sorbonne have not been so brazen but, until Michel Vovelle occupied the chair, none was willing to deal with the reality of civil war or with popular counterrevolution within France itself. Opposition could justify the Terror but in their hands the Terror became strangely antiseptic and the opposition to the Revolution quite abstract.

François Furet began from this point. He wanted to question every aspect of what he called the 'vulgate', the received opinions about the Revolution. But like Alfred Cobban before him, he often reversed the received opinions. He rarely reformulated them. If the Terror derived from circumstances, Furet said it derived from pre-conceived ideas; if popular movements imposed themselves on the polity, ideology drove the Revolution; if there was a good Revolution that a bad Revolution overwhelmed, this bad Revolution was implicit from the beginning; 1793 was embedded in 1789; the Declaration of the Rights of Man was an illusion, it enshrined a single totalizing national will; nothing that happened between 1789 and 1793 really mattered: each revolution was the same, the one telescoped into the other.

Analytically and empirically, this will not do. There are similarities, it is true. The language justifying the murders of de Launay and Berthier de Sauvigny and others in 1789 was identical with one set of the justifications for the slaughter in the September Massacres. But the Terror did not codify into law such appalling events. Instead, its intent was to punish traitors and rebels. How the men of 1789 had arrived at such a point was a process. The emergence of opposition from a very early point, the failure of Louis XVI to keep his word faithfully to abide by the spirit, and not only the letter of the Constitution, the tendency of the revolutionaries from the very beginning to stigmatize and criminalize all opposition, the killing of the King which ensured a decade of civil war – events mattered, no one thing drove the Revolution off the rails, at every point decisions, choices, debates, and quarrels mattered.

Much of what Furet wanted to say was a reflection of a very old debate about where the Revolution went wrong. Furet thought it went wrong from the start; Mathiez, Lefebvre, and Soboul, all of them holders of the chair of the French Revolution at the Sorbonne, thought it went wrong after 9 *thermidor*, when criminally corrupt politicians compromised with the counterrevolution. Choosing when to terminate the account of the Revolution or pronouncing when it all went wrong is often a political judgement, however. More relevant for us is to ask why the Revolution was so violent and why it persisted for so long. For Furet, the answer was the inner need of Jacobinism to create enemies, its propensity to attribute any reverse to largely imaginary conspiracies. For others, the answer is the internal logical inconsistencies within a contrived definition of Jacobinism that eventually exploded in dreadful bloodletting. Attempts like this are one-sided: most Jacobins who pronounced on public matters were earnest bores, especially before the crisis of 1792. Theories that represent Jacobinism as sinister, of course, minimize the importance of real conspiracies and real rebellions all over the country; they also deny the agency of their actors and even their authenticity.

The dialectic of the relations between provincial history and the national government did not work like chain of command driven by ideas, with the impetus given from the top and with provincials left at receiving end, inert and acted upon. In some ways the action was reversed. It was the thousands of local struggles between the clergy and their opponents in the provinces which lay behind the legal restrictions on refractories, behind the early attempts at repression, behind much of the war agitation and so on, down to the dechristianization campaign and beyond. The Terror itself was a response to treason on the frontiers and to rebellion in the west. It was resistance to a particular and local version of the Terror in the Midi that lay behind the federalist revolt in 1793. The suspension of the King was imagined first in the provinces and the provincial National Guards had a crucial role in bringing it about.

The real problem then becomes why the Revolution was opposed at all, how the apparent unanimity of 1789 became the snarling, ghastly series of local anti-revolutions and counterrevolutions that appeared as early as 1790. The rhetoric of the Revolution constantly proclaimed the purity and majesty of the people and explained opposition as the result of hidden conspirators playing on the *naïveté* and trust of ordinary folk. What this rhetoric failed to perceive was how fluid the issue of loyalty was at the beginning and how loyalties were decided over time. Moreover, this rhetoric was not only dangerously simple, it was harmful. A decade's experience showed that shedding the country of priests accomplished none of the goals of fixing a republican and democratic civic order. After the expulsions or the forced resignations, ordinary people did not embrace republican ideals, despite a huge propaganda effort. Instead they resisted, or they tried to escape the cultural nightmare the revolutionaries imposed.

One way of explaining why there was so much opposition is to begin with who had a stake in the new order. Catholic peasants and artisans in the Midi could take some satisfaction in the agony the Terror imposed on the Protestant merchant and professional élites that exploited them, but with this exception, there was very little in the revolutionary settlement for people with little or no property. Farmers, sharecroppers, labourers, the semi-skilled or the unskilled, the poor and the marginal were left to make their own calculations of whether a revolution no one had anticipated had left them better off than before. The Civil Constitution compounded the difficulty of this decision. Women were often significant in this calculation and their reactions had a decisive role to play, not only in the initial rejection of the Civil Constitution but throughout the period. For many families also, higher taxes and the burdens of the abolished feudalism were added to the costs of operating land. This meant the entire class of tenant farmers, a large and significant group, had a grievance. If they could bring along their neighbours, as they did in the west, the result was civil war. Elsewhere, there was constant turmoil, sporadic insurrection, resistance to conscription, and all the rest.

Every historian of the period has emphasized the importance of the war. It reduced the margin of error enormously. Dissidence that local officials once managed with an admitted high-handedness and disrespect for the rule of law and due process, now became much more dangerous. As the war extended to nearly the whole of Europe, the Republic made more and more demands for the sacrifice of persons and treasure, but those whom the Jacobins threatened or who had gained nothing, had no reason to support the ideals of a Revolution that seemed to have been made without them. As the *assignat* deteriorated and finally collapsed, even the life of urban consumers and of ordinary conscripts in the armies of the Republic must have been miserable.

There was a Terror in France in 1793–4 because there was an armed opposition against the Republic, an opposition that the Jacobins were right to suspect was often treasonous. The British did not have a hand in every opposition movement but in 1793, they were exploring how to aid the most menacing one, the Vendean insurrection. Later, they attempted to aid the *chouans* and profit from the civil war to advance their own strategic interests. Their aid to the federalists at Toulon is notorious but how much they financed the murder gangs and how much they supported the aspiring assassins of Bonaparte is so far unknown. There was certainly some hard evidence to link the foreign plot and the domestic plot.

That was not enough to justify the Terror, of course, although it does show that the revolutionaries were not hallucinating and that they were not 'schizophrenic'. Yet their rhetoric and their actions were not calmly gauged either; instead, they were astonishingly beyond what a traditional military defence might require. How they got so far beyond a measured response is a problem but that rhetoric and that behaviour were not present, even implicitly, by any conceivable stretch in 1789. There was a language of vengeance and retribution, as in the lynchings in Paris; there was a language of renewal, as in almost everything Robespierre said and wrote in 1789. But none of this predicted what came later. The lynchings were not revolutionary government. Robespierre's grim moralizing was unusual. Nowhere could one forecast the language and the

action of the maximalist terror, let alone the dechristianization of the
Year II in the rhetoric of 1789. The revolutionaries came to adopt the
maximalist perspective partly because, as Patrice Gueniffey has argued,
revolutionaries competed among themselves to invent the most *outré*
language, and partly because the language became more extreme as the
perceived peril increased.

In the end, beneath the incredibly confusing sequence of events, beneath the Revolution's moments of glory and horror, beneath the broader
trends about which professors debate and will always debate, beneath all
of this, it is impossible for people at the start of the twenty-first century to
avoid one great and unpleasant reality about the Revolution: the revolutionaries drove very large numbers of women and men to a profound
revulsion against them and all their works when they stripped away the
markers that gave their lives meaning. The revolutionaries dismissed all
this as worthless and idiotic and arrogated to themselves the right to
crush its every expression. The resistance to these policies was so great
that the dictator recognized it, but he did it practically alone. That was
his genius: he saw how to end the French Revolution. The price to be
paid was political liberty. In the end, therefore, the vast weight of ancient
peasant France imposed itself upon the government, at the expense of
many of the ideals of 1789. This too should be seen as the result of a
popular movement, one of the most profound revolutions of the revolutionary epoch.

But that was not the end. There were still histories to write. After the
fall of Bonaparte, the survivors of the Revolution undertook a spiri-
ted debate among themselves and with the newly emerging generation of historians. All of the surviving *conventionnels* asserted over and
over again that the Terror was a response to foreign invasion and
domestic subversion. One of them, Jacques-Charles Bailleul, deputy
from the Seine-Inférieure, castigated Mme de Staël for imposing a distinction between a constitutionalist revolution and the Terror, a distinction between a good and bad Revolution. Girondin though he had been,
Bailleul insisted that the uprisings against the Revolution – 'the conspiracy of the privileged' – were criminal acts and that self-defence was 'a
necessity, a duty'. Excesses were the responsibility of lone individuals,
not inherent in the Terror itself. In other words, Bailleul defined the
Terror in its minimalist version. Almost all of the surviving *conventionnels* did this. In defending the Republic, the Convention saved France
from invasion and dismemberment.

There was so much more that could have been said. There was nothing, or almost nothing about the dechristianization campaign. Their
silence on this issue showed that the immense cultural gulf that existed
between the ruling élites and millions of ordinary people would continue

well beyond the Revolution. There was a passing mention that bad things happened at Nantes and Lyon but the inference was these events were peripheral, committed despite the Committee of Public Safety's wishes, not because of them. No one wanted to reflect on the great black hole of the Revolution, the revolutionary tribunals and military commissions. Thus was born the 'thesis of circumstances', a theoretical statement that had its roots in the Revolution itself.

In applying the 'thesis of circumstances' to the King's trial, the survivors showed how elastic the term is. Although some like Carnot, Thibaudeau, and even Fouché regretted their votes and wished it had been otherwise, almost all of them justified the execution as a political necessity, an act that had to be understood in its context. The claim that the King was guilty had almost entirely disappeared; none claimed the execution founded a new epoch; none claimed it was a measured act of self-defence.

This reasoning from circumstances had an enormous effect on the generation of young historians of the Revolution. It has been, and for some historians still is, the dominant paradigm. But it was an historical construct that its exponents designed in order to explain and justify.

This phenomenon of the interaction between living actors and a younger generation shows up very clearly in the case of René Levasseur [de la Sarthe]. He wrote defiant memoirs that brought their publisher a prison sentence in 1829 but they emphasized only a truculent patriotism and his commitment to the 'Rights of Man'. In other words, Levasseur defined himself as a defender of France against foreigners and as a man of 1789. His memoirs say nothing about his vote against Louis XVI and very little about his experience as a representative on mission in the west or on the frontiers. Unlike most of his colleagues, he wanted to rehabilitate Robespierre's reputation. He did it by quoting without attribution the letters of Marc-Antoine Jullien from Nantes in 1793, and by smearing the reputation of many other deputies: 'tigers with a human face'. He also shifted attention from acts to motives. The Montagnards were 'headstrong and generous men [who] in the middle of a necessary anarchy, thought to establish the foundations of a happy and tranquil regime, but based on the most complete equality and the most absolute liberty'.

The eulogies at his funeral evidently said nothing about his terrorist phase, but represented him as a stern democrat, an ardent patriot, a giver of free medical treatment to the poor (an important trope in the 1830s but not in the 1790s) and certainly not as a violent man; that is, they presented him much as the men of 1848 presented themselves. By the 1890s, eulogies over his grave in Le Mans clearly showed that local republican politicians had read Aulard.

As the revolutionary generation died off, as Fouché, the old dechristianizer, was laid to rest in the cathedral of Trieste; as Prieur de la Marne,
member of the Committee of Public Safety, claimed all the Vendeans
received a trial in his sketchy memoirs; as the Emperor kept the interminable evenings going on St Helena with his endless talk; as old Barère sat on
his rocking chair with his huge white beard scaring schoolchildren by his
bloody reputation; as all these men died off, there was another French
Revolution being created, this time by the historians, a revolution that the
historical actors helped them understand. This is a Revolution that continues. This French Revolution is not over.

Bibliography

This bibliography is based upon three others, the first reprinted in my *Revolution and Counter-revolution*, pp. 443–70; 'The French Revolution: A Bibliography of Works in English,' and finally the whole bibliography for this work available at my website at the University of Maryland. What follows on these pages is an abbreviated version of this latter bibliography.

Abbreviations

AHR	*American Historical Review*
AhRf	*Annales historiques de la Révolution française*
AN	*Annales de Normandie*
Annales. H.S.S.	*Annales. Histoires. Sociétiés*
Annales. E.S.C.	*Annales. Economies. Sociétiés. Civilisations.*
EHQ	*European History Quarterly*
FH	*French History*
FHS	*French Historical Studies*
JMH	*Journal of Modern History*
Mln	*Modern Language Notes*
Rf	*Révolution française*
Rhmc	*Revue d'histoire moderne et contemporaine*

Websites

David Andress's site is well-maintained and comprehensive; it has many useful links: http://userwww.port.ac.uk/andressd/homepage.htm

Jack Censer's site is also available as a separate CD-ROM along with an introductory handbook. It is a collection of images, texts and audio accompanied by intelligent commentary: http://chnm.gmu.edu/revolution/

Research aids

Bessieres, Yves, and Patricia Niedzwiecki. *Women in the French Revolution (1789): bibliography.* Brussels, Washington, D.C., 1991.

Bonin, Serge, and Claude Langlois. *Atlas de la Révolution française.* Librairie du bicentenaire de la Révolution française. Paris, 1987. The volumes on space, religion, popular societies and Paris are especially recommended.

Caldwell, Ronald J. *The Era of the French Revolution: A Bibliography of the History of Western Civilization, 1789–1799.* 2 vols. New York, 1985.

Fierro, Alfred, André Palluel-Guillard, and Jean Tulard. *Histoire et dictionnaire du Consulat et de l'Empire.* Paris, 1995.

Jones, Colin. *The Longman Companion to the French Revolution.* London, New York, 1988. Inexhaustible source of information.

Lucas, Colin, and Bibliothèque nationale (France), eds. *The French Revolution Research Collection. Les Archives de la Révolution française.* Oxford, 1989. See http://gallica.bnt.fr

Ross, Steven T. *Historical Dictionary of the Wars of the French Revolution.* Historical dictionaries of war, revolution, and civil unrest; no. 6. Lanham, Md., 1998.

Scott, Samuel F., and Barry Rothaus. *Historical Dictionary of the French Revolution 1789–1799.* 2 vols. Westport, Conn., 1984.

Tulard, Jean. *Dictionnaire Napoléon.* Paris, 1989.

General histories

Andress, David. *French Society in Revolution, 1789–1799.* Manchester, 1999.

Aston, Nigel. *Religion and Revolution in France, 1780–1804.* Washington, D.C., 2000.

Bosher, J. F. *The French Revolution.* New York, 1988.

Censer, Jack Richard, and Lynn Avery Hunt. *Liberty, Equality, Fraternity: Exploring the French Revolution.* University Park, Pa, 2001.

Connelly, Owen, and Fred Hembree. *The French Revolution.* Arlington Heights, Ill., 1993.

Doyle, William. *The Oxford History of the French Revolution.* Oxford, New York, 1989.

—— *Origins of the French Revolution.* Oxford, New York, 1999.

—— *The French Revolution: a Very Short Introduction.* Oxford, 2001.

Forrest, Alan I. *The French Revolution.* Oxford, Cambridge, Mass., 1995.

Martin, J. C. *La France en révolution, 1789–1799.* Paris, 1990.

—— *Révolution et contre-révolution en France: 1789–1989: les rouages de l'histoire.* Rennes, 1996.

—— *Contre-révolution, révolution et nation en France: 1789–1799.* Paris, 1998.

Mayer, Arno J. *The Furies: Violence and Terror in the French and Russian Revolutions.* Princeton, N.J., 2000.

Popkin, Jeremy D. *A Short History of the French Revolution*. Englewood Cliffs, N.J., 1995.

Sagan, Eli. *Citizens & Cannibals: the French Revolution, the Struggle for Modernity, and the Origins of Ideological Terror*. Lanham, Md. 2001. The lurid Revolution.

Schama, Simon. *Citizens: a Chronicle of the French Revolution*. New York, 1989. Provocative, always interesting.

Stone, Bailey. *The Genesis of the French Revolution: A Global-historical Interpretation*. Cambridge UK, New York, 1994.

Whaley, Leigh Ann. *Radicals: Politics and Republicanism in the French Revolution*. Stroud, 2000.

Interpretations and debates

Censer, Jack R. 'Commencing the Third Century of Debate.' *AHR*, xciv (1989) 1309–25.

Cox, Marvin Rountree. *The Place of the French Revolution in History*. Boston, 1998.

Crouzet, François. *Historians and the French Revolution: the Case of Maximilien Robespierre*. Swansea, 1989.

Darnton, Robert. *What was Revolutionary about the French Revolution?* Waco, Tex., 1990.

Desan, Suzanne. 'What's after Political Culture? Recent French Revolutionary Historiography.' *FHS*, xxiii (2000) 163–96.

Fehér, Ferenc. *The French Revolution and the Birth of Modernity*. Berkeley, 1990.

Gueniffey, Patrice. *La politique de la Terreur: essai sur la violence révolutionnaire, 1789–1794*. Paris, 2000. A major contribution.

Kaplan, Steven L. *Farewell, Revolution: Disputed Legacies: France, 1789/1989*. Ithaca, 1995. Important.

Lewis, Gwynne. *The French Revolution: Rethinking the Debate*. London, 1993.

Livesey, James. *Making Democracy in the French Revolution*. Cambridge, Mass., 2001. [What democracy?]

Martin, J. C. *Une guerre interminable: la Vendée deux cents ans après*. Nantes, 1985.

Netter, Marie-Laurence. *La Révolution française n'est pas terminée*. Paris, 1989.

Petiteau, Natalie. *Napoléon, de la mythologie à l'histoire*. Paris, 1999.

Poussou, Jean-Pierre. 'Massacres, terreur et vertu.' *Histoire, Economie et Société*, x (1991) 55–69.

Soboul, Albert. *Understanding the French Revolution*. New York, 1988.

Sonenscher, Michael. 'The cheese and the rats: Augustin Cochin and the bicentenary of the French Revolution.' *Economy and society*, xix (1990) 266–74.

Furet

Baker, Keith Michael. 'New Work on the Old Regime and the French Revolution: A Special Issue in Honor of Francois Furet – In Memoriam: Francois Furet.' *JMH*, lxxii (2000) 1–5.

Bien, David D. 'Francois Furet, the Terror, and 1789.' *FHS*, xvi (1990) 777–83.

Christofferson, Michael Scott. 'An Antitotalitarian History of the French Revolution: Francois Furet's *Penser la Révolution française* in the Intellectual Politics of the Late 1970s.' *FHS*, xxii (1999) 557–611.

Furet, François, and Mona Ozouf. *A Critical Dictionary of the French Revolution.* Cambridge, Mass., 1989.

Judt, Tony. 'On Francois Furet (1927–1997).' *The New York Review of Books*, xliv no. 17 (1997).

Mosher, Michael. 'On the Originality of François Furet: A Commemorative Note.' *Political Theory*, xxvi (1998) 392–96.

Sutherland, Donald. 'An Assessment of the Writings of Francois Furet.' *FHS*, xvi (1990) 784–91.

Woloch, Isser. 'On the Latent Illiberalism of the French Revolution.' *AHR*, xcv (1990) 1452–70. A commentary on the *Critical Dictionary*.

Old Regime

Bell, David Avrom. *Lawyers and Citizens: the Making of a Political Elite in Old Regime France.* New York, 1994.

Bossenga, Gail. *The Politics of Privilege: Old Regime and Revolution in Lille.* Cambridge UK, New York, 1991.

Chartier, Roger. *The Cultural Origins of the French Revolution.* Durham, N.C., 1991.

Darnton, Robert. *The Forbidden Best-sellers of Pre-revolutionary France.* New York, 1995.

Doyle, William. *Venality: the Sale of Offices in Eighteenth-century France.* Oxford, New York, 1996.

——*Jansenism: Catholic Resistance to Authority from the Reformation to the French Revolution.* Houndmills, New York, 2000.

Farge, Arlette, and Jacques Revel. *The Vanishing Children of Paris: Rumor and Politics before the French Revolution.* Cambridge, Mass., 1991.

Fitzsimmons, Michael P. *The Parisian Order of Barristers and the French Revolution.* Cambridge, Mass., 1987.

Garrioch, David. 'Parish Politics, Jansenism and the Paris Middle Classes in the Eighteenth Century.' *FH*, vii (1994) 403–19.

Hunt, Lynn. *The Family Romance of the French Revolution.* Berkeley, 1992.

Jones, Colin. 'The Great Chain of Buying: Medical Advertisement, The Bourgeois Public Sphere, and the Origins of the French Revolution.' *AHR*, ci (1996) 13–40.

Kaiser, Thomas E. 'Madame de Pompadour and the Theaters of Power.' *FHS*, xix (1996) 1025–44.

—— 'The Evil Empire? The Debate on Turkish Despotism in Eighteenth-Century French Political Culture.' *JMH*, lxxii (2000) 29.

Lemarchand, Guy. 'Troubles populaires au XVIIIe siècle et conscience de classe: une préface à la Révolution française.' *AhRf* 61, no. 1 (1990) 32–48.

Merrick, Jeffrey. *The Desacralization of the French Monarchy in the Eighteenth Century*. Baton Rouge, 1990.

Van Kley, Dale K. *The Damiens Affair and the Unraveling of the Ancien Régime, 1750–1770*. Princeton, N.J., 1984.

—— *The Religious Origins of the French Revolution: From Calvin to the Civil Constitution, 1560–1791*. New Haven, Conn., 1996.

Congresses and collections

Aerts, Erik, and François Crouzet. *Economic effects of the French Revolutionary and Napoleonic Wars: session B-1: proceedings, Tenth International Economic History Congress, Leuven, August 1990*. Studies in social and economic history; v. 4. Leuven, Belgium, 1990.

Association pour la célébration du Bicentenaire de la Révolution française en pays de France. 'Les Paysans et la Révolution en pays de France: actes du colloque de Tremblay-lès-Gonesse, 15–16 octobre 1988.' Tremblay-lès-Gonesse, 1989.

Baker, Keith Michael, Colin Lucas, François Furet, and Mona Ozouf. *The French Revolution and the Creation of Modern Political Culture*. Oxford, New York, 1987.

Brive, Marie-France. *Les Femmes et la Révolution française: actes du colloque international, 12–13–14 avril 1989, Université de Toulouse-Le Mirail*. Toulouse, 1989.

Duport, Anne Marie. *Religion, révolution, contre-révolution dans le Midi 1789–1799: colloque international tenu à Nîmes les 27 et 28 janvier 1989*. Nîmes, 1990.

Forrest, Alan I., and Peter Jones. *Reshaping France: Town, Country and Region during the French Revolution*. Manchester, New York, 1991.

France. Comité des travaux historiques et scientifiques. *La Révolution française et le monde rural: actes du colloque tenu en Sorbonne les 23, 24 et 25 octobre 1987*. Colloques du C.T.H.S. 4. Paris, 1989.

'Les Résistances à la Révolution: actes du colloque de Rennes (17–21 septembre 1985).' Paris, 1987.

Reinhardt, Steven G., and Elisabeth A. Cawthon. *Essays on the French Revolution: Paris and the Provinces*. Arlington, Tex., 1992.

UMR TELEMME (Research group: France), and Centre méridional d'histoire sociale des mentalités et des cultures. *Les fédéralismes: réalités et représentations, 1789–1874: actes du colloque de Marseille, septembre 1993*. Aix-en-Provence, 1995.

Université de Rouen. Institut de recherches et de documentation en sciences sociales. *La Révolution française et les processus de socialisation de l'homme moderne: textes des conférences, communications et rapports présentés au colloque international de Rouen, 13–14 octobre 1988.* Rouen, Paris, 1989.

Vovelle, Michel, and Danielle Le Monnier. *Les Colloques du Bicentenaire: répertoire des rencontres scientifiques nationales et internationales.* Paris, 1991.

——*Le tournant de l'an III: réaction et terreur blanche dans la France révolutionnaire.* Paris, 1997.

Events, 1789–92

Andress, David. *Massacre at the Champ de Mars: Popular Dissent and Political Culture in the French Revolution.* Suffolk, UK, Rochester, N.Y., 2000.

Blackman, Robert H. 'Building a national assembly: theories and practice of political representation during the Early French Revolution, 1789–1795.' Ph.D., University of California Irvine, 1998.

Clifford, Dale Lothrop. 'The National Guard and the Parisian Community, 1789–1790.' *FHS*, xvi (1990) 849–78.

Fitzsimmons, Michael P. *The Remaking of France: the National Assembly and the Constitution of 1791.* Cambridge, UK, New York, N.Y., 1994.

Garrioch, David. 'The Everyday Lives of Parisian Women and the October Days of 1789.' *Social History*, xxiv (1999) 231–49. Sets the events in a long term context. Important.

Guilhaumou, Jacques. *Marseille républicaine (1791–1793).* Paris, 1992.

——*L'avènement des porte-parole de la République (1789–1792): essai de synthèse sur les langages de la Révolution française.* Villeneuve-d'Ascq, 1998.

Kates, Gary. *The Cercle social, the Girondins, and the French Revolution.* Princeton N.J., 1985.

Lucas, Colin. 'The Crowd and Politics between Ancien Regime and Revolution in France.' *JMH*, lx (1988) 421–57.

Lüsebrink, Hans-Jürgen, and Rolf Reichardt. *The Bastille: a History of A Symbol of Despotism and Freedom.* Durham N.C., 1997.

Margadant, Ted W. *Urban Rivalries in the French Revolution.* Princeton, N.J., 1992.

Margerison, Kenneth. *Pamphlets & Public Opinion: the Campaign for A Union of Orders in the Early French Revolution.* West Lafayette, Ind., 1998.

Sampoli, Fabio. 'Politics and Society in Revolutionary Arles: Chiffonistes and Monnaidiers.' Ph.D., Yale University, 1982. Excellent.

Shapiro, Barry M. *Revolutionary Justice in Paris, 1789–1790.* Cambridge, UK, New York, 1993.

Shapiro, Gilbert, John Markoff, Timothy Tackett, and Philip Dawson. *Revolutionary Demands: A Content Analysis of the Cahiers de doléances of 1789.* Stanford, Calif., 1998.

Tackett, Timothy. 'Nobles And Third Estate in the Revolutionary Dynamic of the National Assembly, 1789–1790.' *AHR*, xciv (1989) 271–301.

—— 'Becoming a Revolutionary: Five Future Jacobins in 1789.' *Maryland Historian*, xxi (1990) 3–19.

—— *Becoming A Revolutionary: the Deputies of the French National Assembly and the Emergence of A Revolutionary Culture (1789–1790)*. Princeton, N.J., 1996. Excellent.

—— 'Conspiracy Obsession in a Time of Revolution: French Elites and the Origins of the Terror, 1789–1792.' *AHR*, cv (2000) 690–713.

—— 'Les Deputes de l'assemblee legislative, 1791–1792.' In *Pour la Révolution française: en hommage à Claude Mazauric*, ed. Claude Mazauric, Christine Le Bozec, and Eric Wauters, 139–44. Rouen, 1998.

Events, 1792–94

Bluche, Frédéric. *Septembre 1792, logiques d'un massacre*. Paris, 1986.

Cormack, William S. and Sydenham, Michael. 'Counter-Revolution? Toulon, 1793.' *History Today*, xxxvii (1987) 49–55.

Edmonds, Bill. 'A Jacobin Debacle: The Losing of Lyon in Spring 1793.' *History*, lxix (1984) 1–14.

Hanson, Paul R. *Provincial Politics in the French Revolution: Caen and Limoges, 1789–1794*. Baton Rouge, 1989.

Michael, S., Lewis Beck, Anne Hildreth, Alan B. Spitzer. 'Y a-t-il un groupe girondin a la Convention nationale (1792–1793)?' In *La Gironde et les Girondins*, ed. François Furet, Mona Ozouf, and Bronisaw Baczko, 169–188. Paris, 1991.

Slavin, Morris. *The Making of An Insurrection: Parisian Sections and the Gironde*. Cambridge, Mass., 1986.

Valin, Claudy. *Autopsie d'un massacre: journées des 21 et 22 mars 1793*. Saint-Jean-d'Angély, 1992. Worth comparing to Pierre Caron.

Elections

Crook, Malcolm. *Elections in the French Revolution: An Apprenticeship in Democracy, 1789–1799*. Cambridge UK, New York, 1996.

Edelstein, Melvin. 'Integrating the French peasants into the nation-state: the transformation of electoral participation (1789–1870).' *History of European Ideas*, xv (1992) 319–26.

Gueniffey, Patrice. *Le nombre et la raison: la Révolution française et les élections*. Paris, 1993.

Royal family

Duprat, Annie. *Le roi décapité: essai sur les imaginaires politiques*. Paris, 1992.

Girault de Coursac, Paul, and Pierrette Girault de Coursac. *Enquête sur le procès du roi Louis XVI*. Paris, 1982.

Langlois, Claude. *Les sept morts du roi*. Paris, 1993.

Thomas, Chantal. *The Wicked Queen: the Origins of the Myth of Marie-Antoinette*. New York, 1999.

Religion

General

Aston, Nigel. *The End of An Elite: the French Bishops and the Coming of the Revolution, 1786–1790*. Oxford, New York, 1992.

Cholvy, Gérard. 'La Révolution française et la question religieuse.' *Histoire*, no. 72 (1984) 50–9.

Cousin, Bernard, Monique Cubells, and René Moulinas. *La pique et la croix: histoire religieuse de la Révolution française*. Paris, 1989.

Pérouas, Louis, and Paul D. Hollander. *La Révolution française: une rupture dans le christianisme?: le cas du Limousin (1775–1822)*. Treignac, 1988. Excellent regional synopsis.

Civil constitution of the clergy

Tackett, Timothy. *Religion, Revolution, and Regional Culture in Eighteenth-century France: the Ecclesiastical Oath of 1791*. Princeton, N.J., 1986. Indispensable.

Dechristianization

Bernet, Jacques. 'Les limites de la déchristianisation de l'an II éclairées par le retour au culte de l'an III: l'exemple du district de Compiègne.' *AhRf*, no. 312 (1998) 285–99.

Bossut, Nicole. 'Aux origines de la déchristianisation dans la Nièvre: Fouché, Chaumette, ou les jacobins nivernais?' *AhRf*, no. 264 (1986) 181–202.

Bourdin, Philippe. *Le noir et le rouge: itinéraire social, culturel et politique d'un prêtre patriote (1736–1799)*. Clermont-Ferrand, 2000.

Desan, Suzanne. *Reclaiming the Sacred: Lay Religion and Popular Politics in Revolutionary France*. Ithaca, N.Y., 1990.

Lucas, Colin. 'L'église constitutionnelle dans la Loire après la Terreur.' *Cahiers d'histoire*, xxx (1985) 309–39.

Petite Eglise

Chiron, J., and B. Jaud. *Barbarin: le grenadier de la Petite Eglise: l'histoire de Nueil-sur-Argent de 1789 à 1817*. Maulévrier, 1987.

Laurent, Benoît. *Les béguins*. Saint-Étienne, 1944.

Terror

General

Bossut, Nicole. 'Terreur à Clamecy. Quelques réflexions.' *AhRf*, no. 311 (1998) 49–78.
Darrow, Margaret H. 'Economic Terror in the City: the General Maximum In Montauban.' *FHS*, xvii (1991) 498–525.
Duport, Anne Marie. *Terreur et révolution: Nîmes en l'an II, 1793–1794.* Paris, 1987.
Gaffarel, Paul. 'Marseille sans nom (nivôse–pluviôse An II).' *Rf* 60 (1911) 193–215.
Gough, Hugh. *The Terror in the French Revolution.* Houndmills, New York, 1998.
Wahnich, Sophie, and Marc Belissa. 'Les crimes des anglais: Trahir le droit.' *AhRf*, no. 300 (1995) 233–48.

Terrorists

Bourdin, Philippe. 'Les tribulations patriotiques d'un missionnaire jacobin, Philippe-Antoine Dorfeuille.' *Cahiers d'histoire*, xlii (1997) 217–65.
Monnier, Raymonde. 'L'évolution du personnel politique de la section Marat et la rupture de germinal An II.' *AhRf*, no. 263 (1986) 50–73.

Missions

Guilhaumou, Jacques, and Martine Lapied. 'La mission Maignet.' *AhRf*, no. 300 (1995) 283–94.
Labroue, Henri. *La mission du conventionnel Lakanal dans la Dordogne en l'an II (octobre 1793–août 1794).* Paris, 1912.

Suspects and revolutionary committees

Boulant, Antoine. 'Le suspect parisien en l'an II.' *AhRf* 62, no. 2 (1990) 187–97.
Lucas, Colin. 'The Theory and Practice of Denunciation in The French Revolution.' *JMH*, lxvii (1996) 768–85.
Matharan, Jean-Louis. 'L'arrestation des suspects en 1793 et en l'An II. Professions et répression.' *AhRf*, no. 263 (1986) 74–83.

Tribunals

Arasse, Daniel. *The Guillotine and the Terror.* London, New York, 1989.
Godfrey, James Logan. *The Organization, Procedure, and Personnel of the French Revolutionary Tribunal.* Chicago, 1942.
Lallié, A. *La justice révolutionnaire à Nantes et dans la Loire-Inférieure.* Cholet, 1991.

Mansfield, Paul. 'The Repression of Lyon, 1793–94: Origins, Responsibility, Significance.' *FH*, ii (1988) 74–101.

——'The Management of Terror in Montagnard Lyon, Year II.' *EHQ*, xx (1990) 465–96.

Economic and social

General

Aftalion, Florin. *The French Revolution, an Economic Interpretation*. Cambridge UK, New York, Paris, 1990.

Cullen, L. M. 'History, Economic Crises, and Revolution: Understanding Eighteenth-Century France.' *Economic History Review*, xlvi (1993) 635–57.

Garnier, Bernard. 'L'approvisionnement de Paris en moutons, 1780–1820.' *AN*, xl (1990) 83–101.

Miller, Judith A. *Mastering the market: the State and the Grain Trade in Northern France, 1700–1860*. Cambridge UK, New York, 1998.

Rosenthal, Jean-Laurent. *The Fruits of Revolution: Property Rights, Litigation, and French Agriculture, 1700–1860*. Cambridge UK, New York, 1992.

Vardi, Liana. 'The Abolition of the Guilds During the French Revolution.' *FHS*, xv (1988) 704–17.

Biens nationaux

Bodinier, Bernard. 'La vente des biens nationaux: essai de synthèse.' *AhRf*, no. 3 (1999) 7–19.

Martin, Jean-Claude. 'Acquéreurs de biens nationaux et chouans dans le domfrontais pendant la Révolution française.' *AN*, xxxviii (1989) 265–84.

Money and credit

Crouzet, François, and Jacques De Larosière. *La grande inflation: la monnaie en France de Louis XVI à Napoléon*. Paris, 1993. The best book on the Revolution written in the 1990s.

Hoffman, Philip T., Gilles Postel-Vinay, and Jean-Laurent Rosenthal. *Priceless Markets: the Political Economy of Credit in Paris, 1660–1870*. Chicago, 2000.

White, Eugene N. 'Was There a Solution to the Ancien Regime's Financial Dilemma?' *Journal of Economic History*, xlix (1989) 545–68.

——'The French Revolution and the Politics of Government Finance, 1770–1815.' *Journal of economic history*, lv (1995) 227–55.

Demography and the family

Burguière, André. 'La Révolution française et la famille.' *Annales: ESC*, xlvi (1991) 151–68.

Darrow, Margaret H. *Revolution in the House: Family, Class, and Inheritance in Southern France, 1775–1825.* Princeton, N.J., 1989.

Desan, Suzanne. '"War between Brothers and Sisters": Inheritance Law and Gender Politics in Revolutionary France.' *FHS*, xx (1997) 38.

—— 'Reconstituting the Social After the Terror: Family, Property and the Law in Popular Politics.' *Past & Present*, no. 164 (1999) 81–121.

Dupâquier, Jacques. *Histoire de la population française.* Paris, 1988.

Spagnoli, Paul G. 'The Unique Decline of Mortality in Revolutionary France.' *Journal of Family History*, xxii (1997) 425–61.

Weir, David R. 'Les crises économiques et les origines de la Révolution française.' *Annales: ESC*, xlvi (1991) 917–47.

Growth

Le Goff, T. J. A. and D. M. G. Sutherland, 'La Révolution française et l'économie rurale, 1789–1815,' *Histoire et mesure*, xiv (1999), 79–120.

Sutherland, D. M. G., 'Peasants, Lords, and Leviathan: Winners and Losers from the Abolition of French Feudalism, 1780–1820,' *Journal of Economic History*, lxii (March 2002)1–24.

Toutain, J. C. 'La croissance inégale des régions françaises: l'agriculture de 1810 à 1990.' *Revue historique* 291, no. 2 (1994) 315–59.

Rural

General

Béaur, Gérard. *Histoire agraire de la France au XVIIIe siècle: inerties et changements dans les campagnes françaises entre 1715 et 1815.* Paris, 2000. Excellent summary of issues.

Jones, P. M. *The Peasantry in the French Revolution.* Cambridge UK, New York, 1988.

McPhee, Peter. '"The Misguided Greed Of Peasants"? Popular Attitudes To The Environment In The Revolution Of 1789.' *FHS*, xxiv (2001) 247–69.

Anti-seigneurial

Crubaugh, Anthony. *Balancing the Scales of Justice: Local Courts and Rural Society in Southwest France, 1750–1800.* University Park, Pa., 2001.

Fitch, Nancy. 'Rural Violence and Peasant Politics in Central France, 1789–1794.' A paper delivered at the WSFH, 1991.

Markoff, John. 'Violence, Emancipation, and Democracy: The Countryside and the French Revolution.' *AHR*, c (1995) 360–86.

—— *The Abolition of Feudalism: Peasants, Lords, and Legislators in the French Revolution.* University Park, Pa., 1996.

Pautet, Jean. 'Pierre Mazillier, chef de "brigands" en mâconnais (juillet–aout 1789).' *Cahiers d'histoire*, xxxv (1990) 119–32.

Structures and practices

Ponsot, Pierre. 'Un propriétaire clunysois, son domaine et ses métayers sous le Premier Empire. Réflexion sur l'impact social de la Révolution dans les campagnes.' *Cahiers d'histoire*, xxxiv (1989) 29–40.

Vardi, Liana. *The Land and the Loom: Peasants and Profit in Northern France, 1680–1800.* Durham, N.C., 1993.

Vivier, Nadine, and Alain Corbin. *Propriété collective et identité communale: les biens communaux en France 1750–1900.* Paris, 1998.

Culture

Baecque, Antoine de. *The Body Politic: Corporeal Metaphor in Revolutionary France, 1770–1800.* Stanford, 1997.

—— *Glory and Terror: Seven Deaths Under the French Revolution.* New York, 2001. A masterpiece.

Baker, Keith Michael. *Inventing the French Revolution: Essays on French Political Culture in the Eighteenth Century.* Cambridge UK, New York, 1990.

Bell, David Avrom. *The Cult of the Nation in France: Inventing Nationalism, 1680–1800.* Cambridge, Mass., 2001.

Billy, Pierre-Henri. 'Des prénoms révolutionnaires en France.' *AhRf*, no. 322 (2000) 39–60.

Crow, Thomas E. *Emulation: Making Artists for Revolutionary France.* New Haven, 1995.

Guilhaumou, Jacques. *La mort de Marat, 1793.* Brussels, 1989.

Hesse, Carla Alison. 'The Law of the Terror.' *Mln* 114, no. 4 (1999) 702–18.

Hunt, Lynn Avery. *Politics, Culture, and Class in the French Revolution.* Berkeley, 1986.

Johnson, James H. 'Versailles, Meet Les Halles: Masks, Carnival, and the French Revolution.' *Representations*, no. 73 (2001) 89–116. Excellent on revolutionary mentality.

Kennedy, Emmet. *A Cultural History of the French Revolution.* New Haven, 1989.

Landes, Joan B. *Visualizing the nation: gender, representation, and revolution in eighteenth-century France.* Ithaca, 2001.

Langlois, Claude. *La caricature contre-revolutionnaire.* France, 1988.

—— 'Les dérives vendéennes de l'imaginaire révolutionnaire.' *Annales: ESC* 43, no. 3 (1988) 771–97.

Leith, James A. *Space and Revolution: Projects for Monuments, Squares and Public Buildings in France, 1789–1799.* Montréal, Buffalo, 1991.

Letzter, Jacqueline, and Robert Adelson. *Women writing opera: creativity and controversy in the age of the French Revolution.* Berkeley, 2001.

Outram, Dorinda. *The Body and the French Revolution: Sex, Class and Political Culture.* New Haven, 1989.

Ozouf, Mona. *Festivals and the French Revolution.* Cambridge, Mass., 1988.

Pauvert, Jean Jacques. *Estampes érotiques révolutionnaires: la Révolution française et l'obscénité.* Paris, 1989.
Pressly, William L., and Johann Zoffany. *The French Revolution As Blasphemy: Johan Zoffany's Paintings of the Massacre at Paris, August 10, 1792.* Berkeley, 1999.
Starobinski, Jean. *1789, the Emblems of Reason.* Charlottesville, 1982.
Vissière, Jean-Louis. 'Galejades révolutionnaires.' *Provence historique* 44, no. 175 (1994) 107–14.
Vorelle, Michel. *La Révolution française: images et récit, 1789–1799.* Paris, 1986.
—— 'La queue de Danton, ou massacre et sexualité: violence et fantasmes érotiques dans les lectures de la Révolution française.' *Annales de démographie historique* (1987) 365–77.
—— *Les Images de la Révolution française.* Paris, 1988.

Biography

Ballard, John R. *Continuity During the Storm: Boissy D'anglas and the Era of the French Revolution.* Westport, Conn., 2000.
Braconnier, Martine. *Georges Couthon: conventionnel auvergnat, ou, Les métamorphoses de la Raison (22 décembre 1755–10 thermidor an II).* Saint-Julien-Chapteuil, 1996.
Brown, Gregory S. 'The Self-Fashionings Of Olympe De Gouges, 1784–1789.' *Eighteenth-Century Studies,* xxxiv (2001) 383–401.
Germani, Ian. *Jean-Paul Marat: Hero and Anti-hero of the French Revolution.* Lewiston, N.Y., 1992.
Hampson, Norman. *Saint-Just.* Oxford, Cambridge, Mass., 1991.
Hardman, John. *Robespierre.* London, New York, 1999.
—— *Louis XVI.* London, 2000.
Haydon, Colin, and William Doyle. *Robespierre.* Cambridge, New York, 1999.
Jordan, David P. *The Revolutionary Career of Maximilien Robespierre.* New York, 1985.
Lallié, A. J.-B. *Carrier, représentant du Cantal à la Convention, 1756–1794, d'après de nouveaux documents.* Paris, 1901.
Sewell, William Hamilton. *A Rhetoric of Bourgeois Revolution: the Abbé Sieyès and What is the Third Estate?* Durham, N.C., 1994.
Sydenham, M. J. *Leonard Bourdon: the Career of A Revolutionary, 1754–1807.* Waterloo, Ont., 1999.
Tulard, Jean. *Joseph Fouché.* Paris, 1998.

Clubs and sociability

Boutier, Jean, and Philippe Boutry. 'Les sociétés politiques en France de 1789 à l'An III: "une machine"?' *Rhmc,* xxxvi (1989) 29–67.

Kennedy, Michael L. 'The "Last Stand" of The Jacobin Clubs.' *FHS*, xvi (1989) 309–44.
—— *The Jacobin Clubs in the French Revolution, 1793–1795.* New York, Oxford, 2000.
Peyrard, Christine, and Michel Vovelle. *Les Jacobins de l'Ouest: sociabilité révolutionnaire et formes de politisation dans le Maine et la Basse-Normandie (1789–1799).* Paris, 1996.

Women

Godineau, Dominique. *The Women of Paris and their French Revolution.* Berkeley, 1998.
Hufton, Olwen H. *Women and the Limits of Citizenship in the French Revolution.* Toronto, 1992.
Lapied, Martine. 'La place des femmes dans la sociabilité et la vie politique locale en Provence et dans le Comtat Venaissin pendant la Révolution.' *Provence historique*, xlvi (1996) 457–69.

Thermidor *and Directory*

Baczko, Bronisaw. *Ending the Terror: the French Revolution after Robespierre.* Cambridge UK, New York, Paris, 1994.
Baecque, A. de. 'La figure du jacobin dans l'imaginaire politique (1795–1799): naissance d'une obsession.' *Travaux Historiques* (1988) 61–70.
—— 'Robespierre, monstre-cadavre du discours thermidorien.' *Eighteenth century life*, xxi (1997) 203–21. Macabre, irrésistible.
Bourdin, Philippe. 'Les "Jacobins" du Bois de Cros (Clermont-Ferrand, An v): chronique d'un massacre annoncé.' *AhRf*, no. 308 (1997) 249–304.
Branciard, Jacques. 'Les muscadins de Theize.' *Cahiers d'histoire*, xli (1996) 155–77.
Brown, Howard G. 'A Discredited Regime: The Directory and Army Contracting.' *FH*, iv (1990) 48–76.
—— *War, Revolution, and the Bureaucratic State: Politics and Army Administration in France, 1791–1799.* Oxford, New York, 1995.
—— 'From Organic Society to Security State: The War on Brigandage in France, 1797–1802.' *JMH*, lxxix (1997) 661–95.
Brunel, Françoise. *Thermidor, la chute de Robespierre, 1794.* Brussels, 1989.
Gaffarel, Paul. 'Les Massacres royalistes dans le département des Bouches-du-Rhône aux premiers mois de 1795. Episode de la réaction thermidorienne.' *Annales de la faculté des lettres d'Aix*, iii (1909) 1–66.
—— 'Second Proconsulat de Fréron à Marseille, 31 octobre 1795–22 mars 1796.' *Rf* 69 (1916) 148–60, 313–36.
Lewis, Gwynne, Colin Lucas, and Richard Cobb, eds. *Beyond the Terror: Essays in French Regional and Social History, 1794–1815.* Cambridge UK, New York, 1983.

Lucas, Colin. 'The Rules of the Game in Local Politics under the Directory.' *FHS*, xvi (1989) 345–71.

Luzzatto, Sergio. *L'autunno della rivoluzione: lotta e cultura politica nella Francia del Termidoro*. Torino, 1994.

Peterson, Stephen M. 'The Social Origins of Royalist Political Violence in Directorial Bordeaux.' *FH*, x (1996) 56–85.

Renault, Fabrice. 'Autour de Robillard: pour une microsociologie du banditisme directorial dans l'Eure.' *AN*, xxxix (1989) 313–28.

Wilson, Warren. 'Les journees populaires et la violence collective dans le Vaucluse rural après thermidor.' *Canadian journal of history*, xxviii (1993) 41–57.

Consulate and empire

Alexander, R. S. *Bonapartism and Revolutionary Tradition in France: the fédérés of 1815*. Cambridge UK, New York, 1991.

Ellis, Geoffrey James. *Napoleon*. London, New York, 1997.

Crook, Malcolm. 'Confiance d'en bas, manipulation d'en haut: La pratique plebiscitaire sous Napoleon (1799–1815).' (Unpublished paper).

——*Napoleon Comes to Power: Democracy and Dictatorship in Revolutionary France, 1795–1804*. Cardiff, 1998.

Ellis, Geoffrey James. *The Napoleonic Empire*. Atlantic Highlands, N.J., 1991.

Horn, Jeff. 'Who Are the Elite? The Social Contours of the Notability in the Department of the Aube, 1789–1802.' A paper delivered at the WSFH, 1997.

Sibalis, Michael D. 'Prisoners By Mesure de Haute Police Under Napoleon I: Reviving the lettres de cachet.' A paper delivered at the Proceedings of the Annual Meeting of the Western Society for French History, 1991.

——'Internal Exiles In Napoleonic France, 1800–1815.' A paper delivered at the Proceedings of the Annual Meeting of the Western Society for French History, 1993.

Woloch, Isser. *The New Regime: Transformations of the French Civic Order, 1789–1820s*. New York, 1995.

——*Napoleon and his Collaborators: the Making of A Dictatorship*. New York, 2001.

Memories

Gough, Hugh. 'France and the memory of revolution: 1789–1989.' *History of European ideas*, xv (1992) 811–16.

Lagrée, Michel, and Jehanne Roche. *Tombes de mémoire: la dévotion populaire aux victimes de la Révolution dans l'Ouest*. Rennes-Paris, 1993.

Leveque, Pierre. 'Un canton "rouge" en Autunois aux XIXe et XXe siècles Issy-l'évêque.' *AhRf*, no. 274 (1988) 409–26.

Luzzatto, Sergio. *Il terrore ricordato: memoria e tradizione dell'esperienza rivoluzionaria*. Genoa, 1988.

——'Un futur au passé. La Révolution dans les mémoires des conventionnels.' *AhRf* 61, no. 4 (1989) 455–75.

Martin, J. C. *La Vendée de la mémoire: 1800–1980*. Paris, 1989.

Martin, J. C., and Charles Suaud. *Le Puy du Fou, en Vendée: l'histoire mise en scène*. Paris, 1996. A *lieu de mémoire* created very recently, very effective and well done.

Martin, J. C., and Xavier Lardière. *Le massacre des Lucs, Vendée 1794*. Vouillé, 1992.

McPhee, Peter. *Revolution and Environment in Southern France, 1780–1830: Peasants, Lords, and Murder in the Corbières*. Oxford, New York, 1999.

Roche, Jeanne. 'Cultes populaires dans les forêts du Maine sous la Révolution.' *AhRf*, no. 297 (1994) 439–46.

Regional and Paris

Crook, Malcolm. *Toulon in War and Revolution: From the Ancien Régime to the Restoration, 1750–1820*. War, armed forces, and society. Manchester, New York, 1991.

Forrest, Alan I. *The Revolution in Provincial France: Aquitaine, 1789–1799*. Oxford, New York, 1996.

Garrioch, David. *The Formation of the Parisian Bourgeoisie, 1690–1830*. Cambridge, Mass., 1996.

Lapied, Martine. 'Attitudes collectives et analyse de données: clivages politiques en Comtat Venaissin sous la Révolution.' *Annales du Midi*, xcv (1983) 67–89.

——*Le Comtat et la Révolution française: naissance des options collectives*. Aix-en-Provence, 1996.

——'Une Communauté provençale pendant la Révolution française: les antagonismes politiques à Eguilles.' *Provence historique*, xlix (1999) 305–16.

McPhee, Peter. *Collioure et la Révolution française, 1789–1815*. Perpignan, 1989.

Monnier, Raymonde. *Le faubourg Saint-Antoine, 1789–1815*. Paris, 1981.

Moulinas, René. *Histoire de la révolution d'Avignon*. Avignon, 1986.

Press

Gough, Hugh. *The Newspaper Press in the French Revolution*. London, 1988.

Popkin, Jeremy D. *The Right-wing Press in France, 1792–1800*. Chapel Hill, 1980.

——*Revolutionary News: the Press in France, 1789–1799*. Durham, N.C., 1990.

——'The Provincial Newspaper Press and Revolutionary Politics.' *FHS*, xviii (1993) 434–56.

Vendée and chouannerie

Dupâquier, Jacques. *Carrier: le procès d'un missionnaire de la Terreur et du Comité révolutionnaire de Nantes: 16 octobre–16 décembre 1794.* Pontoise, 1994. Long extracts from the trial records.

Dupuy, Roger. *De la Révolution à la Chouannerie: paysans en Bretagne, 1788–1794.* Paris, 1988.

Gérard, Alain. *'Par principe d'humanité...': la Terreur et la Vendée.* Paris, 1999. Passionate, enormously detailed.

Lallié, A. *Les noyades de Nantes; de l'histoire de la persécution des prêtres noyés.* Nantes, 1879.

—— 'Etudes sur la Terreur. Les Fusillades de Nantes, 1793–1794.' *Revue de Bretagne et de Vendée* 26, no. 6th series, t. 1 (1882) 55–102.

—— 'Etudes sur la terreur a Nantes. La compagnie Marat et autres auxiliaires du comité révolutionnaire.' *Revue historique de l'Ouest* 13, no. 7 (1897) 304–32.

Lebrun, François. 'La guerre de Vendée: massacre ou génocide?' *Histoire*, no. 78 (1985) 93–99.

Martin, J. C. 'La Vendée et sa guerre, les logiques de l'évènement.' *Annales: ESC*, xl (1985) 1067–85.

—— *Blancs et bleus dans la Vendée déchirée.* Paris, 1986.

—— *La Vendée et la France.* Paris, 1987.

—— 'Les disparitions mystérieuses de la population de la Vendée.' *Bulletin d'Information de la Société de Démographie Historique*, no. 52 (1988) 20–34.

—— 'Est-il possible de compter les morts de la Vendée?' *Rhmc*, xxxviii (1991) 105–21.

—— 'Histoire et polémique, les massacres de Machecoul.' *AhRf*, no. 291 (1993) 33–60.

Montrémy, Jean-Maurice de. 'La nouvelle "guerre" de Vendée.' *Histoire*, no. 92 (1986) 70–7.

Petitfrere, Claude. 'The Origins of the Civil War in the Vendée.' *FH*, ii (1988) 187–207.

—— 'La Vendée en l'an II: défaite et répression.' *AhRf*, no. 300 (1995) 173–85.

Sécher, Reynald. *La Chapelle-Basse-Mer, village vendéen: révolution et contre-révolution.* Paris, 1986.

—— *Le génocide franco-français: la Vendée-Vengé.* Paris, 1986.

Military

Bertaud, Jean Paul. *The Army of the French Revolution: From Citizen-soldiers to Instrument of Power.* Princeton, N.J., 1988.

Blanning, T. C. W. *The French Revolutionary Wars, 1787–1802.* London, New York, 1996.

Forrest, Alan I. *Conscripts and Deserters: the Army and French Society during the Revolution and Empire.* New York, 1989.

Index